Life and Terror in Stalin's Russia, 1934–1941

Life and Terror in Stalin's Russia 1934 - 1941

R o b e r t   W.   T h u r s t o n

Yale University Press New Haven and London

Designed by Nancy Ovedovitz and set in Times Roman by The Composing Room of Michigan, Inc. Printed in the United States of America by Vail-Ballou Press, Binghamton, New York.

Library of Congress Cataloging-in-Publication Data

Thurston, Robert W.
Life and terror in Stalin's Russia, 1934–1941 / Robert W. Thurston.
p.   cm.
Includes index.
ISBN 0-300-06401-2 (c : alk. paper)
1. Soviet Union—Politics and government—1936–1953.   2. Stalin, Joseph, 1879–1953.   3. Kommunisticheskaia partiia Sovetskogo Soiuza—Purges.   4. Political purges—Soviet Union.   5. Totalitarianism.   I. Title.
DK267.T52   1996
947.084′2—dc20   95-41333
                    CIP

A catalogue record for this book is available from the British Library.

The paper in this book meets the guidelines for permanence and durability of the Committee on Production Guidelines for Book Longevity of the Council on Library Resources.

10 9 8 7 6 5 4 3 2 1

for Gretchen
  to have and to hold
  to raise some kids
  to edit

Contents

Maps and Tables

Maps

Tables

Acknowledgments

Many people and institutions helped in the making of this book. For grants and other assistance that enabled me to travel and do research, I wish to thank the following: the International Research and Exchanges Board, with funds provided by the Andrew W. Mellon Foundation; the National Endowment for the Humanities; and the U.S. Department of State, whose generosity made it possible for me to spend nine months in Moscow and Leningrad and to return for another short trip. The National Endowment for the Humanities provided money for a research trip within the United States and another to Russia. The University of Texas at El Paso assisted through its grant and University Research programs. Miami University awarded me a Summer Research Appointment and a Grant to Promote Research and Scholarship; in addition, the Office for the Promotion of Teaching and Research made possible the maps and other illustrations. The American Philosophical Society provided funds that allowed me to do research at Harvard University one summer. The Russian Research Center there made me welcome as a Fellow on two occasions, gave me an office, and arranged access to Widener Library and other campus facilities. The Kennan Institute, part of the Woodrow Wilson Center for Scholars of the Smithsonian Institution, gave me a grant for a two-week stay in Washington. None of these institutions is responsible for the views expressed here.

During two stays in Moscow, Katya, Sasha, Anya, Ira, and Masha Urnov provided shelter, warmth, good humor, and conversation, as well as a chance to meet other fine people.

Many scholars offered comments and support. My colleagues at the University of Texas at El Paso and at Miami University gave sage advice and saved me, I am sure, from some grievous tactical and logical errors. In particular, I thank Allan Winkler, Jack Kirby, Carl Pletsch and, especially, Drew Cayton, all at Miami. The latter, though an Americanist, read the entire manuscript at an early stage and made extensive comments, many of which I adopted.

Others who read at least part of this work as it progressed, all specialists in Russian history, are Ron Suny, now at the University of Chicago, and Bill Rosenberg, of the University of Michigan. Arch Getty and Gabor Rittersporn are in a class by themselves for generosity. They furnished many valuable archival citations, as well as other materials, and generally helped me more than they will ever know. I am equally indebted to them for numerous conversations about our mutual interests.

Hugh D. Hudson, Jr., read the entire manuscript carefully and commented extensively on the work. He forced me to rethink key sections and had a lot to do with any merit this book may have. Lars Lih confessed to being the reader for Yale University Press; his many thoughtful remarks about presentation and substance caused me to rework entire sections of the book, all to the good. Karen Gangel, my manuscript editor, helped substantially in smoothing the style and argument. It was always a pleasure to deal with Chuck Grench and Otto Bohlman. I also wish to thank Denis J. Mullally for creating the maps.

Portions of Chapter 5 were previously published in *Slavic Review,* 45, no. 2 (1986), and are reprinted here with the permission of the American Association for the Advancement of Slavic Studies. Portions of Chapter 6 were previously published in *New Directions in Soviet History,* edited by Stephen White (Cambridge: Cambridge University Press, 1991), and are reprinted here with the permission of Cambridge University Press.

More than fifteen years ago my wife, Margaret Ziolkowski, and I formed a profound intellectual partnership. She read every word of this book at least twice and prompted me to make both stylistic and logical changes. I am tremendously grateful, and it is to her that this book is dedicated.

Introduction

In September 1987 I walked out of Sheremetevo Airport and boarded a bus to Moscow. There I found myself staring at an image that embodies the central issue of this book: a portrait of Stalin, hanging on the back of the driver's seat.

Iosif Vissarionovich Stalin was born Iosif Djugashvili in 1879 in the Caucasian mountain town of Gori, Georgia. His notoriety in twentieth-century history is rivaled only by that of Hitler, Pol Pot, or Idi Amin. Leader of the Soviet Union from 1928–29 until his death in March 1953, Stalin presided over his country's rise from second-rate status within Europe to the lofty heights of superpowerdom. But he also presided over, and must be held responsible for, the violent deaths of many people.

Of the twenty-five years that Stalin ruled the country, no period stands out more than the "Great Terror" of the late 1930s. During those years the bizarre Moscow show trials took place, in which dozens of high Communist Party officials confessed to crimes they had not committed. A few were sent to labor camps; most were executed. Arrests swept through the armed forces, the arts, managerial and party elites, and reached down to ordinary people. The meaning and impact of these events is the subject of this book.

My encounters with Stalin's presence continued during that fall of 1987. In October I visited the mother of an émigré friend, an editor for a literary journal. We spoke about the Terror, and I remarked that one intriguing question was whether the arrests had occurred mainly within the elite or had deeply affected all classes. Her answer was immediate and bitter: *all* classes. But a few minutes later, she gestured toward her cleaning woman, who was sitting alone in the kitchen—a clear demonstration that Soviet people were often separated according to intellectual inclinations and education, and a warning that no one could speak for all of them. "My cleaning woman still believes in Stalin," my hostess said; "I really don't understand why."

Toward the end of May 1988, I took a cab through Moscow. The middle-aged driver told me that "no portraits at all are allowed in cabs or other vehicles now. But of course that's directed against pictures of Stalin. There weren't any pictures of anyone else."

I asked the cabbie how he felt about the Father of His People when he was alive. "I was a teenager when he died," came the indirect response. "I lived in a small village several hundred kilometers from Moscow. I was the film projectionist there. One night I was showing a movie and an official came up and told me to stop it. He announced that Stalin had died. Immediately, the whole village went into mourning. No one ordered the people to do that; that's just how they felt."

Two Russian authors recently wrote, "Unquestionably, it is important to understand that 'Stalin died yesterday' [as another writer had put it], but still more important to recognize why Stalin 'lives' even today."[1] How could Stalin exist so vividly and, apparently, positively in anyone's mind given the fiercely negative picture of his rule held around the world?

Roy Medvedev, once called a dissident Soviet historian but in recent years regarded as a representative of Russian liberal thought, has described the dilemma this way: "The longer Stalin ruled the Soviet Union, cold-bloodedly destroying millions of people, the greater seems to have been the dedication to him, even the love, of the majority of the people. When he died in March 1953 the grief of hundreds of millions, both in the Soviet Union and around the world, was quite sincere."[2] Many other reports from the time also indicate widespread grief.[3]

Medvedev's conundrum remains unsolved in previous studies of the Terror.[4] Although a range of explanations for that paroxysm exists, a more or less standard version dominates in the West. With some variations, it is found in such works as Robert Conquest's *Great Terror,* published in 1968 and revised in 1990; Medvedev's *Let History Judge* (1972, 1974, 1989); and Robert C. Tucker's *Stalin in Power* (1990).[5] This picture has recently caught on among the intelligentsia of the former Soviet Union as well. Roughly, it goes like this: in 1922 Stalin became General Secretary (or Gensec) of the Communist Party, a position he made into that of leader. He defeated his party opponents, among them Leon Trotsky and Nikolai Bukharin, by the late 1920s. His victory coincided with the beginning of rapid industrialization and collectivization of the country's farms. In spite of his new status as undisputed leader, Stalin still faced strong criticism within communist ranks. These objections related to the feverish pace of industrialization and, above all, to the devastation of agriculture and the nation's best farmers during collectivization. Already hypersensitive, thirsty for glory and adulation, and paranoid, Stalin reacted strongly to this criticism and demanded the execution of a middle-level party official who had called for his removal.

The standard account continues: at the Seventeenth Communist Party Congress, held in January 1934, Stalin encountered another challenge—this time from Sergei Kirov, the young, dynamic, and handsome party boss of Leningrad (now known as St. Petersburg, as it was before World War I). Stalin easily defeated a movement to replace him with Kirov, but the effort left its mark on his suspicious mind. On December 1, 1934, a solitary gunman killed Kirov outside his office in the old imperial capital. Stalin secretly arranged the murder, which ostensibly benefited him in several ways. It removed a dangerous rival and provided a means to frighten the whole country: a leader had been killed by evil figures intent on destroying the USSR, and any official might be next. The culprits were identified as Trotskyites and other former party oppositionists, now in league with foreign powers.

Then in 1935–36, the argument proceeds, Stalin built a crescendo of tension within the party by purging members of the old oppositions. He moved stealthily to set up the show trials, which took place between August 1936 and March 1938 and resulted in the execution of the major figures who might have acted against him. At the same time, Stalin ordered the execution of the best of the officer corps, many capable managers, and the cream of the party. All were charged, falsely, with treason and sabotage and were shot. Arrests then spread throughout the population.

Supposedly the goal of the *vozhd'* (or "leader," akin to "Führer") in this mayhem was to achieve absolute power. He pursued this end through a "system of terror" in which previous behavior or loyalty counted for nothing; arrests were random. The idea was to frighten people profoundly and keep them constantly off balance so that no organized resistance could arise. By early 1939 the system had been perfected, and the Soviet populace effectively terrorized.

In addition to the damage this massive bloodshed caused to the citizenry and the economy, the usual argument continues, there was another terrible price to pay. The bill came due in June 1941, when the Germans attacked across the Soviet border. The effects of the purges now became evident in the behavior of Stalin's armies, numerous accounts maintain. Demoralized, perhaps turned into dehumanized creatures by the Terror, soldiers surrendered en masse to the invaders or, at the least, were unable to fight effectively. Few wished to defend the communist regime; giving themselves up to the Germans was preferable to living under Stalin. The invaders proved to be even worse than the communists, however, which had the effect of making the Russians want to fight for the USSR. Having won the war because of this grudging support, Allied help, and German mistakes, Stalin maintained political terror in the form of periodic waves of arrests until his death. Again, with some variations, this picture characterizes a large number of works on the period.[6]

This is the orthodox view of Stalinism and the Great Terror. Ironically, in many ways it revised earlier scholarship on the period, which often foreshadowed points I shall make on the nature of Stalinist rule and the relationship between authorities and people. In 1958, for example, Merle Fainsod, then dean of Soviet studies in America, published *Smolensk under Soviet Rule,* an investigation of one region of the USSR.[7] He believed that the Soviet system was totalitarian and dominated by terror during the 1930s, but he also stressed the right of ordinary citizens to complain about their situation;[8] their letters to officials were read and often resulted in investigations and judgments in favor of the protester. Fainsod described the effects of the arrests at the upper levels of the party and army but offered no comprehensive explanation of the Terror. A detailed elucidation had to await the opening of Soviet archives, he believed.[9]

In 1957 Joseph Berliner published *Factory and Manager in the USSR,* based on interviews with émigré Soviet managers and engineers. Berliner went beyond Fainsod in his depiction of a crucial arena of Soviet life characterized by compromise, negotiation, and attempts to satisfy complaints. Managers, far from being cowed by the pressure and threats directed at them from above, had to take risks to survive. To keep up production, they had to try to satisfy their workers.[10]

In *The Soviet Citizen: Daily Life in a Totalitarian Society* (1961), Alex Inkeles and Raymond Bauer stressed terror in understanding the 1930s yet detailed other important sources of compliance, including support for policies in education and the economy.[11] Meanwhile, much of the material in émigrés' memoirs countered the idea that fear of the regime dominated life in the USSR.

By the late 1960s, however, studies of the prewar years concentrated overwhelmingly on terror and its supposed impact as the central features of Soviet existence. These works also explained the mass arrests by identifying Stalin as master planner and executor in a drive for total power. Such arguments have been based largely on memoirs by people who were not close to Stalin and, in one crucial case, by someone who was rarely in the Soviet Union as events unfolded.[12]

This harsher depiction of the 1930s advanced what often appears to be considerable evidence for the argument about the crushing impact of the Terror. Many survivors reported that they feared arrest. They perceived an attack by the state on humanity, culture, and family life, in short on everything outside the narrow sphere of enthusiastic obedience required by the authorities.[13]

Certainly there were millions of victims, though recent evidence from Russian archives indicates that many widely accepted orthodox estimates of the toll were much too high. Even with the new, lower figures, the suffering was immense, and obviously many who were tied to those arrested also paid dearly. The pain involved has led writers like Medvedev to argue that "it's impossible to consider as victims of repression only those who did time in camps or died. In principle all the people were victims of repression."[14] But much evidence contradicts this conclusion. A crucial, unresolved issue is why, between 1935 and 1939, so many people supported violence by the state and even participated in it willingly.

Obviously the term *terror* figures prominently in this book. I use it to refer to swift, wide-ranging, and unjust violence carried out by the state, ostensibly in its own defense. This usage will be capitalized throughout. It is also necessary to say a few words about the term *totalitarianism*—which, despite the way most people seem to regard it, is a theoretical formulation and not a statement of fact—and to refer to the Nazi case. The concept purports to explain how certain modern regimes have ruled largely through coercion, though, as noted, the meaning of the word has varied a good deal in scholarly works.[15] In the public's mind totalitarianism is inextricably linked with Hitler's Germany. Yet the old image of the citizenry in the clutches of the Nazi machine has been, or should have been, shattered forever. A flood of works in recent decades has shown how German judges, doctors, lawyers, professors, ordinary people, and many women as a separate group all actively and sincerely supported the Nazis, at least in the years before war broke out.[16]

The conclusion that the Nazis had great support among the German people does not lessen the crimes of the Reich. In fact, it worsens the picture; instead of a handful of criminals, there were millions involved to one degree or another. Facing this reality is not just a German but a human problem.

Theories of totalitarianism are not so much incorrect as simply irrelevant to most of what went on in Germany or the Soviet Union in the 1930s. Each government wanted to control its people, totally if possible. But that desire must not be confused with what actually happened. For example, each state desired not only complete loyalty from its citizens but also productivity and discipline. These two expectations proved to be almost antithetical, because neither the Soviet nor the German government could take on the task of raising all children by itself.

Such an effort would have been enormously expensive as well as deeply unpopular, as the Soviet experience of the 1920s showed. So, developing respectable adults meant placing responsibility for children's upbringing in the hands of the family, and this in turn meant that loyalty to the family had to be encouraged.

Beyond this sort of dilemma, which can be found in various areas of German or Soviet life, there is the fact that no government has ever been able physically to manage the total existence of a country, or even of a prison, or to foresee all the complications that would ensue from a decision made at the center. Indeed, managers a few blocks away from the Kremlin found that they had to break the law every day in order to get anything done and to survive.

Thus totalitarianism is of some use in thinking about what the Nazi and Soviet regimes wanted, but it does not have much to do with what they got. True, the power of these states to intervene in people's lives was immense. Yet that too is something quite different from ordering events on a daily basis; such intervention, in fact, often produced disorder and other negative consequences for the regime.

Terror and fear are the heart of any analysis that relies on the totalitarian model.[17] It is possible that fear of the state touched vast numbers of Germans and Soviet citizens at some point, though the evidence argues against that conjecture. There were many limitations on speech, many options that were closed, and much coercion and control by the government and the ruling party. But there were also those who were not afraid of the state, and a great deal more was involved in making Germany and the USSR function. Coercion must now be assigned a minor role in analyses of the Third Reich; voluntary support was considerably more important. But for the general public the equation is surely still reversed.

The same is true today among the intelligentsia of the former Soviet Union, partly because the belief that all were persecuted is patriotic, ennobling, and politically useful. The Soviet people are proclaimed not guilty; liberals speak of *Stalin's* crimes, and the general-philosopher-historian Dmitrii Volkogonov writes of *Stalin's* triumph, the people's tragedy.[18] Major documents that would help in drawing a composite picture of Stalinism, for example, records of the Politburo, the highest body of the Communist Party, are not made public, for reasons that remain unknown. But stories of torture and suffering appear in a steady stream. Each one indirectly makes the point that the old Soviet system was bad and must be changed wholesale; this view helps engender support for liberal policies that entail a profound restructuring of the economy. An important message in published memoirs is that any distress associated with change in the form of unemployment or inflation cannot compare with the old suffering under Stalin. The command economy, where supposedly everything was planned from the top and no personal initiative existed, is equated with mass murder and concentration camps, thereby encouraging the notion that the old structure must go. Moreover, during the shift to a market system, those who lived under the Soviet regime are informed, none too subtly, that private activity is generally good, state activity often bad. Politics still conditions the treatment of history in the former USSR.[19]

Of course many true stories of tragedy have emerged in recent years. Stalinism was shot through with heinous crimes, and the old Soviet system desperately needed political and economic change. But portraying the past only in terms of suffering and injustice fails to explain a great deal about it or its persistent appeal.

The old view of Stalinism has been morally and politically comforting in the West, too. We bask in the reflected nobility of the victimization argument. We do not have to think about why and how ordinary people might commit disgusting crimes against humanity. We do not have to examine social or personal forces behind these acts. There is no need to question what we would have done under a Hitler or a Stalin; the state was the culprit.

But what is the state, if millions upon millions are involved in carrying out its functions? In a discussion of whether Nuremburg-style trials should be held for those charged with past abuses and state terror, the legal scholar Aleksandr M. Yakovlev recently remarked that he stood for such action wherever the criminal code permitted it. But he added that "if a majority constantly repeats specific acts, it will be in vain to describe it as a crime. Perhaps there may be atrocities in which the majority of people are involved."[20]

If Yakovlev is correct in implying that the majority participated in state crimes under Stalin, or even that a significant portion of the populace supported his actions, for whatever reason, there is little sense in regarding the state as separated from and dominating society. When a huge number of citizens took part in bodies that exercised public authority, they too constituted the state. It will be more logical to see state and society as intimately linked.

The subject of this book is the most crucial period of the USSR's history before *glasnost'*. I examine what recent reformers there claim they have been trying to reverse; as one Russian writer put it, "Stalin and the Stalinshchina [the Stalin phenomenon, but with a pejorative connotation] are the antithesis" of glasnost' and *perestroika*.[21] Yet ironically, this book also has something to say about how Stalinism helped prepare the way for change when Mikhail Gorbachev came to power in 1985. Ignoring earlier roots of glasnost' leads only to a contradiction:

that it sprang from the same minds that had been deadened by decades of totalitarianism.

In recent studies a more balanced picture of Stalinism, harking back to scholarship of the 1950s and early 1960s, has begun to reemerge. Only some who lived through the period spoke of pervasive fear; others pointed to quite different themes in their experiences. In many areas of Soviet life, Stalin's power was far from complete. Neither workers nor collective farmers were totally under central control, and people often found strategies for developing some autonomy.[22] Strong tensions and differences of opinion existed within the Communist Party, even during and after the late 1930s.[23] The party line was often unclear, and sometimes it was contradictory.

Still, we simply do not know much about important areas of Soviet life in the period of "high Stalinism." For example, the topics of workers' opportunities to criticize local conditions, people's perceptions of their regime and the Terror, and soldiers' morale during the German invasion have not been closely investigated. It is necessary to look further into such areas before coming to conclusions about the extent to which the Terror conditioned people's existence.

Many readers may find grating challenges in this book to opinions they have long held. For those who know the figure of Andrei Vyshinskii, chief prosecutor of the USSR and the leading accuser of the show trials, it will be disturbing to see him also portrayed as someone who worked for justice on other levels. Leading victims of the Terror, for instance, Nikolai Bukharin, shared beliefs and assumptions that facilitated their own destruction. Stalin reacted to events as much as he made them.

Terror was not inevitable in the Soviet system; Stalin did not need mass fear to rule. Other factors were more important in securing popular compliance. An authoritarian and repressive regime enjoyed considerable support in spite of— but also, to some extent, because of—its wide use of coercion. The state's use or threat of force did not result in a "broken" people.[24] This conclusion will be supported both by recently unveiled statistics on arrests and deaths and by people's reactions to their state and society.

Soviet citizens often said that during the 1930s they believed real "enemies of the people" were at work in society, carrying out sabotage. Many survivors indicated support for Stalin's effort to root out such villains. A central theme of this book is that in 1937–38 people were sincere in these statements. At this point such a proposition may seem like sheer nonsense: how could anyone have taken seriously the charges that so-called wreckers (*vrediteli*), among them close companions of Lenin, stalwart fighters for the revolution, had put broken glass into butter and caused explosions in factories? And yet, I argue, people did believe such things. We must examine carefully why in a particular situation these accusations made sense to many, just as the charge that the United States government had been thoroughly infiltrated by communists seemed plausible to many Americans in the early 1950s. Then we will be in a position to see how broad acceptance of Stalin's outlook by Soviet citizens accounted for many actions by both ordinary people and officials.

To some readers these arguments, and anyone who advances them, will seem heretical or even immoral. Other readers will not have prejudged the story, and still others will overcome their initial shock and perhaps distaste and will seriously consider the evidence marshaled here. The issues are important enough to warrant that approach.

Life and Terror in Stalin's Russia, 1934–1941

The Police and Courts Begin to Relax, 1933-1936

Much recent Western literature examines how the Soviet government drew on popular acquiescence, if not on outright voluntary support, in its early years.[1] During the Civil War, for example, the authorities found ways to integrate villagers into the new administrative structures and developed a policy concerning provisions that was acceptable to the peasants, whereby grain was funneled from the farms to the Red Army and the cities, despite the grave lack of consumer goods flowing the other way.[2]

As the Russian Empire fractured after 1917, bloodshed by the Reds was widespread and grotesque—but this was also true of their opponents, the Whites.[3] "Green" bands, nonpartisan groups of peasants who wished in vain to be left alone by all sides, sometimes killed in particularly disgusting ways.[4] Murderous conduct was so prevalent that Boris Pasternak deemed it the norm in *Doctor Zhivago:* "That period confirmed the ancient proverb, 'Man is a wolf to man.' Traveller turned off the road at the sight of traveller, stranger meeting stranger killed for fear of being killed. There were isolated cases of cannibalism. The laws of human civilization were suspended. The jungle law was in force. Man dreamed the prehistoric dreams of the cave dweller."[5]

It would be remarkable indeed if Stalin, who played a leading role in this period, had been immune to its effects. As a member and representative of the Politburo, he served on crucial fronts during the fighting and was close to serious danger many times. Yet biographers often pass quickly over these years of his life, assigning less importance to them than to his inherent megalomania. Even though he had become concerned with his own glory by the late 1920s, earlier he had experienced intense fear, pressure, and finally a sense of triumph in a cause. We know little about Stalin between 1917 and 1921; as researchers delve into former Soviet archives, a fuller picture of him and of the times will emerge. Surely the stress of the Civil War had a powerful impact on his thinking, perhaps as much or more so than any inherent tendency he had to seek power.

The number of Russians killed or wounded in World War I is now estimated at between 7.3 and 8.5 million, excluding losses due to illness or civilian casualties.[6] The death toll from 1917 to 1920 was probably 7–10 million.[7] After 1921 famine and epidemics struck the land, claiming the lives of several million more. Another few million emigrated, especially educated citizens. Altogether, the World War, the Civil War, and their aftermath represented an enormous disaster for the nations of the old tsarist empire. One major result of this carnage was a residue of hatred and bitterness throughout the country. During the fighting enemies had been real and ferocious; when the term "enemies of the people" became so lethally fashionable less than twenty years later, it had a profound resonance among the populace.[8] As Peter Loewenberg has written, "Each cohort [those who have shared a significant common experience] carries the impress of its specific encounter with history, be it war or revolution, defeat or national disaster, inflation or depression, throughout its life."[9] The cohort that passed through the Russian Civil War experienced all those things in large, bloody measure.

More turmoil was to come, in the form of collectivization and the famine of 1932–33. Suffice it to say that by late 1933 the country had emerged from a new series of deadly crises. Former oppositionists like Nikolai Bukharin, ousted from the leadership in 1929 for his opposition to collectivization, were appointed to important if secondary posts. Tempos of industrialization for the second five-year plan, 1933–37, were lower than for the previous five years. Food supplies improved so much by early 1935 that most of the rationing decreed in the late 1920s was abolished. The tone of the press and of leaders' speeches became considerably milder.

The party at this point reversed course regarding "bourgeois specialists," the engineers and managers with prerevolutionary educations who in recent years had been hounded by radical activists in the factories. After 1931, specialists were once more protected from insults and arrest. Other improvements took place in the arts, as the militant groups of the late 1920s, which pushed extreme and authoritarian visions, were brought to heel. On January 21, 1934, the party newspaper *Pravda* proclaimed in capital letters that "SOCIALISM IN OUR COUNTRY HAS WON."[10] At the Seventeenth Congress of the Communist Party, which opened a few days later, Stalin said that "there is nothing more to prove and, it seems, no one to fight."[11]

In July of that year the national police were reorganized and renamed; the old security agency, the Ob''edinennoe Gosudarstvennoe Politicheskoe Upravlenie (Unified State Political Administration, or OGPU) was absorbed by the Narodnyi Komissariat Vnutrennykh Del (the People's Commissariat for Internal Affairs), known as the NKVD. The civil or regular police, called the militia, also joined this agency.

In November 1934 the various republican—as in Russia, Ukraine, Georgia, and so on—commissariats of justice relinquished their control of prisons to the new entity.[12] A statute adopted that month created the Main Administration of Corrective Labor Camps, Labor Settlements, and Places of Confinement within the NKVD.[13] The acronym formed from the Russian words for this phrase was GULAG, the infamous organization so well known from Aleksandr Solzhenitsyn's *Gulag Archipelago,* among many other works.

Besides running the labor camps, the NKVD had various other functions and divisions: it operated fire departments across the USSR; ran the militia; kept track of ordinary civil statistics in registry offices; guarded the borders and maintained internal security troops, which were uniformed; had charge of discipline and crime in the transportation network; and handled state security. The NKVD also supervised geodesic and cartographic work, forestry, and measuring devices.[14] This organization was large, complex, and busy. Of major interest here are GULAG and State Security (Gosbezopasnost' in its shortened Russian version), which was responsible for investigating accusations of crimes against the state. This department carried out the gruesome interrogations and tortures of the Terror.

Some of the most serious problems in police behavior stemmed from the vagueness of the criminal statutes on "state crimes." Infamous Article 58 of the criminal code of the Russian Republic was the fundamental law under which the NKVD operated. Originally adopted in 1926, it lasted into the 1950s. Other Soviet republics had similar provisions in their codes. Article 58 began by defining "counterrevolutionary" as any "action that is directed toward the overthrow, undermining, or weakening" of Soviet authority or its representatives. Espionage or links with foreign governments for the purpose of overthrowing the state were of course prohibited, as were undermining government enterprises and "terrorist acts." The most notoriously flexible section of the statute was 58–10, which forbade "propaganda or agitation containing a call for the overthrow, undermining, or weakening of Soviet authority or for the carrying out of separate counterrevolutionary crimes." Various punishments were prescribed according to the nature of the infraction and its circumstances, ranging from a minimum sentence of three months' imprisonment to execution.[15] Nowhere were the words "weakening" or "undermining" defined, so that almost any negative remark could be considered counterrevolutionary if the regime so chose. As many incidents recorded later in this book will show, criticism of various kinds did exist and was tolerated. But obviously Article 58 gave the authorities great scope for arbitrariness and state coercion.

The laws creating and regulating the NKVD therefore presented serious problems. They reflected an outlook that had developed under the Soviets in the Civil War and deepened, if that was possible, during collectivization. The state reserved the right to deal quickly and summarily with perceived threats to its interests.

Yet from 1933 to 1936 a series of limitations, reforms, and criticisms of the NKVD appeared; relative to the earlier situation, these changes represented substantial progress in protecting individual rights. Although reality was far removed from appearances in this sphere, the general trend of these years was positive. By 1934 the *troiki,* three-person field courts set up by the OGPU in 1932 to deal with the problems and movements of people during the famine, had been disbanded.[16] The police were moving toward regular judicial procedure, so that defendants were somewhat better protected from abuse and arbitrariness.

The judicial collegium of the old police also ceased operations, which meant that the security apparatus decided fewer cases. Instead the law-enforcement "organs," as they were widely called, proceeded more frequently than before through the court system, under the jurisdiction of the Commissariat of Justice. Cases initiated by the political police, however, could still go to special collegia at the *oblast'* (roughly the equivalent of a province) court level or to military tribunals. Judging by records from one locality, the collegia were poorly funded stepchildren of the court system: the one at work in Smolensk had to meet in the hallway of a building and lacked money to pay witnesses. Its members had a reputation for being unfit to serve in the regular criminal and civil courts.[17] If Stalin was already planning to carry out mass terror, the new bodies represented a curious step. Underfunded and understaffed, they tended to complicate and lengthen procedures against arrestees.

The statute creating the NKVD specified that certain crimes involving state security were to be tried under the jurisdiction of the Supreme Court of the USSR. Offenses "such as treason to the Motherland, espionage, and similar matters, are to be turned over to the Military Collegium of the Supreme Court . . . or to military tribunals, according to the [seriousness of] the charge."[18] This stipulation too appeared to limit the security forces' powers; at the least, it complicated their operations.

As early as May 1933 the Central Committee (CC), a body of about 140 that stood just below the Politburo in the party hierarchy, had ordered the national Procuracy (or attorney general's office) to supervise arrests made by the OGPU. In the next year the Procuracy complained to the CC that groundless arrests and ones made without procurators' sanctions were taking place and asked the CC to correct the situation.[19] In June 1935 the Council of Ministers and the CC together specified that without exception the police had to have the approval of a procurator in order to make any arrest. For arrests at the scene of a crime, the NKVD had to obtain the agreement of a procurator shortly thereafter. Party members could be detained only with the permission of their local party organization or of a higher tier.[20]

Important protests against the procedures of the special collegia and arbitrary police behavior now came from virtually the highest levels of the regime. Ironically, one source of objections was the notorious Andrei Vyshinskii, who had been appointed procurator-general of the USSR in March 1935. He became infamous as a prosecutor in the staged show trials of 1936–38, extending his reputation for duplicity as assistant minister of foreign affairs from 1940 to 1949 and as minister from then until Stalin's death, in 1953. Vyshinskii's biography is a curious chapter of a curious age. Born in Odessa in 1883, he was of Polish descent. His father owned a business and earned a good income. While growing up in Baku, an industrial city stirring with labor unrest in the late nineteenth century, Andrei "acquired rebellious convictions and a rebellious past" before graduating from high school.[21] Even so, his ideas did not prevent him from studying law at Kiev University, from which he was eventually expelled for participation in an illegal Marxist circle.

Vyshinskii became a Menshevik rather than a Bolshevik after the Russian Social Democratic Party split into two wings in 1903. Nominally, the Mensheviks were the milder group, as shown by their cooperation with the liberals and their opposition to a socialist takeover in 1917.[22]

In 1908 Vyshinskii served a short prison term for his radical activities. In jail he reportedly met and argued strenuously with a Georgian revolutionary then known as Koba. This fellow inmate was Iosif Djugashvili, who in 1912 took the *nom de révolution* Stalin. Although the two did not meet again until 1918, Stalin, with his excellent memory, surely recalled that Vyshinskii had argued over politics but had never lost his temper.

Through one of those odd loopholes that made the tsarist regime so inconsistent, Vyshinskii was able to return to law school after leaving prison. Eventually he settled in Moscow with his own family. When tsarism collapsed in February

1917, he was active as a member of the Mensheviks, who now split irrevocably from the Bolsheviks and became their bitter antagonists as the Revolution and Civil War unfolded. Yet this past did not hamper him; in February 1920 he joined the Communist Party (Bolsheviks), as it was then called.

Vyshinskii returned to the practice of law after the fighting ended. In 1925 he became rector of Moscow State University, the leading academic institution in the country, in spite of a lack of scholarly credentials. In 1928 he received the sensitive assignment of presiding over the Shakhty trial of foreign and Soviet wreckers in mining. He played the same role in the "Industrial Party" trial of 1930, one of the last official assaults on the old bourgeois specialists. Vyshinskii proved himself an able and articulate defender of the regime's political goals and so seemed just the man to lead the prosecution in the Moscow show trials of 1936–38. With this career in mind, most readers will find it difficult to accept the idea that in 1935–36 Vyshinskii represented a strong voice for moderation in interpreting and enforcing the law. Yet he did.

At this point Vyshinskii did not preside over the judicial system; that was the job of the People's Commissar of Justice, the veteran Bolshevik Nikolai Krylenko, a former naval ensign, hero of the October Revolution, and Civil War commander. Rivals for years, the two now waged a bitter struggle in the press and other arenas against each other's conceptions of law. Krylenko favored the "radical, or nihilist, approach," which had dominated procedure from 1928 to 1931, during the outburst of transformative zeal known as the Cultural Revolution.[23] He advocated the tradition of "revolutionary legality," which in fact went back at least to the Civil War. This concept entailed quick adjudication of all cases— under laws that consciously reflected the regime's bias against the former propertied classes and in favor of the former lower classes—and flexible norms that took into account the political nature of a charge. Law merely gave form to the party's political needs. Like some other Soviet theorists, Krylenko hoped that administrative procedures would eventually replace statutes. Thus he did not believe strongly in legal codes.

Between 1932 and 1936, Vyshinskii stood for the opposite on each of these points, advocating instead due process, careful judgments on the basis of evidence, a strong role for defense lawyers in all cases, firm legal codes that applied equally to the entire population, and a strengthening of law. In short, he tried "to restore important elements of the bourgeois legal tradition."[24] Although their struggle was personal as well as institutional, both Krylenko and Vyshinskii were consistent in the principles they advocated during their debate. Here is an indica-

tion of how discussion and exchanges of fundamentally different views characterized Soviet life through the middle of the 1930s.

One major problem that Vyshinskii identified in judicial procedure concerned
the NKVD's right to operate "in administrative order," without normal rules of
justice or evidence, to exile or send to labor camps anyone it chose for up to five
years.[25] The law provided no guidelines on the separation of such cases from
those that had to go through regular or military courts, except that nominally the
more serious offenses proceeded in the military channel.

In February 1936 Vyshinskii wrote to Viacheslav Molotov, Stalin's right-hand
man in the Politburo and chairman of the Sovnarkom (Council of Ministers), to
call for a reduction of the NKVD's administrative powers. The commissariat's
Special Session (Soveshchanie), its internal tribunal, deliberated without calling
witnesses or the accused, especially in cases of counterrevolutionary agitation
and "expression of terrorist intentions." In the process, serious mistakes could
occur. Vyshinskii wanted the "maximum limitation" placed on the Special Session's right to hear cases; he believed they should go instead through the regular
courts, following normal judicial procedure. For cases that continued in the
Special Session, the Procuracy should be allowed to make a "most careful check
of investigative materials" and to obtain the release of prisoners if it found no
basis for further action.[26]

Vyshinskii cited the authority enjoyed by English judges as a model for Soviet
courts, a suggestion that would have seemed heretical, if not counterrevolutionary, just a few years earlier. Bizarrely enough in light of his emphasis during and
after the later show trials on confessions as proof of guilt, in 1935 Vyshinskii
scorned the idea, which he attributed to the NKVD, that they were sufficient for
an indictment. Instead he believed that attention should be paid to objective
evidence. He publicly attacked the NKVD's secret procedures, because, unlike
open show trials, they "served no educative or legitimating functions."[27] In an
article published shortly thereafter, one of many similar pieces, he warned against
violations of law and poor investigative procedures. He gave several examples of
how not to operate, including the case of an engineer given a sentence of six years
for low-quality output. A later check of the circumstances revealed that the man
worked in an experimental laboratory and was in fact not a wrecker but a "very
valuable specialist." Vyshinskii now demanded "concrete changes" in the courts
and the procuracy to liquidate this "scandalous work, so that it will not provoke
laughter or irritation." He linked these remarks to Stalin's current slogan of
"respect for cadres," issued in May 1935. The new procurator-general cited this

phrase in order to fix greater attention on the rights of individuals in the courts.[28] A series of reforms in 1936 strengthened Vyshinskii's supervision of the Procuracy and reduced Krylenko's role to overseeing the administration of the court system, even though he was now head of the new Commissariat of Justice. In spite of their differences on the philosophy of law, at this point both Krylenko and Vyshinskii argued to party leaders that the use of counterrevolutionary charges had to be limited. Writing to Stalin on March 31, 1936, Krylenko noted the rapidly rising number of such cases handled by the special collegia of the courts. They had ruled on 2,995 charges in the first half of 1935, 5,804 in the second half, and 1,214 in February 1936. The number of *sentences* for counterrevolutionary activity, however, dropped in this period, as will be shown.[29]

Krylenko found that the work of the collegia "makes sense because this is the current form of class war." But the growth in the number of political cases "cannot but produce bewilderment." He referred to popular enthusiasm for Soviet progress and a general improvement in conditions; this "contradiction" with the statistics he cited had led him to examine the quantity and quality of collegia cases. Many of the changes were unnecessary to begin with—for example, those involving cooperative stores on collective farms—and the Supreme Court of the USSR had overturned a number of them. In this action too, of course, the court system displayed leniency.

Krylenko also argued for wide tolerance of critical remarks by ordinary citizens, even in cases of "formally counterrevolutionary" statements. As an example, he mentioned the remark by a peasant that "Soviet power leads not to the improvement of the kolkhozniks' [collective farmers] way of life, but to disaster." If critics such as this had no counterrevolutionary past, no basis existed for criminal action, he contended.

In early 1938 Krylenko was arrested as an enemy of the people and shot, though, as we shall see, on charges not related to his stance of 1936. But in the meantime Stalin left him in a critical post. A much stronger indication that the *vozhd'* did not oppose such lenient views at this point is the fact that Vyshinskii, whom Stalin obviously trusted throughout his life, made similar criticisms a month after Krylenko's letter; perhaps the two coordinated their strategy on this issue. In April 1936, writing to Stalin and Molotov, Vyshinskii pointed out that in a study of eight hundred counterrevolutionary cases, between 30 and 35 percent of the convictions for agitation had turned out to be "incorrect." The NKVD, procurators across the country, and the courts were all applying Article 58–10 "extremely widely" and were simplifying investigations "impermissibly." People were being arrested for "everyday babbling, grumbling, dissatisfaction with the poor work of individual persons or organizations . . . and also for singing popular ditties [*chastushki*] and songs with anti-Soviet contents." Vyshinskii requested the CC to order the Procuracy, the NKVD, and the courts to change their behavior regarding counterrevolutionary agitation. He also wanted the Supreme Court of the Russian Republic to review all cases of agitation decided in 1935 in the regions where this charge had been most widely applied.[30] Unfortunately, we do not know whether the CC acted on Vyshinskii's recommendation. But he remained outspoken and powerful.[31]

Thus in 1935–36, despite his appalling role in the show trials that began in August 1936, Vyshinskii advocated major improvements in legal procedures. Simultaneously he scorned key NKVD practices and urged much greater tolerance of ordinary citizens' criticisms, so long as they did not touch fundamental policy. He and Krylenko demanded further progress in the relaxation already under way.

Part of their motivation was surely the desire to enhance the standing of their particular agencies. As judicial officials, they had a vested interest in promoting limits on the police while expanding their own sphere. But, more broadly, it is clear that by 1935 both men felt that the Soviet regime could substantially lessen its reliance on coercion as a means of maintaining control. Terror, to the extent it served as the linchpin of Soviet governance before the mid-1930s, was an extreme measure applied in the crises of 1918 and of 1929–32, while the collective farm structure was being created. Having passed through the stress of that process and of the famine, and with industrialization well under way, there was simply no need for mass arrests. Nor was that practice—itself a response to events, albeit ones set in motion by the regime—a productive one. Imprisoning or exiling millions, as other societies have learned, entails high economic costs.

The pattern of arrests and executions from 1930 to 1936 supports the picture of increasing tolerance (table 1). After 1930 the number of executions fell in each of the next six years, as did the number of convictions for all crimes for 1931 and 1932. In the following year convictions began to rise again, probably as a reflection of the famine, which engendered complaints and increased movement within the country, and the adoption of the internal passport system. Then, as argued above, the years 1934–36 represented a steady relaxation in the political sphere. Arrests in general declined rapidly and steadily, despite the assassination of

Table 1 Number of Arrests or Investigations by the Security Police and Their Outcome, 1930–1936

| | Arrests | | | |
Year	All Crimes	CRᵃ Crimes	Convictions	Executions
1930	331,544	266,679	208,069	20,201
1931	479,065	343,734	180,696	10,651
1932	410,433	195,540	141,919	2,728
1933	505,256	283,029	239,664	2,154
1934	205,173	90,417	78,999	2,056
1935	193,083	108,935	267,076	1,229
1936	131,168	91,127	274,670	1,118
Total	2,255,722	1,379,461	1,391,093	40,137

Source: GARF f. 9401, o. 1, d. 4157, 11. 201–03, a report prepared for Stalin's successors at the end of 1953.
ᵃCR = counter-revolutionary

Kirov in December 1934. That event, however, helped produce an increase in arrests for counterrevolutionary crimes in 1935, but even then the number remained only a little more than 38 percent of what it had been in 1933.

There is a curious anomaly in the figures for that period: for 1935 and 1936, the number convicted of all crimes is larger than the number arrested. Perhaps some cases from earlier years had slowly worked their way through the judicial system. In other instances, people were not formally arrested but were charged and convicted administratively. The majority of such cases, however, likely involved lesser penalties. It was common for Soviet courts to order "noncustodial" sanctions; for example, a worker would be ordered bound to his job for a time with a reduction in pay. We know that in 1937 and 1938, 53.1 and 58.7 percent, respectively, of all court decisions were noncustodial.[32] The large number convicted for all crimes in 1935–36 is therefore not as alarming as it might seem.

There is the possibility that other repression was never recorded, but the top-secret report of December 1953 was surely a serious effort by the post-Stalin regime to collect the available data. There is no reason to suspect that the new leaders chose to lie to themselves.

The figures for police and judicial action continued to be high into 1936; 91,000 arrests for counterrevolutionary crimes is a great many. But the key issue is how the country was ruled, and in that regard the overall trends were definitely in the direction of less coercion.

Nevertheless, the number of prisoners held in camps and labor colonies for all types of crimes increased by almost 90 percent from 1934 to 1935 (table 2). This rise was due to nonpolitical arrests, because both the number and the percentage of people confined for counterrevolutionary crimes fell significantly. By January 1937 the number of prisoners held for counterrevolutionary activity had begun to fall.

The data indicate that as time went on the authorities were less interested in using the counterrevolutionary statutes, the legal weapon that allowed the most scope for arbitrariness and reliance on administrative methods rather than on evidence. There is no pattern here of increasing terror. During 1936 the whole picture of incarceration began a shift toward fewer political and nonpolitical arrests.

In spite of the sharp increase in the number of prisoners from 1934 to 1936, judicial practice now became more humane and concerned for individuals' rights. A first major step occurred in May 1933, when Stalin and Molotov ordered the release of half of all labor-camp inmates whose sentences were connected with collectivization.[33] In January 1935, the Supreme Court of the USSR exonerated a group of convicted *kolkhoz* officials because procurators had mishandled the investigation and examination of evidence. The court even considered criminal proceedings to punish lower judicial bodies for their conduct.[34] In February 1935, *Sovetskaia Iustitsiia* (*Soviet Justice*), the official journal of the Commis-

Table 2 Political and Nonpolitical Inmates in Soviet Incarceration, 1934–1937

Year	No. of Inmates	No. Sentenced for CR[a] Activity	% CR[b]
1934	510,307	135,190	26.5
1935	965,742	118,256	16.3
1936	1,296,494	105,849	12.6
1937	1,196,439	104,826	12.8

Source: V. N. Zemskov, "Gulag (Istoriko-sotsiologicheskii aspekt)," *Sotsiologicheskie Issledovaniia* 6 (1991), 11. Figures are for January 1 of each year and do not include those confined in prisons.
[a]CR = Counterrevolutionary
[b]Among all inmates held in a given year.

sariat of Justice, published, with evident satisfaction, the story of eastern Siberian courts that had quashed a series of cases initiated under Article 58. The journal maintained that these cases should not have arisen in the first place.[35]

By March of the same year the First All-Union Conference of Justice Workers resolved that "fundamental reconstruction [*perestroika*] of the work of the Procuracy in court is essential." The prosecutors would have to participate systematically in all court sessions, whether in the first instance or in appeals. They would bear "responsibility for each incorrect sentence in terms of the composition of the court and for not protesting [such] a sentence."[36]

In August 1935 the government declared an amnesty for all collective farmers sentenced to less than five years if they were working "honorably and with good conscience" on the kolkhozy. Presumably this decree applied to those peasants punished but not sent into distant exile or prison. The directive did not apply to recidivists or those convicted of counterrevolutionary crimes,[37] but sentences in such cases would have been longer than five years.

Major improvements occurred regarding the law of August 7, 1932, which specified an automatic ten-year sentence for the theft of any "socialist property." This punishment was intended in particular to prevent collective farmers from keeping even small amounts of public produce for themselves. At first the statute was widely enforced, but by 1935 it was rapidly declining in importance. In February of that year *Sovetskaia Iustitsiia* reported with approval that a Siberian court, citing "insignificance," had dropped a charge against a worker for having one and one-half kilograms of grain in his pockets and gloves.[38] Vyshinskii revealed that in 1935 only half of the cases prosecuted under the decree of August 7, 1932 resulted in convictions.[39]

Even more meaningful, a judgment of December 1932 against a female farmer from the North Caucasus tried under the August 7 law was now reopened and held up as an example of hideous injustice. She had stolen three *poods* (about 49 kilograms, or 108 pounds) of wheat after a harvest. A year later the Supreme Court of the Russian Republic reclassified her crime under a less severe law and ordered her release. But a year and a half after that, the North Caucasian authorities had not yet taken action to have her freed. Finally, in April 1935 the Procuracy of the Russian Republic, supposedly following a request from the head of the NKVD camp where she was being held, asked for a review of her case. The procurators noted that she had three young children at home and that her "crime [had] stemmed from a difficult material situation." The woman was ordered released, while those guilty of mistreating her were to be "severely punished."

The editors of *Sovetskaia Iustitsiia*, in which this pathetic story appeared, commented that they awaited word from the North Caucasus on whether the farmer had been freed and those guilty of holding her so long were being brought to court.[40]

The discussion of the case was tantamount to an official statement of judicial policy, so the message to courts around the country was clear: there were to be no more prosecutions for petty crimes under the law of August 7; rather, the courts were to show greater understanding for people committing them. This development marked a profound change from the period just after the adoption of the statue, when the press and courts raged about "class enemies" in the countryside and the need to punish them severely.

In January 1936 the CC and Sovnarkom resolved to check all convictions under the August 7 law. A report issued eight months later showed that of the 126,616 sentences handed down to the beginning of 1935, 97 percent had already been reviewed. In 98,375 cases, or over 80 percent of those checked, charges had been changed to another article of the criminal code. Almost 53,000 sentences had been reduced, though the convicts were still being held. In addition, 40,789 people had been released after reclassification of their cases. In only 19.5 percent of the cases were the original charge and sentence left in place.[41]

Policy toward collective farmers now veered away from arrests even more sharply. In April 1936 Vyshinskii reported to Stalin and other top officials that during 1934–35, 768,989 sentences of kolkhozniki had been reversed. Of these, 337,906 were in Ukraine alone.[42]

In April 1935 a further key pronouncement in the direction of relaxation appeared in *Sovetskaia Iustitsiia*. Aron Sol'ts, a high official in the procuracy of the USSR, had remarked at a conference held the previous December that crimes committed "while we are occupied with construction [of a socialist society]" frequently occur because people "do not know how to build, do not know how to live in the way demanded by their situation." Courts are convicting "our people," as opposed to the "socially alien elements" elsewhere identified so often as culprits. Punishment should have "educational [*vospitatel'nye*] goals,"[43] the logical response if the problem was lack of knowledge rather than criminal intent.

In May 1935, in the pages of *Pravda*, the official party newspaper, the brilliant satirists Il'ia Il'f and Evgenii Petrov lent their considerable prestige and talents to the campaign against judicial harshness. They detailed the disheartening case of a Moscow student, Mikhail Sveranovskii, who had boarded a tram to go to a party one evening. He had had a ten-kopeck ticket when he should have had a fifteenkopeck one. An inspector demanded that he pay a fine of three rubles. Sveranovskii did not have that much money with him; the two got into an argument, and the inspector claimed that the student pushed him. Eventually, despite favorable testimony about his record and character from fellow students and officials at his institute, Sveranovskii was convicted of "hooliganism" and given a two-year sentence.

Il′f and Petrov commented that this was not a "judicial mistake" but something "significantly worse, more dangerous." The people's court judge was an "ignorant person" who "did not see whom he was sentencing." He behaved like a "beginning accountant." The court established the facts of which tram and which line the incident occurred on but made no inquiries as to the character of the accused. With disgust, the authors pointed out the great need for improved reasoning and training within the judicial apparatus.[44] Obviously, ordinary people had to be better protected from arbitrary sentences.

In August 1935 *Pravda* added a weighty editorial voice to this campaign when it announced that "to punish for mistakes—this is the last resort. It is necessary to teach how to avoid mistakes. . . . It's necessary to remember a basic rule: persuade, teach, help." Repression was to be used only in "extreme cases," but even then it should also educate.[45]

Thus, during 1935 party organs and the central authorities of the judicial system issued a series of strong warnings to lower courts and prosecutors alike that petty problems and infractions were not to be considered crimes, that cases of counterrevolution were not to be pressed unless serious, and that careful attention to evidence was the order of the day. Krylenko's and Vyshinskii's protests against NKVD behavior and the wide application of article 58 had a similar thrust.

It may be, as Eugene Huskey has suggested, that improvements in legal norms grew out of the leadership's desire to fit better into the world community; Vyshinskii seemed to endorse this goal in his desire not to see Soviet practice derided abroad. By 1934 Hitler appeared likely to stay in power, and the international situation became truly threatening for the USSR. Because Stalin's government actively sought foreign alliances, the country required an image of respectability to mollify other governments. However, the new moderation within the courts had a domestic as well as international impetus and matched other ameliorating trends of the period. The regime was relaxing in 1935–36.

Violence was a central feature of Russian life during the Revolution of 1905 and again from 1914 to 1921. It came from above, carried out by the tsarist regime, the liberal Provisional Government that followed it, the communists, and other groups in the Civil War. It came from below, fueled by frustration and the perception that any regime's ability to persuade people to follow it and to wield power was often weak. These patterns left deep impressions among the populace, including a collective readiness to become frustrated and to anger in succeeding crises.[46] This was the essential background to the Terror.

Yet by 1934 the Stalinist regime had begun to rein in the police and courts and to institute substantial reforms within them, which changed and softened punitive practices. In the mid-1930s great scope still existed for repression and arbitrariness, but progress was being made toward a fairer, more consistent, and less political application of law. Unfortunately, this trend quickly broke down.

Politics and Tension in the Stalinist Leadership, 1934–1937

By 1934 new opposition to Stalin, especially regarding his handling of the economy and collectivization, had arisen within the Communist Party. The extent of the dissatisfaction, however, is unclear. Glasnost' has not yet revealed the whole story, and may never do so, because in the nature of Soviet politics much would not have been committed to paper. Available memoirs are sometimes contradictory or problematic. Key records, kept in a special "presidential" archive within the Kremlin, are still not open to researchers. Nor can we be sure of the impact of this dissatisfaction on Stalin, though Robert C. Tucker is probably correct that it threatened his pride more than his power.[1]

One major document from the opposition is now available: the Riutin Memorandum or Platform. M. N. Riutin had been a district party secretary (that is, leader) in Moscow associated with the Right at the end of the 1920s. He was expelled from the party in 1930 for spreading "rightist propaganda," which generally meant a much more accommodating line toward the peasants. He continued to live in Moscow, however, working as an economist.[2] His platform, dated August 21, 1932, has now been published.[3]

Riutin referred to Stalin's "personal dictatorship" as "the most naked, deceitful, [perfectly] realized." In the preceding four or five years, Stalin had "broken all records for political hypocrisy and unprincipled political intrigue." He had changed his principles even more shamelessly than bourgeois governments did and had offered a "theoretically illiterate" idea on the development of agriculture. Riutin believed that

> the rule of terror in the party and the country under the clearly ruinous policy of Stalin has led to a situation in which hypocrisy and two-facedness have become common phenomena. . . .
>
> The most evil enemy of the party and the proletarian dictatorship, the most evil counterrevolutionary and provocateur could not have carried out the work of destroying the party and socialist construction better than Stalin has done. . . .
>
> Stalin is killing Leninism, [killing] the proletarian revolution under the flag of the proletarian revolution and [killing] socialist construction under the flag of socialist construction![4]

It is easy to imagine not only the Gensec's wrath at this tone but also the offense to his supporters within the Central Committee.

Riutin also called for a "struggle for the destruction of Stalin's dictatorship," which would "give birth to new leaders and heroes."[5] These words could be taken as advocating terrorism, because there was no sign of an open, organized movement against the government. Stalin could well have interpreted these words as a personal threat.

Following Riutin's arrest in September 1932 one of the top bodies of the party, the Control Commission, expelled twenty other members for belonging to a "counterrevolutionary group" led by him. Among those ousted were the former Politburo members and oppositionists Grigorii Zinoviev and Lev Kamenev, who reportedly had received copies of one of Riutin's works but had not informed the authorities.[6]

Stalin then demanded that Riutin be executed. The motion failed in the Politburo, however. Sergei Kirov, supported by Stalin's friend G. K. Ordzhonikidze and also by V. V. Kuibyshev, strongly opposed the death penalty. Stalin's close associates V. M. Molotov and L. M. Kaganovich abstained from the voting.[7] Sent to a labor camp, Riutin survived until 1937 or 1938.[8]

Stalin did not initiate a campaign against Riutin, who was living peacefully at the time he wrote his memorandum, but instead reacted to events. This fact does not, however, absolve him of responsibility for his harsh response; he caused much of the chaos and damage of collectivization, which in turn provoked a reply from people like Riutin. Here the importance of cause and effect or of who acted first begins to disappear; Stalin was a man initiating and reacting to developments, not the cold mastermind of a plot to subdue the party and the nation. Nonetheless, the significance of specific occurrences and his responses to them is great. This interaction moved him in certain directions, which implies that there would be limitations to his behavior stemming from external conditions. He could also be inclined to adopt less repressive policies, according to his reading of circumstances.

Another episode of criticism, the Eismont-Tolmachev affair, followed a few months later. N. B. Eismont, a Bolshevik since 1907, was People's Commissar of Supply for the Russian Republic. Involved with him in what was called a counterrevolutionary grouping was N. V. Tolmachev, a party member since 1904 and head of a government committee overseeing road transportation.

In November 1932 the chief of Moscow's Communist Academy denounced Eismont directly to Stalin, reporting that Eismont had asked a friend of his to join with him in a group like Riutin's. Three Central Committee members, Emelian Iaroslavskii, Ian Rudzutak, and Pavel Postyshev, questioned Eismont in late November and charged that he had said it would be necessary to remove Stalin, which, they maintained, meant killing him. Eismont denied this accusation but admitted having had a conversation critical of Stalin; he described his mood as "painful" (*tiazheloe*) during these "difficult years."

Postyshev immediately urged the arrest of Eismont, who then left the room. At that point Iaroslavskii and Rudzutak said they thought he had been lying from start to finish. Rudzutak suggested Eismont's expulsion from the party, to be followed by arrest. The other two agreed. In this instance Stalin's close subordinates, not their chief, were the decision makers.

In January 1933 Eismont, Tolmachev, and another man received terms of three years' confinement, a degree of reprisal that may be explained by their case having immediately followed the Riutin Memorandum.[9] The Riutin and Tolmachev affairs surely increased Stalin's wariness; Riutin's language in particular probably made him wary of terrorism.

As the famine and the most frantic phase of industrialization passed, so did most of the strident criticism directed against Stalin. But he was soon to face a personal rather than political crisis. In November 1932 his second wife, Nadezhda Allilueva, committed suicide. Apparently depressed by the situation of the country and her husband's crude behavior toward her, she shot herself after he insulted her at a party.

Biographers have paid little attention to this event, as though it made almost no difference to Stalin. A purported lack of concern on his part can be explained only if he is seen as a monster or as someone whose character had become fixed many years before.[10] This view, in turn, readily lends itself to the idea that he meticulously planned and executed every step of the Terror. According to their daughter, however, Stalin never got over Nadezhda's death.[11] One of his bodyguards recalled that the Gensec frequently sat by her grave at night for hours.[12]

It is therefore likely that he experienced the same unsettling effect that others do after the suicide of an immediate relative: "Very often, it destroys others in the same family, burdening them with an indelible stigma and rupturing the bonds of interpersonal relationships that have endured for years." The survivors may suffer for an extended period from an obsession with the "whos, the whys, the whats and the ifs" and from "disturbing images of blood and violence produced in the mind."[13] This description would appear to fit Stalin. Having occurred shortly after the discovery of the Riutin Memorandum, Nadezhda's death may have filled him with hatred, the desire to project his guilt over her death onto others (namely, his enemies in the party), and suspiciousness.

In 1934 a new political threat to Stalin supposedly appeared. As noted, the Seventeenth Congress of the Communist Party, held in January and February of that year, was marked publicly by political relaxation and reconciliation with former oppositionists. Yet several accounts maintain that a group of prominent party members, including some from the Central Committee, approached Sergei Kirov, party chief in Leningrad and a Politburo member, about the possibility of his replacing Stalin as head of the party.

Kirov is portrayed in the literature as a liberal compared to other leaders; he reportedly won widespread support and affection in Leningrad, partly by being accessible to ordinary people. The origin of this picture, the "Letter of an Old Bolshevik," is problematic.[14] In fact Kirov's liberalism and personal qualities are far from clear; he seems to have supported Stalin on every major policy issue.[15] Compared to some in the party, the vozhd' himself could be considered a moderate in this particular period, as will be shown.

There are other opinions on Kirov's character: a young communist who lived in Leningrad at the time but later defected called him "one of the worst tyrants of the Stalin regime" and claimed that "his invariable savagery towards those who disagreed with the regime is indescribable."[16] The Yugoslav communist Anton Ciliga, who visited Leningrad various times in the 1920s and lived there for a short period before his arrest in May 1930, believed that Kirov was hated in the city because of his punitive treatment of Right Oppositionists and his personal corruption.[17] These comments raise serious doubts about the argument that Stalin distrusted Kirov for his liberalism and popularity.

Legends describe the Leningrad chieftain as energetic, charming, and handsome, though in films he appears even shorter than Stalin, who was about five feet three inches tall. Kirov had joined the Bolshevik Party in 1905. Forty-seven years old at this point, he was ethnically Russian, unlike the Gensec.

Whether Kirov informed Stalin of the effort to replace him is uncertain; in any case, Stalin supposedly knew of the move. Kirov went ahead and addressed the Party Congress, to great applause. He spoke about Stalin in adulatory tones, calling him "the great strategist of liberation of the working people of our country and the whole world."[18] Perhaps he was playing a double game, but it would have been out of order to say anything less of Stalin at such a gathering.

The other aspect of the threat to Stalin at the congress was that, reportedly, of the 1,225 (or 1,059 in some accounts) voting delegates, 166 may have voted against his membership in the Central Committee. But an investigation conducted under glasnost' found only that 166 ballots were *missing*, that the original number of paper ballots is unknown, and that it is impossible to be sure how many delegates voted against Stalin.[19]

Even if 166 did oppose him, that number represents only 13.5 percent of those attending. Perhaps such a high proportion within a group already screened for loyalty alarmed Stalin, but this is double speculation. Any threat to him from within the party remained minor; whether he saw it that way or not is another issue.

An event then occurred that is widely accepted in both the West and the ex-Soviet Union as the opening of the Terror. On December 1, 1934, a lone gunman assassinated Kirov in the corridor outside his Leningrad office. The killer, Leonid Nikolaev, is usually thought to have been Stalin's tool in the affair. Supposedly the Gensec achieved two goals with a single shot: he eliminated a dangerous popular rival and moved further toward frightening the entire country into submission. Stalin used Kirov's murder to proclaim the existence of enemies everywhere and to begin a hunt for them, thereby preparing the people for the idea that they had to watch one another carefully. They would be thrown off balance, unable to resist, and he would impose his will on them.[20]

Some evidence appears to support this view of the murder. Nikolaev penetrated the Smolny Building, the party headquarters in Leningrad, and reached the second floor outside Kirov's office without being stopped. No bodyguard protected the local leader at that moment. Within days Nikolaev and several others charged as coconspirators were put to death, which could indicate a quick cover-up by Stalin. In any case, the vozhd' took advantage of the shooting to repress former oppositionists.

But there are many problems with the idea that he had Kirov killed. Evidence recently released from Russia shows that, contrary to many accounts, the police did not detain Nikolaev three times near Kirov, on each occasion mysteriously releasing him despite the fact that he was carrying a gun. He was stopped only once, and the circumstances were not suspicious. He had not received the gun from a Leningrad NKVD officer, as is typically claimed, but had owned it since 1918 and had registered it legally in 1924 and 1930.[21]

Nikolaev had a diary with him at Smolny, but instead of showing that the party's enemies helped him in his attack, which would have been logical if Stalin had planned the shooting, it indicated that he had acted alone. Kirov's bodyguard was not present at the fatal moment because his boss had called to say he would stay at home that day. Kirov went to his office anyway, only to meet Nikolaev by chance. The latter, who had a party card that would automatically admit him to the building, had gone there to ask for a pass to an upcoming conference.[22] The origin of the story that Stalin was involved lies with an NKVD defector named Alexander Orlov, who spent most of the late 1930s in Spain and indicated that he had been two or three steps removed from those directly involved. He wrote that one NKVD officer, a friend of his, cautioned him that talking about the murder was "dangerous" and that it was "healthier not to know too much about it." But then in fall 1935 other friends in the NKVD supposedly talked freely to him about Kirov's death.[23] If Stalin did arrange the affair, it is doubtful that policemen who knew something about it would risk personal disaster by discussing the case with anyone. And an even higher-ranking police defector, G. Liushkov, who was serving in Leningrad at the time of the murder but fled to Japan in 1938, told his handlers abroad that Stalin had nothing to do with the murder.[24] Moreover, the Gensec would have had to rely on Genrykh Iagoda, then head of the NKVD, to carry out his plan. Such involvement would have been far from safe, as Iagoda had been a leading figure in the party for some time. He was later arrested and tried in one of the Moscow show processes; it is unlikely that Stalin would have allowed him to testify publicly with such a terrible secret.[25]

Just after the murder, Stalin called in two top officials, Nikolai Ivanovich Ezhov, a member of the Central Committee (CC), and Aleksandr Kosarev, chief of the Young Communist League (Komsomol). He told them to "look for the killer among the Zinovievites." Years later Ezhov told the CC that at first relations between himself and Kosarev, on the one side, and the secret police, on the other, were poor; the latter did not want to help. Finally Stalin warned Iagoda that "we'll smash your mug [if you don't cooperate]."[26]

Stalin did not trust his police to carry out the investigation and assigned other leaders to monitor its progress, a decision that made Iagoda unhappy and suggests that he was not part of a conspiracy. On this basis alone it is doubtful that Stalin planned the killing with the help of the NKVD.

On the day after Kirov's death, his bodyguard, Borisov, died under mysterious circumstances. Riding in the back of an NKVD truck on his way to see Stalin, Borisov supposedly suffered fatal head injuries in an accident that somehow hurt no one else. Various writers have seen this incident as an indication of Stalin's desire to cover his tracks further by eliminating another witness. But the Gensec's personal bodyguard reported that his chief was upset at Borisov's death and expressed sharp dissatisfaction with the policeman accompanying him.[27]

No evidence has ever emerged to tie Stalin directly to the killing. Generally the materials advanced to support this connection are on the order of Orlov's: someone who supposedly knew about Stalin's role told someone else about it, who wrote down the tale years or decades later.[28] Stalin's successor, Nikita Khrushchev, who had much to gain in the attacks he made on his predecessor in the 1950s and 1960s by tying him to Kirov's death and who did not hesitate to link him to other murders, never produced clear proof. In early 1991, six years into glasnost', an important Soviet scholar and politician announced that, judging from available archival materials, "L. V. Nikolaev planned and perpetrated the murder alone." Files on the case "contain no information implicating J. V. Stalin and agencies of the NKVD." Stalin "did not know of and had no relation to the organization of the attack on Kirov." The author of the report, Aleksandr N. Iakovlev, added that various questions required further study, for example, the structure of the guard system around Kirov, Iagoda's whereabouts before the shooting and whether he met with Stalin at that time, and the conduct of the Leningrad NKVD.[29] Such issues will probably always remain open, because any other participants in the murder would have tried to avoid leaving a paper trail of their crime.

None of this demonstrates that Stalin did not order the murder—it is impossible to prove such a negative. But given the problems with the claim that he did, the simplest answer to the question of who killed Kirov is likely to be the correct one: a disturbed man, Nikolaev, planned and carried out his act by himself. Some reports suggest that Nikolaev believed Kirov was involved with his wife or that he blamed him for his problems in the party.[30] It is also possible that the shooting originated within the police, as an effort to bolster their importance in the eyes of Stalin and the party, or because Iagoda wanted to eliminate a leader who persecuted former oppositionists. This view is in opposition to Kirov's usual image as a liberal; but, as we have seen, and as other accounts have argued, the evidence for that picture is shaky.[31]

On one level, it does not matter whether Stalin was behind the killing or not. The road from Kirov's murder to the mass arrests of 1937 was long and full of twists and turns. Nor does assigning blame for the deed remove the importance of examining police behavior and response to it; the Terror had a dynamic and almost a will of its own.

Whatever Stalin's actual role in Kirov's end, he reacted quickly. On the day of the murder he and his closest associates traveled to Leningrad by train, where they intervened in the case and questioned Nikolaev. Within a week he had been convicted of the murder and executed; he was not saved for a show trial to make a point for Stalin.

On that same fateful December 1, a new law on "terrorist organizations and terrorist acts against employees of Soviet power" was adopted. Investigations of such crimes were to be completed within ten days, and cases were to go directly to a court—which kind was not specified, though presumably the military tribunals were meant—and to be heard without defense or prosecution lawyers. No appeals were permitted, and the "highest measure of punishment," execution, was to be applied "quickly."[32] Because this law was adopted on the day of Kirov's death, many works have argued that it must have been prepared in advance, further indicating Stalin's involvement. But the entire statute, less than a page long and consisting of only five points, could have been composed in a matter of minutes. Regardless of how it was written, it became the crucial document of the Terror.

Whether Stalin ordered Kirov's murder or not, another issue remains: did he use the event to frighten the populace? The answer is no, at least not immediately. Given the final official version of the Kirov affair—that enemies of the people had struck down a top party member—his death should have evoked concern about internal saboteurs. Nothing in the press, the major speeches of the day, the debates over judicial policy, or the overall atmosphere of 1934–35 suggested that the regime intended to repress anyone but a relatively small number of terrorists and former oppositionists.

If Stalin did not arrange the killing, then he would have been frightened by it. In that case he would have begun to lash out at perceived enemies; this notion fits the pattern that began in December 1934, and it is this reaction that matches other evidence on Stalin's behavior. One might note here that in some gulag camps conditions worsened considerably after Kirov's murder. "Politicals" who had been convicted previously of terrorism and espionage were now isolated in separate barracks behind barbed wire and were not allowed out to work.[33]

This move appears to have been motivated by fear of the politicals, because the authorities gave up their valuable labor and spent considerable sums to segregate them even within the prison camps. It may be that Stalin believed such efforts would persuade the public and lower-ranking police officers that a substantial danger existed from enemies. But if so, he missed many opportunities to make the point publicly.

After Kirov's death, Zinoviev, Kamenev, and others were arrested, particularly in Leningrad, on the charge of complicity in the murder. Zinoviev received a ten-year sentence and Kamenev a five-year one. But the police could not show that the "Moscow Center," their purported organization, "knew about the preparations for the terrorist act against Comrade Kirov."[34] If Stalin had prepared the whole affair, he would have made sure that the police found or manufactured the evidence he needed.

In mid-January 1935 the CC sent a letter to all party organizations demanding not only the expulsions of Zinovievites but their "isolation" and arrest.[35] Some accounts speak of the deportation of between thirty thousand and forty thousand Leningraders at this point, though the person chiefly responsible for this claim was in Siberian exile at the time.[36] It is certain only that 843 alleged opposition-ists were arrested in the city in the first two months of 1935, that 663 "Zinovievites" were exiled from Leningrad, and that 325 party members were transferred to work in other regions.[37] If thousands of Leningraders were arrested after Kirov's death, most of them were from the old oppositions or even the prerevolutionary nobility and merchantry.[38] Such selective targeting would not necessarily have frightened people outside these categories.

Nevertheless, existing literature often maintains that Stalin then moved to the next stage in his plan to crush the nation: the Communist Party purges of 1935 and 1936. In Russian these operations were called *chistki,* or "cleansings," a word that applies to cleaning clothes or peeling vegetables. In their first stage the reviews took place at the level of the party cells, or "primary party organiza-tions," which existed in any sizable enterprise or organization. The assembled cell members would discuss the performance and background of each communist and would then vote for ouster, reprimand, demotion, or retention. In large cells, a review board might have this power. Members who received sanctions could appeal to higher party bodies for reversal of a decision.

The internal party reviews of 1935–36 were not "blood purges" that neces-sarily resulted in tragedy. Expulsion at this point did not always mean arrest or even loss of one's job. The oblast' committee in Smolensk specifically directed lower organizations not to dismiss ousted members "wholesale" from their work. They were to be removed from leading posts but otherwise not touched unless they were discovered to be enemies of the people or "socially dangerous ele-ments," a phrase encompassing former priests, kulaks, other former "exploiters," and ordinary criminals.[39]

As shown in the previous chapter, arrests increased in 1935, but the number of political cases declined. The press did not demand a heightened search for enemies at this point. Instead, the policies of relaxation continued. Schools and other organizations for children decreased their emphasis on political education and awareness well into 1936.[40] In short, Kirov's death made little difference in policy and did not stop the trend toward moderation.

However, the first Moscow show trial, held in August 1936, marked a sharp deterioration of the political atmosphere. This time Zinoviev and Kamenev were convicted of new political crimes and executed. The show trials, including two others held in January 1937 and March 1938, are often taken to be the key events of the Terror. Stalin indisputably planned the trials, moved carefully to manufacture evidence, and destroyed his targets. In this light the Terror appears as a grotesque sham, for the show trials had nothing to do with fair judicial procedure. Evidence was faked or nonexistent. Crude errors crept into the state's cases; for example, one defendant in the trial of August 1936 claimed, in what was undoubtedly coerced and manufactured testimony, that four years earlier he had received instructions on conducting terrorism from Trotsky and his son Lev Sedov at the Hotel Bristol in Copenhagen. But the only hotel of that name in the Danish capital had been demolished in 1917.[41] The prosecuting attorney, Vyshinskii, used endless vicious phrases about the accused and seemed more an inquisitor than a lawyer.

Yet the show trials were not concocted out of thin air. In 1932 Trotsky and his son had indeed formed what they termed a "bloc" with dissidents inside the USSR, though the two did not engage in terrorism and were not foreign agents. Material in the Trotsky papers demonstrates that the 1936 show trial was based, albeit crudely and exaggeratedly, on evidence regarding the bloc that a Soviet agent had obtained abroad. Sedov had been able to communicate with his father's sympathizers in the USSR through letters carried in and out by tourists or European communists. Pierre Broué, Trotsky's recent biographer, writes that "Sedov always maintained contacts [un relais] in Moscow."[42] During the first months of 1932, for example, Trotsky sent letters through his son to the former oppositionists Karl Radek, Grigorii Sokol'nikov, and Evgenii Preobrazhenskii. The first two were later show trial defendants.

In May 1931 Sedov met in Berlin with Ivan N. Smirnov, a Civil War commander, close friend of Trotsky's, and former leading oppositionist.[43] At the time of the meeting, he headed the important Gorky auto factory. According to Broué, negotiations began in June 1932 among dissidents inside the USSR with the object of forming a bloc.[44] In October, a Soviet official named E. S. Gol'tsman (or Holzman), a former Trotskyist, also conferred with Sedov in Berlin and gave him a secret government memorandum on economic conditions in the USSR. It appeared the next month in *Biulleten' Oppozitsii* (Bulletin of the Opposition), an émigré socialist journal.

Gol'tsman also brought Sedov a proposal from Smirnov. Supposedly Smirnov had broken with Trotsky in the late 1920s, but he now proposed that a united opposition, to include Trotskyites, Zinovievites, and others, be formed inside the Soviet Union. Trotsky was excited by the prospect but cautious about his followers' participation in the bloc. It could be only a loose coalition, not a merger of groups against Stalin.

A short time later, Sedov informed his father that the bloc had been formed and that it included Trotskyites and Zinovievites. Unfortunately, however, Smirnov and others had been arrested "by accident" in connection with different matters. Sedov went on to assure Trotsky that "the lower workers [of the bloc] are safe."[45] In early 1933 Sergei Mrachkovskii, also a Civil War hero, who had been arrested in 1927 for running an underground opposition press, began to circulate a political platform inside the USSR. Sedov later sent a copy to Trotsky; the text has not surfaced.[46] Mrachkovskii was again arrested and in 1933 was sent to Siberia, probably in connection with this activity. It must be noted that these developments are not mentioned by Alexander Orlov, still the key source for Western accounts arguing that Stalin fabricated the show trials from nothing.

These discoveries of clandestine activities undoubtedly induced Stalin to pressure the party and police for the arrest of opposition members. From February to April 1936, 508 of them were detained by the NKVD. After some of Trotsky's personal materials were found in the possession of one arrestee, Stalin responded by having Ezhov attached to the investigation. Iagoda then suggested to the Gensec that Trotskyites linked to terrorism should be tried and shot under the law of December 1, 1934. Local NKVD units were told that their "chief task" of the moment was to find and destroy all Trotskyite organizations "at maximum speed" (*maksimal'no bystro*).[47]

Along with Zinoviev and Kamenev, Smirnov, Gol'tsman, and Mrachkovskii were defendants in the trial of August 1936. Probably guilty of nothing more than talking about political changes, these men, according to Western standards of justice, did not deserve punishment. But they had engaged in opposition, had had contacts with Trotsky and leaked secret documents to the West, and had wanted to remove Stalin, all of which they had lied about, while proclaiming their complete loyalty. These points provided material for Stalin's suspicious mind. Why were such people lying? How many more like them existed, and what were their real intentions? Given the Trotsky bloc and the language of the Riutin Memorandum, it might have been easy for people less morbid than Stalin to visualize terrorism at work in some of the many industrial accidents of the period. He embellished matters considerably and told massive lies of his own—but the evidence just given suggests that at this point he took steps to eliminate people who had misled him and conspired with an archenemy, Trotsky. This decision, though unjust, was not part of a plan to create political terror.

Ezhov played a significant role in the events of this period. Head of the NKVD from September 1936 to December 1938, his name became so associated with the Terror that at the time educated Soviet people called it the "Ezhovshchina," which might be translated as the "Ezhov phenomenon."[48] Therefore, at the time Ezhov was identified with the Terror more than Stalin was, a telling comment on where people felt responsibility lay.

Ezhov was born in 1895. At the age of fourteen, he became a metal worker in the highly politicized Putilov Factory in St. Petersburg, where he apparently remained until at least 1917.[49] Thus he came of age in one of Russia's most radical occupations, at a time of sharp and increasing tension between workers and employers in the metal-processing industry. Strikes were frequent in the years just before World War I, as labor and management struggled over control of production and issues of dignity, for example, the way supervisors addressed ordinary hands.[50] Perhaps this background made Ezhov less tolerant of managers and bureaucrats, on whom the Terror of the late 1930s fell particularly harshly.

During the Civil War he served in several areas as a frontline commander, where he had plenty of opportunities to battle real enemies. From the end of the fighting until 1927, he worked as a provincial party official. In that year he moved to Moscow and into a job in the Central Committee apparatus, though his exact position is not known. During the worst period of collectivization, 1929–30, he was deputy commissar of agriculture, so that he must have been keenly aware of the violence spreading across the country. By late 1930 he was back in the CC organization, this time in the personnel department. In 1933 he worked on the purge of party members.[51] At the Seventeenth Party Congress he was elected a full member of the CC, skipping the usual apprentice stage of being a nonvoting candidate member. At the beginning of 1935 he was selected to head the Party Control Commission, a body with oversight responsibilities in certain sectors of the economy, party, and government. His inspectors roamed the country looking into charges of malfeasance and abuses of power.[52] Thus, before his appointment as head of the NKVD, his staff had functions paralleling those of the police, though without the right to arrest. During this period of party work Ezhov learned a great deal about what was wrong with the country. Only about five feet tall, he was pleasant-looking, judging by photographs. Some who said they knew him described him as a decent man before his quick rise to Stalin's side. The renowned poet Osip Mandelshtam and his wife, Nadezhda, author of a compelling memoir of the period, met Ezhov at a government villa in the early 1930s and noted that he smiled a good deal and was "a modest and rather agreeable person."[53] A Russian who claimed to know Ezhov in the same period wrote that he "made the impression of a good lad, a good comrade. His conduct in 1936–38 is explained by illness: he went crazy from what he saw."[54]

Others present a different portrait of Ezhov, for example, as a man who had become deranged long before his police service: "In the whole of my long life I have never seen a more repellent personality than Yezhov's," noted a source purporting to be Nikolai Bukharin.[55] Alexander Orlov likened Ezhov to the Moscow slum children who enjoyed tying paraffin-soaked papers to cats' tails and setting them on fire.[56] But it is not clear that Orlov knew him well. Dmitrii Volkogonov, Stalin's Russian biographer, says that in early 1937 Ezhov reported to his boss reeking of alcohol but does not cite a source for the story.[57] It is therefore impossible to know the real Ezhov; the most we can say is that he was Stalin's man.

Ezhov's election to full membership in the Central Committee had already demonstrated Stalin's support, and by early 1935 he had moved even higher in the Gensec's favor. In February a plenum of the CC chose him as a secretary of that inner circle, putting him just a step below Politburo membership and giving him great supervisory responsibilities within the party.[58] It was at the end of the same month that he became head of the Party Control Commission. In that capacity, he wrote a manuscript a short time later in which he claimed that former oppositionists were likely to become counterrevolutionaries. Soon after, he told a deputy head of the NKVD that "according to the opinion of the Central Committee . . . there is an undisclosed center of Trotskyites that must be found and liquidated."[59] In this observation, of course, he appeared prescient, for the bloc did in fact exist.

As head of the Control Commission, Ezhov now became responsible for overseeing the purges, the operations within the party to remove anyone unworthy of membership. Exactly what that phrase meant is hotly debated in the West; as noted, one point of view argues that Stalin aimed to crank up political tension and root out political opponents in 1935–36; another maintains that the purges were not largely political operations but, rather, mundane housecleaning, through which party members who had demonstrated incompetence or lack of interest in socialist affairs were removed.[60] The first interpretation supports the contention that Stalin planned each step of a campaign to extirpate enemies and frighten the country; the second, the lack of a plan on his part and a low level of political anxiety resulting from the party ousters. Whichever definition one uses, Ezhov held a highly sensitive post. By early December 1935, he was sitting among Politburo members at a national conference, while Iagoda was nowhere to be seen.[61]

On December 25, Ezhov delivered a report to the Central Committee entitled "The Results of the Check of Party Documents," as the purge of 1935 was called. Like all key papers of this period, the report was marked "strictly secret" and was probably available only to a handful of high officials outside of the CC itself.

Ezhov called the purge "that huge work on the unmasking of enemies of the party and work on the introduction of order into party management." In the previous seven months these efforts had been "at the center of attention of all party organizations."[62] Thus he emphasized both strains mentioned in Western accounts, housekeeping and a hunt for opponents. In fact, to understand what occurred, the two interpretations can and must be reconciled, for they were part of the same process. Although the majority of members ousted were passive, criminal, or inept, the political side of the purge became increasingly important for party members and the country as a whole. It seems beyond doubt that Ezhov was appointed to head the purges because he had become so involved in the hunt for enemies within the party.

He went on to tell the CC that "secretaries of regional [party] committees, personally checking the documents of each member and candidate of the party, carefully conversing with each communist, often unexpectedly . . . discovered obvious enemies of the party among those whom they had considered model communists."[63] The opposite also occurred, Ezhov noted: the secretaries sometimes found excellent people among those they had earlier considered incompetent. But his main concern was clearly unveiling enemies.

On July 1, 1935, he continued, there had been 1,660,537 communists and 681,245 candidate members, a probationary status, for a total of 2,341,782. By early December, 1,915,894 had gone through the check of documents, and 175,166, or 9.1 percent, had been expelled from the organization. Of that number, 13.6 percent were candidates and 8.1 percent full members. In addition, more than 80,000 party cards were still being checked; "experience shows," said Ezhov, that about 50 percent of those would be taken away.

Reasons for expulsion during this purge varied: 1,788 (1 percent) were "spies, suspected of spying, or linked to spies"; 35,777 (20 percent) were termed former White Guards and kulaks; 5,507 (3.1 percent) were Trotskyites and Zinovievites;

"swindlers" and "scoundrels" numbered 14,879 (8.5 percent).[64] Together these categories account for 33 percent of expulsions. All the rest were either "passives," people who did not bother to attend meetings or pay dues, or those guilty of some nonpolitical infraction, for example, drunkenness. Because almost 70 percent of those ousted from the party, or 77 percent if swindlers and scoundrels are included in this group, lost their party status for commonplace reasons, it might appear that politics played a small role in the purge of 1935.

But numbers alone do not tell the story. For, immediately after giving this information, Ezhov moved to what constituted the real importance of the purge for himself and, by extension, Stalin. This passage of the minutes is printed in boldface: **"In all organizations where the purge was carried out, the check of party documents additionally uncovered many deeply evil [zleishikh] enemies of the party."** For example, in Kareliia, which borders on Finland, 20.3 percent of the members were expelled in the first round of the purge, and 19.5 percent were forced out in a second round. In the second group were 58 spies or people linked to spies and 196 White Guards and kulaks. Ezhov also made it clear that central party officials had demanded and obtained higher purge rates from local organizations during the course of the check. At first the Far Eastern Krai, a group of oblasti, had expelled only 1.6 percent. But after "work" by a commission of the Central Committee sent to the area and "correction of mistakes" by local leaders, the purge rate quickly climbed to 8 percent. Altogether, 130 spies, 68 Trotskyites and Zinovievites, and 442 White Guards had been discovered in the *krai*. The same story was repeated in other regions.[65]

Two points are worth stressing here. First, the hunger of the center to turn the purge into a political event complete with the unmasking of enemies is unmistakable. Regional officials dragged their heels in this task, probably above all because they did not want to lose capable people to the purge. Local party leaders, or for that matter any local officials or managers, were forever caught between the demands of politics and those of production. Satisfying one side could easily mean trouble on the other; to lose effective subordinates might mean a decline in efficiency or production, which would in turn bring about unwanted attention, reprimands, or punishments from the center. But not to root out "enemies" upon Moscow's command could mean major trouble as well. The national leadership, not responsible to anyone, became suspicious when local officials failed to carry out whatever demand was being stressed at a given moment. This dynamic helped to bring on the Terror in 1937.

The second important point in Ezhov's remarks is that the number of spies and actual or potential internal enemies "discovered" in the purge, though far lower than the the number of passives and minor miscreants, was in fact substantial. At least in the official rhetoric of the day, not a great deal distinguished "spies" from White Guards, kulaks, Trotskyites, and Zinovievites. From the Stalinist viewpoint, they may have operated from different perspectives, but they were all seen as threats to the USSR.

Considered this way, the 43,072 discovered in these categories up until December 1935 was large, especially considering that many of these people had held responsible posts. Imagine the outcry, and the fear, if in 1948 the FBI had announced that more than forty thousand enemies of the United States had been discovered operating inside the country's ruling bodies. The allegation that one person, Alger Hiss, had been a Soviet agent was enough to send America into a minor frenzy, even though our enemies were on other sides of the oceans. Forty thousand real and desperate foes, all presumably busy recruiting others, could inflict tremendous damage on any country. If members of the CC believed Ezhov, and there is no indication that they did not, then they had reason to be worried. But as yet they would not have thought that the state intended to exterminate them as well; instead, Ezhov's remarks prodded them, as part of the leadership, to concentrate on rooting out the alleged enemies.

Ezhov noted that the NKVD had already begun to arrest groups of Trotskyites that the purge had unmasked within the party, for instance, nine individuals in Odessa. Next on the podium was Lavrentii Beria, who was to succeed Ezhov as head of the NKVD in December 1938. At this point Beria was first secretary or chief of the party in the Transcaucasus area, which included Georgia, Armenia, and Azerbaijan. He announced that the NKVD had arrested 1,020 enemies of the party in his bailiwick from the start of the purge to December 1, 1935. Following him, a stream of other Central Committee members mounted the rostrum to give similar figures for their areas.[66] From such reports enemies appeared to have been present in every area of the country.

Ezhov's conclusion and the committee resolution on what remained to be done were mild, however. They did not emphasize a further hunt for enemies, though obviously the security forces would continue to look for them. Rather, the message was that the party had to select members much more carefully than it had in the past. Ezhov mentioned cases in which local party organizations had run campaigns to recruit new members wholesale and that in 1931 in one *raion* (district) of Uzbekistan party cards were awarded to one hundred female collective farmers as "premiums" for good work.[67] Such practices had allowed enemies to penetrate the party. The remedy was not to rampage through its ranks in search of enemies, much less through the population as a whole, but to be more careful in initial admissions and then to supervise cadres closely. The plenum resolved that there had been "shameful chaos" in party records and in admissions. "The most important task" at hand was to strengthen the work of "cleansing the ranks" of the party of "enemy elements." To this end vigilance and discipline had to increase;[68] this stock formula, however, appeared in countless documents of the period.

More important in setting a tone for the meeting, and therefore for the party as a whole, was Ezhov's opening statement. Although he too called for more vigilance, he concluded that in the check of documents, party organizations had "cleansed themselves of harmful, foreign [in spirit], and unjustified" people. The organizations had "brought order into the records of members and candidates of the party, reconstructed the work of the party apparatus," gotten to know their members better, and advanced capable ones.[69] In short, the call for more vigilance was almost pro forma, but the thrust of Ezhov's remarks was that severe problems had been corrected and that now everything was all right.

Or nearly so. Party cards had to be exchanged for new ones in 1936. In other words, there would be another purge. Ostensibly a matter of furthering the campaign for order in party records—the CC directed "principal attention" not toward uncovering enemies but toward "passives"—great opportunity nonetheless existed to turn the exchange of cards into another search for political opponents. Yet at this juncture the situation seemed well in hand. The NKVD, still under Genrykh Iagoda, had apparently found the worst nests of harmful elements.

During this time Ezhov continued to rise in the ranks. In March 1936 he appeared in the press as one of six leaders, including Stalin, Molotov, and Commissar of Defense Kliment Voroshilov, who greeted a delegation from Soviet Georgia.[70] In July, with Stalin and four other Politburo members, Ezhov, though only a Central Committee member, was a pallbearer at the funeral of the president of the Academy of Sciences.[71] Clearly he was close to Stalin months before he became head of the NKVD, whereas Iagoda was never in the inner circle.

When the CC gathered again in June 1936, the proceedings were generally dull. Ezhov spoke again, however, on the results of the latest purge, the exchange of party cards. To date about 3.5 percent of those who had gone through the exchange had been expelled. Roughly half of those were passives, often called "ballast," Ezhov informed the group.[72] At another moment in the same speech, he said that more than two hundred thousand communists (presumably counting candidates and full members) had been ousted.[73] Taking the check of documents and the exchange of cards together, in the year since July 1935 approximately 17.7 percent of the membership had been forced out of the party. Therefore to describe these events as measures to introduce orderly record keeping and to remove incompetents is inadequate. The membership had been combed twice, or even three times, for both enemies and passives, and a major chunk had been cut out of its ranks. Granted, all those expelled had the right to appeal, and many were in fact reinstated. But they too had often been deeply upset. Thus the purges did constitute a major political development.

Ezhov was clear about the political thrust of the purges in June 1936. Of the two hundred thousand expelled, he told the CC, "a fairly significant group, as you know, consists of our most evil enemies, all sorts of spies and White Guard elements, scoundrels, rascals, swindlers and simple thieves. A significant part of these has been arrested."[74] The number caught by the NKVD had grown since he addressed the party leaders in December 1935.

Ezhov was considerably more pessimistic about the results of the purges than he had been six months earlier. He asked, "Can we say that those Trotskyites, Zinovievites, Ukrainian nationalists, deserters from foreign states and others, expelled from the party but not arrested because of the lack of a sufficient basis," now refrained from "subversive counterrevolutionary work?" Typical of Stalinist speech making, the question required a negative answer.

And so the sense of danger increased. Yet Ezhov backed away from making an all-out hunt for enemies the order of the day. He followed the question about subversion with the remark that the "main mass" of those excluded were not enemies and insisted that expellees were to be treated humanely. He cited the story of an engineer ejected from the party in 1936 for concealing his social origin; his raion committee wrote on its decision that it would not object to his being employed in his speciality. Yet, even though the engineer applied at dozens of places and there was a strong demand for people with his training, no one would hire him. Finally Ezhov's own agency, the Commission of Party Control, interceded, and the man found work. At this point Ezhov's formula might be summed up as vigilance, great care in admissions to the party, careful supervision of cadres, and avoidance of blanket judgments about those expelled. He was in effect warning against injustice, an indication that at this time the leadership was directing its efforts toward finding perceived enemies within the party. No hint of great danger, and certainly none of panic, appeared in Ezhov's speech.

A manuscript in the Hoover Institution archives presents information that fills out the course of events considerably. The document was written by A. F. Almazov, who claimed to have served as an officer of the NKVD border guards for eighteen years before emigrating during World War II. He reported that an important affair involving former oppositionists came to Ezhov's attention in early 1935. An NKVD agent with close ties to leading former oppositionists had decided to betray his comrades, but opposition sympathizers within the security organs—of whom Iagoda was supposedly one—arrested him first. The agent was able to escape from a transfer point and to reach Ezhov, a logical person to turn to because of his position as head of the Party Control Commission. Ezhov took the story to Stalin, who ordered a full investigation. The inquiry revealed no terrorist intentions, no common plans among the Bukharin "Rightists" and the Zinoviev "leftists," and no links between them and foreign powers. But it did supposedly turn up attempts by them to open channels with émigré Mensheviks, Socialist Revolutionaries, and Trotskyites. This story, of course, seconds the evidence already given on Trotsky's bloc after 1932. As a result of this communication to Stalin, Ezhov eventually took Iagoda's place as head of the NKVD.[75] Almazov's report cannot be confirmed elsewhere, but if true it would help explain the switch. It would also clarify Stalin's newly heightened, deadly antipathy toward the former oppositionists, and the onset of a much higher level of political tension by August 1936.

If the Almazov story is wrong, declining confidence in Iagoda on Stalin's part may be sufficient to explain Ezhov's rise. After all, the NKVD was responsible for finding enemies, but in fact Ezhov did more to uncover them in his capacity as director of the party purges. Iagoda was also reportedly sympathetic to former oppositionists, something Viacheslav Molotov believed into the 1980s.[76] Although Iagoda participated in preparing political trials through August 1936, he may also have tried to limit the damage among former party critics. On the investigation records of some prisoners, he wrote comments like "nonsense" or "impossible" next to several of the more lurid assertions.[77] Such remarks may well have made Stalin suspicious of him.

Meanwhile, the international situation was growing steadily worse. The Germans reoccupied the Rhineland in March 1936, effectively ruining France's ability to rush into that vital industrial area and cripple German production in the event of war. Another considerable portion of the Versailles Treaty had been gutted, and Germany emerged strengthened and emboldened. In July the Spanish Civil War began. Although no one could foresee its seriousness at that point, it represented another threat to socialism in general. Italy was simultaneously pressing its own fascist adventure in Ethiopia, begun in December 1935.

These events surely made Stalin more nervous than ever. But internal affairs probably had more to do with his decision to stage the show trial. First, the cumulative effects of finding so many enemies within the party must have been telling, if he in fact believed that they were enemies. Information on Trotsky's bloc may have reached Stalin at this juncture. Third, shortly before the trial, the Soviet military attaché in London, Corps Commander Vitovt Putna, was recalled to Moscow and arrested. Several sources indicate that he and other officers were plotting against Stalin.[78] If accurate, such reports alone could explain the Gensec's decision to hold the trial; he would have become increasingly suspicious and perhaps wanted to send a signal to other oppositionists.

Local party bodies sometimes reacted to the Zinoviev-Kamenev trial by showing heightened concern for enemies.[79] Still, at least one local NKVD unit, at the town of Tumanovo, in Smolensk oblast', remained relatively quiescent. Even after the August 1936 trial, the party cell of the Tumanovo police discussed editorials in *Pravda* and various local concerns but paid virtually no attention to internal subversion.[80] Up to that point, the increased emphasis on political vigilance was confined largely to the central and regional party leadership.

In September Stalin sounded another grim note when he removed Iagoda as head of the NKVD. In a telegram sent from a vacation spot on the Black Sea to members of the Politburo, Stalin and a relatively new lieutenant of his, Andrei Zhdanov, urged that N. I. Ezhov be appointed police chief: "We deem it absolutely necessary and urgent that Comrade Ezhov be nominated to the post of People's Commissar for Internal Affairs. Iagoda has definitely proved himself to be incapable of unmasking the Trotskyite-Zinovievite bloc. The OGPU [Unified State Political Administration] is four years behind in this matter. This is noted by all Party workers and by the majority of the representatives of the NKVD."[81] Naturally, the Politburo approved Stalin's new choice.

What did the four years refer to? Western writers usually answer that the phrase meant the Riutin Memorandum.[82] But in December 1936 Ezhov mentioned, once again in a speech to a Central Committee plenum, "the formation at the end of 1932 of a Zinovievite-Trotskyite bloc on the basis of terror."[83]

Something new was clearly under way with Ezhov's appointment. But his selection as head of the NKVD did not immediately inaugurate a different policy toward enemies. Stalin himself specifically downplayed any potential problems from such elements as late as the end of November. In a speech on proposals for changes in a draft of the new constitution, he urged restoration of the right to vote to former "nonworking and exploitative elements." Their classes had been destroyed, and the Soviet Union had become an "invincible power." He scoffed at any threat they might pose: "It's said that there is a danger that elements hostile to Soviet power can crawl into the supreme organs of the country, someone from the former White Guards, kulaks, priests and so on. But what's there to be afraid of? If you fear the wolf, don't go into the forest [a Russian proverb]." If any of the wrong types were elected to responsible positions, it would mean that propaganda work had gone badly, and "we would fully deserve such shame."[84] His speech contained no hint that "enemies" would have to be dealt with by force.

On the local level, Soviet architects, to name one group, were already boiling with zeal to find enemies within their midst.[85] But at one of the most important Leningrad factories, the Kirov works, a party cell meeting on January 18 featured no talk of enemies.[86] Within the Tumanovo NKVD, at a meeting held on January 19, 1937, the party cell discussed hooliganism and crimes in rural areas; there was not a word about enemies. On February 1 the cell considered the twenty-fifth anniversary of the Prague Party Conference and resolved to raise "vigilance in the struggle with the *remains* of unbeaten enemies of the party and the people in everyday practical work."[87] In other words, this was a humdrum meeting and a stereotypical resolution, indicating no urgency about present problems with saboteurs and spies. Thus even the January 1937 show trial, this time involving second-rank Bolsheviks like the publicist Karl Radek and the industrial executive Grigorii Piatakov, both former Trotskyites, did not necessarily produce local calls for blood.

In February 1927, when the party secretary in Belyi raion of Smolensk oblast′ faced charges from the rank-and-file members that his methods were "dictatorial and arbitrary," the head of the local NKVD came to the man's defense. He argued that the members should not discuss management of the party organization.[88] The police, often called NKVDisty, had not yet reached the point of always looking for victims, or perhaps they feared for their own skins if local leaders with whom they had worked turned out to be enemies. Whatever the case, there was still no mass terror.

But hidden from public view, ugly changes were unfolding within the Central Committee. At another plenary session, called in December 1936, Ezhov once again held center stage, launching a new series of dramatic charges that involved more former opposition leaders. At the August trial, Zinoviev and Kamenev had mentioned a "reserve center" of terrorists that existed in addition to the "basic center" of the Zinovievite-Trotskyite bloc. In the reserve group were Piatakov; Radek; Grigorii Sokol'nikov, a former candidate member of the Politburo; and L. G. Serebriakov, a former secretary of the Central Committee. All had once been Trotsky's followers. Ezhov informed the CC that these men, now under arrest, had confirmed the information given earlier by Zinoviev and Kamenev. The job of the reserves had been to supply replacements for the basic center if its members were discovered. But Piatakov had begun his wrecking work even before Zinoviev and Kamenev were arrested. He carried out his task more effectively than the Zinovievite center had, because he enjoyed more trust from the government and possessed more links with the periphery. Here Beria interjected, "And foreign connections, too." Ezhov resumed his speech, noting that more than 400 Trotskyites and Zinovievites had already been arrested in Ukraine. Among additional examples he cited, 120 had been found in Western Siberia, more than 200 in the Azov-Black Sea area, some 300 in Georgia, and 400 in Leningrad.[89]

Piatakov "admitted" that in spring of 1931 he had met in Germany with Trotsky's son Sedov, who passed him a directive on terror in the Soviet Union. According to Ezhov, Piatakov told the police after his arrest that "I, unfortunately, gave my agreement." Here the stenographic record notes "noise, movement in the hall." Beria once more interrupted: "Bastard!" Ezhov responded, "Worse than a bastard."

Piatakov, he continued, then set up terrorist organizations through his Trotskyite friends but did not yet give them the order to act. That came only in 1935–36, "more accurately at the beginning of 1936," after which these groups tried to assassinate Molotov, Ordzhonikidze, and Kaganovich. There was also a plan to poison all the leaders of the government at a Kremlin banquet. "You understand, comrades," Ezhov went on, "that I am speaking here only of those facts in the direct testimony [of the arrestees] and of confirmed facts." Ominously, he announced that "I assume that we have many, many undiscovered cases."

He then read a number of excerpts from prisoners' statements, in which they admitted causing accidents in military factories and on railroads. One direct link had been found between Trotskyites and a White Guard organization working in biology. Sokol'nikov had confessed that for all these "little groups," the Riutin memorandum was "in essence the acceptable program." Sokol'nikov had linked all the terrorist activity to Radek and Mikhail Tomskii, a former Politburo member and trade union chief.

At this point a connection to Bukharin began to surface. Tomskii had been one of his partners in the "Right Opposition" of 1928–29, which opposed forced collectivization. Zinoviev, Ezhov stated, had also pointed to the Right in his pretrial testimony; Kamenev had done so in the trial itself. Four rightist leaders, Rykov, Tomskii, Bukharin, and Uglanov, knew of the Trotskyite-Zinovievite bloc and "completely shared its aims," Ezhov announced. At that, Bukharin, present as a candidate member of the Central Committee, asked to speak; he was ignored.

Ezhov continued that other sources had confirmed the testimony about knowledge by the Right of terrorist plans. In particular, L. S. Sosnovskii, a follower of Trotsky in the 1920s and later a journalist under Bukharin at *Izvestiia,* had told the NKVD that his boss had accepted the Riutin platform. Three other former oppositionists had testified that a Right Center of Bukharin, Rykov, Tomskii, and two other men had decided to turn to terror. Ezhov and the Politburo member Lazar Kaganovich had then brought Rykov and Bukharin face to face with other rightists; the two Stalinist henchmen had "had no doubt" that the two under suspicion "were informed of the Trotskyites' decision to turn to terrorism and sympathized with it." This remark was obviously not evidence at all, but it fit the mood of the session.

Before turning to Bukharin's reply, let us consider the state of mind of the other Central Committee members at this point. First, what did they really know? The answer is, precious little. Bukharin, Rykov, and all the others mentioned by Ezhov had been oppositionists at one time or another. There was the Riutin memorandum, with its virulent charges against Stalin. Kirov was dead by an assassin's bullet. Finally, the number of accidents in Soviet industry had been extremely high. All this occurred in a threatening international context, in which foreign powers wished the USSR ill. Now Nikolai Ezhov, in all likelihood someone with a good reputation, brought forward a new series of charges.

To come to the decision that Ezhov was lying, those present at the December 1936 plenum had to make several mental calculations. They had to conclude that the testimony gathered by the police was false, which could only mean that those arrested, who had all served in high positions in the party for years, had been tortured. Such a possibility was as yet unthinkable; no precedent existed for torturing party members who had been in good standing until their arrests. If torture had occurred, then Stalin must have known about it. But why would he have authorized physical methods and arranged "confessions"? The usual theory says that he wanted to cement his position completely; the Central Committee records, however, give no indication that serious resistance to him existed within it or within the party as a whole, except among former oppositionists. This sentiment, such as it was, had last appeared three years earlier, at the Seventeenth Party Congress. So anyone deciding that Stalin needed torture to gain confessions from the arrestees also needed to believe that he was mad; yet he had led the party to some important successes, at least from the point of view of industrial development, and major domestic crises seemed in the past. Therefore an apparently capable leader, by the standards and conditions of the contemporary USSR, had to be deemed insane in order for one to find a hole in Ezhov's presentation. And striking at former oppositionists had little to do with the vast majority of the Central Committee in 1936, which had never resisted Stalin. Thus the cases of Piatakov, Sokol'nikov, Serebriakov, Bukharin, and the others did not suggest that Stalin had a broader attack on the party in mind. For all these reasons, it would have been both psychologically safer and more logical to accept what the top leadership said was happening. And who could know for sure that the confessions were false?

In fact, not only staunch Stalinists but also Bukharin accepted the charges against many others, though of course not against themselves. Bukharin tried to play by Stalin's rules in defending himself to the Central Committee when he was allowed to speak, on the same day that Ezhov had presented his charges. The former rightist and "favorite of the party," as Lenin had called him, began on a personal note: "Comrades, it is more than difficult for me to speak, for perhaps I am speaking for the last time before you." He urged greater vigilance throughout the party and help for the "corresponding organs," that is, the police, in wiping out "the bastard who is busy with wrecking acts." He remarked that he was happy all this had surfaced before the coming war. "Now we can win."[90]

Beria then broke in to sneer, "You [addressing him with the familiar form *ty,* which is condescending except when used with a close friend] would do better to say what your participation was in this affair. You say what you were doing there."

Bukharin replied that "everything is a lie." After meeting with Sokol'nikov at the time of the August trial, Stalin's aide Kaganovich had told Bukharin that the leadership believed he had nothing to do with the terrorist affairs. Then the procuracy had informed him that the investigation of his activities was closed. Kaganovich interrupted to say that that decision had been juridical but that now the matter was political. Obviously, loose standards of evidence would apply in this kangaroo court.

Bukharin, now adopting a somewhat pathetic tone, responded by saying, "For

God's sake, don't interrupt me." He denied having political conversations with Sokol'nikov or the journalist Sosnovskii. He claimed he had never read the Riutin Memorandum. True, in 1928–29 he had "conducted an oppositionist struggle against the party." Yet neither at that time nor afterward had he had "one atom of a conception of platforms or [specific political] aims." He asked plaintively, "Do you really think that I'm that kind of person? Do you really think that I can have something in common with these diversionists, with these wreckers, with these scoundrels after 30 years of my life in the party and after everything? This is really some kind of madness."

MOLOTOV: Kamenev and Zinoviev were also in the party for their whole lives.
BUKHARIN: . . . Many people here know me.
BERIA: It's hard to know a soul. . . .
BUKHARIN: Why didn't they [the wreckers] harm the party from the other end, to ruin a lot of honest people and get their hooks into them? Why, tell me? (Noise, movement in the hall). . . . How to defend oneself in such cases [against the testimony of others]? How to find a defense here?

His specific counterthrusts were weak. He told the CC that he had once visited the renowned scientist Ivan Pavlov. The old scholar, who had not emigrated, had been openly critical of Soviet policy. Bukharin recalled that he had persuaded Pavlov that the government's program was good. However, Bukharin noted helplessly, he had not told anyone else about his conversation with Pavlov, who had died in 1936, or a similar one with the French writer Romain Rolland, who was abroad. Bukharin asked, somewhat incoherently, "Why did I do this if I am a wrecker and if I hate Comrade Stalin, whom I in fact love, if I hate the leadership of the party, which I in fact love, and if I thundered earlier [in 1928–29] against that cause for which I am ready to die. Life is not dear to me, I'm fed up with all this, but there is political honor! (movement in the hall, sceptical laughter)." Bukharin confessed that he had talked frankly with Karl Radek, who, he agreed, was a traitor. Striking another pathetic note, he admitted having spoken to Radek only because he, Bukharin, was completely alone, and in those circumstances a person "will be drawn to any warm place."

When Stalin asked Bukharin why people would lie about him, he replied that he did not know. Bukharin acknowledged that there had been a Right Center, which would have been unnecessary if it was Stalin's fictitious creation. But, Bukharin went on, he had not seen one of its key members for years and did not know another, one Iakovlev. Regarding the latter, Bukharin said he had reported the man's antiparty speeches to the Central Committee. Tomskii had never said anything to him about links to Zinoviev. "I am in an idiotic position," he complained, to which a voice from the floor replied, "True!" Bukharin concluded by saying that "either I am absolutely one hundred percent a son of a bitch, or all the rest falls away."

His attempt at defense could not have helped him much and probably strengthened Stalin's hand vis-à-vis the great majority of the Central Committee members. Bukharin had offered nothing concrete in his favor except his denunciation of Iakovlev—but that could have been interpreted as a smokescreen. The point about speaking to Pavlov and Rolland was worthless. All that Bukharin really counted on was his long service in the party and his personal honor; he asked people to take his word about his honesty over the testimony of numerous others. And he himself said that he had struggled in the late 1920s against pressure on the peasants. But by 1936 it appeared, correctly or not, that that policy, culminating in collectivization, had enabled industrialization to take off.

Again, to accept Bukharin's words required any listener to reject Stalin and to think the worst of him. And yet Bukharin had accepted the gist of what Ezhov had said, including, especially, the need to hunt for enemies. Bukharin had recognized wrecking by Zinoviev, Kamenev, and others; he had acknowledged that there was a Right Center of opposition, and he had been the clear leader of the Right. It looked bad for him that Tomskii, his close associate during the 1920s, had committed suicide rather than face the accusations against him. Bukharin could not openly state, even if he suspected it, that torture had been used to gather testimony. Such an assertion would bring into question Stalin's right to lead and, more broadly, the whole Soviet structure. Obviously Bukharin's audience could not stomach that idea. He was therefore caught, as he put it, in an "idiotic position." Unfortunately, he appeared to be the idiot, or worse.

Stalin spoke next, but available records note only that there is no stenographic report of his speech. Rykov followed him with a defense similar to Bukharin's; he repeated that the charges were all lies. Finally Molotov mounted the rostrum to sum up the position of the leadership. Of all that he had heard from Bukharin and Rykov, he said, only one thing was correct: it was necessary to investigate the matter in the most attentive way. As for all the rest, "I don't believe one word of theirs." Voices replied, "Correct."[91] Bukharin was politically dead; in little more than a year, he was tried and executed.

One more document from his case requires discussion: a letter he wrote to

Stalin while in prison, dated December 10, 1937. In it he begged the Gensec to allow him either to work at some cultural task in Siberia or to emigrate to America, where he would be a faithful Soviet citizen and would "beat Trotsky and company in the snout." If it was necessary to die, Bukharin pleaded, let it be from an overdose of morphine, not by shooting.

More important for understanding his fate and the course of the Terror was his admission that some sort of "conference" of his young followers had occurred in 1932. Apparently one of them had said in Bukharin's presence that he wished to kill Stalin. Bukharin now acknowledged that he had been "two-faced" about his followers and had not informed the authorities of their discussions. He had believed at the time, he claimed, that he could lead them back to the party. As for the accusations that he was linked to foreign espionage services and had fostered terrorism, all that was false.[92] But by this time Bukharin had lied repeatedly to Stalin and the whole Central Committee. Even though his behavior did not warrant the death penalty, Stalin had serious reason to distrust him.

On January 23, 1937, the second show trial, of Piatakov and several others, began in Moscow. Naturally they were convicted of organizing wrecking in conjunction with the Germans and Japanese. Piatakov, Serebriakov, and other defendants received the death penalty; Sokol'nikov and Radek each got ten years' imprisonment.

Following the trial, Grigorii (Sergo) Ordzhonikidze, Piatakov's old boss at the Commissariat of Heavy Industry, died suddenly. Officially, the cause of death was listed as a heart attack, but it appears beyond doubt that he committed suicide. Historians usually accept the second version and add that Stalin was closing in on Ordzhonikidze; realizing what was happening politically and in despair over recent executions, including his brother's, he took his own life.[93]

The arrest of various subordinates of Ordzhonikidze's before and after his death does not prove that Stalin was conducting a campaign against him, for the same thing occurred around men like Lazar Kaganovich and Nikolai Shvernik, the national trade union leader, whom Stalin continued to trust and employ. Just before Ordzhonikidze killed himself, he had several long conversations with Stalin. Why the vozhd' would have devoted so much time to someone he planned to destroy is curious; perhaps Stalin recognized his old friend's disturbed state of mind and tried to calm him down. In any event, the suicide had to be hushed up. But the available evidence is not convincing that Stalin planned to liquidate someone who had served him loyally, had not been in the opposition, and still held key assignments. The traditional image of Stalin demoniacally moving to arrest even close friends does not stand up in this case.[94] If he did mean to crush Ordzhonikidze, this maneuver was a departure from all that had gone before, when only leading oppositionists had been accused. The exception was Abel Enukidze, expelled from the party but not arrested in 1935. But there was no campaign by Stalin against Enukidze before his troubles began, and he was at liberty long after his expulsion. Enukidze's story is too full of twists, turns, and contradictions to suggest a plan to destroy him.[95]

The Central Committee gathered in yet another plenum at the end of February 1937. Andrei Zhdanov, a candidate member of the Politburo and party leader in Leningrad, gave one of the first speeches. He took a mild approach to problems within the party, calling repeatedly for increased democracy and criticism within it, and mocked the rush to arrest people. He related a story from a recent party cell meeting on a state farm, at which the communist Salirov reported on his own activities. The gathering adopted a resolution on the matter, quoted by Zhdanov in full: "Heard: Salirov's report on himself. Resolved: to arrest Salirov." This provoked "general laughter" from the CC.[96] If Zhdanov's address had set the tone for events to follow, they might have developed quite differently. But that was not to be.

In place of Ordzhonikidze, Molotov gave a report on February 28 entitled "The Lessons of Wrecking, Diversion and Espionage of the Japanese-German-Trotskyist Agents." Why was Ordzhonikidze ever entrusted with such a crucial report if Stalin had lost faith in him? Arresting him after such a task would have reflected badly on Stalin himself.

Molotov informed the Central Committee that in early January, before the trial, Piatakov had confessed to having carried out sabotage on Trotsky's orders. Molotov continued by giving a lengthy description of specific wrecking across the country, complete with testimony from saboteurs who had been arrested. Occasionally voices from the floor called out the names of other wreckers. He cited several cases in which the guilty either were former oppositionists or were connected to them.[97]

But once again Molotov specifically and firmly disdained a campaign aimed at everyone who had ever opposed the party line, including Trotskyites. He cited a telegram that Stalin had sent the previous December to the municipal party committee in Perm. There the director of an aviation motor factory, a former Trotskyite, one Poberezhskii, was being persecuted "because of his former sins." But in view of the fact that he and his subordinates, who were also suffering, "now work with a good conscience and enjoy the full confidence of the Central Committee," Stalin asked the city secretary to protect them and "create around them an atmosphere of complete trust." He requested the secretary to let the CC know quickly of measures taken to help the group. It is hard to imagine a more direct and forceful statement that every oppositionist was to be evaluated on his or her merits and record; there was to be no witch-hunt.

Molotov's recommendations for action were along the same lines. More Bolshevik tolerance for objections was needed: "We must prove our ability to cope with criticism," even the unpleasant sort. The way to deal with enemies was through correct education of cadres, selection of employees, and methods of leadership. In short, Molotov did not assign a prominent role to the police.

He was followed by a parade of speakers—including such stalwarts as Kaganovich and Beria—who listed wrecking in their respective areas; blame for the situation again seemed apportioned so evenly that no one particularly stood out. This sharing of the problem would have applied to Ordzhonikidze as well, had he been there. Apparently all who spoke were required to be explicit about sabotage in their jurisdictions. When Ian Gamarnik, First Deputy Commissar of War and head of the Army Political Administration, gave no names of wreckers but mentioned only "a series of cases," both Stalin and Molotov criticized him. Gamarnik stubbornly replied, "I said what I know."[98]

Some speakers received criticism from the floor, particularly from Molotov and Beria, concerning people they had hired and trusted; others who made similar admissions, for example, Voroshilov and Beria himself, escaped condemnation. If there was some rule at work, it seemed to be that any attempt to shift blame or share it with someone else brought immediate objections: this was not owning up to one's responsibilities. Thus when B. P. Sheboldaev of the Ukrainian party organization said that Ordzhonikidze had recommended one unmasked enemy and Kaganovich knew another, Molotov retorted, "Why mention Comrade Kaganovich here, where were you looking?"[99] Nikita Khrushchev, then party leader in Moscow, came in for similar comments from the floor.[100]

On the other hand, a direct statement of regret about using the wrong person could elicit support from the listeners. E. G. Evdokimov said that he had known the accused Iakov Lifshits a long time. "I considered that this figure could not be bent, that he could only be broken." To this Voroshilov added, "Correct, many thought so."[101]

Stalin was mild and supportive toward Stanislav Kosior, first secretary of the party in Ukraine. Kosior admitted that in his area there had been a lot of "family-ness," meaning that he had created a network of people connected directly to himself and had sometimes resisted central directives. Such practices were now condemned as likely to let in enemies. Kosior regretted not having enough "Bolshevik sagacity and decisiveness." Stalin interjected: "If you had told us, we would have helped." When Kosior dwelled further on his errors, Stalin said, "No matter, people learn from mistakes."

KOSIOR: That's true. But the price is too high.

STALIN: A good product is not bought cheaply. (General laughter).[102]

The knowledge that Evdokimov and Khrushchev survived the Terror, while Gamarnik, Sheboldaev, and Kosior were executed, does not clarify matters. No clues to Stalin's psychology surface here. Almost every speaker took some personal blame for not being vigilant enough, including Kaganovich, clearly a man who remained close to Stalin until the latter's death. Each had to name names of wreckers who had worked under him.

This pattern reduced somewhat the threatening tone that otherwise would have been the main characteristic of Ezhov's speech, delivered on March 1, after most of the party leaders and economic chiefs had spoken. He complained that those on the rostrum before him "have not understood completely the concept or the agenda [*postanovka*]" of wrecking, nor the tasks before the party in combating it. None of the government commissars present—which included Kaganovich and Voroshilov—had called him to report suspicious people. More often than not, some comrades tried to defend accused Trotskyites and wreckers when the question of their arrest was raised.[103] Ironically, Stalin had taken the same position regarding the factory director in Perm. So, by criticizing everyone equally but not singling anyone out by name, Ezhov deflated his own remarks. As the speech continued, however, he singled out Grigorii Grinko, Commissar of Finance, and Nikolai Shvernik, head of the labor unions. Ezhov sharply criticized the second man for defects in the national insurance program, administered by the unions, and for industrial explosions that took workers' lives. The unions were supposed to oversee working conditions and safety in industry. "Does the National Labor Union Council really not bear responsibility for what happened in Kemerovo, Gorlovka and other places?" Ezhov asked rhetorically, citing two well-known explosions. Regarding Grinko, Ezhov was equally critical, announcing that he had to basically reconstruct his work.[104] Of these two targets, Shvernik outlived Stalin, whereas Grinko was tried and executed in 1938 as a wrecker. Ezhov's criticism did not mean arrest, even though in Shvernik's case his "errors" included incidents that had already been called sabotage in the courts. Ezhov also listed the numbers of wreckers from various commissariats convicted in the preceding five months for the Russian Republic alone. The figures varied widely from ministry to ministry, but like the criticism and confessions of poor vigilance, the accusations were spread so broadly that they tended to diffuse the blame among all government chiefs. The high number was 228 wreckers, in education; the next highest was 141, in light industry, followed by 137, in communications, which at the time was run by Kaganovich. Grinko's Commissariat of Finance, so loudly thrashed by Ezhov, had spewed out only 35 wreckers.[105]

At this point the following criteria applied: it was a) bad to have hired a lot of people who turned out to be wreckers; b) good to have discovered wreckers in one's bailiwick; c) bad to try to shift blame for having wreckers away from oneself; and d) good to judge each person on his or her merits and not to fire former oppositionists wholesale. All these conditions amounted to a political tightrope from which many were to fall. But up to this point Central Committee members had no reason to feel directly threatened.

More important, they may have believed in the enemy threat. In appears that in late 1936 Ordzhonikidze had wavered in his judgment of his longtime subordinate, Piatakov. In a speech Ordzhonikidze gave in early December, he departed from his notes to say that he had spent many sleepless night wondering how wrecking could have occurred in the Commissariat of Heavy Industry. He asked Bukharin, ironically, what he thought of Piatakov and appeared to agree with the reply that it was hard to know when the latter was telling the truth and when he was speaking from "tactical considerations."[106] According to Bukharin's wife, Anna Larina, Ordzhonikidze met with Piatakov in prison at this point and asked him twice if his testimony was entirely voluntary. Upon receiving the answer that it was, Ordzhonikidze appeared shaken.[107] If he had doubts about a man he had worked with and trusted for years, those in the CC who were more distant from Piatakov certainly felt surer of his guilt. His past as a leading Trotskyite would have added to the suspicions. If this chain of reasoning is correct, the question for members of the party's elite would therefore have been not whether treason had existed but its present scope.

On the next day, March 2, Molotov was the major speaker. The heart of his remarks was an enumeration of Trotskyites, or more precisely "members of anti-

Soviet Trotskyist organizations," arrested in government commissariats (that is, not in party bodies) from October 1, 1936, to March 1, 1937. Presumably referring to the entire USSR, Molotov's total was 1,984, though this number did not include the ministries of defense and foreign affairs or the NKVD. Molotov then accusingly posed another rhetorical question: "Is it correct that our economic managers have not helped with the unveiling of wrecking, but even hampered it?" Speakers had not yet touched on this issue.[108] In doing so, Molotov returned to Ezhov's tone, though still in nonspecific terms.

At last Stalin took the floor. On March 3 he presented an address entitled "On Shortcomings of Party Work and Measures of Liquidation of Trotskyite and Other Double-Dealers." He began by charging that sabotage and espionage, in which "Trotskyites have played a fairly active role," had occurred in almost all government and party organizations.[109] The agents of this nefarious work had reached not just lower levels but "some responsible posts" as well. Many leaders at the center and in the provinces had been "complacent, kindhearted, and naive" toward the wreckers, which had helped them get into high positions. Often the enemies were masked as Bolsheviks.

Of course there had been great successes for the party, but achievements could breed complacency. Wreckers had to produce some successes for the Soviet Union in order to worm their way further into people's confidence. This possibility was especially dangerous at the time, because Trotskyism had changed from a political movement into a band of active wreckers and murderers. The problem of sabotage had become so great that discussion would no longer work; "uprooting and destruction" were needed to combat contemporary Trotskyism.

Still, Stalin did not call for massive purges of the party, even for those guilty of complacency and indirect aid to the wreckers. His signals were terribly mixed. First, he claimed, there were only a few Trotskyites, and they represented not an "organic" but a temporary phenomenon. The whole situation could be dealt with by political means; party cadres had to be carefully reeducated to awareness of the great danger. Local leaders were to attend political refresher courses lasting from four to eight months. Finally, a six-month conference entitled "Questions of Internal and International Politics" would be arranged. One wonders who in the leadership would work, and how anyone would be on the lookout for enemies, while engaged in all this studying. Stalin's emphasis in coping with the danger was on reeducation, not on mass arrests. There was no point in retraining anyone not deemed basically trustworthy.

The vozhd' offered one suggestion often considered tantamount to a death sentence for the Central Committee.[110] From the lowest party cell through the republic level, two substitutes were to be chosen for all secretaries. (The word Stalin used was *zamestiteli,* which frequently means "deputy" or "assistant.") These substitutes were to take part in the courses just mentioned. With the adoption of this measure, each member of the Committee supposedly understood that Stalin planned to replace him once or even twice. But this conclusion is illogical. To begin with, it will not do to portray Stalin as extremely crafty and secretive about his project for terror in most instances but as perfectly open in this one. Announcing his intention to important people would only have hurt his cause, because it gave them warning and a chance to prepare resistance. Second, the secretaries were to attend the various courses, leading them to expect not death but a return to their positions after such a major investment had been made in their careers. Third, replacements already existed in the form of "second," "third," or other designations of secretaries at various levels. Finally, it was the secretaries themselves who were to choose their deputies, not the central party apparatus. This gesture again indicates confidence in the regional officials. Taken as a whole, the overall thrust of Stalin's first report was not toward Terror.

On the same day Stalin spoke, the Central Committee resolved that, at a minimum, Bukharin and Rykov knew of the terrorist activity of the Trotskyite-Zinovievite center and hid it from the party, thereby aiding terrorism. They also knew of other terrorist groups organized by their "pupils and followers." Far from struggling with the terrorists, the two rightist leaders encouraged them. The CC voted to expel Bukharin and Rykov from the party and to turn their case over to the NKVD.[111]

Stalin now changed his tone, though why is not clear. His speech of March 5 was considerably milder than his first remarks, ambivalent as they were. Diverting too much attention from the economy to "party-ideological work" was wrong and would "cost us no fewer victims" than ignoring the internal threat.[112]

It was necessary to hunt down active Trotskyites but not everyone who had been casually involved with them, Stalin announced. In fact, such a crude approach could "only harm the cause of the struggle with active Trotskyist wreckers and spies." Even more surprising given his first set of remarks, but paralleling his December 1936 telegram in defense of a former Trotskyite, Stalin allowed that some people had long ago left their fellows and now "conduct the fight with Trotskyism no worse, but even better than some of our respected comrades. . . . It would be stupid to discredit such comrades." Each case of expulsion from the party for connections with the former oppositions should be dealt with carefully.

Instead of his opinion in the first speech that Trotskyism was terribly dangerous, Stalin now said that its strength was "insignificant."

His first address, though ominous in spots, had by no means called for terror; his second reduced the emphasis on political awareness. To combat problems in the party, he stressed the need to learn from the masses and pay attention to criticism from below.

A resolution adopted by the Central Committee during the February-March plenum continued to take a mixed approach toward the problem of enemies. For example, every railroad accident was to be carefully investigated for wrecking. The "chief task" of the government commissariats was to "root out to the end the Japanese-German-Trotskyite agents." Echoing the theme sounded in the meetings, the resolution also declared that care had to be exercised in selecting cadres, promoting young employees, raising technical qualifications of staff, and educating officials in political courses.[113] On March 5 yet another resolution refrained from comment on the danger of enemies and simply restated the scheme of courses for party secretaries outlined by Stalin.[114]

The only plenum speech published immediately was Andrei Zhdanov's. His remedy for the party's difficulties, including the presence of internal enemies, was to hold secret elections at each level of the organization, a procedure intended to break up familyness and put candidates at "the head of criticism." At present they were simply waiting for complaints to come to them.[115]

Obscuring the message of the plenum even more were the facts that no Central Committee resolution was published after the meeting and that Stalin's speeches did not appear in the press for weeks, until the end of March and the beginning of April. If he wished to prepare the ground somehow for mass terror, he was making it difficult for his audience to sense his goal. Altogether, his indications about the danger of enemies in March 1937 were contradictory and might have inspired reactions ranging from confidence to deep fear, depending on which part of which speech one took to be central. Because virtually every speaker had admitted to having had grave problems and wreckers under his command, with the trouble still identified overwhelmingly as coming from former oppositionists and White Guards, all members of the Central Committee could feel relatively safe.

There was even less reason for apprehension to spread to lower-ranking party members. Stalin had identified only some party leaders as worthy of blame, and only in his first speech.

As his words were published, the hunt for enemies began in some locales, for instance, within the NKVD group at Tumanovo.[116] It is interesting that the police there took their behavioral cues not from any internal NKVD or party directives but from the press. So far, the central leadership had not arranged a concerted drive to produce terror. Nor, despite an initial flurry of reactions to Stalin's words and some noise about enemies in the newspapers, did truly massive arrests begin. They came only in June, following the execution of leading military officers.

This affair began more or less in August 1936, just days before the first Moscow show trial opened, with the arrest of two senior officers.[117] The first, detained on August 14, was Vitalii Primakov, a Bolshevik since 1914, a cavalry commander during the Civil War, and a corps commander since 1935. Then on August 20 Vitovt Putna, the corps commander and Soviet military attaché to London mentioned earlier, was arrested. He had been a Bolshevik since 1917. Both men had taken part in the Trotskyist opposition in 1926–27.

Until May 1937 Primakov categorically denied any kind of counterrevolutionary activity, though he wrote to Stalin that after breaking with Trotskyism in 1928 he "had not completely severed personal contacts with Trotskyites." Putna, on the other hand, quickly admitted to participation in current "Trotskyist-Zinovievist centers" and an organization within the Soviet military. He named Primakov as a member.[118] It is not clear whether they were tortured at this point. Meanwhile, one of the defendants at the August show trial referred to Putna as an "active participant" in terrorist work.

The next major event occurred in April 1937. Marshal Mikhail N. Tukhachevskii, one of the best-known officers in the Soviet Union, a colonel under the tsarist regime, and then a Civil War hero for the Reds, had been scheduled to travel to London for the coronation of George VI. But now Ezhov wrote to Stalin claiming that a "foreign source, worthy of complete confidence," had informed him that the Germans were planning to assassinate Tukhachevskii during his stay in Britain, with the goal of stirring up international trouble. The Politburo responded by removing Tukhachevskii from the Soviet delegation.[119] So far there was no hint of a lack of confidence in him; the decision was taken for his own protection.

But then several officers being held and tortured by the NKVD named Tukhachevskii as a plotter against the government. After this, it is certain that Primakov and Putna were tortured, and they too began to name high officers, including Tukhachevskii, as members of a plot. A new round of arrests among such men began in mid-May; Tukhachevskii was finally taken into custody on May 22.[120] On a single day, June 11, a military court made up of other high officers tried eight men in camera. Found guilty of treason and espionage, all were executed the next day. But Tukhachevskii had not engaged in treasonous collaboration with the Germans. In 1957, during Khrushchev's anti-Stalinist campaign, a Soviet military court found a lack of evidence for all charges against the marshal and rehabilitated him, or rather his name.[121] Someone had framed him—at least on the charge of conspiring with the Germans against Stalin.

B. A. Viktorov, who was procurator of the Western Siberian military district and in 1955 worked on an investigation of the Tukhachevskii affair, has recently supplied additional information. Viktorov quotes a written statement by the investigator A. P. Radzivilovskii, who worked in the Moscow oblast' NKVD in 1937. He was investigating another high officer, Brigade Commander M. E. Medvedev, who had been expelled from the party for Trotskyism or, according to another account, for squandering state funds.[122] One of Ezhov's aides, M. P. Frinovskii, called in Radzivilovskii. Frinovskii gave the investigator a new assignment: "It is necessary to develop the picture of a large and deep plot in the Red Army, whose uncovering would bring to light the huge role and services of Ezhov before the Central Committee." Radzivilovskii then worked on Medvedev—how is not made evident, but we can easily imagine—obtained the desired "evidence" of a plot, and passed his report upward.[123]

Ezhov and Frinovskii had Medvedev brought to them. He promptly told them that his statement was false. Ezhov then ordered his subordinates to "return Medvedev by any means to his previous testimony." When this was accomplished, Ezhov took the material, which now had Medvedev saying that he became aware of a plot within the Red Army in 1931, to the Central Committee. This event occurred on May 8, 1937; five days later Ezhov ordered the arrest of a former secret policeman, A. Kh. Artuzov. Undoubtedly under terrible pressure, Artuzov told Ezhov that earlier in the decade he had received material from Germany that implicated Tukhachevskii in a plot. The marshal's arrest followed.

One by one, the generals were severely beaten to obtain their testimony. Tukhachevskii's "confession" had gray-brown stains on it; the 1955 investigation determined that they were blood. In 1938 Frinovskii was arrested; he told a court that for the generals Ezhov had ordered him to use investigators who had some sort of "sins" on their records. The NKVDisty had to be aware of these taints; in other words, they had to be people who realized that their superiors "fully held them in [their] hands." Frinovskii gave the judges his view that the generals' testimony often came not from them but from the investigators. He claimed that he did not order this practice but that he and Ezhov "knew and encouraged" it.

The accounts of two NKVD men therefore show that Ezhov personally drove the generals' affair forward. Of course, Stalin may well have been behind him, issuing orders. But the impression these reports make is one of Stalin reacting to information as it came to him, not initiating matters. During the investigation he met with Ezhov almost daily, and from May 21 to 28 he also met regularly with Frinovskii. Such close attention to a case that would never come to public trial suggests that Stalin wanted not to manufacture evidence but to learn what the police had found. He might have pushed Ezhov forward in this case in order to investigate something he feared. That Stalin and the Politburo reacted to Ezhov's report about a plot to murder Tukhachevskii in London suggests that the Gensec did not have a plan to proceed against the officers; indeed, the whole picture of long investigations, NKVD behavior, and Ezhov's role is one of material making its way up to Stalin.

Another variant was offered by the ex-NKVD officer B. A. Almazov. In one of his manuscripts in the Hoover Archives, he claimed that a real military conspiracy against Stalin existed. Planning to rely on several army units and on political prisoners as their main forces, Tukhachevskii and his followers intended to surround the Kremlin, arrest key leaders, and kill Stalin in one quick blow. But they were discovered in 1936, when Putna was recalled to Moscow. Sensing danger, he left a packet of incriminating materials in the Soviet capital with someone he thought he could trust, his brother-in-law Elagin. Instead the latter immediately took the documents to the Central Committee. Putna was arrested and quickly confessed—this point is not quite accurate, as we have seen— naming Tukhachevskii and others as his coconspirators.[124]

It must be noted that Almazov offered different versions of the background to the "generals' plot."[125] Yet he was not alone in claiming that a real conspiracy against Stalin existed in the armed forces. A. V. Likhachev, a Red Army officer who served in the Far Eastern military district for six years prior to his ouster from the service in 1937 or 1938, also maintained that such a plot was under way and provided extensive details about it. He insisted that he was not directly involved but that he knew many officers who were. They told him that Tukhachevskii and Gamarnik had begun to lay plans in 1932 (that fateful year once again). The affair centered in the Far East, where most of the plotters had served. Putna was stationed there for several years in the early 1930s. High-ranking civilians in places like Leningrad, Smolensk, Kalinin, Tula, the North

Caucasus, and Siberia were also involved. Gamarnik, trusted completely by the Kremlin, often traveled as its emissary to outlying military districts; he maintained communications among the conspirators.

The chief plotters did not feel that they could trust their troops to follow them against Stalin (an interesting comment on popular loyalties), so they planned to stir up the men by announcing that foreign infiltrators had taken over NKVD headquarters in Khabarovsk, the administrative center of the Far Eastern Army. Once the troops had attacked the building and blood had been shed, it might be possible to turn them against the regime. (How? Why?) In another version of the plan, an attack on the leadership was to take place inside the Kremlin simultaneously with the Khabarovsk action. But all was in vain; although Likhachev does not say how, the plot was discovered before it could unfold.[126] His account is indirectly supported by an ex-Soviet officer who said that his brother had been involved in a "Tukhachevskii group" in 1935.[127]

Such testimony fits well with the picture of the "military affair" developed here. There is no direct evidence other than Almazov's manuscript that reports of plots in the armed forces reached Stalin in late 1936 or early 1937, but that event would explain why he approved arrests of high officers, closely followed the long incarceration of Putna and Primakov, and finally permitted them, as well as others, to be tortured. Putna had increased Stalin's suspicions by almost immediately speaking of Trotskyist organizations in the military, which would have been plausible in light of Stalin's knowledge of such groups among leading members of the Communist Party. In the process of searching for the plotters, innocent people suffered.

Another way of looking at all this, based on material such as prison conversations among people far removed from decision making, has dominated the literature and must be mentioned here. Several reports maintain that in December 1936, a White émigré general, Nikolai Skoblin, reported to high German officials that Tukhachevskii was plotting with members of the German general staff to overthrow Stalin. Skoblin said that his motive in incriminating Tukhachevskii was to take revenge on him for abandoning his former tsarist officer cronies and joining the Reds during the Civil War. The Nazis decided to take this piece of information and build on it. By early 1937 they had prepared a major dossier linking Tukhachevskii to them as a traitor, including his forged signature on fabricated documents.

Why would the Germans have done that? One argument is that Skoblin took his charges to Reinhard Heydrich, chief of the Nazi Party's Security Service

(*Sicherheitsdienst*, or SD). Heydrich, a former naval officer who had been thrown out of the armed services on moral grounds, saw a chance to "humble the German officer corps." He went to Hitler with Skoblin's information and, with some difficulty, persuaded the Führer to allow a case to be fabricated against Tukhachevskii. The major goal then became to undermine the Soviet army.[128]

It is clear that the Germans did prepare compromising material on Tukhachevskii and passed at least part of their work on to Moscow through the Czechoslovak government, which apparently believed in the marshal's guilt and sincerely wanted to warn Stalin.

A number of Western writers have argued that, once again, Stalin arranged the affair. They identify Skoblin as an agent of the NKVD, which means that he was acting on Stalin's orders. As Robert C. Tucker puts it, the Gensec hoped that the Germans would swallow the bait that the White general dangled before them and work for Tukhachevskii's undoing.[129] The Nazis obliged, and Stalin used their efforts to convince other Soviet leaders that a conspiracy against them was under way. Stalin's motives were severalfold: to get rid of dangerous, independent men among the military leaders; to frighten the country and the party officials around him, thus further preparing the ground for massive terror; and to placate the Germans, with whom he wanted close relations, by destroying his best military officers. The weaker dog rolled over and bared its throat to the more powerful one.

But this explanation relies on the Nazis' alleged, albeit unwitting, cooperation with Stalin's plans. He could not have been sure that the Nazi leaders would become involved in this matter, or that if they did they would fabricate the kind of material he wanted. And he would have had no control over the timing of their actions, hardly an appealing prospect. Stalin made no use of the German dossier during Tukhachevskii's trial, strange conduct if the vozhd' had taken so much trouble to have the file prepared in the first place.

It would have been much simpler and more reliable to assign his own police to do the job. With the entire NKVD at his disposal and Ezhov at its head, Stalin had no need to rely on bait dangled before the Germans to concoct a generals' plot.

Furthermore, there is no proof that Skoblin was a Soviet agent. He disappeared shortly after the kidnapping in September 1937 of the White general Evgenii Miller, head of an émigré anti-Soviet organization in Western Europe. Later Skoblin's wife, the singer Nadine Plevitskaia, was tried and convicted in Paris for complicity in Miller's kidnapping. The trial revealed no links to Moscow. Letters seized from the Skoblins were "strongly anti-Bolshevik"; they contained allegations that Soviet and German agents operated in the White Russian community within Paris but did not suggest that Skoblin was one.[130]

Plevitskaia's prosecutor tried to prove that General Skoblin was a Soviet agent and that his superiors had ordered Miller's abduction. But, as the *London Times* put it, "that charge was not substantiated."[131] To be sure, Skoblin's disappearance shortly after Miller's is suspicious, yet that is all that can be said. He may have removed himself from the scene because other White émigrés began to accuse him of helping in the kidnapping. And it is easy to imagine that the Soviet regime wanted Miller out of the way, in order to weaken an organization that attempted to undermine it.

Soviet publications of the glasnost' era have taken still another approach to the Tukhachevskii case. One recent article, reportedly based on archival documents, concluded that the Germans initiated the affair, counting on a suspicious reaction from Stalin. Their goal was to decapitate the Red Army by removing some of its best brains, especially Tukhachevskii, who had stressed the growing power of the German army in speeches and articles.[132] In this interpretation, the Nazi government's motivation is perfectly understandable.

Dmitrii Volkogonov also finds that the Tukhachevskii case began with the Germans, not with Stalin. He cites some of Ezhov's reports to the Gensec as the case unfolded. The first of these, Volkogonov writes, was grounded in the claims of Russian émigré groups in Paris that Soviet officers were committing treason. At first Stalin paid no attention, but then other claims of disloyalty among officers began to work on his mind. When the Czechs passed on the German forgeries, they "sharply strengthened [Stalin's] suspicion of Tukhachevskii." Only then did the NKVD begin to gather materials for a case against him. Because he had had close contacts with German officers dating well back into the 1920s, in connection with secret and open Soviet-German military collaboration, it was not hard to produce information that appeared incriminating.[133]

Glasnost' has not yet cleared up this affair and perhaps never will. In all likelihood the conspirators, if in fact they were, did not write down much. For their part, Ezhov and the NKVD as a whole would not have spelled out their intentions. But the most likely interpretation is that something—either "evidence" coming from the Germans or internal reports of treason—frightened Stalin. His contradictory remarks at the Central Committee plenum of February–March 1937 also show that he was feeling his way along in this period.

If Stalin wished to eliminate stalwart, independent men from the military, why did he leave a number of outstanding officers like G. K. Zhukov and V. I.

Chuikov, both brilliant commanders during the war, untouched? Officers like A. V. Gorbatov were arrested, tortured, and sent off to camps for years by the NKVD but were then released in 1939–41. The most plausible explanation for such a sequence of events is that for a time Stalin genuinely suspected some officers of real crimes. As for the theory that the Gensec wanted to placate the Germans, for which direct evidence is scanty indeed, it is hard to see the sense in cutting off the flower of the armed forces. Because thousands of capable Soviet officers were purged from the services during the Terror, the military emerged weakened. This decrease in force would only have encouraged the Germans to be more arrogant. It does not take the hindsight of the postwar period to judge that such a concession to Germany, which had already begun rapid rearmament, would have been absurd in 1937. Soviet involvement in a European war was a distinct possibility. At any time in the late 1930s, Stalin would have been much better off leading from strength. After all, the USSR was threatened not just to the west but also, simultaneously, by another old and powerful enemy to the east, Japan. The two countries would fight in the summers of both 1938 and 1939. Instead of trying to win Germany's tolerance by showing that the USSR was no military match for the Reich in the immediate prewar years, the Soviets were busily developing new weapons, expanding the armed services, training new officers on a vastly increased scale, and reorganizing their forces in preparation for war. These trends signaled the Germans, or should have, that the USSR could be a formidable enemy.

The results of the generals' arrest and of the Terror that followed also cast doubt on the idea that Stalin was catering to the Germans. The mass arrests weakened the Soviet economy, as will be shown. It is unlikely that in the hostile world of that period Stalin would have damaged both his military machine and industrial production to show Hitler that he meant him no harm. Such an explanation is too contrived.

It is better to rely on the newly published documents and statements by those more directly involved at the time. From their reports, one of several fairly simple explanations can be drawn: either there was a plot, or Ezhov created the appearance of one for his own purposes and aggrandizement, or both. The second interpretation emerges from the glasnost'-era publications of Volkogonov and Viktorov. In any case, Stalin would have believed that a vast conspiracy against him existed in the military and then moved to root it out. But, as the former officer Likhachev put it, the vozhd' could not be sure he had gotten all the heads of the hydra; hence the "mad orgy of the purge" erupted.[134] This notion fits with other evidence already presented on Stalin's behavior during the Terror.

Most works on Stalin written in the West, and now in the former Soviet Union as well, portray him in the 1930s as deeply paranoid, crafty and, perhaps above all, devious. This state of mind is introduced to explain why Stalin would involve the Germans in the "officers' plot," why he turned on old friends in the Terror, and why contradictory signals on arrests emerged from the leadership in 1938.[135] In the past direct evidence on what the vozhd' thought was extremely thin, which is one reason that fictional treatments of the Terror like Anatolii Rybakov's *Children of the Arbat* have been so popular.[136]

It now appears that Stalin and his close associates, having helped create a tense and ugly atmosphere, nonetheless repeatedly reacted to events they had not planned or foreseen. This pattern was also evident in the early stages of collectivization and throughout industrial life.[137]

In 1934 judicial policies, the treatment of former oppositionists, and the political mood all show that the leadership was becoming more tolerant of dissent and less likely to employ coercion. Stalin's outlook changed, however, as more information on enemy activities, either real or fabricated, reached him. His fear of enemies increased, though with serious ambivalence, through March 1937. Then came the Tukhachevskii affair, which caused Stalin's view to harden.

The vozhd' created the Moscow show trials, in which the defendants were, beyond a doubt, innocent of most of the specific charges made against them. He surely intended the trials to transmit the message to the public that organized opposition would not be tolerated—even though, it is important to note, the defendants were mostly members of old oppositions, ones limited in numbers and political impact. Ordinary people would not necessarily have related these convictions to their own lives.

There was, moreover, always a grain of truth to the accusations of the show trials: a Trotskyist bloc had existed in the USSR, and Bukharin did know of a center, albeit a small one, organized against Stalin. At least one of Bukharin's followers spoke of killing the vozhd'. Putna was probably guilty of treason. The Germans fed the Gensec information incriminating Tukhachevskii, and evidence from various sources points to a plot in the army. Ezhov relayed damaging material on officers to his boss. With some justification, Stalin saw dangerous opposition developing around him. He was almost certainly mentally disturbed in some way and therefore blew the dissent out of proportion. But he was not plotting a campaign against the nation.

Stalin and Hitler can be compared with regard to their perceived opponents. Hitler believed from an early age that the Jews were a cancer attacking the German people and set out to eliminate them and other "undesirables." Evidence of their activity one way or the other was of no consequence to him. Stalin's terror of the late 1930s was a reaction, however grossly exaggerated, to information he received on threats to himself and the USSR. His thinking, however, changed dramatically over time. In this analysis Stalin is less of a one-dimensional monster and more of a human being, though a terrible one, than in other treatments.[138]

WHAT'S THE DIFFERENCE?

A Fitzpatrick cartoon of 1918, captioned "What's the Difference?" The word *czarism* has been crossed out on the back of the throne. All the elements of the typical Western view of Stalinism were in place before Stalin was: the noble people are ruled by a gangster relying purely on force. (Reprinted with permission of the *St. Louis Post-Dispatch*.)

Leaders of the Communist Party, 1934. *Top row, from left:* Kliment Voroshilov, Lazar Kaganovich, V. V. Kuibyshev; *bottom row:* Grigorii (Sergo) Ordzhonikidze, Stalin, Viacheslav Molotov, Sergei Kirov. (Private collection.)

Sergei Kirov listening to an unidentified man. (Private collection.)

Caption to the photograph on the left: "Comrades Stalin, Kaganovich, Voroshilov, Molotov, Ordzhonikidze by the coffin of Comrade Kirov"; on the right: "Comrades Stalin, Voroshilov, Kalinin and Molotov carry the urn with the remains of Comrade Kirov. 1934." The text at lower left reads: "The basic lesson that party organizations were to draw from the trial in the case of the evil murder of S. M. Kirov consisted of liquidating our own political blindness, liquidating our political complacency, and raising our vigilance, the vigilance of all members of the party." (Courtesy of the Library of Congress.)

Nikolai Bukharin with his friends I. I. Skvortsov-Stepanov and L. M. Karakhan, both important Bolsheviks, Moscow, 1928. (Private collection.)

A. I. Mikoian, Sergei Kirov, and Stalin, 1932. (Private collection.)

Genrykh Iagoda in the 1930s.
(Private collection.)

Mikhail Kalinin and
Viacheslav Molotov in the
Kremlin, 1936. (Private
collection.)

Nikita Khrushchev, Andrei Zhdanov, and Viacheslav Molotov, January 1936. (Private collection.)

Kliment Voroshilov, marshal of the Red Army, and Stalin in 1938. (Private collection.)

Andrei Vyshinskii, 1949. (Private collection.)

Kliment Voroshilov, Viacheslav Molotov, Stalin, and Nikolai Ezhov at the Moscow-Volga Canal, 1937 or 1938. (Private collection.)

The Political Police at Work in the Terror, 1937-1938

A number of survivors recalled that the large wave of arrests among civilians started only after the Tukhachevskii case, in August 1937.[1] To the extent that the Terror expanded to become "great," it did so now and not before. On July 3, shortly after the officers' executions, Stalin and the Politburo adopted a resolution on "anti-Soviet elements," in which they informed Ezhov and all leading party bodies that onetime kulaks and criminals were returning from exile to their home districts after serving their sentences, only to become the "main instigators of anti-Soviet and diversionist crimes." The NKVD was to round up the "most harmful" of them, process their cases administratively through the troiki, revived in the fall of 1936, and shoot them. Other "less active but nevertheless harmful elements" were to be exiled once again. Six days later, a report from Stalin to the Central Committee indicated that the killings had already begun.[2]

On July 30, Ezhov, obviously under Stalin's direction, ordered the NKVD to begin a truly loathsome operation along the same lines. He now expanded Stalin's list of undesirables to include ordinary criminals, returning kulaks, churchmen and sectarians repressed in the past, Whites, and members of political parties and nationalist movements. Many of these were said to be carrying on anti-Soviet activity in industry, transport, and construction.

Such people were to be divided into two categories, one marked for execution and one for exile. For both groups, Ezhov provided "guide" (*orientirovochnymi*) figures for the major administrative units of the country. In Moscow oblast', for example, five thousand were to be shot and thirty thousand exiled; in Leningrad oblast', the numbers were four thousand and ten thousand. There were wide variations in Central Asia. Ten thousand were to be executed in the labor camps.

Ukraine was not singled out. Available data do not cover all oblasti, but nowhere were figures as high as for Moscow and Leningrad. Within Ukraine, the largest projected numbers were for the more Russian areas, around Khar'kov and Donetsk.

For the entire country, 72,950 executions and 177,500 exiles were projected. Local NKVD units could raise or lower the numbers, giving them large scope for initiative, but increases required Ezhov's permission. Operations were to begin on August 5, 10, or 15, depending on the area.[3]

As 1937 and 1938 wore on, police in various areas bombarded Ezhov with requests to boost the permitted totals, though, because relevant archives are still closed, it is impossible to determine if this happened everywhere. Such communications began at least as early as August 15, when Gorbach, head of the NKVD in Omsk oblast', Siberia, asked to be allowed to raise the limit in the first category to 8,000, *eight times* his assigned figure. Requests for increases also came to the center from high party figures, for example, one in August or September from the Central Committee members Anastas Mikoian and Grigorii Malenkov, along with the unidentified Litvin, to have more "Dashnaks [an earlier nationalist movement] and similar anti-Soviet elements" shot in Armenia. In late January of 1938 Stalin approved an additional 48,000 executions and 9,200 exiles in 22 jurisdictions.[4]

What was all this about? First, the centrally designated targets were largely those who had committed crimes or somehow offended the authorities in the past; kulaks, nationalists, criminals, Whites, and church figures all fell into this group. The effort was therefore directed not at the general population but at removal of people already stigmatized. This activity would not necessarily have frightened those still at liberty.

Of course, the NKVD was also interested in anyone currently engaging in "anti-Soviet activity," and it is this aspect of the Terror that prevails in claims that the regime now set out to rule by fear. But a detailed look at police practice in making arrests on this ground will show something else.

A second problem in analysis is that the campaign was unevenly related to population distribution (table 3). Uzbekistan borders on Kazakhstan and is roughly similar to it in climate and topography, yet for the first republic the figures are significantly lower than for the second. For Kazakhstan the guide numbers were broken down by individual oblasti, which had been done only for the Russian and Ukrainian republics.

These variations, and the fact that apparently additional totals were permitted for some areas but not for others, can best be explained by a belief that in certain regions the threat from enemies was much greater than in others. The relatively high numbers for Western Siberia seem related to the military plot about which witnesses spoke. Moreover, nothing in the orders indicates that the guide figures were to be distributed evenly within each jurisdiction, only that the police were to look somewhere for enemies.

Table 3 Numbers of Individuals Targeted for Repression, 1937

| Region | Guide Numbers for | | | % Indicated for | |
	Executions	Exiles	Population	Death	Exile
Moscow oblast'	5,000	30,000	11,971,367	0.41	.25
Leningrad oblast'	4,000	10,000	6,831,743	.059	.15
Belorussia	2,000	10,000	5,196,549	.038	.19
Kirghiziia	250	500	1,369,667	.018	.037
Uzbekistan	750	4,000	6,278,736	.012	.06
Kazakhstan	2,500	5,000	5,120,173	.049	.098
Western Siberia	5,000	12,000	6,584,000	.076	.18

Source: The guide numbers are from *Trud,* June 4, 1992. The population figures are from *Russian Studies in History* 31, no. 1 (1992), 24–27; they are taken in turn from Iu. A. Poliakov, V. B. Zhiromskaia, and I. N. Kiselev, "Polveka molchaniia (Vsesoiuznaia perepis' naseleniia 1937 g.)," *Sotsiologicheskie Issledovaniia,* nos. 6–8 (1990), 3–25, 50–70, 30–52, respectively.

The ten thousand from the labor camps who might be shot is a sign that the regime did not wish to frighten others by these deaths. Little if any outside publicity accompanied such executions, and presumably those who knew of the arrests of these people to begin with would already have received a dose of fear, if that was ever the regime's intention. Nor do the raw data indicate how the directives on arrests were applied or who fell into police hands.

Finally, although Stalin initiated the mass arrests, it is clear that, once more, he was reacting to information and requests coming from lower levels. Perhaps he had a plan to terrorize Omsk oblast', for example—but if so, the idea was extremely undeveloped, because arrests were not spread evenly through the population or through targeted occupational or other groups. In any case, Stalin would not have specified one figure for arrests there in July and then suddenly developed a number eight times as high in mid-August. He would have had no reason to order the Omsk NKVD chief to feed the new total back to Ezhov; a simple telephone call from Stalin to his police commissar would have done the job. Mikoian and Malenkov, who survived politically and physically for years after Stalin, found more Dashnaks in Armenia than their boss, or perhaps than Ezhov, had anticipated. The guide figures and their increases suggest panic at the top levels of government more than a careful plan to frighten the nation.

The same is true of the targets specified in the July 1937 order. After several years of milder policies toward the peasantry (as shown earlier, for example, with regard to the virtual abandonment of the harsh law on theft of socialist property), the regime suddenly turned on former kulaks. After pleas from Vyshinskii and Krylenko in 1936 for leniency regarding "anti-Soviet" remarks, the police were now directed to be extremely tough on this score. Kulaks, recidivist criminals, and priests obviously had nothing to do with the kinds of suspicious figures found within the party during the purges of 1935–36. It was almost as though Stalin and Ezhov simply wanted to arrest someone and turned on the "usual suspects" in the way that old-time police chiefs did in America.

In at least some areas the results were catastrophic. Events in Turkmenistan were especially horrible; beatings and sleep deprivation began in September 1937, though two months later the assistant head of the republic NKVD officially ordered his officers to use "physical methods" on suspects. In December the new republic NKVD chief issued "limits," or target figures, for arrests in the categories of wrecking, spying, and other activities. Police sometimes carried out mass arrests at the markets. Occasionally the NKVD singled out men simply because they had long beards. In February and March 1938 more than twelve hundred were arrested, most of them workers and peasants.

The Turkmenistan events were described and condemned in an internal report of September 1939, surely because they had little to do with Stalin's original directive of July 1937.[5] He had specified that arrests be linked to past or present behavior; the Turkmenistan NKVD violated this order thoroughly. Its activity might be seen as a drive to establish a system of terror, except that once again there was no attempt to evoke fear systematically; the message would have been "Don't go to the market," not "Be afraid that the authorities might arrest you for no reason." Such police conduct was not, judging by the available evidence, what Stalin had originally wanted. The Turkmenistan police were out of control for a time.

Far more were arrested in 1937–38 than the central officials had suggested at first (table 4). The increase of over 700 percent in arrests from 1936 to 1937 shows a dramatic change in the political situation. Executions rose an astounding 315.8 times in the same period. Rather than a planned campaign, this was an explosion of madness or fear at the top.

Ezhov indicated in July 1937 that a total of 72,950 might be shot and that the total of severe punishments, including exiles, could be 250,450. Yet executions alone amounted to more than 2.7 times that number in the next two years. If a "plan" for repression existed in mid-1937, it was not followed.

Table 4 Number of Individuals Arrested or Investigated by the Security Police and Their Fate, 1934–1938

| | Arrests | | | |
	All Crimes	CR[a] Crimes	Convictions	Executions
Year				
1934	205,173	90,417	78,999	2,056
1935	193,083	108,935	267,076	1,229
1936	131,168	91,127	274,670	1,118
1937[b]	936,750	779,056	790,665	353,074
1938	638,509	593,326	554,258	328,618
Total for 1937–38	1,575,259	1,372,382	1,344,923	681,692

Source: GARF f. 9401, o. 1, d. 4157, 11. 201–03, a report prepared for Stalin's successors at the end of 1953.

[a]CR = counter-revolutionary

[b]The figures for 1937 and 1938 occupied a separate page.

These figures may be incomplete. A detailed study of all the information now available from Russian archives, including judicial sources, concludes almost certainly that fewer than 2.5 million people were arrested on all charges in 1937–38. The number shot "was more likely a question of hundreds of thousands than of millions."[6] Again, these figures are appalling—but we must reserve judgment yet on what they meant for how the country was ruled and how the populace perceived the Terror.

At about the same time that the mass arrests began, central NKVD authorities put great pressure on the lower ranks to extract confessions through torture. Physical methods had been the exception since about 1930, when they were employed in a campaign to extract gold from private citizens.[7] But why require confessions at all, if the goal of the regime was to terrorize the populace? It would have been much simpler just to convict people and be done with it. This is one of the nagging questions about the Terror that will be addressed below.

During this period the jails began to fill up (map 1). Severe overcrowding and hideous conditions prevailed in the prisons and in the camps. Every night people were pulled from the cells for interrogation and torture. For example, in 1937, in the city of Zaporozhe, prisoners who refused to sign confessions were forced into a "special small locked closet" in which they could not sit or even turn. After a

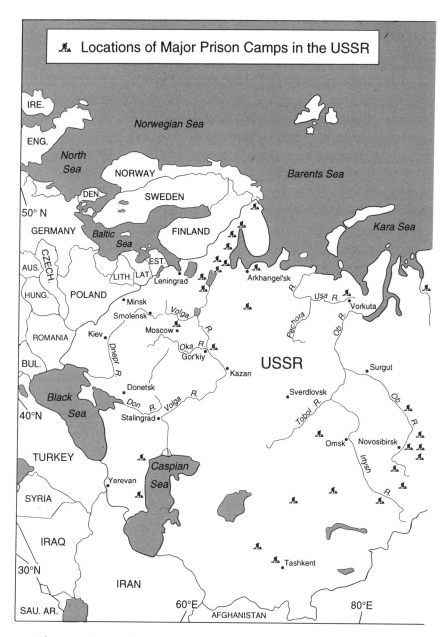

♨ Locations of Major Prison Camps in the USSR

IRE.

ENG.

Norwegian Sea

North Sea

NORWAY

Barents Sea

DEN.

SWEDEN

50° N

GERMANY

Baltic Sea

FINLAND

Kara Sea

CZECH.

AUS.

EST.

LITH. LAT.

Leningrad

Arkhangel'sk

HUNG.

POLAND

Minsk

Usa R.

Vorkuta

Smolensk

Volga

Pechora

Ob R.

ROMANIA

Kiev

Moscow

Dnepr R.

BUL.

Oka R.

Gor'kiy

Kazan

USSR

Surgut

Black Sea

Donetsk

Sverdlovsk

Ob R.

40°N

Don R.

Volga R.

Stalingrad

Tobol R.

TURKEY

Omsk

Novosibirsk

Irtysh

Yerevan

Caspian Sea

SYRIA

R.

IRAQ

30°N

Tashkent

IRAN

60°E

80°E

SAU. AR.

AFGHANISTAN

1. The Soviet Union in 1938

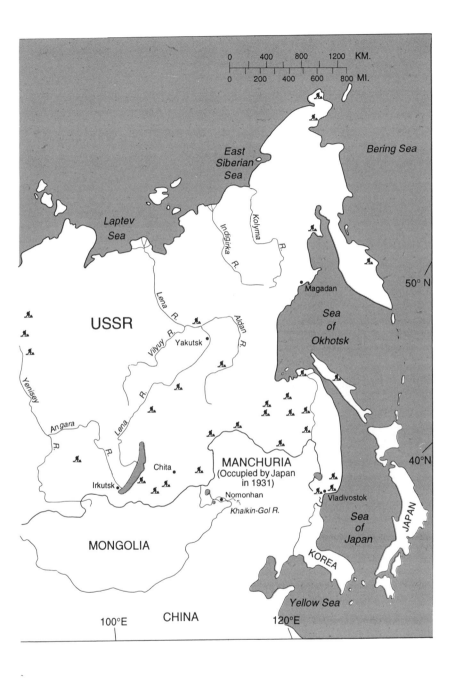

KM.
0   400   800   1200

MI.
0   200   400   600   800

Bering Sea

East
Siberian
Sea

Laptev
Sea

USSR

Kolyma R.

Indigirka R.

Lena R.

Aldan R.

Vilyuy R.

Yakutsk

Yenisey

Angara

Lena R.

R.

Chita

Irkutsk

MONGOLIA

100°E

CHINA

120°E

Nomonhan
Khalkin-Gol R.

MANCHURIA
(Occupied by Japan
in 1931)

Magadan

Sea
of
Okhotsk

50° N

40°N

Vladivostok

Sea
of
Japan

JAPAN

KOREA

Yellow Sea

while the victims would begin to sink down from fatigue and lack of air. Then the guards would enter, revive them, and begin the process all over. This treatment resulted in "horribly swollen legs."[8]

According to other accounts, NKVDisty repeatedly struck and kicked their victims. Professor L. was beaten in 1937 with a board studded with nails.[9] In *Gulag Archipelago* Aleksandr Solzhenitsyn catalogs tortures used at this time, including extremely bright lights, intense sound, psychological tricks, extinguishing cigarettes on the skin, and crushing men's genitals.[10] Although such stories are deeply disturbing, it is still necessary to analyze why such events occurred.

Torture by governments or armed forces has, of course, a long and sad history. Authorities use it when their standards of behavior are low and or when they desperately seek information from someone they consider to be guilty or knowledgeable about criminal activities. Investigators must usually develop a particular attitude toward the victims they face. As two American psychologists, H. C. Kelman and V. L. Hamilton, have observed, "When a group of people is defined entirely in terms of a category to which they belong and when this category is excluded from the human family, moral restraints against killing them are more readily overcome."[11] Clearly the decision to torture someone also becomes easier to make when personal attitudes combine with external pressures and this dehumanization of the victim is at work.

The record of earlier torture in Western Europe provides further perspective on Soviet methods. Michel Foucault notes that in old regimes, including France until 1789, evidence was not regarded as neutral information. Slight evidence indicated slight guilt; at a "certain degree of presumption" of guilt, punishment began. Torture constituted both punishment and inquiry, because "one could not be the object of suspicion and be completely innocent."[12] This premodern psychology resulted from a fear of forces beyond the state's control, for example, witches. Much the same outlook prevailed under Stalin, whose government also faced many issues it could not regulate effectively.

It is worth reiterating that the international situation of the USSR in the 1930s was extremely tense and that the country had experienced war less than twenty years earlier. People could imagine war breaking out again, and the regime did its best to play up that possibility from about 1927 on, partly for purposes of exhorting its people to great sacrifices. Official vocabulary at home was full of military references: the "industrial front," the "literacy front," and so on. "There are no fortresses Bolsheviks cannot storm," ran a widespread slogan of the late

1920s. The media communicated a constant sense of struggle with powerful elements, usually portrayed as the minions of evil, for example, kulaks. Visual images of enemies were of monstrously deformed people or dragons. The regime trained its citizens to see the enemy as less than human or even antihuman. Such indoctrination struck a chord with many, because life during the Civil War had taught them that enemies capable of terrible deeds did exist.

The theory of an "authority situation," in which government servitors consider the authorities over them to be legitimate, may also help explain torture. In such a situation "the moral principles that generally govern human relationships do not apply" for many. If officials perceived as legitimate order violent actions, "people's readiness to commit or condone them is enhanced. That such acts are authorized seems to carry automatic justification for them. Behaviorally, authorization obviates the necessity of making judgments or choices." A new moral code, "linked to the duty to obey superior orders," comes into force.[13] Authority situations have helped produce barbarous acts in many cultures, including the My Lai massacre by American troops during the Vietnam War.

Did NKVD officers normally perceive their superiors, that is, the Stalinist regime, as legitimate? The answer must be yes, whether because of the privileges police received, the screening for loyalty undergone in recruiting, or a conviction that the state was remaking the country in the right direction. The combination of NKVD attitudes toward the regime and the international and domestic context during the last half of the 1930s produced great potential for violent treatment of suspected enemies.

Another problem that strengthened police willingness to obey arbitrary orders and to abuse people in custody was the low level of education throughout the repressive and, for that matter, the judicial apparatus. In 1929–30 no more than one-quarter of raion police chiefs had taken the two-month training course all were obliged to complete. In 1935 almost two-thirds of the Procuracy's investigators, who were supposed to look into every criminal case, had no legal training; 60 percent had no education beyond elementary school. Half of all judges had no legal training, including forty-one of the fifty-six on the Supreme Court of the Russian Republic. To make matters worse, turnover among all judicial employees was high even before the Terror.[14] These difficulties coarsened everything the police and the judiciary touched, while their ignorance inclined them to accept what they were told by high officials. How could they know any better?

Marxism also played a role in setting the stage for torture, even though Marx would have endorsed the practice only during a civil war, if at all. But his emphasis on class struggle, not individual behavior, could tend to dehumanize opponents. The irony here is that by 1937 those arrested as "enemies of the people" were often from social groups of which the Soviet regime approved. Yet the point remains that the NKVD relied on a vocabulary that described opponents of the regime as representatives of broad groups. It is easier to torture a representative than an individual.

Whatever the psychology of the police, the Terror now moved into high gear. The toll at the upper echelons of society was stunning. Of the 139 Central Committee members elected at the Seventeenth Party Congress in 1934, 4 had died of natural causes by 1939. Of the remainder, 114 had been executed or sent to the gulag.[15] The Presidium (executive committee) of the Supreme Soviet, the parliament, suffered devastation, as did the State Planning Commission (Gosplan). The entire party committee of the city of Gorky was imprisoned in 1937–38, and arrests on that order or close to it took place in many locales among the party leadership. Of the 644 delegates to the Tenth Georgian Party Congress, held in May 1937, 425, or 66 percent, were arrested and exiled or shot.[16] Seven hundred writers attended the First Congress of the Union of Soviet Writers in 1934, but only 50 of those lived to participate in the second gathering in 1954. As many as 90 percent may have been repressed.[17] Among top officials of the foreign ministry who served in the 1920s, a minimum of 62 percent fell in the Terror.[18] Except for Stalin, every member of the Politburo who had served under Lenin was destroyed, including Trotsky, who was murdered by an NKVD agent in Mexico in 1940.

These figures refer to the elite of the country. It would be a mistake, however, to conclude from such information that the whole country was terrorized or that Stalin set out to destroy all opposition to his rule. Masses of evidence contradict that picture.

To begin with, some of the country's most authoritative sources spoke for moderation regarding the enemy threat on the eve of the new campaign against it. Speaking in June 1937 to the city party committee of Irkutsk, Central Committee member A. S. Shcherbakov (who survived the Terror) warned that too much attention was being devoted to enemies. He saw "demoralization" and "confusion" in the party but tried to reassure his listeners: the "basic mass of communists" in eastern Siberia consisted of "strong" and "honorable" people dedicated to the Central Committee and to Stalin.[19]

On July 2 *Pravda,* the party's national newspaper, published a broader, more authoritative statement decrying the scope of accusations. It denounced a provincial paper for calling local collective farm chairmen enemies without any evidence. Such reporting was "at least political hooliganism" and an "original form of wrecking, with which it is necessary to struggle decisively."[20]

But a dilemma existed: people could act too hastily in denouncing others, or they could wait too long and be accused of lack of vigilance. No clear party line existed; this situation mirrored Stalin's ambiguity in the two speeches he gave at the Central Committee plenum of 1937, as well as Andrei Zhdanov's criticism of arrests at the same time.

A few people detained by the NKVD were released in 1937; for example, a professor was arrested in October, held for two months, rehabilitated, reinstated in his old position, and given back pay.[21] Some exonerations occurred in the army during 1937. Enough such cases are known to cast doubt on the usual picture of unrelenting terror in this period.[22] Altogether, 364,437 prisoners were released from the gulag in 1937, though the meaning of this figure is not clear.[23] Some had undoubtedly completed their sentences, whereas others were ordinary criminals. Yet in spite of such figures repression generally built through the rest of the year.

In this atmosphere *Pravda*'s cautious note of early July was drowned out by repeated, frantic calls to get the enemies. After Ezhov received the Order of Lenin later that month, the same newspaper remarked that "enemies still are and will be. In place of the unmasked spies the fascist intelligence agencies will undoubtedly try to plant new ones. . . . The NKVD already has and will have even more millions of eyes, millions of ears, millions of arms of the toilers."[24]

But as arrests mounted and the country desperately needed guidance, Stalin offered little. He said or wrote nothing for public consumption between March and October 1937, except for brief comments on a textbook of party history. Worse still, Stalin contributed to the inconsistencies of this period. In October he made a brief speech to executives and model workers in the metal and coal industries. Managers in these areas were a particularly ill-fated group at the time. First he criticized them for "not always understanding the heights to which history has raised them in the Soviet system." Next he reassured them that they had "every basis to enjoy the people's trust and love" and that "the people's trust in regard to managers is a great thing, comrades." Then in the next sentence he reversed course once more and remarked that "leaders come and go, but the people remain. Only the people are immortal. Everything else is transitory."[25] Stalin's intentions toward the managers were therefore far from clear, and listeners could conclude either that they were trusted and valued or that they lacked comprehension and were expendable.

In December the Gensec conveyed a sense of unease to electors gathered in Moscow for the selection of deputies to the Supreme Soviet. Stalin was their candidate. Electors, he informed them, must be sure that they are not only "dispassionate in battle and merciless toward enemies of the people, as Lenin was." They must also be "free from any kind of panic, from any similarity to panic, when the cause begins to become complicated and on the horizon there is the outline of some kind of danger, that they are also free from any sort of panic, as Lenin was free [from it]."[26]

Stalin must have dwelt on the problem of panic because it preyed on his mind. In his public statements, which were all that the population heard, Stalin provided no leadership whatsoever during the worst of the Terror. Rather, he was consistently inconsistent. Was this a deliberate strategy to keep the population off balance? If so, he followed this tactic too briefly for it to be effective.

The evidence on Stalin's thinking and behavior in this span remains fragmentary; he approved lists of people marked for execution supplied to him by the NKVD,[27] but why he felt such deaths were necessary is not clear. He may have had a grand plan to secure his own power, or he may have been convinced of their guilt. Before deciding what happened at the highest level of the regime and why, one must examine police behavior during the mass arrests.

In 1939 the NKVD numbered 366,000 employees, including camp guards, military forces used for internal security, the regular police (militia), fire departments, and the political police.[28] Considering all of its functions, this was not a vast organization in a country of 169 million people. For our purposes, the key section of the NKVD was State Security, and within that department, the investigators and secret informers.

Almazov, the former colonel of the NKVD border troops, maintained that the typical raion police organization had between six and fifteen "operational employees."[29] In Belyi raion of Smolensk oblast', documents show that the local NKVD consisted of eight employees, one of whom was a building inspector; another was probably a secretary.[30] About ninety-one thousand people lived in Belyi raion before the war.[31] Having between eight and fifteen employees per ninety-one thousand people, or from one per eleven thousand to one per six thousand, suggests shallow knowledge of the population's affairs.[32]

Thinly populated northern raiony, according to one ex-policeman, did not necessarily have their own NKVD organizations in the 1930s but only local "plenipotentiaries" with staffs of three to five.[33] Another ex-policeman recalled that in the Murmansk area the NKVD had eight to ten employees, whereas in the

Far Eastern Krai up to fifteen were on the job per raion. For Leningrad, with its population of 2.4 million, no more than thirty served.[34] That figure must not have included the ordinary police or prison staff.

It is not known how many of the NKVDists listed in these examples were members of the militia or carried out nonpolice functions and how many were from State Security. In the countryside probably few policemen served in the second branch. This appears to be the case in Belyi raion, where the NKVD group investigated such things as alleged beatings of children by the director of an orphanage. The subsequent report went not to higher levels of the NKVD but to the local party organization.[35] The police also operated a "grain inspectorate" in Smolensk oblast' and in 1936 were responsible for "the support of construction" of a Minsk-Moscow highway.[36] The commissariat had much to do besides hunting enemies.

Only scattered data are available on the number of secret informers used by the police. A former NKVDist claimed that every Moscow building had several informers, from the superintendent to the doorman, and that in addition there was always one collaborator for every five or six families.[37] But more specific information from ex-policemen shows much less surveillance of the population. One believed that in the city of Kuibyshev in 1938, when the inhabitants numbered over 400,000, the militia had "about 1,000 informers at a minimum."[38] The statement suggests uncertainty about the figures, but at face value it would indicate one informer per four hundred residents. State Security may have had its own informers; but if so, it is curious that this émigré did not mention them. Because the militia and State Security were two branches of the same organization, both did not need to maintain simultaneously *seksoty* (*sekretnye sotrudniki,* or secret coworkers).

Still another former policeman, who said that he had directed all informers in Khar'kov, reported that fifty paid stool pigeons worked in the city in 1940.[39] Their responsibility was to secretly monitor a population of 840,000, at a ratio of 1 per 16,800 inhabitants.[40]

Each factory that was middle-sized or larger had a "special department" (*spetsotdel*) responsible for security matters; this was either staffed by secret policemen or reported to them. Hiring, promotion, and business trips were of particular concern.[41] During the 1930s military plants, a sensitive category, had a much higher concentration of NKVD personnel and informers.[42]

Evidence on police monitoring of the population as a whole suggests that it was not nearly so extensive as many Western accounts have argued. "Operational employees" were not numerous enough to handle reports from thousands of informers at any one time. Of course, other observation occurred, for example, by party members and union officials, but such figures were known. Therefore, in the presence of such people citizens could adopt the behavior necessary for self-protection.

The process of informing is problematic. How much time would be needed for one official to read and absorb a detailed report by an informer on the activities of one target citizen in a single week? After all, even mundane activities would have to be covered for agents to show that they had not overlooked large chunks of the subjects' lives. In fact, this is "much of the information" in the recently opened files of the Stasi, the former East German secret police. They contain "detailed accounts of everyday events such as visits to the grocery store or telephone conversations of a strictly social nature."[43] In all likelihood, NKVD files hold similar material.[44]

According to a recent report, the Stasi, surely more efficient in a small, homogeneous country between 1945 and 1989 than were their Soviet counterparts in the 1930s, employed more than one hundred thousand people, with "tens of thousands more report[ing] occasionally to Stasi officers." Their information was "collected with a Prussian sense of efficiency and love of order, making Stasi one of the best-documented Communist security forces."[45] The East German police kept "roughly 6 million personal files in a country of 16 million."[46] This may sound so far like ruthlessly efficient totalitarianism. But imagine processing files on 6 million individuals, constantly updating and checking them, cross-referencing them, and so on. The Stasi material contains some 2,125,000,000 sheets of paper that would measure about 125 miles in length.[47] The magnitude of the task is mind-boggling.

A writer who skimmed his fifteen-volume file found that Stasi agents were obsessed not only with documenting but also with inventing alleged acts of political opposition. "On the one hand, they were more painstaking and concentrated than I thought. On the other hand, there's a lot they did not know. It changes my image of the state security force. It was large and all-embracing but actually very ineffective in much of what it did. Imprecise—not exactly sloppy, but it did not perform as it should have."[48] In retrospect, this imprecision seems unavoidable, even in an area as small as East Germany, where the population was stable and the authorities could quickly identify dissidents. The more information gathered, the more difficulty in keeping track of and processing it into usable form.

If in the 1930s the Soviet police kept files on a similar portion of the populace, which seems altogether unlikely, they would have had 63,300,000 files to cope with. These would have been drawn from an extraordinarily mobile population, constantly on the move between places and jobs, in the world's largest country. And this before computers, electric typewriters, or even correction fluid! In Kazakhstan, admittedly a backward area at the time, 120 raiony had no telephone links with their own regional administrative centers, let alone with the republic capital or Moscow.[49] In October 1938, 75 percent of the village soviets and 84 percent of the machine-tractor stations, which supplied heavy agricultural equipment to the kolkhozy, had telephone service.[50] But that would have left many thousands of villages—often soviets covered more than one village—without telephone service. In Belyi raion, local party officials regularly traveled to outlying areas by horse or bicycle, which must have been a bit grueling in winter.[51] In 1935 the Commissariat of Justice urged that every "village district people's investigator," the officials responsible for probing rural crimes, should be given a bicycle for transportation. Without them, these investigators often had to walk up to seventeen miles to the scene of a crime and back.[52] With few exceptions, the Soviet Union was terribly inefficient, as most who visited it realized, even at its most rigid Brezhnevian point.

Suppose, however, that every official possessed rapid communications and modern equipment; how much time, and how many people, would be needed to shape 63 million files into manageable information for superiors? The answer is, definitely more time and personnel than were available at the local level in the Soviet police. Even if half the nation had been employed to report on the other half and process the incoming information, the system must have operated with staggering inefficiency. That is in fact the way the NKVD behaved in the Terror.

To even approach coverage of the entire population by a network of informers, which was not the case, would have produced such an overload of material that the whole scheme would have been clogged beyond usefulness. In monitoring some 37.5 percent of East Germany's population, Stasi personnel "accumulated far more information than they could possibly analyze or use. Ultimately, they drowned in their sea of minutiae."[53]

Any security police force has a choice: it can watch relatively few citizens in depth and gain a modest amount of useful material, or it can try to observe a large part of the populace, in which case its files become unmanageable. And the bigger the organization, the more chances that its findings will leak back to the public through typists, clerks, and other ancillary personnel.

Besides such inherent problems, when the NKVD's agents and secret informers fanned out among the populace, they were often ineffective at gathering information. One reason was because many were recruited against their will and they did not behave according to police requirements. A manuscript by an unnamed former NKVDist listed "numerous difficulties" in recruiting and managing informers among students. First, because of their "lightmindedness," youths did not believe in the power of the NKVD and were not easily frightened by it. Second, students regarded denunciations of one another and professors as "extraordinarily shameful" and would quickly establish who the informer was. The consequences for the stool pigeon could be "extremely bad." There were regularly cases of students who had somehow been recruited as informers not only refusing to make reports but also revealing their role to their fellow students.[54] The former director of an institute of higher education confirmed this testimony and also cited the beating of a known informer by fellow students.[55] Several émigrés maintained that they were able to refuse when the NKVD asked them to become informers.[56] An army officer who emigrated after World War II said that during the Ezhovshchina, "the NKVD asked me to get information about others [in the service], compromising information. I told them plainly that I gave them objective information about those I know." The police threatened him with jail and used a "rough, physical manner" but did not arrest him.[57] A Ukrainian math teacher born about 1910 believed that if the police asked someone to become a seksot, it was possible to refuse "by saying you have the wrong kind of character but are always ready to report any facts about a saboteur or spy to your superior." He felt that "in such a case the secret police cannot force you to become an agent."[58]

Two émigrés said that seksoty at their workplaces were not only known to all but were out to protect, not damage, their coworkers.[59] These two and another ex-Soviet citizen believed that secret informers posed no threat to them at all.[60] Several other émigrés were sure that they could identify police spies and that it was easy to avoid them.[61] Nadezhda Mandelstam wrote that "the penetration of the world at large by the secret police was organized on a grand scale." But she also believed that people knew who the local informers were.[62] Two former workers indicated apprehension about seksoty, but neither mentioned any trouble because of them.[63] Obviously, there was no guarantee that all informers would be known, and many arrests resulted from their work. In a large number of places, however, they were clearly not effective. In any event, informers sometimes worked with the best of motives, to protect their country.

Considerable testimony indicates that the NKVD network by no means touched the lives of all Soviet people. "Which of your relatives or friends ever had a run in with the secret police?" an interviewer asked an ex-Soviet auto mechanic, obviously expecting a list in reply. "None of them," came the pithy answer.[64] A metal lathe worker born into a peasant family in 1919 reported that in his home village the "NKVD simply didn't bother very much with people." None of his relatives ever had any serious dealings with the police.[65] Ordinary factory workers and collective farmers in particular frequently reported no contact with the security apparatus.[66]

The NKVD gathered information in other ways, of course; the most common method was to check backgrounds through identification documents and official biographies, especially employment records. It appears that the police often did not have their own files on the citizenry. One man served on a district draft commission with an NKVD employee and a party representative; they gathered data on prospective draftees by "writing to the civilian's home address and the place of work."[67] The same appeared to be true of job changes; a supervisor in a dairy-products plant reported that the personnel director, "who was always a representative of the NKVD," gathered any information he could on new employees—after they had begun work in the enterprise—from their previous workplaces.[68]

The party's records of its own members, however, were in terrible shape: for example, in 1935 almost one-half of the party cards in Leningrad, the country's second largest city and a sensitive military area, were fundamentally flawed. Alterations and erasures had been made, names were misspelled, and birth dates were wrong, among other problems.[69] Zhdanov complained in July 1935 that the Saratov municipal party organization did not know how many members it had; some said 23,000, some 17,000. In 1934–35, almost 5,400 members arrived in the city from other places, while 6,454 left. "What is this, if not a revolving door!" exclaimed Zhdanov. During the two previous years, in just 36 local party organizations in Saratov, 136 secretaries (chiefs) and party organizers had been changed.[70] The rapid turnover of both leaders and followers would have made it impossible to keep track of party members' biographies or even of their location. Any files on the general population were surely in much worse condition.

The constant movement of Soviet citizens greatly complicated record keeping. About 23 million people migrated from rural areas to Soviet towns between 1926 and 1939, and often these newcomers and many born in the cities continued to move from place to place in search of adequate housing and employment.[71] Thus, efforts to gain information from ordinary records could have been even more unreliable than the use of informers. Even when the NKVD questioned people, it did not always know their true backgrounds, for example, that the parents of a woman interrogated but released in 1937 were kulaks.[72] The police never learned of one man's connections to the Socialist Revolutionary Party in the Civil War, even though he lived in Moscow and met regularly with "many of my old SR pals."[73] In at least two cases, and probably numerous others, the NKVD set out to arrest people who were long dead.[74]

The sources provide many accounts of citizens who concealed their "defective" backgrounds. A man who worked as a chief economic planner in an enterprise from the late 1930s until 1944 was the son of a priest and had spent the years 1929 to 1932 in a theological seminary; no one discovered him.[75] A former White officer held the sensitive post of bookkeeper in a Donets River Basin (Donbass) factory from 1937 to 1941 without being caught.[76] One man obtained a new passport in 1933 by charring the old one so thoroughly that only the name was legible; he claimed that it had been burned accidentally in an office fire. The local militia obligingly gave him a passport without the old notation that he had been arrested in 1929.[77] Another man got a new birth certificate from a doctor simply by saying that his old one had been lost.[78] People from the wrong political or social origins thus found ingenious ways to get new, "clean" documents giving their backgrounds as workers or poor peasants, the favored children of the new regime.

Apparently the NKVD's problems in keeping track of people caused it to check biographies carefully, especially in the hysterical atmosphere of 1937–38. At that time any delay in production or accident on the job tended to bring in the police to scrutinize the backgrounds of those involved. A typist for the railroad workers' union in Simferopol recalled that if "there was a train accident, sabotage had to be traced, and a wrecker had to be found."[79] The journal of heavy industry, *Za Industrializatsiiu* (For Industrialization), announced in February 1937 that "every industrial accident must have its name and patronymic."[80] The patronymic is the middle name of every Russian, so the idea was that someone, a wrecker, caused every accident. As one policeman later commented, "You may be chief engineer, but if you make one slight error . . . they will drag up your past, to find out if any relation had ever been repressed or arrested, or if anybody you knew had ever spoken against the Soviet power."[81] An engineer who had "something fishy" on his record, as a naval intelligence officer put it, would receive particularly close attention from the spetsotdel in his plant.[82]

These cases and remarks concern ways the police reacted to events, not initi-

The Political Police at Work

ated them. This point strongly suggests that the NKVD did not try to impose any particular policy on the country; it handled security matters, however solidly or thinly based in reality these might have been. When the police moved beyond central directives regarding arrests, as in Turkmenistan, they were not carrying out a state policy.

To be sure, Stalin and other leaders had created a situation in which accidents "had patronymics." But it would not have been possible to call forth such a mood if the population had not contributed to it readily.

Background checks had to proceed through the muddle of records, and surely the NKVD's files degenerated even further during the Terror, for two reasons. First, the constitution of 1936 thoroughly reorganized the police at the union, republic, and autonomous republic levels. Only units on the krai and oblast' level were unchanged.[83] Second, and more important, great turnover in the leadership of the NKVD occurred in both late 1936 and early 1937, as Ezhov took over, and again in late 1938 and early 1939, as Lavrentii Beria assumed control. One ex-NKVDist guessed that up to three thousand of Iagoda's men were arrested; another who worked in the Special Section of the army noted that almost all of its "old employees" were removed in 1939.[84]

Arrests within the police occurred between these periods as well. A former student in an NKVD school remembered a telling incident that took place at a Kiev train station in July 1938.

The narkom [people's commissar] of the NKVD of the Ukrainian republic stepped on the platform to speak to us. About ten minutes after his speech started, a car drew up and five men in civilian clothes stepped up to the narkom and invited him to come into their car. We knew immediately that he had been arrested. Then his assistant, the chief of the militia, stood up to speak. Five minutes after he began to speak another car came and took him away too. Then they asked the Commissar of our school to speak. He said, I'd rather not, I am afraid I may be arrested too.[85]

Even if this example is extreme, rapid turnover did occur. The new executives needed considerable time to become familiar with the cases and records already in existence, and quite possibly Ezhov's group never fully accomplished that task. Surely the NKVD's lack of knowledge about the populace made it more nervous and more likely to react badly when pressed to find enemies.

The police dug deepest into backgrounds when individuals were promoted; arrests often resulted. This heightened scrutiny helps explain the otherwise baffling pattern so commonly found of promotion followed rapidly by arrest. "A. Dneprovets," detained in Dnepropetrovsk in 1937, reported that people under consideration for advancement in that city often refused it: "Such promotion led directly to careful checking by the organs of the NKVD, and checking . . . the matter is well known . . . to arrest!" Dneprovets, earlier a militia employee, maintained that at the height of the Terror appointments to important positions in the city were made only after long conferences among officials, including the head of the oblast' NKVD.[86] This picture hardly indicates a campaign to spread fear.

Conversely, a tsarist guards officer who became a director of state farms in the 1930s—one man who by most secondary accounts should have been a prime target—had no trouble. In 1937–38 "he sat at home without any work. As a result he was able to avoid arrest. He never registered or had to tell of his past."[87] The Old Bolshevik Viacheslav Karpinskii, a party member since 1898 and a dedicated "Lenin loyalist," lived peacefully through the Terror. Perhaps this was because he was semiretired by 1937.[88] Apparently no one checked on pensioners, though orthodox theories of the purges would suggest that their political experience presented an intolerable threat to Stalin.

On occasion the wrong kind of person penetrated the NKVD, which gives an indication of its poor investigative abilities. One NKVD officer was the son of an executed kulak, another the son of a tsarist officer arrested in the Civil War.[89] Another man, an imperial officer who went on to fight on the White side against the Reds, reported that a friend of his with the same background entered the police in the 1920s and saved many former White officers. Eventually rising to become deputy director of the NKVD in the Ukraine, the man was exposed and shot in 1937.[90] Here a real enemy of the Soviet state had wormed his way into a powerful position.

Uncovering false identities during the party purges of 1935–36 surely contributed to the Terror, as discussed earlier. Ezhov's speeches to the Central Committee indicate that he put tremendous pressure on his subordinates to find other concealed enemies within the party and economic organs. People of the "former" classes, such as tsarist officers, merchants, and kulaks, suffered discrimination under the new regime because of the judgment that their strata had collectively exploited the common people before the Revolution. But many of the old oppressors had the need, talent, and initiative to get new documents and then to reach responsible positions. As official awareness and concern about such cases increased, so did the desire to hunt them down. A vicious cycle was under way.

Colonel Almazov wrote that concealing one's past or even changing one's name guaranteed a death sentence in the Terror, whereas almost any other "crime" might get a lesser penalty.[91]

The other side of the coin is that a number of prominent ex-Mensheviks who had not concealed their past survived; examples are Andrei Vyshinskii and Ivan Maiskii, ambassador to England. The Terror was also lenient toward the "bourgeois specialists," which included technical personnel, scientists, and administrators educated before the Revolution.[92] Former opponents who had not concealed their pasts were not considered a major problem. The great emphasis of 1937–38 was on hidden opponents, and the key word was "unmasking." The central authorities pursued those they perceived as real, concealed enemies.

The difficulties of record keeping help explain another mystery of the purges, the NKVD's apparent inability, and even lack of interest, in tracing suspects who moved around.[93] When the teacher Vladimir Samarin fled arrest in December 1937, he went first to the city of Voronezh and then to the hinterlands of Voronezh oblast'. There he worked openly as an instructor in an agricultural college.[94] Evgeniia Ginzburg relates several such cases, one involving a former newspaper editor who continued to publish in *Pravda*.[95] The confusion in the nationwide efforts of the NKVD suggests severe bureaucratic incompetence.

Other patterns of the Terror further counter the standard theories. If the intention of the NKVD was to spread fear of the state, in many instances it engaged in overkill. Arrests sometimes centered around one place, one enterprise, or one position. In the Kalmyk Autonomous Republic, as many as 70 percent of the journalists and writers and 80 percent of party and government leaders were arrested, a witness reported.[96] A butter expert and 32 colleagues received an assignment in 1937 to go abroad. He lost his job before the trip, but the others went, and all suffered arrest on their return. He was spared.[97] That same year a resident of Dnepropetrovsk claimed that not one person who held a responsible post in that city remained at liberty.[98] As a newspaper writer recalled, "In one week in early 1937 we had three or four different editors."[99] Some areas of industry experienced awesome carnage: in one coal *kombinat,* or network of coal mines, of 170 top executives at work in October 1938, only 17 had been in their positions more than a year, and 126 had been employed in their present jobs for five months or less, a degree of turnover that can best be explained by arrests.[100]

According to some reports, entire groups of men were taken in one swoop by the NKVD. "Almost all the male inhabitants of the little Greek community where I lived [in the lower Ukraine] had been arrested," recalled one émigré.[101] Another reported that the NKVD took all males between the ages of seventeen and seventy from his village of German-Russians.[102] Such concentrations of arrests far exceeded any level necessary to discourage others from opposition, had that been the goal of the regime.

The corollary to the pattern of a high concentration of arrests in some cases is that in other settings few or no detentions occurred. As noted, some émigrés mentioned a lack of contact with the police. One rural worker said, "I had no difficulty with the NKVD. No one in my family had difficulty with them or was arrested."[103] Several army veterans, including officers, also reported no relations whatsoever with the secret police.[104] A psychiatrist working with a group in Kiev from 1927 to 1940 recalled that no arrests had occurred among its members: "In this collective there were Party and non-Party people, and we all were very close to each other. It was the work that brought them together."[105] N. Otradin, who worked in a factory located on the upper Volga in the late 1930s, noted: "The terror proceeded more above—only rumors reached us, down below: at our factory and in the settlement attached to it no one suffered then."[106] Former workers of the Likhachev auto works in Moscow said that they had simply "not noticed" many arrests in the factory.[107] The Terror was too erratic to have been a planned operation with the goal of spreading fear.

The importance of the NKVDists' attitudes toward their work deserves a more detailed examination. In some stories, the police clearly knew they were arresting innocent people. For example, an order reportedly arrived in Tashkent to "Send 200!" The local NKVD was at its wits' end about who else to arrest, having exhausted all the obvious possibilities, until it learned that a band of "gypsies" (Romany) had just camped in town. Police surrounded them and charged every male from seventeen to sixty with sabotage.[108]

NKVDisty sometimes demonstrated a willingness or necessity to repress the innocent by writing out confessions for accused persons.[109] By early 1938, a repulsive "socialist competition" to catch the most spies and saboteurs had developed within the police of the Kirghiz Republic.[110] A story related by a former Soviet prosecutor shows that the NKVD pressed its members for more arrests. The head of the Leningrad oblast' police told a sergeant that in one raion the NKVD had discovered a Socialist Revolutionary (SR) organization with forty-five members, "but in your Volotovskii raion you think there are no counter-revolutionaries." Within a short time a similar plot was "discovered" in the sergeant's bailiwick, complete with an SR, kulaks, and religious sectarians—

again, segments that could be called old categories. "The case will go to the troika," said the sergeant. "We do everything by order."[111]

Vadim Denisov, a former NKVD officer, recalled that investigators' "quality" was determined by the number and seriousness of cases they handled. Because of this internal pressure, the police often created wholly fictitious cases. They usually relied on some incident or other, perhaps an accident in a factory, which they then turned into a case of wrecking by forcing a confession from a production supervisor.[112] Ezhov, too, appears to have demonstrated his quality by promoting fictitious persecutions, as the Tukhachevskii affair shows. To be sure, this duplicity took place in a context that demanded the unmasking of enemies, and Stalin bears the ultimate responsibility for creating this atmosphere.

Concocted crimes, however, do not necessarily mean that it is the policy of central authorities to manufacture cases. Law enforcement agencies have long forced confessions from innocent people and have tried to boost the image of their own efficiency by "solving" crimes on the basis of such material. Stasi agents behaved this way, for instance, as did Iraqi personnel in the early 1990s.[113]

Of the manufactured Soviet cases, what reached Stalin were simply reports that a certain number of people had been unmasked as saboteurs in a given area. He received regular briefings on "political" cases from V. V. Ul'rikh, assistant president of the national supreme court. In 1937 Ul'rikh provided a weekly summary "of the general number" sentenced for terrorist acts, spying, and sabotage, according to Dmitrii Volkogonov.[114] It is possible that occasionally Stalin saw individual confessions, but he could not have judged their content. Denisov remarked that the cases initiated by the police were more "refined" and appeared to be "very realistic";[115] if so, Stalin's suspicious mind would have interpreted them as true. Volkogonov, who examined the Gensec's personal files, remarked that his subject "always believed" police reports about treason.[116] Acting on this assumption, Stalin would then press the police for even more arrests, worsening the vicious cycle in which the NKVD already worked.

Fictitious cases are usually presented as the norm of NKVD activity, and Denisov claimed that all investigations were 95 percent spurious.[117] Referring to another man's arrest, an émigré reported that an NKVDist told him he did not care if a prisoner was guilty or not; he had a plan to fulfill, set from above.[118]

But other evidence suggests that the police often believed they were pursuing real enemies. Beck and Godin, the pseudonyms of two men arrested during the

Terror, wrote that S. L. Prygov, assistant head of the NKVD in Kiev, had a reputation as a brutal examiner but "turned out to be kind and gentle to the point of sentimentality." More important, they considered him to be "a believer [in the regime and its policies] with no doubts or hesitations." They found that "at the end of the Yezhov period the great majority of the young examining magistrates were more or less genuinely convinced of the guilt of the 'enemies of the people' and of the reality of their confessions."[119] Victor Kravchenko, later an émigré, recalled a conversation with an NKVD officer, an old childhood acquaintance of his. The man told him, "If you fell into our hands, it certainly wouldn't be without reason. . . . Purges are absolutely necessary. The Politburo is more than right about that." He went on to speak of "the immensely important objective of the Politburo, to free the country of traitors and of spies." This man was so committed to his work that he named one of his children Stalina and the other Feliks, after the first head of the political police, Feliks Dzerzhinskii.[120]

Officials recruited the "best Communists" for the NKVD, based on their achievements, records, and dedication, wrote G. A. Tokaev, himself a young party member in the 1930s.[121] In 1938 Mikhail Gorokhov, an engineer, was assigned by the Gorky City Party organization to the NKVD. "I felt satisfaction; I was even proud," he wrote.[122] As part of their training, he and his fellow students calmly watched the torture of a peasant, believing that it was necessary in order to get information from a dangerous enemy. Gorokhov described NKVD recruits as "Party members, simple boys, who have been told that 'enemies of the Socialist society' try to wreck our Soviet system and kill our leaders, and that these wreckers must be exterminated. The fellows do what they are told and quietly accomplish their job."[123] Not only "simple boys" believed what they were told; Gorokhov himself had already received higher education.[124]

A former investigator testified in the 1950s that "Ezhov's authority in the organs of the NKVD was so high that I, like the other employees, did not doubt the guilt of individuals who were arrested on his direct orders," despite a lack of suspicious indications. The officer continued, "I was convinced of the guilt of such an individual even before the interrogation" and then used "all possible means" to obtain a confession.[125] Other accounts also indicate that security policemen accepted as truth the idea that enemies had to be uncovered and eliminated.[126]

One émigré described an incident in 1938 in which an NKVD officer beat fifty-two suspects over a four-month period, trying to get them to admit membership in an anti-Soviet organization. Finally it became clear even to the policeman that there was no such group. But, he told one victim, "to find a gram of gold, it's necessary to sift tons of sand."[127] Here three points are worth stressing: the NKVDist believed that "grams of gold," meaning real enemies, were out in society; to the police, beating suspects seemed a reasonable way to learn the truth; and the investigator finally realized that he was dealing with innocent people. His purpose was to uncover crimes, not to terrorize.[128]

A former member of the security police reported an illustrative incident from May 1937, during the arrest of Tukhachevskii and his fellow officers. One of them was R. P. Eideman, a corps commander. Although he was a suspect, no "compromising materials" on him existed. But the NKVD knew that he was a friend of General A. I. Kork, who had already been implicated more directly. An agent whose voice closely resembled Kork's telephoned Eideman, impersonated his friend, and "warned" him that he might be arrested at any moment. The NKVD watched Eideman's reaction and arrested him as he was about to flee in his car.[129] The Eideman incident would have made the NKVDists who partici- pated in or heard about it feel that the commander had acted like a truly guilty person; he seemed to know exactly what the Kork impersonator was talking about and why.

Sometimes the security forces reacted energetically to trivial incidents. During the worst of the Terror, Stalin's portrait disappeared from a wall of an institute in Kiev and was finally discovered in a men's room. NKVD men "came in masses." Meetings of students and staff were held, and the police demanded that the guilty party be revealed. Everyone was questioned several times. This process went on for an entire month, but the culprit was never found.[130] The great resources devoted to the affair indicate that the NKVD took this matter seriously and expected to find an evil hand behind it.

The behavior of the NKVD's lowest level further illustrates its members' attitudes. The unit at Tumanovo in Smolensk oblast' responded to developments more or less the way the general population did. As noted, it took its cues for action from the party press, not from any internal NKVD directives. The same sorts of conversations, criticism, and self-criticism occurred in this party cell as in non-NKVD cells at the same time. Soviet police were part of their society and were not immune to widely held beliefs and concerns. Aleksandr Solzhenitsyn, who lived through the period as a young man and was able to describe it with such power thirty years later, asked, "Where did this wolf-tribe appear from among our people? Does it really stem from our own roots? Our own blood? It is our own."[131]

The Role of Evidence in Arrests

To the extent that the NKVD wanted to root out people it deemed dangerous to society, it paid attention to evidence of wrongdoing. In numerous instances this was done quite carefully. The chief of a department in a construction trust was accused in 1937 of "deep and secret sabotage," a charge that, by most accounts, would automatically warrant a one-way trip to Siberia. Yet the man had noted "every telephone call in writing and attached it to my files, maybe this saved me later." The documents showed that he had warned that problems in construction would develop; the responsibility was not his, and he was not arrested.[132]

An engineer in Leningrad was ordered to build a plant twice as big as was practical. Realizing the defects inherent in the blueprints, he and the chief of the planning department wrote out a report to that effect and signed it. When the project turned into disaster, they were not arrested. "They could not do anything against us," he said. "This is the usual path of the Soviet specialist. He covers himself with official notes."[133]

It was possible for an engineer or executive to express reservations about a project to the plant spetsotdel. "In such a case the engineer will be safe," said the naval intelligence officer already quoted.[134] A dairy-products technician related an incident in which an NKVDist found that a milk bottle at his plant contained broken glass. A policeman gave the technician forty minutes to explain how this had happened. He discovered that a bottle had been broken in production but that workers had not taken enough care in removing the glass from the vat. Three of the workers and a laboratory accountant were arrested, but the technician went free.[135]

Victor Kravchenko was director of a plant in Nikopol in late 1936 when he was accused of ordering unnecessary equipment from abroad in order to help wreck the Soviet economy. Although he was harassed repeatedly by the local NKVD, he finally found documents that cleared him in an old briefcase. After that he had further encounters with the police and was beaten by them, but he was never arrested. At some point in 1938, a regional party control commission removed a prior reprimand from his record; subsequently he received more important assignments.[136] It is remarkable that the NKVD would beat a man without arresting him, which suggests that a local unit wanted Kravchenko under its control but feared that he could not be convicted of a crime. In any event, the police here too displayed a concern for evidence.

During the same year, security officers were highly suspicious of one of

Valentina Bogdan's brothers-in-law, a railroad official, about a problem on his line. They questioned him up until several hours before his death from cancer.[137] Such conduct was pointless unless the police were seeking information on a perceived crime. The naval intelligence officer, who worked closely with the NKVD at various defense plants, insisted that its agents looked for "wicked intent" in accidents and that it was police psychology to anticipate such motivation. However, he continued, if the chief of the spetsotdel was an "experienced man" who knew the plant well, he might react to a report of an accident or production delay in a "friendly manner." In other cases the chief would investigate the problem to determine who, if anyone, was at fault.[138]

An incident from Murmansk reported by an ex-NKVD officer further illustrates police concern for gathering evidence. The date is not certain, but the story took place while the troikas were operating, so it occurred under Ezhov. Several reports from informers about a port employee led the local NKVD to open an investigation of him—another indication that the police responded to "signals" from outside its ranks. But after working on the case for almost a year, the officer in charge found no stains on the suspect's record; he was "a person completely loyal to the Soviet regime." The investigator realized that pursuing the matter through arrest would not succeed. A trial, even if held in a special session or troika, would fail. The case was closed.[139] But if there had been any problem in the suspect's record, the NKVD might well have hung a charge on him. Still, the police did not behave randomly in this instance but considered both denunciations and proof of guilt or innocence. The same pattern appeared in an investigation of a people's court judge conducted in Smolensk oblast' in spring of 1936.[140]

As the mass arrests unfolded, officials' fear of sabotage seemed strongly focused on citizens whose backgrounds were suspect. On the other hand, the "right" social origins were sometimes helpful when the police did investigate. A case in 1937 concerned a female Ukrainian worker who got a splinter in her eye on the job. Her reaction was to jump back from her machine, which went out of control and was damaged. The NKVD arrived and at first announced that she had injured herself on purpose, in order to wreck the machine. But after two days she was released.[141] Surely the woman's social standing helped her cause. In another case a man and his older cousin, who lived with the family for four years, had the habit of engaging in frank political discussions. The NKVD called in the younger man and told him that the cousin, a party member, had denounced him. The police did not detain the former but merely told him he should no longer let the cousin in his house. This lenient treatment probably related to his being a worker and a Red Army veteran from the Civil War.[142]

A Ukrainian engineer, born in 1915 into a white collar family, was never arrested. "Suppose I had made a mistake in production," he told an interviewer; "I would be called to the spetsotdel." There an official would check his background and would "not do much to me." When asked, "And if you had been the son of a worker?" he replied, "Oh, this would have been better."[143] A Kalmyk man reported that his uncle had been jailed in 1935–36 for possession of an old gun. He was released after an appeal to Mikhail Kalinin, president of the USSR. In 1937 the uncle was declared a bourgeois nationalist and thrown out of the party, whereupon he went to work as a simple collective farmer. The NKVD then investigated him, but he appealed again to Kalinin, "playing up his origins as a son of a batrak [landless peasant]." Kalinin again interceded, and the uncle was not arrested.[144] In these cases, the authorities' prejudice in favor of some social categories indicates a belief that enemies were not likely to be found there.

If NKVDisty did scent an enemy, they and other officials frequently took a great deal of time for investigations and often kept arrestees in prison for months and even years before settling their fate. Victor Herman reported being beaten by one interrogator for fifty-five nights beginning in July 1938.[145] Thirty investigators worked on Konstantin Shteppa, keeping him constantly awake on the "conveyor" system, in which agents hounded arrestees around the clock, for about fifty days in the spring of the same year. Curiously, none of the police were interested in the findings of those who had questioned Shteppa before.[146] This lack of concern points to several possibilities: the terrible inefficiency of the police, a desire of each officer to build both his own case and his reputation in the eyes of his superiors, or a lack of trust on the part of NKVD leaders toward their underlings.

It was not unusual for a detainee to undergo multiple interrogations. R. V. Ivanov-Razumnik, Victor Kravchenko, Mikhail Boikov, and Evgeniia Ginzburg were among those who reported long and numerous sessions. Arrested in May 1937, an army officer spent twelve months under investigation before his release from prison.[147] Beck and Godin claimed that interrogation often lasted, with interruptions, as long as a year, though for educated people the process was longer, up to two and a half years.[148] Indeed, Nina Kosterina's father, a party member and a journalist, spent twenty-six months in prison under investigation.[149] A man from a Caucasian Mountain nationality spent two years in jail beginning in 1935. At times, eight interrogators questioned him for twenty-four hours at a stretch.[150] There are many such stories. They do not make sense if the purpose of the regime was to terrify the population, to acquire cheap labor, or to cement Stalin's position, all usual explanations of the Terror. These cases are, however, logical in the light of a hunt for feared enemies. The intensive, costly use of personnel and facilities in these instances meant, after all, that resources were unavailable for other prisoners or suspects still at large.

NKVDists at least occasionally believed the confessions they obtained, feeling that force had finally induced evildoers to reveal the truth. According to the writer known merely as A. T., one prisoner "admitted" organizing a detachment for an uprising; he described it as composed of three hundred members equipped with rifles, machine guns, and two airplanes. The investigator believed it all, though he did not want to note the airplanes. Subsequently, the NKVD arrested everyone the prisoner had named as participants in his "plot." In another case, an eighty-six-year-old man was so desperate to stop his investigator's harassment that he dreamed up a plot to place a bomb in a shaft dug under the Kremlin. The policeman responded that such an act would have required fifty men and demanded their names. Finally the prisoner named about thirty. The next day his investigator cursed and beat him for misleading them; the NKVD had driven around the city looking for men who had been dead for twenty years or more. The old man then had to come up with more names of conspirators.[151] The other side of the same coin is that Alexander Weissberg's investigator refused his offer to sign anything the police cared to concoct after months of questioning in 1937.[152]

As many stories cited here show, at the height of the Terror the police were interested in finding out who was closely linked to anyone accused of counter-revolutionary crime. Those people were in turn arrested. This scenario is the opposite of the randomness posited in theories of terror. Instead, suspects were pulled in because of specific connections, suggesting once more police belief in guilt at some point in the chain.

The interest of the NKVD in seeking guilty parties and evidence on their cases was stimulated by denunciations it received from the public. A professor's assistant told the Leningrad NKVD in 1938 that his boss was involved in a plot to kill Andrei Zhdanov, the city's party chief. After seven months in jail, the professor was exiled to Central Asia.[153] A Ukrainian *prorab* (supervisor of foremen) in a machine-building plant maintained that "very often a worker would make a declaration [about problems on the job] to the procurator and one copy goes to the NKVD. Then he will sign it simply 'worker.' This is to protect himself."[154] An assistant mechanic on a collective farm, born in 1925 and admittedly young to know personally about such things, though probably relying on his parents' experience, told an interviewer that "if a member of the kolkhoz goes to the NKVD and says that the chairman of the kolkhoz said so and so or did such and such against the regime, the NKVD will come and arrest the chairman of the kolkhoz."[155] Accusatory letters to the authorities produced investigations, for example, an anonymous missive of 1935 charging that the judge of a "people's court," one of the lowest rungs on the judicial ladder, had concealed his true social origin.[156] In the hope of receiving lighter punishment, an army deserter arrested by the NKVD invented a plot and accused other soldiers at liberty of disloyalty.[157]

In another incident, the police held a man who, without being tortured, readily confessed to wrecking and who had indeed caused the destruction of state property, namely, millions of piglets. "Professor Microbiologist Zion" (need it be said that this is a pseudonym?) had in good faith developed a method of inoculating suckling piglets against swine fever. His directions, which were followed across the country, ended in disaster: piglets caught the disease instead of receiving protection from it. Charged with criminal wrecking, Zion understood the seriousness of his situation and decided to play the role of penitent saboteur. He "confessed" to the murder of the piglets and pronounced himself a "weapon" in the hands of the USSR's enemies. In so doing "he evoked some sympathy, even with the officer in charge of his case, by reason of his sincerity and the plain and comprehensive picture that he made of the crime." He received a death sentence at first, but a Special Commission commuted it to ten years' imprisonment. After he served his time, the professor "preferred to live and work in Eastern Siberia."[158] His investigator, and perhaps his judges, believed his confession.

Recent studies of architects and astronomers in the Terror show clearly that problems, personal tensions, and denunciations had built to a high level inside these groups by the mid-1930s. Only after this trouble had been brewing did the NKVD enter the picture.[159] In general, suspicious information of any kind or quality coming from the outside fit the picture of enemy activity as portrayed by the leadership, whetted police appetites, and bolstered their certainty that more traitors existed. Because the great majority of suspects were hardly inclined to confess voluntarily to their vicious crimes, the police saw torture as a proper way to gather information.

Two of the more sensational memoirs mention cruel experiments on prisoners, akin to Nazi activities during the war.[160] More sober accounts deny any deliberate, Nazi-style cruelty by the NKVD.[161] Other stories describe helpfulness on the part of the police, even to the extent of warning families of imminent arrest.[162] One man who had the same investigator for three separate arrests, briefly at the end of 1934, in 1936, and again in 1941, experienced even greater consideration: "After the inspector saw that I was unjustly accused the first time, he advised me the second and third times of my arrest to say nothing and that I would be cleared." And he was.[163]

Interrogators used torture and degradation frequently, but these methods were intended to extract confessions, not simply to debase individuals. Once admissions were obtained, torture ceased. At least some NKVD men, having decided that the accused were innocent, behaved decently and protected subjects. Evidence, or belief in a person's guilt or innocence, was again the criterion determining treatment in these cases; policy and practice did not aim to terrorize citizens.

Another indication that the NKVD did not always fabricate evidence is that physical intimidation was far from universal, even at the peak of the Terror. The man just mentioned, a newspaper editor, was not tortured during any of his three arrests.[164] A Belorussian man jailed at the end of 1936 was held for two months, interrogated without physical methods about a brother who had lived abroad, then released. He subsequently found work as a school inspector, obviously a sensitive post.[165] The authorities investigated him, cleared him, and renewed their confidence in him. Among the well-known memoirists held through the worst part of the Terror but not tortured were Ginzburg, Weissberg, and Ivanov-Razumnik.

The portrait of NKVD work given thus far would be rounded out if real plots and terrorist groups, besides the apparently nonviolent Trotskyist bloc, existed in the USSR during the 1930s. The police apparently had reason to fear such activity, in that various sources report resistance and conspiracies. If such intrigue did exist, one should not find it surprising, considering the depth of feeling against the regime provoked, for example, by collectivization or affronts to ethnic sensibilities in a country with many nationalities but dominated by Russians. Even if such reports are exaggerated or completely false, the point remains that they were transmitted by word of mouth and believed in the Soviet Union; the police undoubtedly heard them, too, and perhaps believed them, as did various émigrés. Mikhail Boikov claimed that in July 1936 members of a terrorist organization shot at President Kalinin while he was at a resort.[166] G. A. Tokaev mentioned several groups that discussed assassinations and professed membership in one of them.[167] We may recall the reports that a plot against the government existed in the armed forces. Roy Medvedev, without specifying his sources, recounts several attempts on the life of Sergei Kirov in 1934 that constituted a "real hunt" for him.[168] Perhaps Stalin was stalking Kirov, but even in that case few NKVDists would have known the truth, although many would have heard of the hunt.

More precise and corroborated evidence on conspiracies concerns Azerbaijan. An army officer claimed that a group of his fellow Azerbaijanis, including a number of other officers, wanted to secede from the USSR in the 1930s. In 1936 the NKVD discovered the network, arrested almost all the officers, transferred others, and broke up the Azerbaijani Division of the army.[169] Another report confirms the existence in Azerbaijan of an "independent group which fought against the regime underground." It took its plans from "Western powers." In 1938, the respondent said, about fourteen hundred members of the movement were arrested, twenty-eight of whom were shot.[170] An Azerbaijani worker repeated the story.[171] News of these cases would have spread throughout the NKVD, raising the suspicion that yet other plots remained undiscovered.

What emerges from this tangle of brutal physical pressure as well as fair treatment, of quotas and demands to confess as well as attention to evidence, is a lack of pattern. There was no plan outside of the guide figures, which pointed to past behavior, not present or future activity. A system of terror would rest on frightening the population in order to achieve broad submission; this goal depends not on actual crime but on some selection of specific targets whose arrest will convey the message to people still at liberty that they may be next.[172] But if arrests involve those suspected of identifiable actions, and the investigations that follow are serious inquiries into those deeds, the public as a whole is not the target. Suspected criminals are.

Careful investigations were hardly the usual practice during 1937–38, however. An atmosphere of panic had set in, reminiscent of the European witch-hunts, lynching in the American South, or McCarthyism. As in those cases, fear of enemies became sharply pronounced within the Soviet regime. The police often speeded up their inquiries, dehumanized their captives, and used brutal investigative methods so extensively that justice was denied on a massive scale. But survivors' accounts suggest that the police tortured and shot largely because they felt they had to get to the bottom of a huge conspiracy that threatened the nation.

Still, numerous reports indicate that even at the peak of the Terror, evidence often made the difference in a case. The NKVD detained people because of some connection with misdeeds, accidents, someone else already arrested, or a denunciation. If in the worst period these connections were often flimsy, they still existed in some fashion. Without that kind of suspicious link, or when clearly protected by documentary evidence, people were either not touched or were exonerated in investigations.

Even fabricated cases grew out of identifiable connections or problems. Scripted charges do not in any event demonstrate general police insincerity, since officers could have acted to frame someone they genuinely suspected but against whom evidence was flimsy. Moreover, concocting cases in some instances and believing in real crime in others are not mutually exclusive position.

Arrests were not typically random. Many accounts show that the NKVD pursued people suspected of espionage and sabotage, deemed crimes in any country. This hunt for enemies occurred in a context of energetic encouragement from above and denunciations from below.

The NKVD and Soviet Society

Rather than constituting an organization suspended above society and dominating it, the police were part of society and had to tailor their actions to social and demographic conditions. The difficulties that the NKVD had with informers, its need to rely on civilian records to check backgrounds, and its frequent lack of knowledge about individuals all strengthen this impression, which emerges even more clearly in documents from the local level.

First, NKVDists did not necessarily live better than other people. Such works as Rybakov's *Children of the Arbat* depict agents as supplied and housed far above the average level, and a former policeman maintained that they were always well off. They received high pay and had access to prized goods at special closed stores.[173] In 1939 a group of jurists claimed that newly hired NKVDists earned more than 1,000–1,500 rubles a month, in addition to enjoying various benefits, a uniform allowance, and other perquisites.[174] This would have been excellent earnings, equivalent to a factory director's salary. By contrast, many factory workers earned only a few hundred rubles per month and had far poorer access even to ordinary goods.

In Smolensk oblast', however, three NKVD men and their families were housed in the kind of abysmal quarters that other people inhabited. One agent transferred to the area in October 1935 did not have his own apartment for his family of four but only a damp corner with relatives. The children could not study under those conditions, and the policeman was sick. Such was his situation, even though he had been in the security organs from "the first days of the revolution." One other NKVDist in the same local branch had similar housing, and another who was supposed to be transferred to this organization had not been because no satisfactory quarters could be found for him.[175]

Police had to follow party discipline, if they were members, and were subject to purges and exclusions. A middle-level officer was expelled from the party in December 1935 by a local organization because he had released a swindler from custody. Driven out of his apartment as well, he protested the decision to the oblast' party committee in May 1936, writing that the blame for the release was not his. This man had suffered substantially for months at the hands of a local party group, though he remained in the NKVD and had the powerful position of assistant chief of a gulag camp.[176]

Shortly before this, a Smolensk regional party committee (*raikom*) had not been afraid to exclude the local head of the NKVD from its executive bureau and to request higher party authorities to remove him from his police post. However, the oblast' party committee (*obkom*) found the raikom's complaint unfounded and reinstated the man in the bureau.[177] This did not mean that the higher-level body feared the NKVD at this point. Although in June 1936 the obkom removed a lower organization's reprimand of V. I. Sychev, head of a raion NKVD, for breaking party rules, this occurred only after Sychev "recognized his mistake" and explained that it had not been on purpose.[178]

In July the obkom took much firmer action against a former head of the NKVD unit in the Monastyrshchinskii raion. A man named Fetisov had committed suicide after being excluded from the party during the 1936 purge. "Comrade Fetisov was marked down as among the alien elements incorrectly, according to unverified materials of the NKVD." His father had been called a kulak but in fact had been a worker for fifty years. Neither the regional party committee or the local NKVD checked with Fetisov's home raion. For this fatal mistake the former head of the Monastyrshchinskii police, Filippovich, was given a "strict reprimand" by the obkom. It went on to say that it was "impossible that he should have a directing role in the organs of the NKVD" and asked the Central Committee to confirm its resolution regarding him.[179]

The party, judging from one "strictly secret" document in the Smolensk archive, did not appreciate high-handedness by NKVDists in moving people from job to job. In October 1937 the obkom complained to regional secretaries and the provincial head of the NKVD that, without its agreement, the police in a number of raiony were selecting people for various kinds of "soviet-party work." The obkom resolved that this activity was incorrect and that such appointments could be made only with its approval.[180]

An extreme example of party action against a policeman in this period involved I. M. Matskevich in 1935. A military tribunal of the Internal Guard, part of the NKVD, removed him from his position as a rank-and-file policeman and sentenced him to eighteen months' confinement. Matskevich had abused his post on occasion, arrested citizens while drunk and beaten them, and stolen 127 rubles of state funds. His appeal was rejected, whereupon he wrote to the Special Sector of the party Central Committee. But that body merely sent the complaint back down to the obkom, whose own investigation confirmed the original report.[181] How the whole affair started is not evident in the sources, but it is clear from this and the other cases just discussed that the party in Smolensk did not fear to criticize or even help discipline the NKVD in 1935–37.

Although the atmosphere became more tense with the August 1936 show trial, the head of a raion NKVD in Kuibyshev oblast', east of Moscow, was not reelected to the executive committee of the district party organization. He "had not been sufficiently present in the work of the party organization" to merit reelection.[182] This important setback in his party career occurred while he still held his NKVD post, indicating that local party members did not defer at that time to police power.

The party continued to affect police matters into 1937, too. In another NKVD group in Smolensk oblast', this one a special unit concerned with roads and transport, a member of the party committee questioned an arrest order issued in March by a Major D'iakonov. The critic, a man named Khon, was not identified specifically, so was apparently an ordinary party member within this NKVD organization. He objected to an order by D'iakonov that a young engineer, Machul'skii, be placed under administrative arrest for ten days. The engineer was a party member, which was why the affair could be discussed at a party cell meeting. Khon believed that the engineer deserved a strict reprimand, "but we should remember the decision of the plenum [of the party Central Committee in February–March 1937] on individual approaches to people." Machul'skii was fresh out of a technical institute and lacked experience. Khon remarked, "I don't want to accuse Comrade D'iakonov here, who did not know Machul'skii completely"; probably the assistant head of the local NKVD unit, a nonparty man, had not reported to the major on the affair with "sufficiently objectivity."[183]

The sources contain no further information on this case, but several points from the available material are striking. First, a low-ranking NKVDist felt able to challenge a relatively high-ranking officer, surely because the affair was a party as well as police matter. Second, the planned arrest was only for ten days, indicating again that not all incarcerations resulted in shipment to the gulag. Finally, there were people within the party and the NKVD willing to speak against the overuse of arrest even after the February-March Central Committee meeting; as of March 1937, the hysterical hunt for enemies had not begun.

Two other cases from Kuibyshev oblast' show that criticism of the NKVD from within the party continued later into the year. In May, representatives of local organizations presented to raion secretaries the "accusation" that leaders of NKVD and other party cells were "unsatisfactory" in educating communists.[184] In June the remonstrations from lower party ranks were stronger yet. "Communists sharply corrected their leaders," reminding them of Stalin's message that Bolsheviks had to practice "honest and open recognition of their mistakes." The heads of several cells had behaved badly during recent party elections and had not been sufficiently self-critical in their reports. Raion police chief Panov evoked strong feelings among party members, who charged that he had worked "especially poorly" on political studies with rank-and-file militia members and was a "bad leader" who had lost his "revolutionary vigilance." Although he had known for a long time that the assistant head of the political department (of the local soviet?) was a Trotskyite, he had kept silent about it until the party purge of 1936. Another man was elected party organizer of the cell in place of "politically bankrupt" Panov.[185]

Perhaps Panov had been marked from above as ripe to fall, and ordinary party members were turned loose on him. But he was only one of several local leaders criticized in Kuibyshev at this point, and the fact that such severe remarks about him came from the rank and file and were published in a party journal fits a broader pattern of the late 1930s: low-ranking people were encouraged to criticize their superiors, with significant results. The populist nature of the Terror is evident here and also a year later, when another NKVD party cell in Kuibyshev oblast' witnessed only slightly less strident criticism of its *partorg,* the member chosen, often by secret ballot of the members, to head it.[186]

Even while the worst of the frenzy was going on, the outside public could sometimes influence police practice. Several army officers were arrested in 1936 for saying during their oath of loyalty that they would *not* serve the working people. After two months in jail, reported one, "we got off, however, because our major intervened for us."[187] In 1937 an army captain was arrested, and his apartment in Kiev confiscated. His wife, who had been caring for her sick mother at home, was supposed to move about sixty miles away. Worsening her situation was the fact that her father and brothers had been tsarist officers and had emigrated to Yugoslavia. She went to the head of the passport office at militia headquarters in Kiev and told him the whole story. He supplied her with a permit to live in the city for a month.

At the end of that time, he called her in and accused her of being an enemy. He also required her building manager and a minor official from her residence to see him; but instead of fearfully denouncing her, both spoke in her favor. In her own defense, the woman said she could not be held responsible for her husband's deeds. Finally the official gave her a permanent residence permit for Kiev and even said he greatly appreciated her frankness; "his office only saw people with long stories and lies." Later an official at her workplace complimented her for not hiding her family's story. "For this reason the party and the spetsotdel left me alone," she commented.[188]

In this account the police responded positively to favorable recommendations, even though the husband was in a particularly sensitive category and his wife's family background was almost as bad as one could have in Soviet eyes. Tragedy occurred here, but once more the NKVD's actions reveal a distinction between perceived enemies and innocent people. Clearly the woman's frankness saved her, underscoring the point made earlier that the worst crime of the Terror was to lie about one's circumstances.

Sometimes a spirited defense spared people. A man working as a public works engineer in Kislovodsk came close to real trouble in 1937 after the arrest of his father. A "representative from Moscow" arrived in the town and ordered the son to conduct an investigation in another region. But on orders from the regional party committee, which set out to protect him, his chauffeur deliberately made him late to the train station, then took him back to the committee headquarters, where a meeting was under way to decide his fate. To the Moscow representative's surprise, the engineer walked in and was allowed to refute all the charges made against him. Others around him were arrested, but he was not.[189] In this instance local party officials defended a person in whom they had confidence, at the risk of incurring the wrath of the center.

Other cases are similar. A woman and her ex-kulak husband worked on the southern Donets railroad in the latter half of the 1930s; the reader will recall that the rail network was under direct NKVD supervision. The spetsotdel called her in "many times" for questioning and at one point told her she had to leave the job because someone with her personal connections to a kulak could not hold such a responsible post. But her boss always defended the couple because they "were the best workers," and they remained in their positions.[190]

Two incidents in the life of General Petr Grigorenko, later a prominent dissident, illustrate both the possibility of making a strong defense against accusations and the concern of the security forces for evidence. In 1937 Grigorenko, then a young officer, was in charge of defense fortifications in an area of Belorussia. A military commission rated them all unsatisfactory against chemical attacks, which should have guaranteed Grigorenko's arrest, given that Tukhachevskii had just fallen. But Grigorenko did not budge and was able to prove that the commission had performed the tests incorrectly, out of ignorance. Instead of being arrested, he was called to study at the General Staff Academy. The NKVD did, however, haul in three members of the commission when they returned to Moscow.[191] Of course, they were not guilty of anything but lack of knowledge, but they could not prove that.

While Grigorenko was at the Academy, two officials of the party cell in his class saw to it that repressions "simply were not permitted to develop and gain momentum" within the group. These men were the cell secretary, a Major Safonov, and his deputy secretary, a Colonel Gaidullin. In the fall of 1937 a colonel in the class, M. N. Sharokhin, was accused by the political commissar of the academy, one Gavrilov, and its Smersh chief, unnamed in the account, of having served with people who had been arrested. ("Smersh," the military counterintelligence agency, was an acronym for "Death to Spies.") The two political officers attended the party cell meeting and insisted that Sharokhin's "case" be put at the head of the agenda. Safonov replied coolly that it would be considered last. Finally, he read out the charge against Sharokhin and asked if there was a motion to "take cognizance" of the document. At this point the commissar spoke hotly.

"What do you mean, take cognizance of?" Gavrilov jumped up.

"What do you propose we do?" Safonov's voice took on a serious tone.

"We have to call to party account a Communist who failed to observe enemies," Gavrilov said.

Very quietly the Smersh chief uttered an aside: "I'm sick and tired of having to arrest party members."

As if he had been burned by this remark, Geniatullin jumped up and spoke with his strong Tatar accent.

"Listen here, comrade, do you have specific facts against our party member? If so, set them forth!"

"I don't have to tell you everything I know."

Geniatullin exploded. "Where do you think you are? You are in a party organization! You are a Communist? You are talking about a member of our organization. It is your duty to put all facts out on the table. Otherwise we will charge you with disrespect for the party."

Safonov also threatened Gavrilov with a report describing his conduct as "not befitting a Communist" if he did not reveal his information. He did not, and the party cell in fact passed a resolution condemning his behavior and transmitted it to his party organization. He was rebuked there and soon disappeared from the academy. Grigorenko's own cell did not consider a single case of ties to enemies of the people, and no one in his class was arrested.[192]

In a somewhat similar incident, a woman who worked as a secretary in a factory outside Kiev had been exiled at one point; her husband was arrested after Kirov's murder and died in exile. Around 1938—she could not remember the exact year—an NKVDist demanded to see her personnel file. The plant director, who outranked him in the party, refused. A week later the policeman came to her and said, "I, too, realize that you are an excellent worker, and I am not going to do anything about your case."[193]

Thus even during the worst period, managers, neighbors, and party members found it possible to defend people who had fallen under suspicion. These cases depended on the presence of brave people willing to resist the police. Although defiance was difficult, such incidents could and did take place. The security organs did not ride roughshod over the public's objections at these moments. Outside pressure affected the security apparatus, particularly when considerations of high performance at work were concerned. Support for those under a cloud could sometimes make the difference in police behavior, possibly by persuading officials that the subject of inquiry was trustworthy. In these stories the suspected people were usually accused not of committing crimes but of being in contact with enemies. Each example of someone close to arrest but not taken, however, represents a break in the chain of repression that characterized the Terror in its Great phase.

Most important in these stories for an understanding of the dynamics of the Terror is Grigorenko's comment that accusations never built up momentum in his class. If Colonel Sharokhin had been condemned by his party cell, not only he but also those connected with him—the others in the room, and more besides— would have been liable to arrest. Perhaps his defenders realized that and took the shortest way out. Nevertheless, they considered it possible to defy the police and got away with their resistance. The essential point remains that no one in the group was arrested; no chain reaction began, no hysteria took hold. Nothing fed the Terror from outside NKVD ranks.

In the stories just recounted, the regime did not try to crush the people. Rather, these incidents illustrate the close connections between police and society. On the other hand, once someone was arrested on the basis of any suspicion, outside intervention rarely helped.

In the Gulag

The image of Soviet prison camps etched into the public mind in the West, and now in the former USSR as well, is the one portrayed by Solzhenitsyn in *Gulag Archipelago*. This world unto itself is shown as a vast tableau of bitter cold, hideous brutality practiced on the political prisoners by camp personnel and ordinary criminals, and unbearable labor. Some of the most graphic descriptions come from *Kolymskie rasskazy* (Kolyma Stories), by Varlam Shalamov, for many years a political prisoner in the gulag system. Writing of the Kolyma region, in farthest northeastern Siberia, Shalamov remembered that "they didn't show thermometers to the workers, but it wasn't necessary—they had to go out to work at any temperature. Anyway, the old hands could determine the degree of frost almost exactly without a thermometer: if there is a frosty fog, that means that outside it is 40 degrees [Centigrade, which at that point is the same in Fahrenheit] below zero; if breath upon exhaling goes out with noise, but it's still not hard to breathe—that means 45 degrees; if breathing is noisy and there's a noticeable shortness of breath—50 degrees. Below 50 degrees spit freezes on the fly. Spit had been freezing on the fly already for two weeks." Under these conditions, "breakfast was sufficient, at the most, for one hour's work, then came tiredness, and the cold penetrated the whole body 'to the bone'—this popular expression was by no means just a metaphor."[194]

The worst place to be sent was the Siberian gold mines. There, Shalamov reported, men died like flies during the worst of the Terror. In the winter of 1938 the administration in Magadan, the headquarters town of the Kolyma camp system, decided to send prisoners on foot to the northern goldfields. "Of a column of 500 people over the 500 kilometers to Iagodny 30–40 made it. The remainder settled on the way—frozen, starved, shot."[195]

Yet although these conditions existed and claimed many lives, they do not provide the whole story of the camps. Such accounts do not even fully describe the situation in Kolyma. Another man who spent considerable time there was somehow able to emigrate later to the West. He did not deny the harshness of the region, but found it possible to live and work there, including a stint of three years in the mines and three years in "different technical jobs."[196]

Camp conditions varied tremendously according to place and time, and sometimes strange bright spots existed. A newspaperman arrested in 1936 remembered that in the next year his camp, part of the Pechora-Vorkuta complex in the north, had a theater and a huge library. "After a year of what was for me a very interesting experience, the camp theater was disbanded." Then he was transferred to a geological laboratory and trained there until 1941, when he was released. Conditions in the second place were "bearable."[197] A camp at Chib′iu also had its own opera-dramatic company into 1938, staffed with performers from the capitals.[198]

Conditions in a camp also depended on its distance from Moscow, probably because of transportation difficulties and the increasing possibility of corruption as more people handled supplies. Gustav Herling reported that the situation at the Second Alexeyevka camp in the heart of the Archangel forest was much worse than at Yercevo, which was in a more accessible place. A prisoner who had been in both told him that "the farther away from Moscow, the worse the conditions became."[199] Margarete Buber (Neumann) noted that the greater the distance she and her fellow prisoners got from the center, "the smaller our rations became."[200]

New difficulties arose as the Terror grew. The prisoner Joseph Berger found that "in general the older camps were better than the new ones [opened in 1937–38], where the living conditions were appalling, the supplies unorganized and the administration poor."[201] Thus *some* of the homicidal situation in the gulag was not the result of a calculated policy but arose from the immense distances, the poor transportation system, and the inevitable graft that plagues most prison networks and that was endemic in Soviet life anyway.

As the system expanded, deaths in the camps rose from 20,595 in 1936 to 25,376 in 1937 and 90,546 in 1938.[202] These figures relate only to the actual camp population and not to labor colonies or places of exile, though in those sites the death rate was usually lower.

Into 1936, Iagoda and Vyshinskii at least sporadically expressed concern about conditions in prisons and the gulag; in February Iagoda issued a secret order to the NKVD to stop "coarse treatment" of inmates, for example, keeping them in "isolator" cells, often deprived of heat or even light, without good reason. Such acts continued despite a "whole series of my orders." To back up his demand for improvement, Iagoda announced the removal or arrest of officials in several camps and promised that "all administrative personnel will be arrested for similar errors."[203]

The situation deteriorated markedly when Ezhov became police chief in September 1936.[204] Certain prisoners were then kept "under special surveillance" in the camps, a sign that they were considered especially dangerous.[205] In early 1937 the administration of a camp in the far north warned prisoners that "the worst enemies—the KRTD [counterrevolutionary Trotskyite activists]" were coming. "You must not let them wreck," said the commandant. "Help us, Soviet people, in the struggle with counter[-revolution]."[206] Beyond the bizarre quality of a security officer's asking political prisoners to prevent their fellows from committing sabotage, the story indicates that the NKVD took the crimes of the new arrivals seriously.

Much the same attitude appeared at the Siberian Ukht-Pechorsk camp complex. According to a man who was there, the guards "affirmed only one 'truth,' that all the inmates were 'enemies of the people,' and consequently their enemies too." The guards related to the convicts with "terrifying inhumanity."[207] Although some of this behavior undoubtedly stemmed from the guards' own undesirable situation, stuck as they were in the middle of nowhere, much of it came from their belief in enemies.

Another heretofore baffling phenomenon, the purge within a purge of 1937–38, further indicates that this belief existed within the regime and the NKVD. Nothing whatsoever was accomplished for the economy, the spread of fear, or the consolidation of Stalin's rule by shooting the "remnants of the Trotskyite opposition" in one camp.[208] This new kind of blow fell in Ukht-Pechorsk during the summer of 1937, according to another former prisoner there. The engineer Kanev (a pseudonym) was baffled: "There seemed no reason why the Kremlin's vengeance should reach to the poor victims already toiling their lives away in the labor camps, but it did." In 1938 executions for anti-Soviet propaganda occurred in his locale.[209] NKVDists now began to torture inmates within the camps and to demand new confessions;[210] in other cases prisoners already in camps were brought back to jail and their investigations, with all that term implied in 1937–38, were reopened.[211]

Other stories strengthen the conclusion that during the Terror, the police regarded politicals already in the camps as dangerous people who had to be removed even from other prisoners. A man arrested in 1928 for the attempted murder of an official in the North Caucasus remembered that "in 1936 I was doing a good job fulfilling my norms, but in 1937 I and many other political prisoners were isolated and put into separate camps and we did not work on the railroad during that time. I was in an isolator [a type of prison] from November of 1937 to August 1938, with others in a jail in the city of Svobodnyi in Siberia west of Khabarovsk. Many prisoners were shot and there was terrible confusion regarding the feeding and some prisoners got too much food and others got nothing." In 1938, NKVD officials reexamined the cases of all the political prisoners in this facility; their sentences were increased or they were shot.[212]

In the Vorkuta camp system, located in the far north, rearrests and interrogations of inmates occurred frequently in late 1937, and a prison within the mines was set up. The targets of this new campaign were "anybody sympathetic to Trotskyism" or anyone who told a political anecdote.[213] Guards executed a large number of prisoners, perhaps a thousand or more.[214] The purge within a purge seems to have been especially bad within Vorkuta and within Dal'stroi (Far Eastern Construction, a huge NKVD labor complex), from which there are numerous reports of shootings.[215] In Sergei L'vov's camp, "the worst time for all of us came after the big trials in Moscow. It was evident that orders had been received to select from among the prisoners a prescribed number—the worst among the 'counter-revolutionaries'—and execute them."[216]

Margarete Buber (Neumann) reported that one night in "1938–39," most likely in 1938, arrests of all the free exiles in the Kazakh steppe, presumably the most productive of the repressed labor, took place.[217] The NKVD now created a network of informers within the gulag to report on the prisoners, especially the counterrevolutionaries.[218] Perhaps the police expected to learn something incriminating regarding people still at liberty, but that possibility only raises the question of why the NKVD did not simply fabricate cases against those it wanted to arrest. Instead, the goal in this instance was to punish further the worst enemies of the people within the camps.

This episode is best explained by reference to hysteria reaching into the police ranks. Camp inmates, of course, were already isolated from the rest of the population. Escapes did occur, 58,264 of them in 1937, but probably most were from the less tightly controlled labor colonies.[219] To get away from the north or the far east was virtually impossible, considering the terrain, distances, and climate. There prisoners usually posed no further threat to the regime, if they ever had. Yet now the leadership apparently regarded even this degree of sanitation as insufficient—but only for politicals, not for all prisoners. Fortunately this aspect of the bloodletting passed quickly, albeit too late for many. Persecution of prisoners already in the gulag took place under Ezhov; such reports cease after Beria took charge of the NKVD in late 1938.

Different kinds of camps and exile with widely varying features and regimens existed, indicating that gulag practice was not simply to hold or destroy innocent people. Prisoners were treated according to the nature and degree of the crimes for which they had been convicted. The NKVD colonel Almazov reported that inmates sentenced to administrative exile were often hired by the camps as free workers.[220] The gulag administration did not need to house, guard, or feed such people, whose productivity was higher than that of the regular prisoners. An Avar man arrested in 1937 went to a state farm in Kazakhstan, part of a colony of such NKVD facilities. "We all worked very hard in the hope of eventual freedom," he recalled. Nor did he report any starvation at his site.[221] A young Russian man arrested in the same year was sent to a factory in Arkhangel'sk. Not kept under guard, he was taught how to use a power saw for wood. "I learned and worked hard on this machine," he said later. This man was not a political prisoner; people in that category worked in the forests under guard and had a high mortality rate.[222] Instead of being used for economic gain, politicals were typically given the worst work or were dumped into the less productive parts of the gulag.

The difference in treatment for the two categories of prisoners is also illustrated in the memoirs of Victor Herman. He contrasted the camps Burepolom and Nuksha 2, both near Viatka, in the north of Russia. In Burepolom there were about three thousand prisoners, all nonpolitical, in the central compound. They could walk around at will, were lightly guarded, had unlocked barracks with mattresses and pillows, and watched western movies. But Nuksha 2, which housed serious criminals and politicals, featured guard towers with machine guns and locked barracks and allowed no correspond.[223]

These points about conditions within the camps cannot be explained by reference to economic goals or to some desire to spread fear within the populace. They begin to make some sense only if the NKVD saw some prisoners as traitors and therefore more dangerous and worth less as human beings than others. The same point explains the different kinds of sentences handed down by the NKVD tribunals: exile; camp for five, ten, or twenty years, with or without the right to correspondence; or death. Obviously the Soviet government bears responsibility for the slaughter of prisoners through cold, hunger, and overwork. But the story of the camps in 1937–38 suggests that those deaths were not usually planned. It made little sense to take great time and trouble shipping many thousands or millions of prisoners across the whole USSR only to starve them to death, at a time when the railroads were desperately overworked and short of equipment. Such people could have been executed more cheaply and easily at the scene of imprisonment.

In the early part of 1938, some camp commandants repeatedly urged central officials to send them more prisoners for the "labor force."[224] There were probably two reasons for such requests: first, the camps' production plans had been raised arbitrarily; and second, inmates were dying at an alarming rate, having reached 6.9 percent of the camp population in 1938.[225] But demands for more convict labor were not part of a coherent economic scheme, given the desperate shortage of hands in places where productivity was much higher.

The secondary literature has often argued that many people were arrested to provide cheap labor. However, any economic rationale for the camp system disappeared as the mass arrests of 1937 began. Earlier in the decade, prisoners and exiles more often worked at their specialties, as did a Russian man who lived near the Usbirlag after his arrest in 1933.[226] At that time prisoners could shorten their sentences by overfulfilling the work norms. The newspaper *Perekovka* of the White Sea–Baltic Combine, marked "not for distribution beyond the boundaries of the camp," lists ten prisoners released early in 1936 for good performance.[227] Here were powerful incentives to work hard.

Other productive options were open to inmates at this point. In early 1935, the same paper mentioned a course in livestock raising held for prisoners at a nearby state farm; those who took it had their workday reduced to four hours.[228] During that year the professional theater group in the camp complex gave 230 performances of plays and concerts to over 115,000 spectators.[229] In no way were conditions in the camps before 1937 particularly good—far from it. But until then at least the gulag contributed with some logic to the economy and provided incentives for prisoners to work.

As the new enemies entered the camps, however, the situation deteriorated rapidly. Old hands in Dal'stroi told a newcomer that earlier conditions had been considerably better. Dal'stroi had been "unquestionably the best in the USSR, both in its regime, with the lowest mortality rates, and in the cultural level of its administration." But all that changed at the end of 1937; "all traces of liberalism were gone." Arrests took place among the free employees of the camp while watchtowers, barbed wire, and machine guns appeared.[230] The new inmates were taken seriously indeed.

The food situation had generally been tolerable in the gulag under Iagoda but quickly became abysmal under Ezhov.[231] Up to 1937 free men and inmates, though never politicals, were used as armed guards. Camp newspapers and bond drives existed until then;[232] although it is ironic and cruel to collect money for the state from prisoners, it is at least an indication that they were still regarded as participants in society to some degree.

But in 1937–38, Kolyma prisoners, for example, discovered that rations were often too low and work too hard to sustain life. The death rate was high, and productivity extremely low.[233] After 1936, the Kolyma institutions in particular were more holding areas for enemies of the people than they were labor camps. Vladimir Petrov, like others who went there, reported that when the men in his group of prisoners reached the area in 1938, they were "unfit not only for work, but for living."[234] Even the most obtuse regime would not have treated people that way had it wanted to receive the benefit of their labor.

Once in Kolyma, according to one prisoner, enemies were singled out for the "heaviest jobs."[235] Another claimed that in February or March 1938, the head of Dal'stroi ordered political prisoners assigned exclusively to "heavy physical labor." Camp administrators were specifically forbidden to issue extra rations to such inmates, who could be fed only according to fulfillment of work norms.[236]

What labor the politicals did accomplish was often of little or no value.[237] Many leading scientists, engineers, and other specialists were arrested.[238] To put such people to work chopping wood and digging for gold made no economic sense. These changes underscore the point that until 1937 the camps may have had an economic purpose or at least provided some economic incentives to prisoners; at the height of the Terror they did not. The arrests, as Chapter 6 will show, damaged industrial production, the most important sector of the economy. S. Swianiewicz, an economist and prisoner in the gulag for a time, believed that the extension of forced labor in the late 1930s could not have "brought any net gain." Costs of investment were lowered in some respects, but on the other side of the ledger the expense of maintaining the "machinery of coercion" ballooned.[239] He did not attempt to calculate the cost of putting highly trained people to work at menial labor.

A copy of the Soviet economic plan for 1941 fell into German hands during the war. It revealed that 19 percent of capital construction was listed under the heading of the NKVD, leading various writers to argue that the police ran a vast and vital economic network by that time. But this figure does not indicate that 19 percent of capital construction was *performed* by the NKVD, only that it was carried out on its account.[240] Because the police were responsible for so many matters, ranging from geodesic surveys to supervision of the railroads and maintenance of the border guards and internal security troops, considerable construction, including that carried out by ordinary hired labor, was required to run the commissariat as a whole. In 1941 facilities along the borders also expanded rapidly in defense of the new territories brought into the USSR after September 1939. The unfree population was not large enough to play a vast role in the Soviet economy by 1941, especially given the extraordinarily wasteful ways inmates were used and the restrictions on work by many politicals.

If the Terror had been either a campaign to frighten people or to boost the economy, gulag inmates would surely have been shifted from chopping trees to making armaments after 1938, when the Soviet Union began to concentrate more than ever on production for the coming war. Labor shortages occurred throughout the economy, and transportation could have been put to much better use than carrying prisoners and their supplies. But no such transfer of labor took place.

Sometimes, perhaps even frequently, NKVDisty fabricated cases for their own purposes. But little suggests that Stalin ordered such behavior for his own goals. A policy of terrorizing the nation would not have required such creations.

The guide figures did imply that innocent people, for example, priests and ex-kulaks, would be arrested. But this did not mean that Stalin was going after people without blemishes on their record, in his eyes, and arrests of the previously tainted people he pointed to in July 1937 did not provide examples that would have frightened the rest of the citizenry. Nor were recidivist criminals and the like a serious political threat to the Gensec's position. In any case, the guide figures and the quotas for arrest, as far as can be concluded from the evidence, appear to have made up a relatively minor part of all arrests; the original numbers of July 1937 were far below the eventual toll.

On the other hand, a belief in enemies often appeared within NKVD ranks, prompting members to search for evidence of crimes and often to torture inmates. Arrests frequently centered around certain occupations or positions; this was because people in those roles were more likely than others to have the kinds of responsibilities or make the sorts of mistakes that the NKVD would check carefully during the Terror. Nevertheless, even in the worst period people reported that they escaped incarceration when they could offer specific evidence indicating they had not engaged in wrecking. Unfortunately, the burden of proof to demonstrate innocence was on them. This reflected the hysteria of 1937–38 but was to change.

Within the gulag the authorities typically distinguished politicals, who were considered especially dangerous, from other prisoners. The former were used unproductively and allowed to die at the height of the Terror with little or no thought for economic purposes. All of these aspects of NKVD behavior in the worst years point toward the handling of perceived enemies.

The NKVD, by no means an all-knowing, all-powerful organization, depended on the citizenry for information and cooperation; its members were produced by Soviet society and history, especially the Revolution and Civil War, which did so much to shape police, or at least their parents. Citizens at liberty in the 1930s could influence the NKVD and even forestall arrests in some instances. Whether repression occurred at the height of the Terror often hinged on the appearance of panic in a given group, above all at the level of a party cell, an enterprise, or other local institution. Once accusations of treason or sabotage began to fly, it proved extremely difficult to halt the momentum of emotions and subsequent arrests. But a skeptical attitude toward charges in the first place could prevent this tragic pattern from developing. In any event, numerous people who lived through the period reported no arrests around them.

At higher levels in the party or government, emissaries from the center sometimes appeared to stir up trouble and provoke new arrests. It appears that in some cases Stalin attacked many regional officials[241] but that, owing to his demands or to their own beliefs, such figures sometimes became extremely zealous in their own hunts for enemies.[242] Why did the vozhd' push the Terror hard from above?

Stalin's conduct and intentions not only for 1937–38 but also for earlier years are illuminated by an examination of NKVD behavior in the Terror. The party purges of 1935–36 were "housekeeping measures" and also intensely political, but they were not the beginning of a planned assault on the party, let alone on the nation as a whole. Instead, given that in the next two years the police more often than not searched for those considered to be genuine enemies, Stalin seems to have become steadily more worried as the purges uncovered alleged spies and Trotskyites. Finally he struck at them, almost incoherently.

During 1937 and 1938 events spun out of the control. It took some time to reestablish the semblance of order, at least to the extent that it had existed before the fall of 1936.

4 The Terror Ends

In January 1938 the atmosphere began to change dramatically, though the pattern of arrests did not yet follow suit. At a meeting of the Central Committee in the middle of the month, speakers scorned excesses in the purges and repressions, while calling repeatedly for increased attention to appeals for reinstatement by ousted communists. Georgi Malenkov, director of the Central Committee's department of cadres though still not a member of the committee itself, reported to the session on the party purges of 1937. About one hundred members had been expelled, twenty-four thousand in the first half of the year and seventy-six thousand in the second.[1] This is a stark indication of how tension soared after the Tukhachevskii affair.

Malenkov emphasized that the Commission of Party Control, still headed by Ezhov, had discovered that "very many" of the appeals for reinstatement "correctly objected" to expulsion. In the majority of cases that the commission had examined, from 40 to 60 percent of those thrown out of the party had been reinstated. Malenkov reminded the CC of Stalin's objection in March 1937 to a "heartless bureaucratic" approach to communists. He then specifically tore into Pavel Postyshev's record as first secretary in Kuibyshev oblast', where more than 1,300 appeals had not yet been examined. In 1937, 3,237, or 7.4 percent of all party members, had been expelled in the oblast', and 70 party cells had actually been disbanded after being devastated by expulsions.[2] The Communist Party had been virtually crippled in parts of the oblast', as it had been elsewhere.[3]

The Central Committee now signaled a change of course for its remaining members and, by extension, for the whole party apparatus and the police. Malenkov recounted several examples of misdeeds at the local level. For example, in Perm a communist named Liforov was expelled in 1937 for opposing the expulsion of another man, Lavrenov. Lavrenov was quickly reinstated, which of course should have cleared Liforov immediately. But his appeal went unanswered for nine months, during which he was unemployed. Meanwhile, two other communists were thrown out of the party because of their links to him. The last fact provoked laughter from the assembled CC.[4]

It is already obvious that the NKVD did not automatically arrest people expelled from the party. Malenkov now gave some precise figures on this subject. In one district of Kuibyshev oblast', 50 of 210 communists had been ousted, but the NKVD found no basis for arrest in 43 of the cases. The Central Committee of the Azerbaijan Republic expelled 279 communists on one day in November 1937; of them, the NKVD arrested 63.[5] Two points stand out here: first, the NKVD began to investigate people after they encountered trouble in their party cells, not before; and second, it appears that the security organs investigated each charge rather than proceeding randomly. This surmise fits with other evidence on police behavior and with the tenor of the national Central Committee meeting in January.

The new tone of politics quickly became public, as a stream of newspaper articles and editorials denounced false denouncers and called for greater care in handling cases of accused party members. In *Pravda* of January 19, a separate box at the top of page one contained part of a resolution passed by the CC plenum. Although the message was still to root out enemies, it put even more stress on the need to display "maximum carefulness and comradely concern in deciding questions of expulsion" from the party. Now the "most evil traitor" was no longer the Trotskyist or the agent of a foreign power but the "masked enemy," the "careerist-communists" who tried to advance or cover their own mistakes by denouncing others.[6] On January 26, *Pravda* announced in the lead editorial that it was time to "rehabilitate those unjustly expelled [from the party], severely punish slanderers!"[7] These were strong indications that people making accusations without proof would fall themselves. The public had to calm down, and the Terror had to abate.

Even before the Central Committee began to curb expulsions, the legal system began to approach crime more carefully. An order of November 15, 1937, to all procurators of Soviet railroads mentioned the incorrect classification of cases as counterrevolutionary instead of malfeasance or the theft of socialist property, which carried lesser penalties.[8] Given the mood of that fall, this was a major step forward.

By early 1938 this tendency had progressed significantly. Procurator-General Vyshinskii then informed Molotov of a case involving a rural official who had been arrested for wrecking. An investigation showed that he was guilty merely of a sloppy attitude toward his work. Vyshinskii ordered him released; only disciplinary action was to be taken against him.[9] Procuracy documents thereafter mentioned many instances of groundless counterrevolutionary charges and warned procurators not to pursue them. To cite one example, one hundred party members in Omsk had been arrested without cause.[10] Too late for the victims, the Procuracy protested to the NKVD against shooting men who were supposed to have been exiled instead;[11] but this was at least a move to check the power of the police, and it augured well for the future.

At this point the tendency toward ameliorative measures was checkered. On January 24 the leadership council of the national Procuracy ordered all of its lower officials to review cases involving Article 58–10, having to do specifically with counterrevolutionary agitation, in which the sentence was less than five years. The goal was to see if any reason existed for appeal, with the object of *increasing* the punishments.[12]

Nonetheless, Vyshinskii and the Procuracy as a whole soon not only improved their procedures and insisted upon greater attention to evidence but questioned the whole course of the Terror. On February 19 Vyshinskii informed Stalin and Molotov that conditions in the "biggest camps" were unsatisfactory and "in some cases completely unbearable." He cited, for example, a Siberian camp about five miles from the Manchurian border in which five hundred inmates lived in cold, dirty barracks. "The more dissolute elements" were taking rations and clothes away from the others. Elsewhere the food situation was "catastrophic," and in one camp typhus was raging. "Those responsible have been brought to justice," he informed his superiors. He had told Ezhov of the situation but asked Stalin and Molotov to "instruct" the NKVD as well.[13] No evidence has appeared to indicate that in 1937 top Soviet officials cared particularly about how gulag inmates were faring; by early 1938 this attitude had changed.

In an order to the Procuracy of February 25, Vyshinskii touched on the essence of the Terror. In "a whole series of cases, raion procurators are incorrectly bringing charges of counterrevolutionary crimes." With the object of "overinsuring" themselves, procurators were wrongly classifying cases under Article 58. Clearly trying to slow the momentum of the Terror, Vyshinskii now stipulated that procurators at each level had to have approval from a superior procurator to bring counterrevolutionary charges.[14]

At the same time, complaints about injustice from the public to the Procuracy shot up. In January 1937 there had been about thirteen thousand; this rose to sixteen thousand in February. In January 1938 twenty-five thousand complaints reached Vyshinskii's nationwide staff; in the first twenty days of February, as a reaction to the new tone from the party, some forty thousand complaints were made.[15] The people of the USSR had not been cowed into silence during the Terror; now they protested widely.

In mid-March Vyshinskii continued to work against mass political arrests when he complained to Stalin and Molotov about improper counterrevolutionary charges against railroad personnel. He noted that during 1937, procurators took cases to the courts and obtained convictions with ten-year sentences for mere "formal violations of the rules of technical exploitation, in the absence of harmful consequences and evil intentions." Vyshinskii proposed that all such cases be reviewed in the four months following.[16] There is no record of a response; if Stalin committed his answers to paper, the relevant documents are still inaccessible in the Kremlin archives. But, as we will see, a policy of reviewing at least many of the cases involving Article 58 was in place by the end of the year.

In early February Vyshinskii also began to condemn the use of torture. He informed Ezhov's assistant Frinovskii that, according to a military procurator in Kiev, prisoners there had been beaten and forced to stand for long periods. Vyshinskii's concern was partly practical: the ill treatment had become widely known in the area after some of the abused had been released "owing to the complete groundlessness of their cases." Yet Vyshinskii appeared to be genuinely angry; he referred to "*direct fabrication of cases*" and demanded that the guilty NKVDisty be arrested.[17] "Slanderers," or false denouncers, were convicted of wrongdoing by July 1938 at the latest and were sent to prison.[18]

In late March the Procuracy Council referred in general to "beating of honest Soviet people," which it ascribed to penetration of its own agency by enemies. All procurators were now instructed to "strengthen the principles of judicial Soviet democracy" and to oppose sentences they disagreed with.[19] At the same time Vyshinskii wrote to Ezhov to protest sleep deprivation and threats against a prisoner, which induced him to sign a statement that he was in an anti-Soviet group. The procurator-general planned to investigate and bring the guilty to justice.[20]

Two days later Vyshinskii wrote to Malenkov, again mentioning enemies within the Procuracy. "In a number of places," he indicated, citizens had been prosecuted without cause. As a result, higher levels of the Procuracy and judiciary had quashed many cases.[21] Within weeks Vyshinskii's officials were busy across the country investigating charges against prisoners and cases already decided, with an eye to weeding out the groundless ones.[22] In June he ordered procurators to refer all cases involving the death penalty to him personally or, in his absence, to a deputy.[23] Then on July 25 the Procuracy Council required *all* counterrevolutionary cases to be cleared by the procurator-general's office in

Moscow; a staff of twelve people would be assigned to review them.[24] As of August 1, no new cases were to go to the troiki, though in fact some did.[25] These changes represented further major steps toward halting the Terror.

By early August an oblast'-level prosecutor had been tried, on Vyshinskii's initiative, for bringing political charges without sufficient evidence. The accused had also classified some ordinary crimes, for example, malfeasance, as counter-revolutionary. *Pravda* announced that this "overinsurer," who had carried out orders of enemies of the people, had received a five-year sentence.[26] In October the former prosecutor of the city of Omsk was sentenced to two years for sanctioning illegal arrests without "penetrating the essence of the case."[27] These reports were powerful indications to the justice system about how not to operate.

In the same month a political case moved on appeal to the Supreme Court of the Russian Republic, which converted the charge to an ordinary criminal one. Vyshinskii then stepped in and took the matter to the Supreme Court of the USSR, where it was overturned entirely.[28] By this time the judiciary had switched almost completely from facilitating the Terror to opposing it.

Vyshinskii, never a hero but brave enough to criticize the NKVD while Ezhov ran it, remained in important positions for the rest of Stalin's life. Without the Gensec's approval, the Procuracy would never have taken the steps it did to protest and curb the Terror.

Another account from the same period helps to illuminate thinking at the highest levels. In the spring of 1938 A. S. Chuianov, a relatively young party member, was transferred unexpectedly from work in the Central Committee apparatus to be first secretary of Stalingrad oblast', the highest office in that province. After receiving his new assignment, Chuianov went immediately to pick up clothes appropriate to his status from a special stock and then directly onto a train for the trip south.

He received no detailed instructions on what to do, especially in regard to the hunt for enemies. When he arrived at his new post, the head of the oblast' NKVD, Sharov, came to see him and brought a list of cases for his signature. But Chuianov insisted that they review the actual case materials together. Sharov objected hotly that this was "lack of faith in the organs." Chuianov replied that his suggestion to work together indicated trust but that to sign a list without seeing the evidence would be a crime. After looking at the materials all night with a lower NKVD officer, Chuianov informed Sharov that his attitude toward them was "negative." Investigations had been conducted in violation of Soviet laws and in opposition to decisions of the party and government. "I propose," he went on, "to end all [these] cases for lack of a basis and to free quickly all the arrestees under investigation."

When Sharov threatened to inform Moscow, Chuianov told him to go ahead. Some three hours later, a call came from Georgi Malenkov at the Central Committee:

MALENKOV: What have you done there? They've informed me that you propose to release a big group of enemies of the people, whose investigations have already been completed.

CHUIANOV: Yes, I've gone through the investigative files and have proposed the release of those arrested without foundation.

MALENKOV: Go through again more carefully and with a broader perspective. I warn you: you will answer for an incorrect decision.

Chuianov persisted and succeeded in obtaining the releases, together with job reinstatements for the innocent.[29]

Malenkov's telephone call shows that he really did not know whether the prisoners were guilty or not; he would have accepted without question a decision by Chuianov to keep them in jail. Once more, the lack of leadership from above is obvious. Chuianov had to act on his own, according to his personal interpretation of the situation in Stalingrad. Because the Central Committee meeting of January 1938 was fresh in his mind, he chose to examine the evidence and to regard each case individually.[30] Another man in his place might simply have signed Sharov's list, thereby condemning another group of innocent people. But by this point, or earlier, the NKVD had relinquished a great deal of power; conscientious party officials could thwart the agency, while Vyshinskii repeatedly challenged its practices.

Chuianov's account demonstrates that the NKVD had been out of control at the regional level, if not nationally. This fact does not in any way lessen Stalin's responsibility for what happened. But all the evidence assembled here suggests that the Terror had two tracks: on one, Stalin pushed events forward personally, arranging the show trials and demanding, in a muddled way, that hundreds of thousands be arrested in 1937. On another level the police fabricated cases, tortured people not targeted in Stalin's directives, and became a power unto themselves. The vozhd' apparently wanted only certain cases concocted and only certain figures coerced into making confessions, probably when he harbored deep suspicions against them. Such people were at the top of society and government or had once been oppositionists.

Stalin feared that numerous other enemies were also at large and drove the police to find them, but he did not intend to terrorize the populace as a whole. After January 1938 the abuses of the Terror were brought under control—albeit gradually, in that the leadership could not be sure that all the real enemies had been found. But by then it was also clear that in the course of the hunt, many (or too many) innocent people had been made to suffer and that the party and economy had been weakened.

Local communist organizations across the country began to scramble to reinstate purged members and to distance themselves from the earlier hysteria.[31] The communists of the Tumanovo NKVD in Smolensk oblast' were nearly frantic in their efforts to expose their earlier mistakes and end false denunciations. On January 22, three days after *Pravda*'s editorial on slander, the Tumanovo NKVD cell met in a closed session and resolved to "take to heart" the Central Committee resolution on recent mistakes. In the Tumanovo organization the cases of expelled members had received "insufficient individual study." Still greater "vigilance" was needed, but it was to be directed primarily toward unmasking careerists, who were "trying to beat honest communists and sow panic in the organization and by this means distract the attention of communists from the struggle with real enemies of the party." Several members admitted that they had made mistakes in denouncing others; one felt compelled to announce that in urging the expulsion of another, "I wasn't a careerist."[32]

Individual study of each case meant considerably greater attention to evidence than before. The mention of panic indicates some realization among the Tumanovo members that they had been acting hysterically. Finally, the thrust of this and other evidence is that the period of wild denunciations, in short the Terror, was over in Tumanovo. From this point on, meetings there were relatively calm affairs that included criticism of members and outsiders but no specific charges of wrecking.[33]

Then from March 2 to 13, the third and last Moscow show trial was held. Bukharin, Iagoda, and Rykov were the major defendants. Far from willingly rendering Arthur Koestler's "last service" to the party by confessing, Bukharin took every opportunity to subtly discredit his opponent, the state prosecutor Vyshinskii. Bukharin was playing a deadly game not for himself but for others; he knew he had forfeited his own life, but he wanted to save his wife and infant daughter. At the same time, he tried to leave the impression that something was fundamentally wrong with the state's case. He repeatedly denied connections with foreign police, for example, or with foreign espionage work. He rejected the charge of complicity in the murders of Kirov, the writer Maxim Gorky, and others.[34]

This last show trial also sent out the signal that the worst of the Terror was over. The major spies and enemies, who were former members of opposition groups, had been caught. Together with the Central Committee's resolution on false denouncers as the most serious enemy, the trial heralded a major new direction.

Yet local and central practice did not shift entirely overnight. Months after the Central Committee's warning against false denouncers and shaky evidence, provincial party organizations were still expelling people for links to enemies.[35] Arrests continued, though at least occasionally the results were milder than in the previous year. An economist jailed at this point remembered that "since it was 1938, when the storm of the terror began to subside, they did not find any act of political sabotage," merely malfeasance and wasting of funds. He did not go to a camp but received the light sentence for that period of "minus six": the right to live anywhere but in the country's six major cities.[36]

Ezhov must have felt increasingly uncomfortable as secret and open acknowledgments of NKVD misdeeds mounted during 1938. Toward the end of August, Lavrentii Beria was appointed Ezhov's deputy, even though the two men had had little prior contact. This was Stalin's way of checking his police chief's behavior more closely. Then in the early fall two of Ezhov's key subordinates were dismissed.[37]

The NKVD chief was so reduced in status by October 11 that Vyshinskii could write to him with a report of massive, illegal arrests in the Iakutsk Autonomous Republic. Worse yet, the local NKVD did not arrest real enemies in the region, Vyshinskii claimed.[38] Undoubtedly this letter, or an idea of its contents, reached Stalin as well.

By the fall of 1938 Ezhov's leadership of the NKVD was under steady fire from various directions. The regime responded officially on November 17, in a joint resolution of the Sovnarkom and the party Central Committee. This document went to thousands of officials across the USSR in the NKVD, the Procuracy, and the party, down to the raion level. Thus, the acknowledgment that grotesque mistakes and injustice had occurred spread widely—hardly the action of a government that wanted to continue frightening its citizens.

The resolution began by stating that in 1937–38 the NKVD had carried out "major work" in destroying enemies of the people. More remained to be done in this sphere, but the struggle now had to adopt more "perfect and reliable methods." This was all the more necessary because the "mass operations" of the preceding period, with their "simplified conduct of investigations and trials," had led to "a number of serious shortcomings and distortions in the work of the organs of the NKVD and the procuracy." Enemies of the people and foreign spies had penetrated the security police and the judicial system and had "consciously . . . carried out massive and groundless arrests." NKVDisty had completely abandoned careful investigative operations and had recently adopted "so-called 'limits' [quotas]" for arrests. Agents had wanted only to obtain confessions from arrestees, regardless of evidence or lack of it.

The resolution went on to say that many prisoners had not been questioned until long after their arrests. Protocols of their statements were often not kept, or if taken down, were full of changes made by the police. Vyshinskii's staff also stood accused: the Procuracy had not worked to improve its procedures, and enemies had entered its ranks. All this had happened because the NKVD and the Procuracy had tried to "tear [their] work" away from party supervision.

Sovnarkom and the CC therefore resolved to prohibit "any sort of mass operations relating to arrests and exiles" by the NKVD and the Procuracy. Henceforth arrests would require a court order and the sanction of a procurator. Exile from a border area was permitted in "each individual case" only with the approval of the Sovnarkom and the CC. The troiki, so instrumental in raising the tempo of the Terror, were immediately disbanded.

When requesting a procurator's sanction for arrest, the NKVD had to produce incriminating materials, which the Procuracy was required to verify. State attorneys were specifically directed not to permit groundless arrests. NKVDisty had to follow strictly the procedures of the criminal code on investigations, including interrogation within twenty-four hours. All questioning had to be under the supervision of procurators, who were responsible for seeing that any violations of the specified procedures were corrected. Vyshinskii was ordered to create a special group of procurators dedicated to this task. The resolution concluded with a warning to all members of the NKVD and Procuracy: "no matter who the person," any party guilty of the "slightest violation" of the directive and Soviet laws would be brought to the "strictest legal accounting."[39]

Vyshinskii quickly echoed the main points of the resolution in an order to the Procuracy. He added that all cases that had passed through the troiki or the NKVD's Special Sessions but had not yet reached sentencing had to be returned to the NKVD for further investigation. There could be no more prolonging of jail or camp terms for inmates. Local procurators had to meet with local NKVD heads to make all this clear to them.[40]

The Terror had ended. Although the resolution never mentioned the word *torture*, it tacitly recognized that physical abuse had occurred widely. And although there was still considerable room in a closed and secret system for violating the laws and tormenting prisoners, the highest authorities of the land had made clear their desire to end mass arrests, stabilize the country, and restore a much greater level of justice.

Ezhov had to go. On November 23 he wrote to Stalin asking the CC to release him from his post. He took responsibility for failing to notice that several of his close subordinates had attempted to conceal their own links to conspiracies. There were other, "completely intolerable shortcomings" in the NKVD's work, and it had been widely penetrated by enemies and foreign agents. Ezhov continued that he had been satisfied with destroying only the upper level and part of the middle reaches of this infestation. Many enemies were left in the NKVD.

He stressed that he had proved unable to cope with the task of running a "huge and responsible commissariat." He had seen mistakes in the NKVD but did not bring them to the CC's attention. He had recommended people for promotion who later proved to be spies. Two high NKVD officials had defected or disappeared. For all these reasons, he asked to be released from his job, though he claimed that the NKVD had generally performed well in destroying enemies.[41]

On November 24 the Central Committee voted to oust Ezhov; on the next day it approved Beria's appointment as Commissar of the NKVD. Remarkably, Ezhov retained his other positions, as one of the secretaries of the CC, narkom of Water Transport, and head of the Party Control Commission.[42]

According to a memorandum left by a delegate to the Eighteenth Party Congress, which opened in March 1939, Ezhov was still free then, though several of his top aides had been arrested. At a meeting of the Council of Elders, apparently an informal group of top delegates within the Central Committee, Stalin called Ezhov forward. The Gensec asked him who various arrested NKVDists were. Ezhov replied:

> "Joseph Vissarionovich! You know it was I—I myself!—who disclosed their conspiracy! I came to you and reported it. . . ."
> Stalin didn't let him continue. "Yes, yes, yes! When you felt you were about to be caught, then you came in a hurry. But what about before that? Were you

organizing a conspiracy? Did you want to kill Stalin? Top officials of the NKVD are plotting, but you, supposedly, aren't involved. You think I don't see anything?! Do you remember who you sent on a certain date for duty with Stalin? Who? With revolvers? Why revolvers near Stalin? Why? To kill Stalin? And if I hadn't noticed? What then?!"

Stalin went on to accuse Yezhov of working too feverishly, arresting many people who were innocent and covering up for others.

Ezhov was arrested a few days later. Roy Medvedev reports that he was shot in July 1940, after being held in a prison for especially dangerous "enemies of the people."[43] A recent Russian publication confirms that Ezhov was arrested in 1939 and shot in 1940, "for groundless repressions against the Soviet people."[44]

Although this account of Ezhov's fall cannot be confirmed from other sources, it is compatible with the image already offered here of a Stalin who was genuinely afraid of plots against him. It may also be that the vozhd' staged an act for the Council of Elders, though there would have been no need to do so. But at face value his words once more indicate deep suspiciousness bordering on hysteria. Surely people with revolvers were sent to guard Stalin, but he saw them as potential assassins.

If Ezhov was kept in maximum security for more than a year rather than shot right away, one might conclude that Stalin hoped to get information about other enemies from him. The story also rings true in Stalin's charge that Ezhov had arrested too many, given what followed. Those who lived through the whole phenomenon did not call it the Ezhovshchina for nothing; the worst of it matched the tenure of that tiny man whose bland but decent-looking face so often appeared in the Soviet press from September 1936 to late 1938.

His replacement, Lavrentii Pavlovich Beria, is frequently discussed in Russian émigré or glasnost'-era sources as one of the most loathsome monsters of a loathsome system.[45] Reportedly he was a sex maniac who cruised Moscow in an official car, ordering his NKVD thugs to grab attractive young women off the streets for his personal use. They were never seen again.[46] A Georgian, as was Stalin, Beria was born in 1899. He joined the Communist Party in 1917. According to Stalin's daughter, who hated Beria and blamed him for her father's actions, Beria was imprisoned during the Civil War by his own side on suspicion of working for the Whites. Kirov demanded that he be shot as a traitor; only the renewal of fighting saved him.[47] Such hearsay, however, smacks of the worst sort of unsubstantiated Moscow rumor.[48]

Beria rose through the security apparatus in the 1920s to become its head, first for Georgia and then for the whole Transcaucasian region, which included Azerbaijan and Armenia as well as Georgia. He probably first met Stalin in the mid-1920s when the Gensec vacationed in Georgia. In 1931 Beria became first secretary of the party for his native republic; in the next year he was named first secretary for the entire Transcaucasus.[49]

Like Ezhov, Beria was selected for full membership in the Central Committee in 1934, skipping the candidate stage. Evidently by this time Stalin had great confidence in him. In 1935 Beria returned the compliment by publishing a fawning volume entitled *On the Question of the History of the Bolshevik Organizations in Transcaucasia*. In it he cleaned up Stalin's past in the region, clarified where he was born and began his revolutionary career, and glorified the Gensec as the only Bolshevik hero of the area worth considering.[50] Through these and probably other acts, Beria strengthened his boss's faith in him.

Western and Russian glasnost' literature on the Terror typically considers that Beria's appointment to head the NKVD did not significantly change police practice, at least in qualitative terms.[51] In Nikita Khrushchev's famous "Secret Speech" of February 1956 to the Twentieth Communist Party Congress, his first denunciation of Stalin, he cited a telegram sent by the Gensec in January 1939 to various officials around the country, including heads of NKVD organizations. In it Stalin wrote that the Central Committee had authorized "physical pressure" on suspects in 1937 with permission of the CC itself. The 1939 telegram reaffirmed that "the Central Committee . . . considers that physical pressure should still be used obligatorily, as an exception applicable to known and obstinate enemies of the people, as a method both justifiable and appropriate." Khrushchev then suggested that police torture continued freely and even increased under Beria.[52] Because part of Khrushchev's purpose in the speech was to show his archenemy and political opponent after Stalin's death in the worst possible light, this claim must not be taken as a definitive statement.

Beria's negative image, richly deserved because of the many injustices that did occur under him as head of the security organs, has nevertheless wrongly overridden the firsthand evidence of what happened when he replaced Ezhov. Boris Men'shagin, a defense attorney in Smolensk, commented that Beria "right away displayed astonishing liberalism."[53] Arrests "fell away practically to nothing," as the inmate Alexander Weissberg put it.[54] Although millions remained in the camps and countless relatives of victims still suffered, a new and much improved policy was in place.

Political repression declined acutely in 1939–41 (table 5). Unfortunately, the categories used for this period are not directly comparable to the ones the police employed for 1930–38. But the available data show that executions in 1939 and 1940, apparently for political crimes alone, amounted to only .6 percent of the number put to death in 1937 and 1938. The rise in executions in 1941 is explained by the upsurge in suspicion that accompanied the German invasion.

In late 1938 prison and camp inmates regained the rights, allowed under Iagoda but lost with Ezhov, to have books and play chess and other games. These improvements alone were of major significance to people under lock and key. Investigators now addressed them using the polite form *"vy"* instead of the condescendingly familiar *"ty."* This too was an important change for the better, because it represented a major increase in the human dignity accorded prisoners.

Police have a much harder time torturing people they regard as individuals rather than as dehumanized captives. It is therefore no surprise that torture once again became the exception, contrary to Khrushchev's assertion. Abuse did occur sometimes; for instance, in May 1939 the foreign ministry official Evgenii Gnedin was beaten in Beria's presence.[55] Such cases after Ezhov's fall appear to have been limited largely to people taken from the highest levels of government, the army, or society; another example is the treatment of Marshal Vasilii Bliukher, arrested in October 1938. But prisoners like R. V. Ivanov-Razumnik, Mariia Ioffe, and Abdurakman Avtorkhanov, among others, reported that physical methods ceased where they were being held when Beria assumed control of the police.[56]

On Christmas Day 1938, Ivanov-Razumnik was summoned from his Moscow

Table 5 Repression in 1939–1941

	Sentences		
	For CR[a] Crimes	*For Article 58-10*	*Executions*
1939	63,889	24,720	2,552
1940	71,806	18,371	1,649
1941	75,411[b]	35,116	8,001

Source: GARF f. 9401, o. 1, d. 4157, 1. 201.

[a]CR = counterrevolutionary

[b]This number must not have included executions of Soviet troops in the field.

prison cell for an interview with an assistant district prosecutor. He informed Ivanov-Razumnik that over a period of fifteen months his NKVD interrogators had violated laws and official procedures by refusing to record his objections and counterevidence. The prosecutor now noted all of Ivanov's rebuttals "with great care." To the prisoner's disappointment, the case had to be sent back to the NKVD; but in the meantime the official agreed to inform Ivanov's wife of his whereabouts and to let her send him money. Within a few months he was released.[57]

As we have already seen, however, the events of 1938 rarely proceeded in a straight line. Executions continued at a ferocious pace for a time after Ezhov's loss of power: on December 12 Stalin and Molotov signed orders to shoot 3,167 persons.[58] It seems that they could not bring themselves to reverse cases that had gone past a certain point.

Mildness, improved practices, and increased sanity dominated in other spheres, however, particularly in the judicial system. Acting under a law adopted in August 1938, by the fall the Supreme Court of the USSR intervened frequently in criminal proceedings. The court "began reviewing convictions in political cases and at the same time requiring strict standards of evidence in criminal cases of all kinds."[59]

A case from Smolensk illustrates the changes in court procedure in 1937–38, while demonstrating that even in the worst months some officials kept their heads. In November 1937, courageous Boris Men'shagin became defense attorney for a group of veterinarians and agricultural administrators accused of spreading an epidemic among cattle. At their trial, conducted in a regular court, Men'shagin requested expert testimony to determine whether the men had infected healthy animals. His motion was denied, and eight defendants were sentenced to death.

At the request of the convicted men's wives, Men'shagin traveled to Moscow and was able to see Vyshinskii personally, even though by law the case could not be appealed. Upon hearing that the court did not permit expert testimony, Vyshinskii promised to look into the trial record. He did, and in January 1938 an appeals court ordered the case sent back down for retrial. Even after this rebuke, the lower court returned a verdict similar to the original one. But then the Procuracy took the case to the Supreme Court of the Russian Republic, which ordered another retrial. This time, in March 1939, the process was "much calmer," and the defendants received lesser sentences. Some were considered to have served their time already, but one got eight years and another was convicted of anti-Soviet activity. Finally, yet another appeal to the Russian Supreme Court led to a judgment in which all eight men's "crimes" were reclassified as "negligence" toward their duties. Considered to have served their time already, all were freed.[60]

This long saga is another indication that the regime set out not to terrorize these men or their relatives but to try them for perceived crimes. Bouncing from court to court was torture in its own way, of course, but a much simpler, cheaper, and more direct route could easily have been found if the goal was to make them and their relatives afraid of the state.

Men'shagin's comment about the calmer proceedings of the appeals illustrates the change from the panic-stricken atmosphere of 1937–38, when members of the judiciary were typically unwilling or afraid to take much time on cases, to the mood of 1939, when a new attitude prevailed toward charges of wrecking.

Men'shagin's story also underscores the need to separate the Moscow show trials from the bulk of the Terror. Vyshinskii's conduct was radically different in the ordeals of the former oppositionists than in the case of the agricultural specialists from Smolensk. In the first instance, he helped carry out grotesque miscarriages of justice based on fabricated evidence. In the second, he insisted that evidence be considered rationally and objectively, and he followed his words with deeds.[61] The show trials differed in purpose from arrests of nonoppositionists, which included the vast majority of the population. The Moscow trials were intended not just to punish former leading figures for their minor lies and intrigues but to indicate that any more such activity would not be tolerated. Arrests lower down in the populace related more to perceived crimes.

Paralleling Men'shagin's tale, the story of repressions among military officers in the Terror provides a stark illustration of its rapid rise and fall (table 6). The large jump in the number of officers in trouble from 1936 to 1937 followed a similar pattern. Figures for 1938 declined significantly, and the tremendous drop for 1939 shows clearly that a new policy had come into effect.

Reinstatements occurred in the same span: in 1937, 4,544 of those discharged for political reasons or arrested were returned to their posts; in 1938, 4,089; and in 1939, 152. This total of 8,785 leaves 19,900 unaccounted for. For the air force, 5,616 men were discharged in 1937–39, of whom 892 were reinstated,[62] leaving 4,724, or a total of 24,624 in both branches, whose fate is unknown. Unfortunately, a precise breakdown of why air force officers were ousted is not available; judging by the infantry figures, probably about 85 percent left for political reasons. No data have been published on the navy, which had far fewer personnel

Table 6 Dismissals from the Army (Not Including the Air Force), 1935–1939

Year	No. of Dismissals	Reason Given
1935	6,198	discharged
1936	5,677	discharged
1937	4,474	arrested
	11,104	discharged for "ties to plotters"
	15,578 (total for 1937)	
1938	5,032	arrested
	3,580	discharged for ties
	4,138	discharged because of ethnic origin or connections[a]
	12,750 (total for 1938)	
1939	73	arrested
	284	discharged for ties
	357 (total for 1939)	
Total	28,685 (for 1937–39)	

Source: The data for 1935 and 1936 are from F. B. Komal, "Voennye kadry nakanune voiny," *Voenno-Istoricheskii Zhurnal,* no. 2 (1990), 24. Figures for 1937–39 are from "O rabote za 1939 god. Iz otcheta nachal'nika Upravleniia po nachal'stvuiushchemu sostavu RKKA Narkomata Oborony SSSR E. A. Shchadenko, May 1940," *ITsK,* no. 1, 1990, 188–89. Komal's data generally correspond to this source, except that he does not count those discharged because of ties to an ethnic group.

[a]Includes officers from the German, Polish, Korean, and other "border peoples," as well as men connected to such peoples in some way. These officers were removed from the armed forces in June 1938 by order of the Commissariat of Defense.

than the army. Citing archival sources, F. B. Komal gives the figure of 31,397 officers forced out permanently from all services, to one fate or another, in 1936–39.[63]

As the table shows, only a minority of discharges among officers were because of arrests. Even of those incarcerated, more than 1,400 were reinstated in the infantry alone.[64] Not all who were forced to leave the services permanently were arrested; A. V. Likhachev, for example, the man who described the military plot against Stalin, was not. In fact, according to Komal's data, 9,579 of the 36,898 infantry officers ousted in 1937–39, or about 26 percent, were jailed; the previous table yields a figure of one-third.[65] And of those imprisoned, relatively few were convicted: 3,188 for all the services in 1937–39 (compared to only 263 in 1936). A recent Soviet military commission that investigated these convictions found that about 10 percent were "justified," though why was not specified.[66] This may be another indication that a plot against Stalin did exist.

In 1937 the Soviet armed forces readmitted 4,661 ousted men. At the direction of the party Central Committee, the Commissariat of Defense created a board in August 1938 to receive complaints from dismissed officers. More than 30,000 appeals and petitions came to it. As a result, 6,333 officers regained their old status in the services in 1938, and 184 in 1939, totalling 11,178 in three years. In addition, 2,416 won changes in the terms of their dismissals, presumably from political to less serious grounds. By 1939, more air force officers were reinstated (867) than arrested (344).[67]

It should be mentioned that a recent Soviet article by G. Kumanev gives much higher arrest and execution totals. He claims that from February 27, 1937, to November 12, 1938, Stalin and his associates Molotov and Kaganovich sent to the NKVD "sanctions for the shooting" of 38,679 military personnel. This figure refers only to the army, including the air force. Considering executions in the navy and in the army before and after the dates he cites, Kumanev estimates that about 50,000 of the "command staff" of the armed forces perished in the Terror.[68]

The other sources just cited have several merits compared to Kumanev's work: they are internally consistent, are much more comprehensive, and contain specific archival references. The first data follow the up-and-down curve of the Terror through 1937–39. Kumanev's total for 1937–38 is precise, but his article refers only to unspecified "archival materials."

In the other, detailed accounts of what happened, the fate of 24,624 army and air force officers who left the service in the Terror is unknown.[69] Not all of them were killed or imprisoned. More than two-thirds of the 9,600 officers arrested were acquitted, and many were reinstated. This pattern indicates that the regime at least believed it was investigating a real plot. If the goal had been to terrorize the military, far fewer would have been exonerated. Clearing the names of two-thirds would only have convinced other officers, and anyone on the outside who learned the details, that the authorities acted on the basis of evidence, not with the intent of instilling fear of the regime in the military.

The impact of these dismissals on the armed forces is hard to determine. To begin with, the percentage of officers permanently removed for any reason is unclear, since the number of officers was growing extremely rapidly as new graduates poured out of military schools in preparation for war. But two frames from this moving picture are available: 6.9 percent of all infantry officers in the ranks as of 1936–37 had been dismissed but not reinstated by May 1940; the figure for officers active in 1938–39 was 2.3 percent.[70] Older works commonly suggested that 50 percent of all officers had been purged, with most shot.[71] This number resulted from overestimating the number arrested and greatly underestimating the size of the officer corps.

The totals supported by recent, detailed evidence were in all likelihood too low to spread a sense of fear among officers still at liberty, especially because those discharged usually had some connection to one another, as the phrase "ties to plotters" implies. Thus men outside such networks could feel that only certain officers had been chosen for repression, and those for clear reasons. In any event, as officers who were party members (and a great majority were) passed through a purge in their units, they were checked on a number of specific points. Did they work efficiently? Had they ever been out of the country? What was the family background? Any connections to the Old Regime or the old exploiting classes? Any criticisms of the party or links to the old oppositions? A wrong answer to any of these questions could lead to ouster from the party. Then the expelled officer's dossier would be turned over to the NKVD.[72] The purge within this group of officers was an effort to find those most suspicious according to Stalinist standards.

By late 1938, cases moving through the regular judicial system mirrored the story in the armed forces; the civil courts now handed down acquittals much more frequently than in the previous eighteen months. The brother of one émigré had been a highly successful director of a state farm before his arrest. When his case came to trial, "those who had accused him were given 10 years apiece, and he was returned to his former station." Later he was promoted to head a military factory, a sensitive post to say the least.[73]

A further logical and crucial step in improving judicial practice came on the last day of 1938. The Supreme Court of the USSR resolved that Article 58 could be applied only when criminal intent could be proven.[74] The courts had already begun to throw out Article 58 cases or reduce them to less serious offenses.[75] Concerning accidents in production, prosecutors now had to show intent to wreck, making it next to impossible to prove the charge without a confession. Because torture was no longer widely used, such admissions were not forthcoming. On the basis of interviews with émigré lawyers, Peter Solomon has concluded that "party officials, rather than the security police, influenced the work of Soviet courts after 1938."[76] The judicial foundation of the Terror was severely weakened.

At about the same time, the Special Collegia in the oblast' courts, to which the NKVD had previously sent most of its political cases, were eliminated. In effect the Collegia had been special tribunals to serve the NKVD. By this point the regular courts had received a good deal more autonomy, accompanied by efforts to strengthen their standards of procedure and evidence. Unfortunately, the NKVD simultaneously gained the right to have its own special boards, essentially a return to the standard practice of the years 1918–34.[77] Military tribunals also continued to handle political cases after 1938, but their standards of evidence may have been reasonably high.[78]

In April 1939 I. T. Goliakov, president of the USSR Supreme Court, published an article that indicated a broad new departure for the use of law. He argued that the statutes of August 7, 1932, on theft of socialist property, and of December 1, 1934, on terrorist acts, were appropriate for the second phase of socialist development, which had now passed. The first stage had involved liquidation of the exploiting classes; the second eliminated remaining capitalist elements. But the 1936 constitution had introduced a new epoch that emphasized the defense of citizens' rights and interests, bolstering the courts, and fighting external enemies.[79] Obviously this claim was mostly a vicious farce from fall 1936 to December 1938, and the words and practices of Soviet courts after that hardly reached the best of Western standards. But judicial procedure improved vastly compared to what had gone just before.

To the chagrin of NKVD officers, by late 1938 the Procuracy reclaimed its right to oversee the security organs. In December, for example, Vyshinskii sent an investigator to the city of Gorky in response to an anonymous letter from inmates about abuses. Vyshinskii wrote to Beria on the December 20 to inform him that dozens of prisoners had been beaten there and in the town of Balakhna; some had died. Such "spy cases" had already been terminated and the accused had been freed. In another nineteen cases the previous NKVD investigations were being checked.[80]

Local security chiefs protested to their superiors about the conduct of procurators, apparently to no avail. One incident involved a procurator in Leningrad who upbraided an NKVDist "in a sharp tone" while in the presence of prisoners. The lawyer demanded polite conduct toward arrestees from the police; he also asked a group of more than one hundred prisoners for instances of abuse and names of those who had committed them. Many inmates "slandered" the NKVD in response, according to the Leningrad chief's report. Prisoners began "naked rejection" of testimony they had given previously and demanded that their investigators be changed. Beria passed the letter of complaint from his subordinate to Vyshinskii but limited himself to asking for the latter's "instructions."[81]

In June 1939 Vyshinskii left his post as procurator-general to become deputy chairman of Sovnarkom, second to Molotov. This demotion was surely related to the performance of the Procuracy in 1937–38. As noted, however, Vyshinskii later held several extremely sensitive positions, including foreign minister and ambassador to the United Nations.

His replacement as head state attorney was Mikhail Pankrat′ev. A group calling itself "workers of the Procuracy of the USSR" sent a letter to Zhdanov in October 1939 criticizing their new director for his inability to stand up to Beria on the issue of freeing those wrongly accused. The message asserted that the new NKVD chief was "not burning with desire to free totally innocent people, but on the contrary is conducting a definite policy to hinder this effort and is using his authority to maintain the 'honor of the uniform.' "[82] There is no record that Beria's critics suffered as a result of their views.

Although this letter belittled Pankrat′ev, he did in fact try repeatedly to gain the release of innocent people, with some success. For example, Beria reported to him in October 1939 about an earlier affair in East Kazakhstan oblast′. The NKVD commissar admitted that beatings had occurred there in 1937–38 but protested a court decision of June 1939 that overturned several convictions. The court had not "appraised the facts of wrecking work" by the accused. A "Japanese spy" still at large in the area had to be arrested. Beria also "considered it essential" to change the court decision, reinvestigate the case, and arrest the NKVDisty who carried out falsifications.

Pankrat′ev did not back down. He replied to Beria with many details of beatings and falsifications, actions mentioned by the NKVD chief only in passing. The court decision to free the nine prisoners involved was correct. Pankrat′ev would decide on the arrest of the alleged spy only after the return of the investigators he had sent to the scene.[83]

Other prisoners were released on the initiative of the Procuracy between late 1938 and the German invasion in June 1941.[84] In a check of sixty cases sent to the Special Session of the Mordvin Autonomous Republic by its procurator, apparently in 1939–40, fifty-two were quashed completely, three were allowed to go forward in the Special Session, and the remaining five were sent to the regular courts.[85]

In March 1940 Pankrat′ev, together with Commissar of Justice N. M. Rychkov and Supreme Court President Goliakov, wrote to Stalin asking for a major review effort for counterrevolutionary cases decided in 1937–39 by the Military Collegium of the court, one of the major sources of convictions. These cases had been handled without witnesses; the only evidence introduced was the testimony of the accused, which could not be checked against other materials. Some sentences had already been reversed, whereas others had been sent back to lower courts for retrial. Now the three judicial officials asked Stalin for a review of a "significant number of cases and removal of sentences."[86] Thus, it was not a lack of courage or determination on Pankrat'ev's part that kept more people from being released; instead, Stalin gave him insufficient support. Once again, the Gensec behaved ambivalently: he at least approved the new departures of late 1938 but did not push them to their logical conclusion.

As for the situation within the gulag, it began to improve even before Ezhov's fall from power. A former prisoner recalled that "in 1938–1939 a change for the better occurred in most of the camps;"[87] in another place the same man maintained that no starvation took place in the gulag in those years.[88] One prisoner, having described horrific death rates in Kolyma late in the winter of 1938, reported that several camp administrators were removed at the end of April or early May, charged with wrecking by causing high mortality. Labeled "enemies of the people," they disappeared into the hands of the organization they had just been helping to direct.[89]

Vladimir Petrov received pay at a Magadan camp for his work as a miner and then as a draftsman in 1938 and 1939. He was also sent to a hospital to be treated for scurvy.[90] Gustav Herling reported that by 1940 his Far North camp had a "decent hospital"; sick men were released from work if their temperatures were over 100 degrees and sent to the hospital for temperatures over 102.2 degrees. He noted the "kindness and helpfulness of the nurses" at the facility.[91] At the NKVD farm where Margarete Buber (Neumann) was held, field-workers were paid according to a rational quota system beginning in the summer of 1939. Skilled workers like mechanics and combine drivers could earn up to one hundred rubles a month.[92] Another former prisoner remembered that "little by little the atmosphere of the camps became less oppressive [after Ezhov's fall]. We were astonished when prisoners whose terms had expired were released, one after the other."[93] Even some with time left to serve were freed, for instance, General A. V. Gorbatov and about one hundred others from his Siberian camp.[94]

In short, the gulag became somewhat more bearable, at least relative to the conditions of 1937–38. One can only speculate on the eventual results of this trend had not other factors intervened; but the new pressures on supply and transport created by preparations for war again led to desperate conditions by mid-1940. With the German invasion, prisoners had the lowest priority, and "famine became the normal condition in many camps."[95]

More remarkable among the changes begun in late 1938, and incompatible with the idea that the population was to stay terrorized, is that the public now received broad notice of police misbehavior under Ezhov. Several open trials of NKVD men who had tortured victims during his tenure took place around the country. Such cases were reported from Moscow, Moldavia, the North Caucasus, Ivanovsk oblast', and the town of Leninsk-Kuznetsk.[96] The last trial is particularly disturbing: the head of the city NKVD, another police officer, and a procurator had cooperated in "exposing" a counterrevolutionary organization of children between the ages of ten and twelve. Placed in the dock themselves, the former enemy hunters could not produce a single fact in support of the charges they had pressed against the children. The court sentenced the procurator to five years and the two NKVDists to seven and ten years. There was no word on the fate of their victims.[97]

The Moscow trial featured five members of the militia who had created "artificial cases"; one policeman was sentenced to death, and others received confinements of up to ten years.[98] In the Moldavian affair, five NKVD men confessed to "illegal methods of investigation" and were shot.[99] According to a former Soviet citizen, probably referring to the same trial, in one courtroom eight women complained that their husbands had been beaten while under arrest.[100] A. Dneprovets claimed that NKVDists were now afraid: they understood that "he who tortures or has tortured the innocent—is an *enemy!*"[101]

One émigré believed that news of the trials spread through the populace "with lightning speed."[102] A former student recalled that "a 'spontaneous' campaign against slander and denunciation was organized" at this point. "It was all too obvious," he continued, "that many people had been using political denunciation as a means of settling private grudges or eliminating personal rivals."[103] The press campaign against false denouncers resumed.[104]

Within the police itself, investigations became much more focused on evidence, and NKVDists became more effective and conscientious about gathering it. A shop chief in a textile mill, arrested in 1937, noted that at first the police he met had little competence. "But already in the last years of my arrest, towards '38, '39, the situation changed, and I saw that people had become more competent." He referred to "a commission" appointed after Ezhov's fall and claimed that it decided to draft people from industrial production and higher education into the NKVD.[105] This is exactly what happened to Mikhail Gorokhov, the former policeman mentioned in Chapter 3. The shop chief met one of the new-style NKVD officers after his release; he described the agent as "an engineer, a competent man and an agreeable person."[106] The former prisoner S. Swianiewicz also found that by the final years of the decade many NKVD men had backgrounds in engineering or technical education. They were "concerned with technical and industrial sabotage."[107] In cases of what had been labeled wrecking in production, investigators now asked engineers for their opinions.[108] One émigré recalled that a friend of his, a party man, was "sent to check on the work of the NKVD" after Ezhov's downfall.[109]

The new security officers whom Dneprovets encountered were "very polite."[110] When General Gorbatov was finally released in March 1941, his investigator drove him to a friend's house and gave him his telephone number. "If anything happens," the man told Gorbatov, "ring me at any time. You can count on my help."[111] Perhaps this officer was trying to cover himself, but his gesture fits the overall pattern of new police behavior.

Under Beria, a purge swept through the NKVD, removing most of Ezhov's lieutenants and many in the lower ranks as well.[112] A man from Khar'kov claimed that of the city's investigators, "25% were arrested and exiled or shot, 50% were fired or transferred, and 25% remained" after Beria's accession.[113]

At the same time, the NKVD lost various functions and responsibilities that had been part of its operation since 1934–35. It no longer directed geodesic and cartographic matters, forestry, and measures and measuring devices. Much more significant, in February 1941 the NKVD was split into the Commissariat of Internal Affairs (still called the NKVD), which contained the regular police, and the Commissariat of State Security (NKGB).[114] This change made it somewhat harder for the political police, located within the NKGB, to gather information and handle cases as arbitrarily and rapidly as they had in the previous few years. The new structure was the forerunner of arrangements in the last decades of the USSR, when the militia was separated from the KGB, the body responsible for internal security.

Political charges and arrests had by now declined steeply, and the Stalinist leadership had cut back police responsibilities and power substantially. Yet it was unwilling to give up the tsarist and Soviet tradition of recourse to quick administrative judgments as opposed to slow standardized legal procedure. The Stalinist leadership was committed by mid-1938 to "the creation of a functioning legal order . . . existing side by side with terror administered by the security police."[115] But by the end of that year the sphere allotted to the legal order had grown rapidly and widely relative to the sphere of terror, which in this case means summary judgments of political suspects.

Speakers at the Eighteenth Party Congress, held in March 1939, consistently suggested that the struggle against internal enemies was largely over. Beria announced that the NKVD still had "extremely important tasks" and that not all enemies had been discovered. But he spoke about this problem mostly in the past tense and pointedly stated that troubles in the economy could not be explained solely by reference to sabotage. The gist of the difficulty was that managers had not yet mastered "the Bolshevik style of leadership." President Mikhail Kalinin spoke of "significant changes in the functions" of the security forces. Molotov said that foreign governments might try again to undermine the USSR, and their efforts would have to be answered by Soviet authorities. Yet he emphasized that the most important tasks for the state were educational, meaning that cadres, rather than being arrested, would be shown how to work more efficiently.[116]

Perhaps the most remarkable speech of the congress was Andrei Zhdanov's. He announced that although mass purges had served a useful function in the past, they had become outmoded in an era when the country's capitalist elements had been eliminated. Moreover, "the negative sides of mass purges are that the campaign character leads to many mistakes, above all in violating the Leninist principle of individual treatment of people." The purges had allowed enemy elements inside the party to persecute honest members. Following his lead, the congress resolved to ban mass purges and to strengthen the rights of communists at all levels to criticize any party official.[117]

Zhdanov distinguished the purges of 1935–36 from the hunt for enemies but also linked the two processes. He believed that the "most serious work in cleansing the party of enemies of the people" occurred after the purges. As discussed in Chapter 2, however, this pattern was no accident. The drive to unveil Trotskyites and White Guards in the purges helped produce a hysterical mood within the party, which degenerated into the hunt for enemies of any sort. In this way the mass purges were a prelude to the Terror, though not in the sense of the old argument that Stalin built carefully toward his final goal. Such purges did not occur in the rest of the Soviet period, and without them insufficient hysterical momentum arose inside the party to cause another round of widespread arrests. Zhdanov appeared to recognize the connection between mass purge and terror when he disdained what he called the "biological approach," that is, judging a communist for something a relative had done.[118] This remark was a warning against snap judgments and a condemnation of the earlier atmosphere of suspicion.

Of course, Stalin's words on the subject were the most important. At the

Eighteenth Party Congress he indicated that internal subversion was largely a thing of the past and specifically noted that the punitive organs had turned their attention "not to the interior of the country, but outside it, against external enemies."[119] Between the end of the congress in March 1939 and the German invasion in June 1941, he offered no more comments on spies and saboteurs. The official slogans for the May Day holiday in 1939 contained not a word about the NKVD or enemies but dwelt on the glories and responsibilities of the army, fleet, and border guards.[120]

It is impossible to say how far this liberalization would have gone under other circumstances, but the German attack ended the promising start on reform of the security organs. In July 1941, for instance, the NKVD and the Commissariat of State Security merged again, signifying the return of broader powers to the political police. A new wave of arrests began, though it was much smaller than before. But this story is part of the tremendously heightened fear and suspicion that came with the war.

The most striking feature of NKVD and court practices in 1938 is their erratic quality. In January the Central Committee and the press sharply criticized policies followed under Ezhov, yet he remained at the helm of the NKVD, and large-scale arrests continued until November. Even after his dismissal from that post, he served as a deputy to the Eighteenth Party Congress and did not disappear until months later.[121]

Why events took such a zig-zag course in 1938 is not clear. Perhaps a struggle over the hunt for enemies swirled around Stalin, who determined what would happen but could not make up his mind. The Russian historian Boris Starkov has recently written that in Politburo meetings during August 1938 Zhdanov and A. A. Andreev stressed the poor quality of party cadres promoted during the mass repressions. Soon L. M. Kaganovich and A. I. Mikoian joined them "against Ezhov." Then in the fall, according to Starkov, Stalin proposed replacing Ezhov with Georgi Malenkov. But the rest of the Politburo blocked the Gensec and insisted on Beria, though why is not clear.[122] This version of events is based on material that only Starkov has seen, but it would fit with the accessible sources cited here. Even if Starkov's account is wrong, Ezhov's fall was only one of a long series of moves, dating back to January 1938, that dramatically improved the conduct of the police and courts.

It would not be surprising, however, if strong disagreements on the course of the Terror had existed within the leadership. In the mid-1930s serious differences of opinion emerged among the Gensec's lieutenants over relations with Germany, the tempo of industrialization, and the matter of internal opposition. Figures like Zhdanov stood for more moderate policies, Molotov for harsher ones.[123] After the war these two men and others squared off in political combat over cultural policy, approaches to the West, and the domestic atmosphere.[124] In both periods, Stalin occupied the middle ground and was slow to take a firm stance—which may be how he functioned during the Terror as well.

Stalin was not only a vicious leader but, at crucial moments, a highly ineffective one. He gave no public guidance and may have panicked during the worst period of collectivization.[125] It is possible that during the Terror he was torn between a belief that enemies had to be rooted out and the concern that events were going too far. This hypothesis is borne out by the conflicting speeches he made to the Central Committee in early 1937.

The previous chapter explored Stalin's mentality in that year, including his emphasis on avoiding panic in his December speech. He had little to say on any subject as the Terror careened through 1938. He did not lend his name to the campaign against false denouncers, but neither did he refer much to enemies during the whole year.[126] Otherwise his pronouncements were rather dry; for example, he protested the scheduled publication of a book called *Stories about Stalin's Childhood* (though his letter was not published until 1953) and in a speech offered the prosaic thought that "the future belongs to the youth of science."[127] He seems to have been unwilling or unable to guide events firmly in one direction during 1938, which may explain why Ezhov retained his post for ten months after the party decried the frenzied denunciations so closely linked to his direction of the police.

After Beria took charge of the NKVD, many admissions of mistakes were made, open trials of policemen took place, and some prisoners convicted of political crimes were released. Many such prisoners were not this fortunate, however, even though it was obvious to some high officials that injustice had occurred on a massive scale.

Why was more not done to rectify the many violations of elementary justice and humanity? The answer must lie partly with Stalin; it would simply have been too damaging to his position to show that errors and violence had occurred in thousands or millions of cases. Ezhov had been his man for over two years, and it was risky enough to thrust all the blame onto his shoulders. The argument that problems were all the fault of underlings may work in an "Irancontragate" scandal, but it will not satisfy people who suffer on a vast scale. As the NKVD colonel Almazov argued, it was impossible to release so many witnesses of police practices.[128] Part of the reluctance to reverse the majority of judgments made during the Terror also has to do with the "honor of the uniform," as the procurators put it. To roll back all or even a high percentage of the convictions of 1936–38 would have undermined the credibility of the security agencies and of the state as a whole.

Given the evidence presented thus far on the police and courts at work from 1936 to 1941, what was the Terror about? It is easiest to start with what it was not. In no sense was it an economic policy, nor was it an effort to crush the people and prevent them from even thinking of resistance to Stalin. The Terror was more immense, more complicated, and more erratic than that. Arrests of young engineers after accidents or of a young man because he had a likeness of Hitler in his stamp collection had nothing to do with threats to Stalin.[129] If anything, the purges created more enemies of the regime. They caused severe dislocation and weakness in the party, the economy, and the armed forces instead of serving as a logical procedure in the midst of a dangerous international situation.

Nor does the Terror appear to have been connected with a generational change within the elite, designed to put people who came to political consciousness under Stalin in power or at least to facilitate their rise.[130] Older people were sometimes promoted during the storm; in Stalin raion of the city of Smolensk at least forty-one people born in the nineteenth century advanced in 1937–38.[131] Presumably they had developed some political consciousness by 1924, the year of Lenin's death, or even by 1917. On the other hand, young people who had matured and been trained under Stalin were often taken into custody by the NKVD. Arrests within this group occurred because of problems in production or because of individuals' association with enemies. People of any age without such blots on their records were by and large not touched, though the hysteria of 1937–38 occasionally engulfed even the purest Soviet citizens.

The Old Bolsheviks, those who had joined the party before October 1917, and who were often cited as the key target group in the Terror, were not in fact especially singled out. About 5,000 veterans of the prerevolutionary party were still members of it in March 1939, and 125,000 activists from the end of the Civil War were alive and at work. This group made up only 8.3 percent of the members of the Communist Party but accounted for 20 percent of the delegates to the Eighteenth Party Congress and 73 percent of the Central Committee it elected. One-fifth of the leading officials in the regional and local party apparatus had been members while Lenin was still alive.[132] If the Old Bolsheviks or party cadres from Lenin's era were arrested in the Terror, that was usually because their responsible posts put them in a position to deal with the kinds of problems or associations guaranteed to bring in the NKVD.[133] In this they were no more unfortunate than other administrators with different backgrounds.

Executives in various spheres of Soviet life were often replaced three, four, or even more times in quick succession. This evidence undercuts Zbigniew Brzezinski's argument that people were removed in order to bring in new blood and avoid stagnation, a policy supposedly necessitated because the totalitarian system provided no regular mechanisms for change.[134] No coherent scheme besides cannibalism requires the introduction of new blood four times in the span of a few months. Brzezinski's formulation is far too rational; it does not explain the spasmodic course of the Terror.

Material on arrests and treatment of prisoners also indicates that there was little connection between collectivization or modernization and the Terror. Many young men and women who had not been involved in collectivization or who had served loyally in that campaign suffered ruin under Ezhov. Concealing one's past before or during the Civil War, however, became a deeply serious matter in the Terror.

There were ups and downs in police power; in early 1938 they were reined in somewhat, only to regain full discretion a short time later. But by autumn it became obvious even to Stalin that Ezhov and his men had gone well beyond anything the presence of enemies might call for and had begun to damage the country significantly in the process. As noted, a recent Soviet publication indicated that Ezhov was executed for ordering "groundless repressions." Viacheslav Molotov, Stalin's right-hand man in this period, told an interviewer in the 1970s that Ezhov fell because he "began to assign a quantity [of arrests] to the oblasti, and figures from the oblast' to the raiony. . . . That's why he was shot." The problem was not that the Politburo trusted Ezhov too much, Molotov said in reply to a question, but that "there should have been more supervision over him. . . . There was, but not enough."[135] Of course, Ezhov did not devise the guide numbers of 1937 by himself, but his men had a role in pushing them upward beyond what Stalin originally wanted. Molotov tried to shift the blame away from the Gensec, whom he still respected decades after his death. Yet there is a grain of truth in Molotov's claim that Ezhov went too far. It apparently took almost all of 1938 for Stalin's coterie to come to this realization.

The twists and turns of the year 1938 and the great ambivalence in police practice throughout the Terror cast more doubt on the idea that Stalin planned a campaign against the country. By late 1938, many admissions of grotesque and numerous mistakes began to appear. Neither the beginning, the course, nor the end of the Terror show the hand of a master planner.

What, given all this, was the motive force behind the mass arrests? The simplest answer is that, perhaps beyond the ambiguous guide figures but probably even including them, the Terror was a hunt for perceived enemies. That is, Stalin and his immediate entourage believed in the existence of a large number of real and dangerous foes within the country.

The Gensec's letters to Molotov from 1925 to 1936, at least the ones available to researchers and recently published, indicate that Stalin consistently believed in sabotage. For instance, in the summer of 1930 he wrote to Molotov about wreckers in finance, banking, and the "meat industry" who had to be shot. He appeared to believe the testimony on the finance case brought to him by Iagoda.[136] Lars Lih, editor of the letters, summarized Stalin's concept of governing as "antibureaucrat" and a "continual struggle with class enemies of various types and hues." In 1929–30 Stalin's anger at his perceived enemies, both international and domestic, became "increasingly intense."[137] Unfortunately, few letters are available for the period 1931–36. For the latter year we have exactly one line, and then the correspondence ends. In the published letters, however, addressed privately to a man with whom he had no need for deception, Stalin with evident sincerity expressed the view that enemies posed danger to the country.

Khrushchev, one of the few close to Stalin who left an account, recalled that the Gensec frequently mentioned treason by former tsarist officers serving in the Red Army during the Civil War, a category that included Marshal Tukhachevskii. Stalin was clearly prone to see treason behind various problems, as illustrated by such reactions as his distress "when he heard that horses were being poisoned in the Ukraine" in 1939.[138] After the war he reportedly told Admiral I. S. Isakov, as they walked in a passageway under the Kremlin, that the security troops there were "on guard, sure. . . . But you just watch—they'll shoot you in the back themselves."[139] As noted above, Dmitri Volkogonov concluded on the basis of Stalin's own papers that he always believed police reports of treason.

He equated a threat to himself with one to the country. He then struck at what he perceived to be a genuine danger, rather than creating plots in order to crush any opposition. As the sociologist W. I. Thomas put it, "If men define situations as real, they are real in their consequences."[140] To Stalin, enemies became a tangible, severe threat—in keeping with the definition of paranoia.[141]

Molotov was hardly an impartial judge, but his opinion is worth repeating here, for he never lost his faith in Stalin, even when it became fashionable to do so. In 1970 he reportedly told an interviewer that "1937 was essential. . . . [After the Revolution] remnants of various kinds of enemies [still] existed, and in view of the threatening danger of fascist aggression, they might have united. We were obliged [to carry out] the year 1937 so that in time of war there would not be a fifth column." Molotov applied his thoughts even to "good and dedicated" communists who, it was feared, might have weakened during war. He rejected the rehabilitation of military officers arrested in the Terror; although they were not spies, they had been connected with foreign espionage services. "Most important, at a decisive moment they were not reliable."[142]

Sometime in 1936, Stalin changed course from political relaxation to hyper-suspicion, reminiscent of 1929–30 but more severe. Probably the new tack emerged for a number of reasons: information about the Trotskyite bloc; the worsening international situation created by Germany's growing strength, vitiation of the Versailles Treaty, and the Spanish Civil War; the discovery of many concealed former oppositionists, White Guards, and the like inside the party during the purges; and quite possibly the Stakhanovite movement to boost labor productivity (see Chapter 6). By the summer of 1936 Stalin may have been receiving reports on alleged treason within the armed forces. Ezhov's role was to feed such information to his boss; it was for this reason that Stalin chose him to head the NKVD in September. There is some evidence that the vozhd' lost his self-control at key junctures through 1937 and 1938, which would help explain the contradictory messages and policies toward domestic enemies of those years, particularly the second.

The central leadership ordered the hunt for spies and wreckers, but the police expanded and sharpened it. As this happened, the Terror assumed a momentum and dynamic of its own among the populace. Neither Stalin nor the NKVD acted independently of society.

A brave Soviet border guard and his loyal dog, powerful symbols of the need for vigilance against enemies in the 1930s. This statue, by M. G. Manizer, was commissioned for the Ploshchad' Revoliutsii (Square of the Revolution) metro station, which opened in March 1938. The sculpture was still in place in the early 1990s. (Photo by author.)

Soviet leaders, probably about 1939: Andrei Zhdanov, Lazar Kaganovich, Kliment Voroshilov, and Stalin. (Private collection.)

Aleksei Stakhanov (*center*) with a group of miners, probably 1935 or 1936. (Private collection.)

Participants in a physical culture parade, Moscow, 1938. A trip to Moscow was a dreamlike prize for provincial Soviet citizens in the 1930s. (Courtesy of the Hoover Institution.)

Meeting of workers at the Trekhgornaia Textile Mill, Moscow, 1936. (Courtesy of the Hoover Institution.)

A cafe in Moscow, mid-1930s. (Courtesy of the National Archives, Washington, D.C.)

Milk sellers in Baku, early 1930s. Food sold at the legal peasant markets was important for the diets of urban dwellers and the income of peasants. (Courtesy of the National Archives, Washington, D.C.)

Soviet prisoners taken by the Germans near Augustove, June 22, 1941. Few such men survived until the end of the war. (Courtesy of the National Archives, Washington, D.C.)

Soviet prisoners captured near Demidov, July 15, 1941. Note that the men's clothing ranges from complete uniforms to civilian dress, reflecting the hodgepodge of troops thrown into battle after the first days. (Courtesy of the National Archives, Washington, D.C.)

Soviet soldiers killed in action in the summer of 1941. No place or date recorded. (Courtesy of the National Archives, Washington, D.C.)

Stalin lying in state, March 1953. (Private collection.)

The common man graphically demonstrating his support for Stalin. (Photo by Vladimir Sichov, from *Political Jokes of Leningrad* [Austin: Silver Girl, 1982].)

Fear and Belief in the Terror: Response to Arrest

Stalin, or rather Stalin with a great deal of help, killed millions or facilitated their untimely deaths. He was one of history's leading murderers, and his crimes were truly grotesque.

More precise efforts to estimate the number of victims have produced sharp debates for fifty years. Why dwell on the numbers? Those who suffered and died are no better off if one estimate is favored over another—even the lowest figures denote tragedy on a huge scale. No moral issue is at stake here; injustice was rampant, and there were millions of victims in the eight years of our focus alone. In addition, millions of others suffered because of their ties to the direct casualties.

But, as suggested earlier, the numbers do make a considerable difference in analyzing how the regime ruled and how people responded to it. Imagine a continuum of states ranging from one with no political arrests to one in which everyone is arrested at one time or another, an absurd condition. (Even so, there was a Soviet saying in the 1930s and afterward, which people were not afraid to pass on, that the population consisted of those who had been in prison, those who were, and those who would be.)[1] At the end of the continuum with no arrests or state violence toward dissenters, compliance would presumably be entirely voluntary. Toward the other extreme, involving some level of coercion we can only guess at, people would dread their government so much that they might be cowed into submission.

The population of the USSR in 1939, before the incorporation of Polish and Baltic territory, was about 168.8 million.[2] If during the Terror many millions died at the hands of the state and 7, 8, or even 15 million people were imprisoned or otherwise fettered by the end of the decade, as numerous works have estimated, we might—though this conclusion is far from certain—justifiably speak of a "system of terror," as described in the introduction.[3] At some point a high number of arrests would translate into the quality of terror, or a terrorized population.

We now know that estimates of the order just cited were far too high. At the beginning of 1937, 2,658,000 people were detained as follows: 821,000 were in labor camps; 375,000 in labor colonies; 545,000 in jails; and 917,000 in "special settlements" or internal exile.[4]

By the eve of World War II, the labor camps held 1.5 million, bringing the number of detainees or exiles to 3,593,000.[5]

In 1939, a year for which both population and prisoner data are available, the rate of incarceration was 2,129 per 100,000 population, or about 4⅔ times the American rate in 1992.[6] That figure may seem staggering, but put another way, a little over 2 percent of the Soviet population was under detention.

The police data of December 1953 show that 4,932,556 people were convicted of counterrevolutionary crimes from 1930 to the end of 1941.[7] We might add to that number many of the "socially dangerous elements" mentioned earlier. Complete data on incarceration of these types are not available, but 103,513 of them were held in the gulag in January 1937, and 285,831 in early 1939.[8]

A pool of likely arrestees could be imagined in this fashion: excluding everyone under age twenty and one-third of those over age sixty in the 1939 census would leave just over 89 million adults. Some people under age twenty were arrested, but including two-thirds of those over age sixty should adequately cover the younger inmates. By itself, this information would mean that as of 1939 about 5 percent of the adult pool had been arrested. More males than females were incarcerated; men made up 91.9 percent of the gulag population in 1940.[9] Thus the figure of 5 percent might be raised for adult males. As earlier chapters showed, however, the number under arrest fluctuated wildly. In addition, quite a few people were arrested and convicted on political charges more than once.

Of course, in any society crime is socially and culturally defined to some extent, and many arrests may have been politically colored, for example, the detention of heads of collective farms who found it necessary to juggle the books and were caught.[10] It might therefore seem appropriate to raise the percentage of those arrested for political crimes on the grounds that some infractions of other statutes were simply rational responses to the regime's policies. At the height of the Terror, however, some quite ordinary crimes were called sabotage or wrecking. One such case involved a collective farmer who got drunk at a party in 1937 and punched another guest. Because the victim happened to be a Stakhanovite (a model worker; see Chapter 6), the local procuracy brought a charge of counterrevolutionary terrorism against the farmer. In other cases judges did not distinguish between ordinary hooliganism and wrecking.[11] Therefore some actions that would have been deemed commonplace crimes in other societies were labeled political in the USSR. There is no way of determining how many crimes were reclassified in either direction. Given these ambiguities, it is hard to estimate the percentage of Soviet adults arrested between 1930 and 1941 for political crimes; let us stay with the conservative approximation of 5 percent.

If this educated guess is correct, the impact on society was vast yet much less severe than many older, high estimates have implied. On our continuum of state coercion, analysis must move toward more popular support for the regime.

The question of who was arrested remains. If the Terror fell primarily on highly placed people, the bulk of the populace may have felt relatively safe. Again, more room would have existed in the system for voluntary support. But if the Terror hit all strata hard, the population would have responded differently.

Turning to the issue of "excess" deaths, those beyond what would normally occur in a society, a number of mass graves have recently been uncovered, the best known of which is in the Kuropaty forest, near Minsk. But it is impossible to make a count of such grave sites or, in some cases, a determination of how many bodies lie in those that have been found. Even at Kuropaty, the subject of the most interest, estimates of the number buried vary from thirty thousand to three hundred thousand, rendering extrapolation to a toll for the whole country out of the question.[12] It is therefore far better to rely on the harder evidence on demographic issues, that coming out of ex-Soviet archives, which is reasonably comprehensive.

The official figures of 1953 on executions during the Terror, 681,692 in 1937–38, have already been given; this number refers to both political and ordinary cases. After Stalin's death no reason existed to minimize the toll in an internal, top-secret report. Other deaths that occurred, in particular during interrogation, might have been listed as natural, though this percentage of killings would have been small. A recent study of the few available data on mortality rates in prisons and exile yields a total of 1,473,424 deaths among those in state custody on any charge for the decade 1930–40.[13]

Beginning in 1946 demographers and some other scholars in the West offered estimates of all Soviet excess deaths between the censuses of 1926 and 1939 on the order of 4.5 to 5.5 million.[14] But other estimates, for example, Steven Rosefielde's projection of 20.8 million for the years 1929–39, have received more attention.[15] Evidence from recently opened archives and works published in Russia since glasnost' began show that such figures must be reduced substantially, though not to the earlier, low numbers.[16] Relying primarily on the work of others, Alec Nove cautiously posited a maximum of 10–11 million unnatural deaths in the 1930s, from all causes; of these, "upwards of 7 million were famine

and famine-related." This figure implies "almost 3 million other deaths: in deportation, detention, and shooting."[17] However, some of this mortality was due to the
large number of industrial accidents in the period, for which no specific data
exist.

It is relevant to note that much the same process of reducing estimates has
occurred regarding convicted witches in early modern Europe and Africans
captured for the slave trade. In both cases, earlier high figures based on extrapolation have yielded to lower numbers based on systematic, archival research.[18] The
same is true for the sixteenth-century terror of Ivan the Terrible.[19]

The question of how many will not be settled by this or any other discussion. In
the former USSR claims continue to appear that high totals are correct, though
they are not supported by substantial documentation.[20] Those who see more
deaths or prisoners than are indicated by existing data are abandoning the best
kinds of evidence used in any other field in favor of speculation.

The new numbers of Soviet victims are low, of course, only in comparison to
previous estimates. Eleven million excess deaths and almost 5 million convictions for political crimes in little more than a decade are stunning figures, but
were they enough to produce widespread apprehension and hatred of the regime?
Regardless of one's preferred estimates, it is pointless to assume that a certain
level of repression produced certain responses among the population as a whole;
rather, it is necessary to examine people's perceptions of the regime and the
Terror.

"Only fear" of the regime motivated Soviet people after 1935, wrote Anton
Antonov-Ovseyenko, a survivor whose father and mother perished in the Terror
and who was himself sent to a labor camp.[21] Others echoed his view.[22]

The prominent Soviet writer Ilya Ehrenburg, deeply critical of the Terror after
Stalin's death, had a different sense of popular response to the regime before the
war. "In the minds of millions of people Stalin had become a sort of mythical
demi-god; everyone uttered his name with awe and believed that he alone could
save the Soviet State from invasion and disruption."[23]

These two assessments are diametrically opposed, although a mixture of dread
and awe may have existed in some people's minds. Still, these two statements
express the polarity of response to the Terror and to the Stalinist regime in
general. Neither can be taken as definitive: first, because, as the observations of
survivors, they have equal claims on our attention; and, second, because neither
Antonov-Ovseyenko, nor Ehrenburg, nor anyone else could have known the

attitudes of all Soviet people. No one was in a position to judge the emotional life of the entire country, or even of a city block. Ehrenburg noted that "I can write only about what I have seen for myself: my life in Moscow, the lives of fifty, or perhaps a hundred friends and acquaintances with whom I was in touch at the time . . . mainly writers and artists."[24] If terror had truly reigned, people would have revealed their innermost thoughts only to close confidants; most would not have dared to say what they felt.

Many sources allow an examination of people's attitudes in some depth. Newly available materials from ex-Soviet archives bear on the issue of popular perceptions of the Stalinist regime. The advent of glasnost' has not undermined the validity of older memoirs, written shortly after the period and published or deposited in the open climate of the West. In the United States archival collections have yielded interviews and manuscripts by émigrés not widely tapped before.

A convenient focal point for a study of fear and belief during the Terror is response to arrest, either one's own or others'. At that moment citizens had to make a crucial decision: Did they believe that the given arrest was (1) justified as part of the hunt for enemies, (2) a mistake, though the hunt itself was still valid, or (3) a deliberate attack by the authorities on an innocent person? Descriptions of a system of terror identify the last choice as the common reaction to arrest. It would follow that people perceived massive injustice under which anyone could be next. What do the sources indicate about how commonly citizens felt that way, as opposed to the belief that enemies of the people posed a grave threat to the country? The second position would necessitate regarding the arrests as largely reasonable, even if mistakes occurred.

To pose such issues is to attempt to look into people's souls,[25] when they themselves may not have been able to say at the time or later exactly what they believed. But recollections of the Terror are the major source for any assessment of how people felt at the time; all historians of the period have relied on them, and they will always be essential for its investigation. The results of this inquiry are necessarily imprecise, because fear may be a passing emotion and, in theory, might have affected everyone at some time. Also involved in memories of the Terror are the deepest issues of guilt, complicity, and careerism versus sincerity and ignorance of injustice. Grappling with such dilemmas may have led many memoirists to alter their impressions of the period, if only unconsciously. Some writers probably embellished their accounts to heighten dramatic impact. Nevertheless, certain patterns emerge consistently from firsthand reports.

Memoirs and interviews are especially problematic when examining Stalin's motivation and the reasons behind the Terror, things that few survivors knew about personally, and fewer still recorded. Firsthand accounts used in this book describe what individuals themselves experienced or heard about directly. The memoirs and interviews cited here come from many kinds of people: loyal Soviet citizens and those who helped the German invaders, émigrés and those who stayed at home, foreigners who were arrested and foreigners who remained free. The range in social status among the authors and respondents, as well as the number of sources, compensate to a degree for bias or self-justification. Above all, the value of the personal accounts lies in the broad patterns they reveal.

The Stalin regime evoked loathing and enthusiasm, fear and belief. These emotional responses coexisted and must be probed in some depth to illuminate how Stalinism worked.

Sergei Kirov's assassination on December 1, 1934, is the starting point. Little evidence supports the claim that pervasive apprehension dated from that event. One response, apparently found mostly in the countryside and linked to hatred of collectivization, was delight at his death.[26] The response of urban dwellers, particularly workers, may have been quite different.[27]

For our purposes, the issue is whether or not the assassination made people fear the state. Beck and Godin, still at liberty when Kirov died, believed his murder "was a sign for the masses that the struggle [within the party] had not yet ended."[28] They do not mention any other reaction from below. The young communist G. A. Tokaev detected not fear but relaxation and optimism with the end of food rationing, which occurred at the beginning of 1935: "The public . . . felt a cloud had lifted. . . . There was a new sense of freedom in domestic life; not that food became more plentiful, but it was hard not to draw the conclusion that, if the government could take this step, 'things could not be so bad after all.' "[29]

Some people felt that the assassination meant great danger from internal enemies. Mikhail Shul'man was a party member and the de facto director of the Red Army Ensemble at the time of Kirov's murder, which occurred just before the group was scheduled to give a concert in the Kremlin. In reaction to the event Shul'man insisted that each member of the ensemble be thoroughly searched before the performance. With no prompting, he sincerely believed in the necessity to "raise vigilance."[30] The only fear he felt was that other party leaders might also be the target of terrorists.

Andrew Smith, a radical American worker employed in Moscow in 1934, recalled that other hands at his factory reacted in much the same way to the killing: "No doubt they were badly scared by the sheer audacity of the assassination, and the possibility of future terroristic acts." There were "visible evidences of extreme panic."[31] William Campbell immigrated to Soviet Russia from Britain in the early 1930s. Before becoming a vaudeville and circus star, he worked for a while in an aviation factory. In 1932 his fellow workers told him horrible tales of sabotage—of whole factories being blown up by enemies of the people who had found lost entry passes. "In those days there were widespread fears about sabotage and subversion," he wrote.[32] Lev Kopelev said of Kirov's murder that "now it turned out that a new counter-revolutionary underground had appeared in our country. They wanted to wipe out our leaders. This meant that terror was indispensable."[33] Any fear resulting from Kirov's murder was more often of internal enemies than of the state. People had no more reason to be afraid of the regime after the killing than they had earlier; as discussed above, it is unlikely that more than several hundred arrests occurred in the aftermath of the murder, most of them in Leningrad. The number arrested for counterrevolutionary crimes did rise in 1935, but the total number of arrests and executions fell.

Up to that time, there was little feeling that arrests involved injustice. Joseph Berger, a communist in Moscow and abroad in the 1930s, was incarcerated after Kirov's death. He recalled that any party member arrested in 1935 naturally believed that he was "a victim of a misunderstanding which sooner or later would be cleared up." Most people, by which Berger means a few he knew well, still felt that inmates of the labor camps "consisted overwhelmingly of class enemies and counter-revolutionaries."[34] His report suggests that the arrests were not yet extensive enough to produce the sense that anyone might be next.

Another survivor, Abdurakhman Avtorkhanov, spent much of the 1930s at the Institute for Red Professors in Moscow. Concerning the first Moscow show trial, held in August 1936, Avtorkhanov wrote that "intellectuals knew that this was all a spectacle, [while] foreigners believed [in it], . . . but . . . for the common people this material was too elevated."[35] Victor Kravchenko reported that, judging by the workers in Nikopol, where he managed a steel tubing plant, the "population at large . . . were pretty indifferent to what seemed to them a family quarrel among their new masters."[36] Alexander Weissberg wrote that ordinary people believed the purges were a conflict within the party until the second half of 1937.[37] Nadezhda and Osip Mandelstam spent that year in a provincial city; their landlord, a factory worker, regarded "what was going on as 'a fight for power among themselves [party leaders].' "[38]

These accounts suggest that the majority of Soviet people did not feel the first show trial, its surrounding atmosphere, or perhaps even the later trials represented a threat to them from the state. There is no indication that the Moscow spectacles provoked widespread personal fear of the authorities. And why should the trials have done so? They involved former high party officials and a few prominent physicians, not ordinary people. Even at provincial show trials, the defendants were officials. Ordinary peasants, surely to their delight, played a prominent role in accusing the defendants and complaining loudly in court about their abuses.[39]

Several memoirists specifically remarked that they did not feel anxiety about arrests in 1935 or 1936. Mikhail Shul'man called himself one "of the most orthodox communists" in the 1930s. His Red Army Ensemble was a favorite of Stalin and the people close to him. Because of that backing and his "c'oseness to high military and party circles," he remarked that he "did not know fear."[40] Raisa Berg and Ivan Minishki also specified their lack of fear before 1937.[41]

Sources that do speak of general fright as early as 1935 sometimes contradict themselves. Antonov-Ovseyenko indicates that both he and his father completely supported the regime into 1936 or much later. In June 1936, the father published an article comparing Stalin to a mountain eagle. "He wrote it sincerely, believing that fate had blessed the party by bestowing this Great Leader upon it." The elder Antonov continued to serve the regime faithfully until his arrest in 1938.[42]

Considerable evidence shows that even many of the those close to the centers of power did not feel apprehension, let alone sense its pervasive presence, into 1937 or later. Those who say that they were personally afraid of arrest earlier than that are the exception, not the rule. The accounts that do mention fear almost invariably refer to a situation among the country's elite, not to the population as a whole.[43]

When massive arrests began in 1937, they often came unexpectedly.[44] During 1937 Lydiia Shatunovskaia occupied a Moscow apartment in a building with the ponderous title "House of the Government," also the residence of such luminaries as Marshal Tukhachevskii and General Kork. She was, in short, at the very center of things. Yet "until the year 1937, the circles of this party elite, which were represented by the inhabitants of the House of the Government, lived in plenty and spiritual calm, not deep in thought about how fragile and unreliable their good fortune [was]. They believed and persuaded themselves that everything was going well, that Stalin was leading the country 'along the Leninist path.'" But in May 1937 "thunder resounded" for Shatunovskaia. The "first blow"—not the second, third, or tenth—then fell, against commanders of the

Red Army.[45] Solzhenitsyn repeated the same phrase in *Gulag Archipelago:* "Old prisoners claim to remember that the first blow allegedly took the form of mass arrests" in August 1937.[46] Alexander Weissberg believed that large-scale arrests began only in the fall.[47] According to these accounts, substantial dread of the regime could have arisen no earlier than the late spring of that year.

Whenever the storm began, survivors often had a keen sense that certain categories of the population were much more vulnerable than others; people outside these unfortunate groups did not typically fear arrest. The perception of targeted categories is illustrated in a joke that circulated during the purges: The NKVD bangs on the door of an apartment in Leningrad in 1937. A terrified voice from inside asks, "Who's there?" "NKVD, open up!" comes the reply. "No, no, you've got the wrong apartment, the communists live upstairs!"[48]

The joke finds confirmation elsewhere. Beck and Godin noted that "during the Yezhov period people used to say, 'He's not a party member and he's not a Jew, so why has he been arrested?' "[49] In Moscow during the summer of 1937, supposedly the center of the cataclysm at or near its height, the porter of Shatunovskaia's building came to her door in the middle of the night. Even though the incident concerned only a maintenance problem, the visit shattered her roommate, who was a communist. Shatunovskaia asked her, "Why were you so frightened?" "Oh," the friend responded, "I'm an Old Bolshevik. Do you really not understand that in our times that's enough [to be arrested]?"[50] Although Shatunovskaia does not seem stupid, she did not yet consider that fear was rampant. Instead, during the same summer, "For myself and for my husband I was not afraid. We were non-party *intelligenty,* specialists, and such [people] were still not very threatened in those years."[51]

General Petro Grigorenko believed that except for a fortuitous incident, "I might have reached the very top of that apparatus [the Central Committee of the Ukrainian Komsomol], which would have meant certain arrest and death."[52] A camp prisoner noted after 1937 that "a situation has existed for a long time in which the higher the post occupied in Soviet society, the greater the chances of arrest."[53] Another survivor repeated a saying heard in Vladivostok in the late 1930s: "For a difficult operation, you have to go not to Moscow, but to Magadan [the notorious camp complex in the Far East]"—the reason being that all the good doctors were there.[54] Beck and Godin compiled a list of "arrest-worthy" groups like the "senior and middle ranks of the Communist Party" and those involved in "transport";[55] their categories excluded the vast majority of Soviet people.

Alexander and Lilia Bitak, "the best among the best of Communists . . . began to be nervous with arrests of party members" only in 1938. Lilia then surmised that Stalin was liquidating soldiers of the revolution, the "witnesses of his crimes."[56] She did not indicate that at that late date she considered anyone under threat except such older communists.

An Azerbaijani doctor was convinced that the arrests under Ezhov "only concerned Party politics in Moscow."[57] Regarding 1937–38, an ex-foreman in a milk plant stressed that "those who were arrested were not peasants but [white-collar] employees and mostly Party people. I was glad that they were cutting each other's throats."[58]

A perception that some categories within the officer corps were prone to arrest but other were not appears with crystal clarity in the account of Ismail Akhmedov, a student at a military academy in Moscow at the height of the purges. "We junior officers knew that personally we ran no hazards. We had been as much as told that we were exempt, that we were being groomed for commands of the future."[59]

There were other perceptions that certain social groups were liable to arrest. Workers in Magnitogorsk, where the American John Scott was employed as a welder, sneered at their supervisors: "You're a wrecker yourself," they would say. "Tomorrow they'll come and arrest you. All you engineers and technicians are wreckers."[60] The rank-and-file troops under Grigorenko demanded, "Who is commanding us! Enemies of the people are intentionally putting us in danger of slaughter. All the officers ought to be punished."[61] These incidents indicate a sense that only the elite were targeted for repression and a widespread belief among ordinary people in the existence of enemies.

The notion that members of certain groups were more likely to be arrested also figures in the great reluctance of some to accept promotion at the height of the purges. For the years 1937–38, this factor calls into question the idea that under Stalin upward mobility was a source of support for the regime.[62] Protocols of party cell meetings at the Shamilovo Pig Collective Farm in Smolensk oblast' provide one illustration. On November 14, 1937, the assembled communists of the collective asked one of their members, V. D. Zuzov, to take charge of the pig-breeding station within the farm. Zuzov demurred: "I will not take on the pig farm, I am president of the precinct [party] commission. Earlier I agreed to that job but now I have thought it over. I won't be able to cope with that job." Three people immediately replied that his stance was "not communist" but "rotten."

Zuzov insisted that "I will not take on the pig farm. Do with me what you wish. That's one thing. Second, I stand on a principle. I won't take this job because Chemurov works in the secret section [linked to the NKVD] and I don't like his personality. Until he is removed I won't take [the job]."[63]

Thus, Zuzov took the chance of offending his fellow communists, including one connected to the NKVD, in order to avoid what he clearly considered a greater risk. The new position would have given him too much responsibility or the wrong kind, requiring him to work daily alongside someone allied with the police. Zuzov must have felt that he was better off avoiding a new position, even if he disdained someone responsible for security and opened himself to charges that elsewhere could have been grounds for arrest. In spite of Chemurov's presence at the meeting, however, no one threatened Zuzov with punishment, either then or at the following session.[64]

Reluctance to be promoted or self-demotion to a job with less responsibility also appears in the memoirs of Valentina Bogdan, an engineer in Rostov in the late 1930s. The chief engineer in her mill and a friend of his in a similar position quit to become doormen, their goal being "not to occupy responsible positions any more."[65] Neither man was arrested. "A. Dneprovets," the militia officer arrested in Dnepropetrovsk in 1937, described "the panic reigning at that time in these [city] soviet-party organizations. . . . Comrades who in the past strove for promotion on the party ladder, now with satisfaction and simultaneously with fear refused promotion."[66]

Many other survivors were certain that people in lower positions were arrested much less often than higher-ups. A man who was pulled in while heading a raion soviet put the matter this way: "Work on a responsible post is the road to prison."[67] When an interviewer asked one émigré how a Soviet citizen could avoid trouble with the regime, he replied, "He should be an average worker so that no one will bother him."[68] Such comments show that arrests did evoke dread—of advancement. Terror was producing avoidance of responsibility, which was dysfunctional. Whatever the goal at the top, events were again out of control.

It is difficult to be precise about the social composition of those arrested. Information on the Terror in the Donbass lists several hundred workers as "repressed."[69] We do not know how many were arrested and later released, as occasionally happened even in the worst period. What proportion of workers in the region suffered? How many were arrested for counterrevolutionary crimes, how many for other infractions? Was the story in the Donbass typical, or did the fact that coal production represented a particularly vital and troubled part of the economy make the police more active there?[70]

During 1990 the newspaper *Vechernii Leningrad* published the names of 2,627 people executed in the Terror, usually with their occupations. I noted the jobs of the first 441, considering that to be a random sample. This approach is problematic, for there is no assurance that this list is representative of those executed in the Terror as a whole. Over 46,000 are said to be buried in this one pit, at Levashovskii, but no indication of how this number was calculated appears in the accounts; of this total, the 2,627 individuals named amount to less than 6 percent of the victims, and the sample of 441 a little under 1 percent. Whether some or many of the dead were shot for ordinary civil crimes is not clear; they are called only "rehabilitated citizens." Nonetheless, for lack of broader data, my findings will serve. Of the 441, 39 were workers, by a generous definition; most were carpenters and, judging by the occupations around them, they probably worked on collective or state farms. The two biggest groups in the sample were clerics and peasants, the latter numbering 184. The remainder were bookkeepers, managers, or low-level party officials.[71] Whether the dead in the Levashovskii pit were unusually rural or not is impossible to say. But this case does not demonstrate that workers were frequent victims of the Terror. As shown, archival materials indicate that probably a little over 20 percent of those arrested in 1936–38 were charged with counterrevolution, so there is room for doubt that all the Levashovskii bodies were politicals. It would be equally shaky to conclude that peasants predominated among victims.

Available statistics do not facilitate generalizations about what kinds of people were arrested, though we do know that those who had obtained some secondary or higher education were found twice as often in the gulag in 1937 as in the population at large. In the next few years the percentage of relatively well-educated prisoners rose steadily, from 6.3 percent in 1934 to 12.8 percent in 1941.[72] The educational level throughout the country also climbed in the same years, though not as steeply. People with more education were certainly more likely than others to be arrested.

A broader picture of who the prisoners were must be sought in other sources. Former inmates' comments on the backgrounds of arrestees suggest that workers were rarely jailed on political charges. For example, one account speaks of a prison in 1938 that held a high NKVD official, professors, party cadres, economic employees, and finally "simple people."[73] A survivor of the Terror in the Kalmyk

Autonomous Republic mentioned carnage among journalists, writers, and leaders of the party and government; he said not a word about ordinary people.[74] One might argue that these remarks reflect only the concerns or snobbishness of the observers, but, like other sources already noted, they frequently and specifically emphasized the tendency of arrests to fall on people in positions of responsibility. A former factory timekeeper noted "less [sic] repressions of course upon the working class, but there were arrests among them."[75] In the Harvard Project survey of "non-returnees" after the war, 2,718 respondents completed questionnaires. Those with "administrative responsibility were twice as likely as their nonadministrative peers to report having been personally arrested." Respondents thought that factory managers and engineers were particularly arrest-prone but that workers were not.[76]

When the fear of enemies erupted in any location, it was likely to spread through the populace and result in numerous arrests, because both the citizenry and the NKVD believed in conspiracy and because torture was used to obtain names of additional suspects. This link was one factor that sometimes broke the stereotype of the wrecker as a person in a responsible position and led to arrests among workers. When the chief of the Donbass mine trust entered jail in 1937, fifteen others from his organization followed, down to two or three workers.[77]

Yet given survivors' comments about the relatively low incidence of arrests among industrial workers, it is unlikely that they made up a high proportion of those swept up by the NKVD. Various accounts portray industrial laborers more as actors in the Terror than as victims. Even allowing for exaggeration and personal bitterness, the statement of an engineer who worked in Soviet plants in the worst years is indicative. He characterized the title "engineer" as a "synonym for candidate for concentration camp or execution." The NKVD, he believed, accepted "all denunciations of engineers . . . whether they were written or anonymous or in whatever form they were. Workers took advantage of this to settle their own personal accounts."[78]

High party officials, armed forces officers, writers, industrial managers, collective farm chairs, and other "visible" people were cut down in large numbers. In a curious and deadly way, the key problem sometimes was drawing attention to oneself. This unwanted interest could come through promotion or connection to an accident, but more innocent activities also attracted the keen gaze of the NKVD. The poet Boris Kuzin used to wear a colorful hat around Moscow. "Don't wear that hat," Osip Mandelstam told him. "You mustn't attract attention—or you'll have trouble." And Kuzin did.[79] Victor Herman, whose family moved from Detroit to the USSR in the 1930s because of his father's socialist convictions, became a pilot and parachutist. He later wrote that his tricks in planes "brought me to the point where others began noticing me too much," and that in turn led to his arrest.[80]

Beyond the question of categories, what were popular perceptions of the Terror? As noted, classic histories argue that arrests became so prevalent that the free population understood innocent people were being detained by the millions. Robert Conquest has written that "at the beginning of the Purge those arrested often thought that the other people in the prisons were actually guilty of something, and that only their own case was a mistake. By 1937, the outside public had come to realize that the accused were innocent."[81]

This point is the crux of the claim that a system of terror existed; if correct, fear must have reached a terribly high level, at which people would have believed that absolutely no one was safe. But in fact "the outside public" consisted of individuals who had various kinds of reactions to the arrests then under way.

Much evidence already given here counters the idea that people understood arrests were not linked to guilt. A number of survivors' accounts, however, do support that notion for 1937 or 1938. "Ivan Ivanovich from Zherinka" had his wife sew rubles into his coat because the NKVD was taking all the men in his town.[82] Andrei Lebid, a railroad official on the North Donets line, was worried in August 1937 because he knew that "innocence would be no protection."[83] Yet once again, some of the memoirs that stress the expectation of arrest refer largely to discrete categories of people.[84]

Some witnesses assert that by 1937 virtually no one believed in enemies. For instance, Ismail Akhmedov argued that "even the simplest fool knew that all those thousands were not 'traitors,' 'enemies of the people,' or 'spies.' "[85]

But such claims are undermined by a wealth of other material. Although Alexander Weissberg was one of the first to argue that by the fall of 1937 everyone comprehended exactly that pattern of police work, he recorded his own feeling into 1938—and the sense of others during the next year—that innocent people would not be treated wrongly.[86] R. V. Ivanov-Razumnik remembered that in his cell into 1938, newcomers so often expressed lack of understanding and surprise at their arrests that the old hands spoke of such laments as playing "records."[87] More often than not, citizens considered the purges to be legitimate actions against enemies.

Even when Antonov-Ovseyenko's father was arrested in 1937 and executed the following year as an enemy of the people," his own faith did not waver. He recorded general approval of the campaign against spies and saboteurs but not concern for himself or the sense that terror was operating randomly: "A year had not passed since the death of Antonov-Ovseyenko, and his son was glorifying his murderer. For me, a youth of nineteen, Stalin's name was sacred. As for the executions of enemies of the people, what could you say? The state had the right to defend itself. Errors were possible in such matters, but Stalin had nothing to do with it. He had been and remained the Great Leader."[88]

Antonov also blames his lack of understanding on indoctrination, but the fact remains that he embraced the necessity of the purges. Nothing shook that faith until his own arrest in 1940. Usually only the personal experience of detention shattered such acceptance—but even that did not always change views.

These recollections establish a social context of widespread belief in enemies during the Terror. The assertion is sometimes made that people denounced others to settle personal scores, to advance in their careers, or to gain their apartments.[89] Inevitably such behavior did take place. But the evidence presented here, and a good deal more besides, shows that much more commonly people acted to denounce others because they believed in danger from saboteurs. In that situation, it is likely that the members of the NKVD both imbibed the common atmosphere and reinforced it, as they spoke informally to their acquaintances about cases they had "solved" with the aid of torture. A truly vicious cycle had built up.

Two other perceptions appear regularly: that the scale of the arrests was small and that there was little or no injustice. Aleksandr Solzhenitsyn, born in 1918, noted that he and his peers did not understand "the sort of arrests that were being made at the time, and the fact that they were torturing people in prisons. . . . How could we know anything about those arrests and why should we think about them? All the provincial leaders had been removed, but as far as we were concerned it didn't matter. Two or three professors had been arrested, but after all they hadn't been our dancing partners."[90] Pavel Kuznetsov, a member of the Komsomol, did note that from 1936 to 1939, "among various strata of workers, peasants, students, intellectuals, and the army . . . I invariably observed evidences of discontent and fear, as well as a lack of the necessities of life." Yet once again, his own feelings were different: "I was not yet capable of appraising the situation." He ascribed this defect to indoctrination, which had convinced him that what the "government did was always for the best."[91] For many people, however, indoctrination and official information by no means served as the sole basis of judgment.[92]

Another émigré seconded Kuznetsov's impressions. Nikita Malysh entered a naval school in 1936, later commanded a coast-guard vessel, then completed a three-year course in Chinese, and finally joined military intelligence. In all this he was "inspired by the consciousness of my participation in the establishment of our great socialist state." Despite everything that happened around him and his brother-in-law, including the arrest of a close relative, they believed the Russian proverb so often repeated by survivors of these years: "When wood is cut, splinters fly." They were convinced that "when a new world is being built, injustice and victims are unavoidable."[93]

Andrei Manchur, a soldier who did not return to the USSR after the war, reported the same kind of faith in the system and even in Stalin through the 1930s. "We, Soviet youth, walking around in rags, believed Stalin then, that he was really creating a 'happy life' for us! I believed in this terrible lie until in an army field shirt I went myself to Europe."[94] Manchur's disillusionment arose not from the repression of the period but because he had been led to believe something false about the Soviet standard of living, only to have his illusions crushed when he saw other parts of Europe.

The émigré Lena Moroz, born in 1917, wrote that "owing to my youth and the atmosphere of falsehood which surrounded me when I lived in the Soviet Union, I did not realize the dimensions and the significance of the terrorism exercised by the NKVD."[95] There is no question that the lies told in this period were immense, yet the perceptions of the arrests just noted would have had to change if immediate reality had indicated that the NKVD was winnowing the entire population. After all, people were always well aware of the arrests that took place around them. Raisa Orlova writes that only one person "from those close to us was arrested." She does record others her family knew of, but they had no immediate significance for her.[96] In the accounts just cited and others mentioned earlier, the writers' experience was that the arrests occurred on a small scale. They "didn't understand" that vast injustice was taking place, a comment that appears frequently in the sources, because the world around them did not promote that interpretation. One émigré recounted that "where I lived in Tambov I did not hear about any repressions, mass arrests, and so on. I learned about all this only here [abroad]. . . . I was very surprised to hear all this talk about this terror in Russia. I never heard that neighbors or relatives of neighbors of ours have disappeared."[97]

When Soviet citizens did know of arrests, a number of reports show that often they responded not by assuming a sense of malevolence or injustice on the part of the state but with the opposite conclusion, based on their belief in the widespread existence of enemies and wrecking. This feeling is evident in the recollections of John Scott and Petro Grigorenko, cited above. Colonel Philip R. Faymonville, an American military attaché in Moscow in 1937, reported to Washington on the mood in the Red Army after the second show trial, which ended in late January. His conversations with officers and his "close observation" of the press showed "displeasure and dismay" over events. But this was not fear of the regime; rather, "the recent treason trials have revealed that individuals in the Red Army were and have been for years in communication with the counter-revolutionary element." The guilty parties "were in effect plotting the overthrow of the Soviet government." Faymonville concluded that the trials had "shocked the country."[98] With brilliant hindsight and a chance to examine the transcripts of the trials in a totally different context, we know that they were outrageous fakes. But that was not necessarily the perception of the time inside the USSR.

General Gorbatov recalled his reaction after the announcement that Marshal Tukhachevskii and other top officers had been executed in June 1937:

"How can it be," I thought, "that men who took such a part in routing foreign interventionists and internal reactionaries, men who have done so much to improve our army, Communists tested in the leanest days—how can it be that they have suddenly become enemies of the people?" Finally, after mulling over a host of possible explanations, I accepted the answer most common in those days. "No matter how you feed the wolf, it will always look towards the forest," as the saying goes. There was apparently some justification for this, since Tukhachevsky and a number of those arrested with him came from rich families, and had been Tsarist officers. "Obviously," many people said at the time, trying to puzzle out an answer, "they fell into the nets of foreign intelligence organizations while abroad on duty or to take a cure."[99]

Office workers responded similarly to the arrest of their boss in Lydia Chukovskaia's novel *Opustel' yi dom (Deserted House)*, written in 1939–40 as an attempt "to record the events just experienced by my country, those close to me, and myself."[100]

Nicholas Prychodko reacted the same way in late 1936 or early 1937 to the arrest of a professor he knew. "I began to wonder whether there really was something wrong, for surely the NKVD would not do this to an innocent man!"[101] When the Politburo member Stanislav Kosior was arrested in 1937, General Grigorenko approved: "I blamed everything I discovered about the Ukrainian famine on Kossior. . . . I considered it [his arrest] just retribution for his activities against the people."[102] An émigré also believed that the famine had been caused by enemies.[103] Thus the disaster of 1932–33 may not have frightened people later in the decade, if they believed that the government was arresting those responsible for the famine.

Pavel Kuznetsov's father, who had quit the party in disgust over collectivization in 1930 but was never arrested, "believed the repressions were the machinations of enemies of the people; he wasn't the only one who thought this way." This reverses the usual identification of enemies but nonetheless recognizes their role. Moreover, the elder Kuznetsov accepted the necessity for "vigilance" and harshness: he had the "conviction that whoever ran counter to the regime should be exterminated for the good of the community."[104]

Belief that spies and saboteurs had penetrated the upper echelons of Soviet society was common. Harvard Project respondents regularly expressed certainty that Tukhachevskii was guilty of plotting with the Germans.[105] John Hazard, an American Sovietologist who studied law in Moscow in 1937, remembered that the students he knew usually believed that the marshal was guilty.[106] If citizens considered one of the country's best-known officers a traitor, surely they would have felt unease about loyalty among other strata as well.

A young naval intelligence officer told a postwar interviewer that he had eagerly looked for foreign agents in 1935–38. Even after the war he still believed that "at that time Japanese agents were very active on the Pacific."[107] Valentina Bogdan's maid sincerely believed in enemies of the people in 1937 and considered that domestic servants had a duty to listen to conversations and report events such as the burning of papers. Servants were willingly recruited for this monitoring in the city of Rostov.[108] Markoosha Fischer, the Russian-born wife of an American journalist, also employed a domestic servant who believed in enemies. Niura "truly represented the mentality of the woman and man in the street. . . . She was not bothered by political doubts and accepted every official utterance as gospel."[109]

A. Lunin, who worked in the Soviet aircraft industry, reported that after the arrest of the famous designer A. N. Tupolev there were whispers that he had truly been a wrecker. Some "asserted that he had been connected for a long time" with a foreign power and that he had been preparing to flee abroad, but the security organs got him first.[110] K. Petrus mentioned a "flying cavalry" of Komsomol members who found a nest of enemies in Central Asia in 1937.[111]

Some who lived through the 1930s in the USSR and then emigrated continued to believe that sabotage had been pervasive. A watch repairman thought that many took part in wrecking because they had been bribed from abroad.[112] An émigré who was a student in the late 1930s recalled that his peers felt a mixture of "perplexity, resentment, even disgust" at meetings when they all voted to expel the offspring of arrested parents. "On the other hand," he continued, "there are the 'facts' of domestic sabotage and the 'fact' (accepted by most students) that the 'greedy imperialists have killed millions of persons in wars to conquer new markets and inflate their profits.' Many students go one step further and accept the alleged 'fact' of widespread intervention by 'capitalist agents' in Soviet internal affairs."[113] Such convictions translated readily into support for the hunt for enemies.

A man interviewed after the war commented that "in 1937 and '38, I noticed that the government was trying to do something for the people to better the situation. Also, I saw the government annihilate the enemies of the people, those who were enemies of the building of socialism. And there were many enemies. On the other hand, I had pity for these people. True, there were enemies of the people, but after all, they were unhappy."[114]

The broad belief in enemies undoubtedly contributed to the acceptance of the regime that appears so often in the sources. In 1940 Aleksandr Solzhenitsyn's "faith in Marxism was burning brighter than ever." He wrote, "I believe to the marrow of my bones. I suffer no doubts, no hesitations—life is crystal clear to me."[115] It seems possible that Solzhenitsyn wrote about doubts and hesitations precisely because he did have some and felt a psychological need to disarm them; nonetheless, his operative outlook was one of full support for the regime. A good deal of his faith stemmed from the fact that his own situation was bright: in 1940 he received a Stalin Scholarship to study at Rostov University, which was awarded for his achievement in school and for "social and political activism in the Komsomol." Another part of his complacency grew from his sense, already noted, that the arrests involved only a few people. When he and his first wife met a former camp prisoner, they were baffled by his stories and did not believe they were typical. And all they could tell the man about their own lives concerned their "studies, amateur theatricals, sporting events, and so on."[116]

Other veterans of the era were more psychologically straightforward than Solzhenitsyn about their views. Mikhail Gorokhov, the young engineering graduate trained as an NKVD officer during the purges, reported that "at that time . . . no doubts assailed my mind, and I accepted the accusations as genuine."[117] Raisa

Orlova wrote that "up until 1953 I believed in everything." She would have accepted even her own father's arrest as justified.[118] Dmitri Panin did not believe in enemies, but his wife did.[119]

Even a recognition that some injustice was occurring did not necessarily shake the conviction that enemies had to be rooted out. This pattern is implicit in the remarks of Nikita Malysh, cited above, and of Lev Kopelev: "I convinced myself and others that the main thing had remained unchanged, that all our ills, malefactions and falsehoods were inevitable but temporary afflictions in our overall healthy society. In freeing ourselves from barbarity, we were forced to resort to barbaric methods, and in repulsing cruel and crafty foes, we could not do without cruelty and craftiness."[120]

The belief in enemies is also underscored by a common reaction to a person's own arrest or that of a close relative, namely, that others detained by the NKVD were indeed guilty but that the case in question was an error. Out of such problems might arise anxiety that one could be arrested by mistake; this response does appear, but it should not be confused with fear of a state campaign to terrorize.

A pattern of identifying errors but not injustice extended throughout the purge period. An engineer in a gulag camp reportedly said in 1937, "But I'm not a Trotskyite. I have nothing in common with them!"[121] When the son of Chukovskaia's heroine is arrested in 1937, his mother is convinced that a terrible mistake has been made but that all the other women in line to get information are the relatives of saboteurs or terrorists.[122] The author of the novel later called her protagonist a "generalized model of those who seriously believed in the reasonableness and justice of what had happened." Such people were "the majority" in their understanding.[123] Lydiia Shatunovskaia agreed: "The majority of Soviet people . . . still didn't fully understand at that time [1937–38] the meaning of this wave of massive repression."[124]

Nadezhda Mandelstam wrote that "the young people—whether students, soldiers, writers or guards—were particularly credulous. . . . Even we [she and Osip], with all our experience, were not able to form a proper judgment of all the changes, so what could we expect of younger people?" In fact, Nadezhda met not only young people but also older ones who believed in enemies, and not just at the time but years after as well. She mentions a woman who denounced her husband during the Terror because she thought he was guilty, a landlord in the mid-1930s who prided himself on his role as an informer, and other "true believers" in Stalin and his rule, including women she spoke to in 1953 and 1957. All this is in a book that finds "chronic fear" among the populace and asserts that "everybody is a victim in a reign of terror." In reality, as many passages make clear,[125] Mandelstam is speaking not of the population as a whole but of the intelligentsia, above all the literary elite. Occasionally she tried to penetrate the psychology of ordinary people, but they were alien to her world.

Well into 1937 and 1938, and even when victims came from the prime categories, they or their peers sometimes expressed great surprise at their fate, a reaction indicating that arrests were neither expected nor commonplace. The husband of Lydia Grebin (a pseudonym) was a railroad engineer, an occupation that suffered many arrests.[126] When he was picked up at the end of November 1937, "his fellow workers were thunderstruck. "If they're starting to take people like him," one of them said, "they should have arrested me long ago. . . . Many of my husband's friends, when they heard of his arrest, found it incredible. He never criticized the government."[127] The incident also suggests that prior to her husband's arrest, his fellow workers had seen some justification for other cases.

Grebin's story, of course, indicates a widespread realization that criticizing the regime was dangerous. There has never been any question that the state imposed constraints on expression. The recognition that certain statements could put one in jeopardy, however, did not necessarily mean that people were afraid of the state or that they felt restrictions on freedom of speech were wrong. Among the Harvard Project respondents, only about one-third believed that "people should be allowed to say things against the government."[128] Soviet émigrés to America continued to express strong reservations about freedom of speech into the 1980s.[129] Apparently people still felt that it would threaten the country's security. Second, citizens learned fairly readily what could be said and what could not, and they proved adept at using ritual language and staying within acceptable parameters.

Even if, despite all the evidence presented thus far, extensive fear did reign for a time in the USSR, it could have begun no earlier than the spring of 1937. And it would have lasted no longer than the end of 1938, though the course of the Terror became highly checkered well before that.

Is it possible, however, as some scholars have suggested to me, that survivors repressed or suppressed memories of fear and that in fact they were terrified? It seems odd to maintain that a large body of evidence does not mean what it says and that something quite different was true. But let us examine the issue more closely. One handbook of psychology discusses *repression* as a psychoanalytic term referring to "the unconscious mechanism whereby unwelcome knowledge is kept from the conscious." In contrast, suppression is "the conscious inhibition of a response."[130] So far either might indicate the existence of fear even when people said they were not afraid.

But repression is a slippery word in the psychologists' lexicon. Sigmund Freud did not say categorically that the mechanism was unconscious; sometimes he wrote that it was, once that it was "intentional," and elsewhere that it could be either conscious or unconscious.[131] Anna Freud consistently thought repression was unconscious.[132] Currently, most psychiatrists agree with her.[133]

Still, the elder Freud did suggest that something from the unconscious could make its way into the conscious, with or without the help of a psychoanalyst. It is possible for repression to cease, for example, if one moves to another culture. Recall of unpalatable events should be even easier if the original control was suppression. Yet no weakening of either mechanism, thereby allowing a memory to surface, figures in the dozens of memoirs used for this book.

Moreover, Freud did not argue that unpleasant things in general are repressed; rather, he believed that the things that are repressed are unpleasant. Following his lead, it is impossible to accept that over and over people who lived through the Terror remembered various negative subjects but somehow repressed—and kept on repressing—profound fear from the 1930s. Once again, only a relatively small number claimed that they personally feared arrest before it occurred, if it ever did.

On the basis of some remarks by Freud and other students of psychoanalysis that repression is conscious, or using instead the concept of suppression, we might expect to uncover evidence of deliberate attempts at quashing fright in an especially honest memoirist. But no such confessions have appeared, even though a good many writers are brutally frank about their own rationalizations and misunderstandings on other counts.

Another specialist on repression writes that it "operates to prevent retrieval, not of unhappiness, but of mental contents that would produce conflict in consciousness." One such dilemma occurs when someone cannot act upon an idea because the outcome would be socially unacceptable.[134] Thinking about fear at the time of the Terror might have led to dangerous behavior, for example, to a denunciation of Stalin. Not repressing dread could have produced conflicts that made it hard for an individual to function. But these difficulties would have ceased in emigration, where it would have been more socially acceptable to speak of personal fear during the Terror than to suppress it. People rarely reported fear before their own arrest, however, although they commonly remembered other serious objections to Soviet policies and horrible events in their lives, including torture. These "mental contents," according to the theorists, would also have led to insoluble dilemmas if not repressed. Survivors would not have been selective about excising one kind of bad memory, apprehension toward the regime, but not others.

Recent psychological experiments demonstrate that people tend to remember extremely pleasant and unpleasant experiences equally, because such events stand out much more than milder ones do.[135] This revelation obviously points to a strong tendency to recall something as powerful as deep fear.

Given these findings, concepts of repression and suppression do not support the idea that people somehow widely overrode or erased their real emotions. Both evidence and theory lead to acceptance of what people said about the Terror as reflecting their feelings at the time.

Most reactions to arrest catalogued above suggest that extensive fear did not exist in the USSR at any time in the late 1930s. Usually only those who were actually arrested came to understand that innocent people were being persecuted. Citizens at liberty often felt that some event in the backgrounds of detained individuals justified their arrest. The sense that anyone could be next, the under-pinning of theories on systems of terror, rarely appears. If by the Terror we mean that many innocent people suffered tremendously at the hands of the state, that is a valid statement; to say that all, or probably even the majority, were terrorized is as incorrect for the USSR in the last half of the 1930s as it is for Germany at the same time.[136]

When citizens did understand that many innocents were being arrested, the result was not necessarily broad fear of the regime. Incarcerating loyal, trustworthy people had the effect more of spreading confusion, signaling that obedience was of no value, damaging the economy, and evoking avoidance behavior, hardly desirable results from any government's point of view. In the Soviet case, such arrests often, though not always, turned loyal, dedicated citizens into inveterate haters of the regime and even of socialism itself.[137] The Terror was not a logical system, and it did not systematically produce desirable behavior from the standpoint of the regime. "Order through Terror" is probably a contradiction in terms anywhere;[138] it certainly was in the USSR.

At its height, the Terror often became a mass of bizarre accusations that had little to do with reality or with the goals usually ascribed to Stalin. The denunciations and charges took on a dynamic of their own. In his memoirs, Nikita Khrushchev relates a story from Ukraine during the purges. At a party meeting a woman stood up and said about a perfect stranger, "I don't know that man over there but I can tell from the look in his eyes that he's an enemy of the people." The near-victim saved himself by firing back that he could see from the woman's eyes that she was a prostitute. Khrushchev commented that the man's "quick comeback probably saved his life." If he had begun to protest and defend himself, he would only have fallen under more suspicion.[139] Nestor Lakoba, a Georgian Old Bolshevik, died in December 1936 and was buried with honors. But in the next year he was accused of having participated in a plot on Stalin's life; his remains were exhumed and reburied ignominiously.[140] Emotions ran so high in 1937 that leaders of Young Pioneer detachments, the political organization for children up to age fifteen, believed they saw "counterrevolutionary designations" in the slides members used to hold up their red kerchiefs. The leaders pulled off the slides on the spot and sometimes even summarily expelled children from the Pioneers. At other times leaders found more "'enemy' designations" in the drawings children made in their notebooks.[141] Such insanity was widely criticized in the press during 1938.

When a seventeen-year-old Russian boy tried to enter flight school in 1937, he was rejected because of a grandmother who lived abroad. "The other people looked at me and said, 'See, he has a grandmother abroad, he must be some spy or devil.'"[142] Beginning in 1936, newspaper editors and printers were warned to be careful in dividing words. "Anti-Soviet," for instance, always had to be broken as "Anti-So-," because otherwise a phrase like "Soviet imperialism" might appear on one line.[143] Many arrests for counterrevolutionary activity paralleled the following: a young movie projectionist was picked up in 1938 because a friend had left a cigarette on the floor of the projection booth, igniting a film of Stalin making a speech.[144] A typist in Chukovskaia's *Deserted House* is fired for accidentally typing "Rats Army" instead of "Red Army," as close a match in Russian as in English.[145] Such was the hysterical atmosphere of the Terror.

Beck and Godin reported that trouble overtook a woman pottery artist who had designed ashtrays manufactured by the thousands for hotels. Someone noticed that if the trays were turned upside down and a line was drawn to connect three of its legs, the result was a "Zionist star." She was charged with making the design on orders of "foreign fascism," something that would have been funny in a society that had not gone half mad.[146]

But this frame of mind did not necessarily cause people to bow silently to their circumstances. As the arrests rolled on, they *increased* the chances to criticize, because so many superiors in various settings were now under suspicion. The party cell of an NKVD road-building group in Smolensk oblast' noted a rise in the number of complaints in 1937. Supposedly the reason was that managers "are not dealing seriously with workers' petitions."[147] Collective farm peasants drafted for work by this NKVD unit were not afraid to express their displeasure with conditions on the job in 1937. "Because of the mess which has happened at construction project 199," where the people were "naked," not being paid, and infected with typhus, a report noted in March, kolkhozniki "are cursing Soviet power."[148] There is no record that they suffered for their words, and in fact the description of their plight is sympathetic.

Another case involved a worker arrested in Krasnodar in 1937. The man's family was "dispersed," and his apartment and furniture taken away. After a while he was released and restored to both his job and party membership. He then stood up in a party meeting and criticized the party for allowing such a mistake; nothing was done to help him, but he was not arrested a second time.[149]

At the end of the disaster of 1937–38, the country as a whole was by no means "broken."[150] Acceptable behavior on the eve of World War II included criticism: a raucous meeting of factory workers in 1940 could "criticize the plant director, make suggestions as to how to increase production, improve quality, and lower costs."[151] Of course, criticism had been strongly encouraged during the purges, and local records contain plenty of it.[152] The press strongly endorsed criticism from below at the end of 1938. *Pravda* denounced "haughty answers to critical questions by the Secretary of the Sverdlovsk Party district committee. . . . Such a statement by a party leader does not facilitate healthy Bolshevik criticism and self-criticism. On the contrary, it leads to stopping up, to tying up the initiative of the masses, to putting brakes on uncovering enemies."[153]

Another article announced that "the majority of complaints and statements which have come to me [the author was a deputy of the Supreme Soviet] from the electors are just and legal. 95% of them can be solved on the local level (*na meste*)."[154] The press not only continued to elicit complaints from below but also stressed that officials had to respond quickly and politely.

The quack and self-made agricultural adviser Trofim Lysenko became the leading figure in Soviet agro-biology by the late 1930s, with tragic consequences for the development of both science and farming. Yet "cases of audacious public disobedience" of the charlatan's policies appeared before the war. In this connection a real scientist told Stalin to his face that "organizational measures" were keeping the collective farms from applying sound principles; the man was not arrested. In 1940 biologists were able to start a new journal critical of Lysenko, though they did not refer to him by name.[155] Genuine scientists were able to discuss genetics despite Lysenko's hatred for the discipline.[156]

Nor did everyone kowtow to the NKVD or to party officials; in both 1937 and 1938 Solzhenitsyn, then a Komsomol member, refused the urgings of local party officials to enter an NKVD training institute.[157] At the same time, there were still people willing to listen to foreign radio broadcasts and to trust others to join them.[158] Many people maintained a critical sense or independent judgment, demonstrated also by the sarcastic jokes they told one another about politics and even arrests.[159]

Some people actually enjoyed life during the late 1930s, something the "total fear" theory, and indeed most Western accounts of the period, cannot admit. The predominant view in the literature is that existence went from grim to grimmer to grimmest.[160] But the diary of Nina Kosterina, a daughter of the new elite who was fifteen years old in 1936, records romances, summer outings, and stormy relationships with friends. The first and second (January 1937) Moscow trials had no impact on her life, and she records no sense of personal apprehension until late 1937.[161]

Other émigrés' accounts convey the same impression. Klara Agranovich-Shul'man and her second husband lived in Moscow. "Not suspecting that the echo of that year [1937] would touch us, [we] lived in fleeting happiness and the sensation of joy in our daily lives. The black shadow of the Gulag fell on me only much later, but then I was happy in the love of the many friends around me, [I] found joy in creative work, in the consciousness of my usefulness to people."[162]

Aleksandr Solzhenitsyn had fun as late as the summer of 1939, when he and a friend traveled on the Volga in a small boat.[163] Other accounts also record enjoyable times in the same period.[164] Mass arrests took place but life went on, probably for the majority. Soviet society absorbed great suffering and still demonstrated a capacity for happiness.

Of 1939 in Leningrad, one observer remarked that the young workers, the students, and the newly created intelligentsia remained overwhelmingly loyal. For the students the "first shock" was not the purges but the debacle of the Finnish war in the winter of 1939–40. The same writer indicated that problems of disloyalty in other strata stemmed more from the low standard of living than from any sense of political repression.[165] Lev Kopelev found a "militant Polophobia and Finnophobia in 1939–40," an emotion that suggests strong support for the government.[166] G. A. Tokaev also noticed great patriotism in 1940.[167] John Scott went beyond those comments to discuss widespread optimism in Magnitogorsk in 1939,[168] and Solzhenitsyn wrote that at that point "the brightest of futures lay ahead" for himself and his associates.[169]

In the coming years a broken people would not have fought effectively, let alone put up the tremendous resistance that the Soviet population by and large displayed during World War II (see Chapter 7). Nor can this idea explain why people evinced genuine affection for Stalin during and after the war, which for some continued decades after his death.

No one can judge how many people feared the regime in the late 1930s, let alone how long and deeply anyone experienced that feeling. But the abundant sources touching on this issue indicate, much more often than not, that this response to the situation was limited, in important ways. Such fright occurred within certain categories of the populace. But for the vast majority of the citizenry, if it occurred at all in the late 1930s, it existed only between mid-1937 and some point in 1938.

At any time during that period, apprehension toward the state was surely less important than belief in the authorities and their hunt for enemies. The second outlook, expressed repeatedly by survivors, lent support to the regime's efforts to unveil wreckers. By 1939–41, at least the urban citizens of the USSR often exhibited patriotism, support for the Stalinist leadership and its overall goals, and confidence in their right and ability to criticize important aspects of their situation.

Life in the Factories

With the possible exception of one short period, terror was not the central fact or motivating factor of Soviet existence between collectivization, when it touched many peasants, and June 1941. Other factors were more important in getting the populace to comply with the general goals and structure of the regime, or at least to forego working actively against it. In this chapter I explore some of these other dynamics for one important social group, the industrial workers. Although coercion and manipulation of workers existed on a fairly large scale, the successes of industrialization, the evidence on workers' attitudes already cited, and Soviet performance in World War II compel further inquiry into the nature of the industrial world.

Like many depictions of the Soviet people during the Terror, older treatments of workers were often simultaneously ennobling and demeaning. They were portrayed as innocent sufferers who virtually became saints through their martyrdom. But they were also rarely credited with initiative or influence in their environment, making them appear incapable.[1]

More recent Western investigations have forced revision of this picture by offering considerable insight into, for example, the difficulties the regime encountered in regulating the turnover of workers, labor-management relations, and the Stakhanovite movement.[2]

Yet we still have little understanding of workers' political life in the late 1930s. If Soviet workers were actors and not just objects—typically on the local, not the national, level—did they have any meaningful input and influence in the factory environment? If they exercised such influence, did it give them any sense that the regime was legitimate?

I shall examine the ways workers criticized local conditions and participated in decision making. "Participation" and "criticism" in this context apply to both formal opportunities, through established organizations and forums, and informal possibilities, through contacts and influence on the shop floor. The nature, limits, and results of workers' criticism need to be explored, because these issues are at the heart of workers' sense of whether the regime responded to them meaningfully and positively.[3]

Industrial workers were a fast-changing group under Stalin. Between 1926 and 1939, the number of urban dwellers increased by about 29.6 million.[4] Where there had been 14.6 million industrial workers and members of their families in 1913, there were 33.7 million in 1939.[5] The number of workers doubled between 1928 and 1932 alone, and increased from 3,124,000 in the first of those years to 8,290,000 in 1940.[6]

Even by the end of the 1920s, the new arrivals swamped the more experienced workers in Soviet plants. At the AMO auto factory in Moscow, for example, the number of workers increased from 1,000 in 1927 to 14,000 in 1932. In 1930–31 69.9 percent of metalworkers in the Urals were of peasant origin.[7] This influx lowered the level of skill and the average age in the factories and sharply increased the proportion of illiterates.

Newly hired workers without skill or experience had, of course, low status in the plants, while the old, experienced hands enjoyed high prestige and often served as informal consultants for supervisors. Great disparities also existed between the situations of males and females, even within the same factories or branches of industry; males always had higher standing and were more forthright about expressing grievances. The work environment and the influence of an industry within the government likewise varied between areas dominated by women, such as textiles, and those dominated by men, such as metallurgy. The differences in conditions in turn had a strong impact on how workers behaved.

The chief concern here is not with what might be called the sociology of Soviet workers but with their political culture, though the two spheres are often difficult to separate. In workers' political culture, commonalities were strong across industry, despite the many variations. Present in virtually all Soviet factories were strong Communist Party organizations, official trade unions, norms of output specified for individual tasks, and a production plan set by the government.

A discussion of some aspects of workers' political culture is central to this book. First, workers were supposed to be the rulers of the country, in what was called the "workers' state," until the constitution of 1936. After that document proclaimed the equality of the only three social groups acknowledged to exist in the USSR—peasants, intelligentsia (meaning white-collar or educated employees of any sort), and workers—the latter still enjoyed verbal and sometimes political preference. Was this merely hypocrisy? Or did the authorities find it necessary to provide some substance to claims of proletarian rights?

Workers were also important because during the upheavals of 1905 and 1917, they had demonstrated at least the fleeting ability to alter or even control politics through their dominance in production and communications. Peasants have usually been too scattered, locally oriented, and tied to the land to threaten most political structures in the past or present. Workers, however, have different capabilities. If they band together, they can shut down an economy, as happened in Russia in 1905. Therefore, strong efforts are required either to contain or mollify them in some fashion, or to find an effective combination of the two approaches. Ruling workers largely by force, if it had been possible at all, would have required massive resources from the Stalinist regime, especially considering the rapid growth in the number of industrial hands. But that is not what happened.

Soviet workers rarely lived well. Their real wages fell dramatically beginning in 1928, as the cost of food shot up. Manya Gordon figured that real wages in 1927 were 14 percent above the level of 1913, but that by 1937 they had fallen to only 66 percent of the 1913 rate.[8] In Leningrad the average consumption of meat declined by 72 percent between 1928 and 1933. Milk and fruit consumption were off slightly less, butter by 47 percent.[9]

In 1938 buying a loaf of wheat bread required a Soviet worker to labor for 62 minutes, an American only 17. A liter of milk required 58 minutes of work in Moscow, 26 in London.[10] The average Swedish worker had 2.5 times more purchasing power for food than the average Soviet worker, and the typical American proletarian 4.17 times.[11]

These statistics, however, are not the whole story. First, workers often ate their main meals in factory cafeterias; some 16.2 million wage earners ate in collective kitchens by 1932.[12] Second, enterprises maintained land for gardens whenever possible, so that workers grew some of their own food. Third, more members of families went to work: in 1927 there were on average 1.25 wage earners per working-class family; by 1935 this figure had risen to 1.47.[13] Thus overall purchasing power per family did not slip as badly as prices alone would indicate.

Fourth, the decline in living standards applied mainly to newcomers, so that to contrast the picture in 1928 with that of 1932 or later is somewhat like comparing apples and oranges. For the older, established workers, things did not worsen nearly so much. They earned higher pay to begin with and became even more valuable in light of the flood of peasants into the plants, because the more experienced hands were desperately needed for their skills and as instructors.

Yet the immigrants may not have felt disgruntled in their new environment, because they had often left a miserable situation, even discounting the effects of collectivization. Poverty, filth, ignorance, lack of opportunity, and strong parental control characterized village life across the Soviet Union before 1929. Compared to those conditions, the city may not have been so bad.[14] In 1984 the exiled writer Alexander Zinoviev told an interviewer that

> life in the big cities . . . offered irresistible temptations. Country life was primitive and boring. My family lived on the land. We had a large and comfortable house. In Moscow the ten of us had to make do with a single room of ten square meters—one square meter per head. Can you imagine?! Yet, we *preferred* life in Moscow. [My] own family . . . were peasants. As a result of the collectivization of agriculture, my parents lost everything they had. But my elder brother eventually rose to be a factory manager; the next one to him in age made it to the rank of colonel; three of my older brothers qualified as engineers; and I became a professor at Moscow University.[15]

Here was the pull of the city and its opportunities, including upward mobility, with the exception of the years 1937–38. If Zinoviev's family represented a remarkable case of seizing those chances, the basic pattern was by no means unusual. Those who did not rise nearly so high may still have felt better off away from parental or village control, not to mention the "primitive and boring" existence they left behind.[16]

A fifth reason that workers may not have been dissatisfied with their material circumstances in the late 1930s is that official pay was often not their entire income. Out of sheer necessity, as we shall see, managers discovered many ways to offer more pay than they were supposed to. Even under the official scales, it was possible for supervisors to improve workers' situations by moving them up through the various "grades" that determined rates, assigning them easier jobs, or improving their skills through training. In addition, many a worker had extra sources of income through schemes, scams, and hustles of one kind or another.[17] The government disliked such activity but could not eliminate it.

Finally, living standards improved considerably after the truly miserable point of the early 1930s. Rationing ended in 1935; food prices then remained relatively stable in 1936–37 while wages went up, according to one estimate, by about 30 percent.[18] Workers could feel optimistic about the future. Then the economy again encountered major problems, as production was diverted for the military. War loomed over the country once more. Yet workers could have believed that, except for the imminent struggle, and actual fighting against the Japanese by the summer of 1938, they would have done better.

The major difficulty in everyday life was usually not food but housing. Discussions of the situation were remarkably frank. In 1933, for example, the head of the National Trade Union Council, Nikolai M. Shvernik, noted the existence of apartment blocks with forty rooms per toilet.[19] People found the most extraordinary places to live: at Kuznetskstroi, a huge steel complex in the Urals, the majority of the workers lived in holes they dug in the side of a hill. Even in an established Moscow factory, Elektrozavod, many workers slept on the floor of the plant.[20] John Scott, the American welder who worked in Magnitogorsk, reported that in the city's barracks in 1937 people had thirty-five square feet each. Other workers lived in an area called "Shanghai." Here

a collection of improvised mud huts huddled in a sort of ravine overlooking the railroad yards. The inhabitants were largely Bashkirs, Tartars, and Kirghizi, and had built their dwellings out of materials found or stolen over a period of years. The roofs were usually made of old scrap metal, sometimes covered by sod or by thatch. The same house was inhabited by the family, the chickens, the pigs, and the cow, if there was one. . . . The dwellers in these "zemlyanki" were laborers and semi-skilled workers and their families. Their possession of chickens and goats was witness of the fact that they "were living well" by the standards of Russian peasantry. They had eggs and milk, while the fathers working in the mill supplied a cash income.[21]

This is a fairly dismal picture, yet these people were getting by. Scott's account also underscores the fact that statistics on purchasing power do not take into account food provided by animals owned privately.[22]

Housing improved somewhat after the end of the first five-year plan in 1932, but in 1937 each Soviet urban dweller had an average of 45 square feet of living space.[23] The battle for decent quarters continued, with important implications for worker-management relations.

The trade unions were a major factor in this sphere. During the 1920s they were relatively autonomous. They pressed for workers' rights in regard to employment, wages, safety, housing, and other vital matters. Although they hardly achieved satisfaction for their members in these areas and discontent with union performance was common, they did protect workers in some ways.[24] But by 1928, most accounts argue, the unions were forced to retreat to mere record keeping, targeting capable people for promotion, and spurring everyone on to greater production. Strikes were forbidden. This year is said to mark the "death of Soviet trade unionism."[25] But in fact the unions did not die.

To a degree, workers simply bypassed unions at the end of the 1920s by turning to other bodies. Among these were production conferences, which varied in composition but always included some workers and some supervisors. First held in 1923, the conferences fell into torpor within a few years. But, as a study of Moscow shows, in 1926–29 workers increasingly used the meetings "to vent their hostility toward and grievances with factory administrators and technical specialists."[26]

Meanwhile, the overall situation for labor had moved rapidly from an oversupply to a desperate shortage. For those not promoted or admitted to higher education, this favorable labor market was extremely important. No matter what the political setting, the bargaining power of workers depends most of all on the demand for their services. By the early 1930s, managers desperate for help resorted to whatever blandishments they could muster to attract and keep workers, especially skilled ones. Enterprises sent out recruiters who penetrated barracks on any pretext and "engaged in the ugliest forms of hiring," a practice so common it was labeled piracy.[27] The demand for labor created a situation that overrode the problems of the unions and even the efforts of the regime to control labor through legislation.

The first of these attempts came in September–October 1930, when laws adopted by the Russian Republic (not the whole USSR) specified that the reason for dismissal or quitting a job had to be entered in the books that recorded workers' pay and service. Managers were forbidden to hire people with unsatisfactory records, and employment offices were ordered to withhold benefits from those who violated the laws.[28] In November 1932, another statute declared that workers could be deprived of housing and their ration cards for even one unexcused absence. This measure was followed in December by the requirement that every citizen carry a domestic passport at all times; it was to be shown to the authorities on demand, particularly to arrange a job or housing.[29] Six months later, the government decreed expulsion from housing cooperatives for absenteeism and added further minor restrictions on reemploying those who had quit their jobs.

No further limitations on labor mobility appeared until December 1938, when work books detailing employment records were again required, this time across the USSR. Management collected the books upon hiring and could refuse to return them if workers wanted to leave, thereby tying them to the spot in theory. Two other decrees specified that workers who were even twenty minutes late were to be dismissed and evicted from factory housing.

A law of June 1940 extended the work day to eight hours for those who had previously worked seven and to seven hours for those who had worked six, such as miners; but job norms and pay rates were to be adjusted so that aggregate pay remained at the old levels. Extending a break or arriving to work more than twenty minutes late was supposed to lead to an automatic sentence of corrective labor at the workplace, in addition to the loss of some pay, all seniority, and pension accumulation to that point. Workers had to carry out managers' orders, even if illegal, and could protest only afterward. Most important, workers could not quit without the permission of the director of the enterprise.[30]

These laws are often lumped together and cited as evidence that the regime successfully controlled workers and shackled them to the job.[31] Yet the workbooks and other measures of 1938–39 essentially replicated the law of November 1932, though in a more severe form. The very fact that the government had to try repeatedly to slow down the flux of people in general and workers in particular indicates that it failed.

Conditions in the 1930s dictated that outcome. Industrial executives experienced extreme pressure from both workers, who wanted to improve conditions and pay, and the regime, which wanted to maintain output. Managers had to placate the proletarians to some extent; factory executives regularly commented on the need to relate well to workers and help them in order to get them to perform effectively.[32] After all, workers could easily find other jobs. To cover themselves at higher levels, managers frequently lied about production. They even had a saying for the situation: "It's necessary not to work well but to account well."[33]

Such maneuvers made industrial administrators more vulnerable to arrest in a period of hysteria and intense scrutiny of their activities. A former chief of construction work recalled that during six weeks in 1938 there were twenty-eight separate investigations of his performance, for instance, of how he supervised work norms and allocated wages.[34]

From the start of efforts to control workers' movements, in 1930, the press reported many deliberate violations. Workers *tried* to get fired so that they could move to better jobs; managers balked at compliance because they stood to lose needed workers. Administrators continued to hire without regard to workbooks, and even the labor exchanges went on paying unemployment benefits in clear violation of the law.[35] As for the statutes of late 1932, they were "so harsh both workers and managers now had a clear stake in finding ways to get around them." Administrators openly resisted; the largest engineering plant in Leningrad, for example, refused to discharge absentee workers because it could not replace them.[36] A survey taken in Azerbaijan in December 1932 revealed that only 10 percent of those fired had returned their ration cards and that in many areas workers had not been evicted from factory housing after discharge.[37] Some managers were prosecuted for not enforcing the law, but the legal journals, so full of cases regarding other statutes, published few such accounts. Having tried only half-heartedly to enforce its own policy, probably because some leaders recognized the damage this would cause to production, the regime seemed to give up on the laws by late 1933; the press campaign against violations died away.[38]

For the next few years a curious situation concerning firings prevailed. Managers discharged vast numbers of industrial workers: 22.3 percent were released for truancy in 1934, 18 percent in 1935, and 17 percent in 1936. But being sacked did not necessarily end badly for workers and might not even force them out of the factory. At some plants it was more or less policy to take a worker who had been fired from one shop into another. Workers from one factory of a large combined operation could often easily find jobs in another enterprise under its control.[39]

In truth, the laws hardly slowed down the movement of workers. During the latter half of the 1920s, yearly turnover in Soviet production averaged about 100 percent. That is, for every position, one person was hired each year. Put another way, each worker changed jobs an average of once a year. But that situation was nothing compared to the picture a few years later, when workers began pouring through industry—at the rate of 115.2 percent in 1929 and 152.4 percent in 1930. In coal mining during those two years, turnover increased from 192 percent to 295.2 percent. At the Stalingrad tractor plant, no one knew exactly how many hands were on the job.[40] Some sectors of the economy became virtual sieves; no wonder managers were frantic to entice workers to stay. Because industry stabilized significantly after the early 1930s and fewer new enterprises opened, mobility declined somewhat. But as late as 1938 the average Soviet industrial worker changed jobs every seventeen months.[41]

The campaign of 1938–40 to tighten labor discipline was more far-reaching than the one of 1930–32, and the countermeasures taken by managers and workers more extensive. The imperatives of production and demand for labor had not changed, and once more administrators found it essential to skirt the laws. At the Elektroapparat factory in Leningrad, management did not investigate the reasons for lateness and hence could not say if cases of it were warranted or not. This stance prevented court action against workers. At the Dnepropetrovsk aluminum factory, a shop chief asked the director not to send a case of absenteeism to the prosecutor but to fine the worker. This was done, but the sum was never collected. Such cases stretch on and on.[42] A former power plant executive, after detailing ways he had helped workers avoid charges for lateness, reported that "as a rule, we from the Administration, tried to help the workers and to cover up whenever possible."[43] Such evidence also suggests that when noncustodial punishment occurred, it was often not severe.

Despite demotions or the arrests of some managers for ignoring the laws, workers continued to change jobs at a high rate. At the Elektrosila plant in Leningrad during the first quarter of 1940, 1,873 had been "released" and 1,544 hired, though there were only 5,674 workers in the factory on February 1.[44] In the coal mines of the Makeevka region during 1939, recruits discovered that conditions were so bad that many demanded transfers or simply left. A year later, half of the workers who had signed contracts to stay for at least one year had quit. By the end of 1939, turnover across Soviet industry had returned to the level of 1936–37.[45] A government report of late 1940 admitted that although absenteeism and quitting had "declined somewhat," they were still "extremely significant."[46] This was the situation *after* the labor laws of 1938–40.

In any event, these statutes were part of the reorientation to military production.[47] Two émigrés, a deeply anti-Soviet former supply agent and a former chief engineer in a factory, saw the labor law of 1940 as part of the preparations for war.[48] The new restrictions came at a time when increased discipline was needed to boost productivity and meet the growing threat from abroad. Given the relaxed attitude of the preceding five years toward discipline and turnover, it cannot be argued that the Stalinist leadership intended to hamstring labor's rights for the sake of overall political control. Even if that was the goal, the leadership failed miserably in attempting to achieve it. Social and economic factors limited the regime's power. Once again, policies launched by the state did not turn out as planned, though they did generate resistance.

The Stakhanovite Movement: Workers' Criticism and Rising Tensions

During the night of August 30–31, 1935, Aleksei Stakhanov, a slim, pleasant-looking twenty-nine year old, cut 102 tons of coal in one shift at a Donbass mine. This amounted to fourteen times the prescribed "norm," or quota for production. Although at first the achievement received only moderate publicity, within weeks the "Stakhanovite movement" had spread across the country, through many branches of the economy.[49] Everywhere workers scrambled to set production records. Eventually there were even Stakhanovite mail carriers and waiters, an idea that would have appealed to many a visitor to the USSR in later years.[50] The situation in Soviet industry was already fraught with difficulties. Besides high turnover, there were labor shortages, especially of experienced foremen and skilled workers; bottlenecks in production; shortages in tools, materials, and transportation; friction between managers and workers; and relentless pressure to produce at virtually any cost. Stakhanovism aggravated all of these points.

The movement has usually been described as a drive by the state to coopt leading workers and to squeeze more output from all production personnel.[51] But campaigns to raise productivity were nothing new, and recent research has shown that Stakhanovism quickly became a mass movement in the factories. By September 1936, 22 percent of industrial workers were Stakhanovites, and a further 23 percent were "shock workers," an honorific category one step down.[52]

Numerous problems plagued any effort to raise productivity. In particular, the astonishing number of norms in Soviet factories provided immense scope for connivance within management, tricks by workers, or simple confusion. The Krasnyi Proletarii textile mill had thirty-five thousand norms in 1937, and the Ordzhonikidze Lathe Factory forty-eight thousand, or twenty-seven per worker, in 1936. The champion may have been the locomotive factory at Kolomenskoe, outside Moscow, with a staggering five hundred thousand norms in the spring of 1937, at which time the plant supposedly reviewed and adjusted all of them in the span of fifteen days.[53]

In April 1935, before the Stakhanov movement complicated the picture even more, investigators at the Gorky auto factory found cases in which foremen signed any document put before them. One approved a job order even though the worker's name was falsified; the fictitious man was to receive 682 rubles in pay, a hefty month's salary. Another supervisor signed an order that bore the name Vodop'ianov, then a famous pilot; it was for 1,796 rubles. A different foreman approved an order brought to him to "assemble a good wife on the conveyor." Yet another authorized a worker to "grind off his head." In other instances foremen allowed workers to fill in the details of a job, including pay for it.[54] Probably low-level supervisors acted this way because of the overwhelming paperwork they had to deal with and because workers were happier when they could determine much of their own effort and pay.

In early 1936 norms rose from 10 percent on average in certain industries to 55 percent in others.[55] However, the new targets were often not especially onerous; many workers quickly met them. In one group of four Far Eastern coal mines, for example, only 5.4 to 15.4 percent of the miners were *not* fulfilling the new norms by May 1936.[56] By June 1938, despite further rises in norms, only .7 percent of workers in electrical power could not fulfill them. The same figures for selected other industries were 4.8 percent in coal, 11 percent in chemicals, and 27.9 percent in paper, the highest proportion among available figures.[57] In October of the same year, workers in four factories involved in heavy industry coped easily with norms; average fulfillment ranged from 147.6 to 172.6 percent.[58] Often the workers who could not achieve the new standards quickly had been recently hired and therefore lacked sufficient experience or training to work effectively.[59]

New norms were determined not solely from above but with workers' participation. The union council of Moscow oblast' illustrated this practice in April 1936, when it strongly criticized the administration of the Krasnaia Presnia factory for acting unilaterally on norms. The council resolved to inform the central committee of the relevant union and the Commissariat of Heavy Industry of the transgression, which made it impossible for workers to earn premiums.[60]

Each major branch of industry, some ninety altogether, held a conference in early 1936 to discuss the course of the Stakhanovite movement, how to broaden it, and its impact on production, focusing specifically on norms. These meetings and the discussions on norms throughout Soviet industry at this time provided new opportunities for workers to be heard. In preparation for the conferences, workers in various enterprises at least made recommendations regarding norms, while some reports indicate that extensive discussions took place among the hands.[61]

To cite one example of how the new norms were actually set, 70 percent of those adopted in early 1936 at the Voroshilov factory in Vladivostok were drawn up by technical personnel on the basis of their observations of workers.[62] This practice facilitated slowdowns; as a proletarian from the Stalingrad tractor factory admitted, "any worker will deceive at every step" when being observed for norm setting.[63] In 1928 the national trade union newspaper *Trud* had advised managers that "the chronometrist must approach the worker tactfully so as not to make him nervous and intentionally or unintentionally distort the production process" during norm determination.[64] Supervisors and workers might collude while setting standards, since both sides wished to keep norms at an attainable level: managers wanted workers to be reasonably satisfied; workers wanted to make more money.

Worker involvement in determining norms sometimes resulted in proposals to raise some but lower others, for example, at the Ordzhonikidze Lathe Factory.[65]

Several branch conferences recommended retaining some norms at their current level,[66] whereas others reduced the increases urged by individual factories.[67] That Stakhanovites typically represented workers at the conferences did not mean that the trendsetters could think only of how to boost norms rapidly and steeply. The basic constraints of work in Soviet industry still applied.[68] Soviet workers were not simple recipients of norm increases, just as they have not been in industry elsewhere.[69]

In spite of orders from above, new standards were not always introduced into practice. In May 1936, a turner at the Voroshilov factory in Vladivostok was still following the old norms. His foreman signed job orders without filling in pay rates or specifying the time allotted for completion of the task.[70] A former Donbass coal miner who emigrated remarked that some foremen were "pigs" but that "most of them helped you when they saw that the norms were too high."[71] Foremen were sometimes demanding and bullying,[72] but a number of other ex-workers and supervisors reported largely accommodating relations between ordinary hands and the first tier of management.[73]

If norms were too difficult to achieve, workers would take other jobs, which was frequently easy to do in view of the constant labor shortage. After another round of norm increases in 1939, the Elektrosila plant in Leningrad "lost 7,000 workers. Almost the whole body of workers changed." This took place, of course, after the labor laws of December 1938 designed to control movement. Both norms and the premium system were altered at the same time at Elektrosila, causing pay for some hands to fall 30 to 40 percent.[74] Clearly such thorough turnover devastated production. To avoid this outcome, in 1938 executives of two weaving trusts sent thirty-eight requests to the Commissariat of Light Industry to have norms lowered; in a few cases the commissariat allowed the changes.[75] Acting on their own, managers in the Donbass in "very many" cases raised job rates and lowered norms; in one group of mines this happened four times in 1937 alone.[76] In spite of the regime's loud promotion of regular norm increases, executives risked wrath from above in order to satisfy workers.

For the same reason, managers abused the pay system so much that Shvernik, the national trade union chief, complained publicly in August 1938. Citing two factories that had developed elaborate premium systems, he charged that the pay schemes "were thought up especially to get around the directives of the party and the government that an increase in wages must be accompanied by a growth in productivity and a rise in the skill of the worker."[77] But executives could either follow the rules on pay, in which case they could lose workers and fall into the dangerous position of not fulfilling their factories' production plans, or cater to workers by paying them more, whenever that could be done quietly. Usually the second course was safer, at least as long as the enterprise fulfilled the plan. Workers' ability to leave gave them circuitous but powerful influence within the factories. As the example of Elektrosila shows, they could quit even after the restrictive laws of 1938–40. The size of the country, the necessity to fulfill the plan, and the forces of the labor market systematically eviscerated the regime's attempts to bind workers to their jobs.

This situation, enhanced by Stakhanovism in 1935, facilitated workers' opportunities to influence the whole industrial environment. That fall marked a meteoric rise of the movement in both official rhetoric and the number of proletarians dubbed Stakhanovites. With this upsurge, workers' criticisms often took on a sharp tone. Clothed in their new status as heroes of production, early Stakhanovites articulated the aspirations of workers in general. Strident criticisms of working and living conditions throughout industry quickly began to surface, drawing on support from the highest levels.

Workers began to speak frankly about living standards. A major example occurred at the First All-Union Conference of Male and Female Stakhanovites, held in Moscow in mid-November. Worker enthusiasm was essential to boosting productivity; to whip up zeal, the party leadership encouraged workers to speak out. They needed to feel that the Stakhanovite movement was theirs in a meaningful way. One of the leading worker-speakers was Nikita Izotov, a coal miner who had lent his name to a smaller efficiency movement of 1932–33. With Stalin, Molotov, and other top officials sitting behind him, Izotov was blunt: "Stakhanovites spoke to me and asked me to convey the following to the government: they earn a lot, but there is little to buy. One says: I need a piano, another—a bicycle, a third, a record player, radio and all sorts of cultural goods, which are necessary, but which are not [available] in the Donbass."[78]

Aleksandr Busygin, a stamping-press operator whose stature in the movement was almost as high as Stakhanov's, made an indirect but telling comment at the conference on the economic situation of most workers. Earlier almost all his money had gone for food, "but now, I think, it will be necessary to improve the food, and I'll be able to get new clothes, and even to furnish the apartment better."[79] Thus the leading Stakhanovites took the opportunity to address the national leadership and the country about the plight of workers. Speakers at the conference were surely selected and prompted from above, but their statements signaled the citizenry that workers' complaints were now being encouraged. More precisely, an existing policy acquired new emphasis and dimensions.

Industrial workers quickly followed the outstanding Stakhanovites' lead and began to attack their supervisors in other settings. In December 1935 workers in glass and chemicals in Moscow oblast' spoke up about the failure of managers and technical personnel to supply materials adequately, make timely repairs, and conduct "correct accounting" (that is, to pay well). The problems had come to the attention of the oblast' administration for local industry, which remarked that it was "necessary to end the insufficient development of work on the penetration of Stakhanovite methods."[80]

At a meeting of Stakhanovites and executives of the porcelain industry, also held in December 1935, a molder insisted in his own rambling way that six months before "our bosses lived, but the workers got by (*pozhivali*). . . . [Now] our bosses don't look quite like that, since they are combing their hair, on the contrary, probably they are being combed. . . . And they will look after us at the factory as they should. This is correct. But we don't believe it. We believe it when the director curses—well, okay, you live well, but we live badly."[81]

In fact managers were being "combed" (an expression equivalent to "cleaning up one's act") by their own superiors. At the same session, an official of the People's Commissariat in charge of porcelain production scourged "Comrade Frantsev," a plant manager, for not creating the "essential conditions" or giving workers the support they needed to improve their output. "Shame, Comrade Frantsev," the official scolded, and called for "wider self-criticism" as a means of eliminating the problems.[82] In Soviet parlance "self-criticism" implied frank reviews of one's own and others' behavior on the scene.

Concern for safety figured strongly in a testy interchange between a union official, one Nikotin, and the chairman of the porcelain industry branch conference. Nikotin, president of the factory union committee at the Kalininskii factory, complained in a speech that at the end of 1935 an order circulated throughout the industry to reduce spending on safety by 50 percent. He did not say who issued the order. At his factory the sum allotted fell from eighteen thousand to ten thousand rubles. Through the "stubbornness" of the Commissariat of Light Industry and the central committee of the union, the decision was supposedly rescinded at his plant in February 1936.

But at the branch conference Nikotin learned that all funds for safety at his factory had been eliminated for the year. Here the chair interrupted him: "This

interests us least of all. Tell us how you help the Stakhanovite movement."
Nikotin did not budge. "But this interests us," he retorted. He then detailed safety
problems at the plant, including temperatures above the maximum prescribed by
law and lack of proper work clothing. "We had to bring the head of the shop to
justice within the party and now the case has been turned over to a people's
court."[83] Nikotin refused to be intimidated by a higher official, and he and the
workers around him knew how to use the complaint system to their advantage.

A few months before the Stakhanovite movement began, the journal of the
Commissariat of Justice had remarked that procurators across the country did not
take safety violations seriously enough. Punishments for supervisors were too
"soft," often resulting only in sentences of forced labor, even when accidents had
led to deaths in industry. Procurators were ordered to take part in investigations of
safety violations and to involve workers as well. The article did not mention
wrecking as a cause of accidents, but it was a stern warning to the judicial system
to pay close attention to safety issues and to involve workers more directly in
their consideration.[84]

Stakhanovites had raised criticisms of dangerous conditions and a variety of
other matters by early 1936. Mistrust and resentment of superiors had found
outlets at conferences arranged to implement the new movement. Perhaps some
of the worker-critics deliberately chose to reproach management, in the hope that
they could deflect other hands' resentment away from themselves. A little class
solidarity in the factories might save Stakhanovites from bruised egos or heads at
the hands of other workers, who opposed "rate busting." That is, the less adept
proletarians feared that their production norms would be raised steeply in light of
the Stakhanovites' demonstration of what was possible.[85] But the remarks directed against managers in 1935–36 resounded with sincerity, reflected industrial conditions, and contained significant criticisms.

Some managers had already absorbed the message from above on how to relate
to the Stakhanovite movement. Another worker at the porcelain conference
outlined how supervisors in his factory had responded to his requests for help in
improving output, so that he had gone from making twelve hundred to thirteen
hundred pieces per shift to about two thousand.[86] Such executives understood the
need to become more receptive to proletarians' concerns.

In February 1936 a group in Murmansk joined in the chorus of complaints.
During a meeting of workers from all three shifts at the city railroad depot, strong
criticism of union leaders and management emerged; they had allegedly done

nothing to help ordinary hands become Stakhanovites. Some workers claimed that "whatever you say, however many suggestions you make about removing the defects and disorders in production, no one does anything. On the contrary, later they pressure those who spoke up with criticisms. It's better to keep quiet."[87] This report points to several broad themes. Local officials or managers had tried to stifle criticism, but the National Trade Union journal published the story. In part this was because, as the article again suggests, criticism and suggestions from workers tended to go hand in hand. Encouraging proposals from rank-and-file employees was a key element of the Stakhanovite movement, one that gave them a sense of serious participation in it. Finally, local attempts in Murmansk to silence workers had backfired: somehow they had enlisted the aid of the trade union journal, and dissatisfaction with the pressure on critics had become so widespread among the depot workers that they had turned out at a mass meeting clearly intended to intimidate management and union leadership. The Murmansk officials, with the spotlight of a national publication on them, must have mended their ways.

During fall 1935, the rank and file of at least two factories were able to achieve the firing of supervisors who failed to satisfy them in the new situation. Both cases involved heads of production shops, an important position, particularly in heavy industry. At the Chisovsk metal plant, workers ousted the head of the rolling shop for forbidding them to finish more than fifty tons of metal per shift. "For sabotage of the [Stakhanovite] movement," the head of another rolling shop, this one at the Chernozem metal factory, lost his post "at the insistence of a [production] conference."[88]

These conferences, so prominent in the late 1920s, now began to revive. In October 1935 the party Central Committee and the National Trade Union Council together issued a circular to all union organizations directing them to see that the "basic content of work of the production conferences becomes the struggle for the removal of shortcomings hampering the Stakhanovite movement." Among the problems listed were defects in the organization of production, supply of materials, and the "inertness" of managerial personnel.[89]

Numerous reports indicate that production conferences did in fact respond to the new thrusts of Stakhanovism. In its early phase, the sources imply, all workers in a given setting were welcome to attend the meetings. At the Vostokostal' plant, workers made 87 percent more proposals for changes in production in 1936 than they had in 1935. During September 1935 workers at the Skorokhod shoe factory in Leningrad made 78 proposals at production conferences; in October, after the Stakhanovite movement had gained momentum and publicity, they made 212 suggestions. Two hundred fifty more followed at November meetings.[90]

Proletarians undoubtedly offered many ideas in the hope that they might be recognized as Stakhanovites simply by virtue of such contributions; nevertheless, they probably felt greater legitimacy for the political system because their views were being so widely solicited. This result emerges in an account from a railroad depot in Zagorsk, about forty-five miles north of Moscow. In the fall of 1935 the conferences "began not with words but with deeds." Workers now seriously examined problems in carrying out repairs. " 'Until this time we had the opinion that blabbing was the occupation of the production conferences. Now we see that it isn't that way,' said workers."[91]

At the important Stalin Auto Factory in Moscow, today the Likhachev works, the conferences also changed radically with the advent of the Stakhanovite movement. "At once the production conferences ceased to be boring. Earlier at these conferences foremen spoke most, and [they] spoke about fulfillment of the [production] program only drily. Now the important issues of vital practice are considered there." Workers raised questions about how to improve specific jobs; discussions were concrete, down to which engineers and technicians would help workers and how. These changes improved communications at the factory between technical personnel and ordinary hands.[92] The production conferences had revived as an important arena for workers, one that managers could not ignore.

In these ways Stakhanovism pressured industrial executives to listen carefully to the lower ranks.[93] Four former workers from Moscow's major auto factory insisted that the director, Ivan A. Likhachev, kept his door open for all employees. He spent considerable time among them on the factory floor and always listened to them. If someone made a proposal to him, he would immediately direct a subordinate to follow it up. He enjoyed so much authority in the factory that he could afford to speak frankly if he thought an idea was not worthwhile, a comment that suggests the workers believed other managers lacked such status.[94] Likhachev's approach must have helped not only to save him from arrest but to secure his position for decades.

When N. M. Borodin managed a meat packing plant in Baku before the war, he considered it his duty to spend two hours a day listening to workers' grievances. They came to him with matters ranging from "wages which sometimes were not sufficient to keep body and soul together, or the rudeness of a foreman, to bad living accommodations which were insufficient for an already large family with the prospect of a new baby arriving." They wanted financial help in connection with sickness or a death in the family. Borodin sometimes even acted as a marriage counselor.[95] He too survived the Terror unscathed.[96]

At first some managers resisted the Stakhanovite movement, because it challenged their authority and disrupted their legal and illegal methods of running factories.[97] The regime responded to this foot-dragging with considerable repression among executives from the fall of 1935 to early 1936. In addition, workers also sometimes suffered arrest because they undermined rate busting by assaulting or even murdering early Stakhanovites.[98] Later it became clear, however, that the new norms were not onerous and that the movement was becoming a mass phenomenon.

As this happened, the Presidium of the Supreme Court of the USSR, probably recognizing that a harsh reaction was only likely to increase discontent, announced a change in policy in March 1936. It reported that "in many cases courts have incorrectly judged individual backward workers as enemies of the people for incorrect remarks." Such statements, the court continued, often reflected workers' inability to cope with the new conditions; that is, some could not make the new norms. Workers' negative remarks did not "indicate their opposition to the Stakhanovite movement or sabotage." What was needed was not judicial action but "mass explanatory work."[99] In other words, workers were not to be punished for speaking against the movement; instead, managers and other officials were directed to help discontented proletarians master the new standards.

On the other hand, the attitude of the regime toward managers and their sabotage remained erratic for a time; on March 26 a headline in *Pravda* read, "Open Fire on Saboteurs of the Stakhanovite Movement." Managers and local party leaders had allegedly been holding the movement back.[100] But in addition to the change in court practice, important voices spoke for a milder course. In November 1935, Ordzhonikidze dropped his earlier reference to sabotage of Stakhanovism by managers and stressed that "the best part" of them headed the new drive.[101] In late June 1936, he hedged somewhat by saying that managers were not leading the movement. But to believe that supervisors were saboteurs was "nonsense."[102]

Mixed signals continued throughout this period. In April the official journal of the Commissariat of Justice denounced the prosecution of workers *and* technical personnel for opposition to Stakhanovism, arguing that this practice was a direct violation of Stalin's words in November 1935.[103] What he had said was in fact not quite so beneficent: the "conservative elements of industry" who were not helping the movement should be persuaded to fall in line. Failing that, "more decisive measures" should be taken.[104] Nevertheless, his words did lend themselves to the clear change in court policy in the spring of the next year, when the Commissariat of Justice informed judges and prosecutors that coercion was not to be applied to critics of Stakhanovism, especially when they were workers. This shift followed the improvement in legal procedures and the lessening of tension that proceeded well into 1936.

Even negative remarks about Stakhanovism as a policy, which constituted a direct challenge to the regime, did not always result in arrest. An archival report of late 1935 lists several workers having been excluded from the party or a union or fired for criticism of the movement but does not indicate that they were arrested.[105] A former mining engineer recalled that "in our mine there was an old worker who was not afraid" to say that Stakhanovism was "screwing" the labor force.[106] A woman identified as a "pure proletarian" pronounced the campaign "nonsense" at her factory, but the only result was that managers quietly reprimanded her.[107] When a young woman at one plant got a set of Lenin's works as a prize for her job performance, an old worker called out, "That's what the whore deserves." Laughter and some confusion followed, "but finally nothing was done about it."[108]

In contrast to these negative comments, some émigré workers indicated that they and their peers appraised Stakhanovism much more neutrally or even somewhat positively. The man just cited also said that, beyond the incident with Lenin's works, "you could not observe any isolation of Stakhanovites from the rest of the workers."[109] A former lathe operator called Stakhanovites "people who worked well. Everywhere, there are some who work well and some who do not work so well." Almost as an afterthought to this casual appraisal, he added, "Also, they do what the government wants—they raise the norms." But he indicated no rancor about that fact.[110]

Although the campaign for Stakhanovism and its trail of repression declined during 1936, the legacy of the movement played a role during the Terror. In the hysterical months of 1937 and 1938, workers accused managers of deliberately holding back production. The Stakhanovite Iakov Chaikovskii, a steel maker at the Comintern plant, "sharply criticized the executives of the factory" in the summer of 1937. Earlier the plant had been a leading one, he claimed, thanks to the movement. But now the administration displayed a "formal attitude" toward it, and the situation had regressed. It was necessary "to bring order into production arrangements" so that "big outputs" could be achieved again. In the same report a Stakhanovite from a Khar'kov factory accused management of allowing the movement to develop chaotically. Workers did not know from one day to the next which jobs they would be assigned. All this confusion was linked to enemies in a series of factories.[111]

In September 1937 workers in the machine-tool field refused to use a certain model of lathe, saying that it was too high and too difficult to operate. The charge then arose that the lathe, a foreign machine, had been bought on purpose by wreckers.[112] Workers at the Svobodnyi Proletarii textile mill outside Moscow "exposed" a foreman as a member of Menshevik organizations in 1917–19.[113] Such denunciations from below, coupled with rapid turnover among administrators caused by arrests and their own inclination to move, damaged discipline in industry. Workers had less reason than before to respect or obey their superiors. The laws of December 1938 and January 1939 were probably partly an effort to improve managerial control following the disruptions caused by the Terror, partly an effort to boost production in view of the growing military threat.

Yet discipline was a chronic sore point in industry; from 1934 to the eve of the war, documents from various levels refer to problems.[114] To some extent this lament was a hackneyed theme of the managers, who could use it to explain difficulties in production. Lack of discipline was one of the major reasons the linen industry failed to make its plan in 1938, a high executive said early the next year. He linked the problem to wrecking, probably to be even more on the safe side.[115] The leitmotiv of "poor discipline" reflected not only managers' excuses, however, but also their perennial inability to control workers. Although the Terror hurt order in the factories, it exacerbated existing problems rather than creating a qualitatively different situation.

Even during the chaos and frenzied mood of 1937–38, difficulties within factories did not necessarily prove fatal to managers. In May 1937 a meeting of the *aktiv,* the most energetic employees, consisting of Stakhanovites, engineers, and technical personnel, took place at the Red Star factory. Speakers were not identified by occupation, but Stakhanovites at least listened to a frank exchange of views on production problems. Several participants traded charges about whose fault the difficulties were. But the discussion did not lead to arrest; instead, a member of the aktiv suggested a "simple resolution": the antagonists should "think over all defects, take measures and the matter will go better."[116] This story is reminiscent of General Grigorenko's experience at the Moscow General Staff Academy, recounted in Chapter 3; here, too, arrests were not allowed to gain momentum in the first place. Criticism did not have to mean rancor or repression.

Managers who enjoyed high support within their plants weathered open discussions much better than those who were unpopular.

The regime found it almost impossible to regulate workers, who were able to skirt laws repeatedly, often with the help and understanding of managers. Shortages of labor, especially of skilled people, compelled industrial executives to accommodate workers whenever possible. Repeated efforts to control the flow of proletarians around the country failed each time.

Workers could influence their environment and take part in decision making by leaving one job for another, slowing down their work when it was time to set new norms, denouncing managers, or simply by voicing their opinions. Managers, desperate to fulfill their production plans and facing grave danger if they did not, had to listen.

The Stakhanovite movement gave workers even more opportunity to speak out and to demand improved conditions. Simultaneously, the campaign sharpened tensions in production. At the start of the movement, these problems were mostly between workers, who, by tradition, were seriously divided anyway.[117] But when the new norms of 1936 proved attainable and the whole movement broadened considerably, friction between workers subsided to its old level.

Stakhanovism, however, left serious animosity between workers and managers. Workers tended to blame superiors for the lack of opportunity to become Stakhanovites. Some leading officials agreed, though not without considerable vacillation. By mid-1936, the leadership's concerns about sabotage of the movement by managers and technicians paralleled the new fear of enemies. These two strands of doubt about loyalty did not merge overtly until the Kemerovo explosions in September, when charges of sabotage became prominent; but after that, they fed each other. Piatakov, a defendant in the second Moscow show trial, in January 1937, had been both a former Trotskyite and an industrial executive. Thereafter managers and technical personnel across the USSR were screened more closely than ever before for signs of wrecking and ties to the old oppositions. Workers took an active role in this grim examination.

Finally, the regime's approach to Stakhanovism represents another story of hesitation and contradiction. In a number of basic respects, such as qualifications to be a Stakhanovite, no clear policy ever emerged. More important was the point that from the fall of 1935 into the spring of 1936 the leadership was not united or consistent on the question of whether industrial administrators were sabotaging the movement. Once again Stalinism was not a monolithic phenomenon, and Stalin did not impose a firm policy on the country.

Workers' Institutions for Criticism and Participation in Decision Making

The Stakhanovite movement can be seen as a temporary phenomenon. But a variety of more permanent institutions facilitated expression of grievances and influence on the factory environment.

Although a number of the twenty-six émigré factory employees interviewed by J. K. Zawodny in the early 1950s spoke of the important role fear of arrest played in their lives, their specific stories often convey a different picture.[118] One of his respondents, a former accountant, spoke positively of the way grievances were handled: "Honestly, I have to say that the People's Court usually rendered just sentences favoring the workers, particularly with regard to housing cases."[119] A man who had begun as a worker and risen to become an electrical engineer and finally chief of a shift in a power station reported that "anyone could complain in a formal way, especially when he had the law behind him. He could even write to a paper, and in this way to let the higher officials know about his complaint."[120] This often happened: for example, in the first half of 1935 workers sent two thousand letters to the newspaper of the Voroshilov factory in Vladivostok.[121]

Judging by letters in other factory newspapers, many of the ones to this paper were critical of conditions and people in the plant. Workers at the Svobodnyi Proletarii textile mill in Moscow oblast' wrote to their factory newspaper to demand apartments and improvement of "inhuman conditions" in a barracks and to insist that the plant administration direct a foreman to work better with ordinary weavers and relate attentively to their needs.[122] Similar complaints about housing appeared in the newspaper *Kirovets,* published by the union committee of a metal plant in the Donbass.[123]

The regime regularly urged people to criticize local conditions as well as leaders, at least those below an exalted level. For example, in March 1937 Stalin emphasized the importance of the party's "ties to the masses." To maintain them, it was necessary "to listen carefully to the voice of the masses, to the voice of rank and file members of the party, to the voice of the so-called 'little people,' to the voice of ordinary folk [*narod*]."[124] *Pravda* went so far as to identify lack of criticism with enemies of the people: "*Only an enemy* is interested in seeing that we, the Bolsheviks . . . do not notice actual reality. . . . Only an enemy . . . *strives to put the rose-colored glasses of self-satisfaction* over the eyes of our people."[125] As the Zawodny materials and a mass of other evidence show, these calls were by no means merely a vicious sham that permitted only carefully chosen, reliable individuals to make "safe" criticisms.[126]

Obviously limits existed to the objections one could raise, yet that simple truth also obscures the fact that many important matters were open to frank discussion. An émigré construction engineer, citing his experiences before World War II, remarked about criticism that "the Soviet system is a dictatorship, but on the other side you must recognize that there exists a big criticism of the small and responsible workers excluding criticism of the regime, the Party or the Politburo. No doubt in their authority can be expressed, and a word against the regime, the Politburo or the Party and this is the end of you. You can criticize the secretary of a raikom but it is fairly dangerous. Also you can criticize comrade Ivanov [the equivalent of Mr. Smith] who works as a [second or lower] secretary of the raikom. If you criticize him nothing will come to you." The engineer maintained that such a figure was open to criticism even regarding official duties. "If you do this you defend the Soviet regime by criticizing the way he does his Party work."[127] Speaking out was a good deal safer, it should be added, if the critic had a desirable social background as a child of the old oppressed classes.

What happened when ordinary people took their grievances to the authorities or to the press? A civil engineer interviewed after the war remembered that people frequently complained about the poor quality of construction and that he had to spend considerable time responding. Citizens protested to the city soviet "and then when they see that it doesn't help they write direct to Stalin." Answers would come back to his organization from Stalin's secretariat with a standard message: "We send these complaints to you for investigation and taking of necessary measures." The chief of the entire housing administration in the area would then tell the engineer, "Let me know in three days what has been done."[128]

Numerous examples exist of these standardized replies from central organs concerned with complaints, which, in addition to Stalin's secretariat, included such bodies as the Party Control Commission and the Special Sector of the Central Committee. On the local level, authorities had to respond to replies and directives coming from above.[129] The Party Control Commission, it will be recalled, was headed by Nikolai Ezhov from early 1935 until late 1938. To give one example of how the complaint process operated, in early 1936 a worker at the

Red Handicraft factory complained, apparently to various offices, about corruption, delays in pay, and rudeness by the officials of his *artel'* (a voluntary, cooperative association of workers). Four separate investigations followed, two by the oblast' party committee, one by an official of the relevant union, and one by the oblast' procuracy. Several of these confirmed the accusations, and the artel' leaders had to take steps to correct the situation, while the regional party secretary had to report to oblast' authorities in Smolensk on his monitoring of the affair.[130] Surely the artel' officials then behaved better toward their workers.

Stalin encouraged outspokenness in other ways. In May 1935, as a replacement for the old slogan "Technology Decides Everything," he offered "Cadres Decide Everything." In this context, cadres meant almost anyone, for, he continued, this policy "demands that our leaders display the most careful attitude toward our workers, toward the 'small' and the 'big,' no matter what area they work in."[131] In the city of Smolensk, workers immediately took his words to heart and demanded pay increases.[132] Referring to the new slogan, an article in the major trade union journal in September 1935 lashed out at housing conditions for workers at the electrical stations of Uzbekistan. The article cited one case of six workers living in a single room of forty-three square feet, and another of three families occupying a room of seventy-five square feet. Some employees slept on bare earthen floors.[133]

Sometimes complaining did not go well for the initiator. A lathe operator, working as an instructor in 1936, had a conflict with the raion party committee over his housing. He had gone to the party and his labor union about the problem but had concluded that they wanted bribes from him. At that point he wrote to *Trud,* which published his letter. Immediately the town party committee called him in. "Do you know that it is forbidden to write a letter like that?" an official asked him.[134] The question seems almost surreal, because a national periodical would hardly publish a forbidden complaint.

In another case the local reaction to criticism was more severe. Two foremen at a repair depot of the Viazemsk railroad station in Siberia had criticized the poor performance of their workplace in October 1936. They were charged with making counterrevolutionary statements and in April 1937 received prison sentences, one for five years, the other for two. But in early July, despite the tense atmosphere of the moment, the appeals college of the Khabarovsk oblast' court overturned the judgment and ordered them released.[135]

Regional authorities often differed from national leaders in their reactions to criticism from below. Complaints challenged the power of local officials, and some led to reallocation of scarce resources and unwanted, dangerous scrutiny from above. Provincial satraps therefore sometimes acted severely to throttle or punish criticism.[136]

National authorities took a different view and encouraged criticism from below, primarily for three reasons. First, it was a check on the pretensions and behavior of local officials. Second, it was a way of getting some reliable information about performance. Given the penchant of Soviet administrators to lie about what was happening, frank statements were highly prized at the upper levels of government. Third, workers' ability to criticize made them feel that they played a significant role in their own affairs and that their views were taken seriously. In short, the opportunity to express grievances increased workers' sense that the Soviet system was legitimate. At the same time, national figures and institutions could convey the sense, not without reason, that they defended ordinary people against local despots.

Besides offering informal verbal criticisms and writing to newspapers, workers had other recourse when they encountered problems. They could go to the Rates and Conflicts Commissions (RKKs) within their factory to protest decisions regarding pay, job classification, or dismissal. In these bodies, which had the power to overrule administrators' decisions, the employer and factory or shop union committee were equally represented. If workers failed to win their cases in an RKK, they could appeal to the people's courts or to the central committees of their unions.[137] To cite one illustration of this system's operation, in 1938 the central committee of the union of paper workers considered 796 appeals of RKK decisions, 263 of which were resolved in favor of workers. And in 1939, 1,002 protests reached the union central committee;[138] obviously workers were not afraid to use this means of defending their rights. That so many appeals reached the highest body of this union indicates that even greater numbers of cases went through the RKKs themselves.

A former shop chief in a textile mill recalled how the RKK worked in his section of the plant until 1935, when he moved to a higher position. The RKK "was very good indeed; the worker could go by himself and complain. . . . We wanted to give the worker justice and a good deal as far as we could." Workers with grievances testified personally, and "the larger factories allowed a worker to be represented by an old, experienced worker who was designated by the trade union."[139]

Unions also helped with workers' problems by sending officials called *instruktory* from the organizations' headquarters to factories, where they listened to complaints. These were then transmitted to higher officials of the unions or the government.[140] A story told by a former shop chief in a factory further illustrates, among other things, the role unions could play in handling workers' grievances. He gave no date for the incident, but apparently it occurred just before the war. A young mother in his shop needed to breast-feed her baby three times a day. The distance between the plant and its nursery was almost a mile and a half, so that all she was doing on the job was hiking back and forth. The chief, however, could not release her from production. He described her appeals:

> She went to the Director and he didn't allow her to leave. The poor girl went to her [union] steward, told him her story, but he didn't do anything for her. Therefore, she went, on her own, to the Trade Union Plant Committee. They listened to her and they telephoned to the Director. The Director told them, "Look, this an ordnance factory. I have to fulfill the Plan." Therefore, the Plant Committee, also said No to her. She was so unhappy and so tired that she went to the Secretary of the Plant Party Committee and he told her a story about the country being in danger and said No. So she continued, but the child became ill, and the people among the workers started to get restless and to talk back. Finally, the women workers one day got the steward in a corner, swore at him, shouted, and pushed him around, and all these women told him that something worse would happen to him if he didn't do something about this girl.

Following that incident the union committee advised her to feign illness, which she did. Only then was she allowed to leave the factory.[141]

This story depicts workers who were unafraid to insist on the answer they wanted, to show solidarity with one another over a human problem, and to threaten a minor official with violence if he did not find a solution. Although the factory union committee and the director reacted negatively at first to the woman's problems, they were willing to listen to individual complaints, and this in a plant with forty thousand workers. To be sure, a harsh law created the problem in the first place, but the people on the spot found a way around it.

Thus labor unions exercised some power on workers' behalf in the second half of the decade. Another former worker, later an administrator in a municipal power plant, speaking of the union there before the war, commented that "it was established and acted on the basis of excellent legislation. The directives were also really very good." The union's legal power was "very good because it embraced all possible conflicts which could occur."[142]

Union meetings and elections provided yet another outlet for workers' complaints. Evidence from a number of sessions held in 1937 shows that participants exchanged harsh assessments and criticisms of factory union leadership and working conditions. For example, a female member of the union committee in a shop of the Kazan' linen mill had to defend herself against charges from the rank and file that she had been rude to workers and had withheld passes to resorts.[143]

On occasion, union factory committees even behaved aggressively toward plant directors. In June 1935 the committee of the Svobodnyi Proletarii textile mill heard a report by the director that newly arriving workers would receive apartments or dormitory space. He promised to take care of all shortcomings in housing. The unionists then warned him that if past "disorders" in accommodations reappeared, he would be "brought to the strictest accounting."[144] In view of the frequency with which managers were arrested for abuse of their positions or wrecking, this was not an idle threat. At another linen union session, this one of the oblast' committee in Sverdlovsk, held in December 1937, the members resolved "categorically to forbid the directors of linen mills" to permit overtime in violation of the law. Heads of factory committees were to monitor compliance. Those leaders and the directors were also ordered to hold meetings of workers and employees on raising the wages of the lowest paid, in connection with a government decree of the preceding month.[145] In May 1941, the oblast' union committee of the Smolensk linen workers, after hearing a complaint from an ordinary weaver about pay, overturned an RKK decision against him and obligated the director to pay the worker according to the collective agreement on wages in force in the mill.[146]

Such instances occurred in other industries, too; in February 1938 the central committee of the union of machine-tool workers ordered the new director of a factory to correct various dangerous conditions within two weeks; other problems had to be rectified by December. The committee also ordered the new head of the entire industry to fulfill an agreement on safety signed in January 1938, or the case would be brought to the "corresponding organs."[147] Workers in these instances stood firmly on their rights and relied on central institutions to defend them.

These criticisms and threats from below challenged newly appointed administrators, undercutting the assertion that criticism was allowed only against those the regime had already decided to remove.[148] In another case, speakers at a union election meeting heavily scolded one of their officials, yet he received the most votes of anyone present in the selection of an important commission.[149] Criticism was encouraged and sometimes staged from above, but it was also an everyday occurrence that came from the workers themselves.

The Commissariat of Justice was another institution that heard and responded to workers' appeals. In August 1935 the Saratov city prosecutor reported that of 118 cases regarding pay recently handled by his office, 90, or 76.3 percent, had been resolved in favor of workers.[150] Representatives of the Commissariat occasionally went to factories to solicit or respond to complaints, as happened in Khabarovsk in July 1936.[151]

The Komsomol, often quite active in the factories because of the workers' youthfulness, probably served as a particularly common channel for complaints. Aleksandr Kosarev, its head for years until his arrest in November 1938, received a constant stream of letters on such subjects as pay improperly held back or lack of protective clothing on a job. According to one almost hagiographical account of Kosarev, he reacted to every letter by directing the Komsomol to investigate and report back to him.[152] A more sober document from 1936 mentioned that Kosarev had been able to operate through the Komsomol Central Committee and the national procuracy to win the release of ten workers falsely arrested for fighting. They had received jail terms of up to six years, and their conviction was upheld by an appeals court. But after they wrote to Kosarev about their plight, the national Supreme Court overturned the judgment and ordered those guilty of a "bureaucratic attitude" toward the workers to be brought to justice.[153] Once more, central officials were more lenient and approachable than their local counterparts.

Pressure to satisfy workers' requests also came from regional party officials. A. S. Shcherbakov, a party secretary in Leningrad oblast′ at the time, urged area union officials in September 1936 to meet workers' demands. "It should sound like a formal accusation to you," he said, when workers brought up problems like bedbugs in dormitories, the lack of radios there, or the absence of "concrete help" from factory administrators.[154]

To a fair extent, the Communist Party acted as a gigantic complaint bureau across the country. Party cell meetings and elections also served as forums for grievances and even attacks on superiors. At a meeting of the party committee in Leningrad's Bolshevik Factory, held less than two weeks before the German invasion, a member of the committee announced that in one shop work conditions were "extremely hard" and that the "elementary daily needs of the workers are not being satisfied." There were no toilets, snack bar, cafeteria, or ventilation. These problems had "produced indignation" among the workers, who had started to petition the committee for improvements. Meanwhile, several had attempted suicide, one successfully.[155] Obviously conditions in the plant were desperate, but at least workers could use organizational channels to protest and get a response. Elections for factory party committees featured multiple candidates and debates about their qualifications, during which workers spoke out about their local leaders and conditions.[156]

Hundreds of thousands of workers further enhanced their ability to wield a degree of local power by serving in special inspectorates, commissions, and brigades that checked the work of managers and institutions.[157] For instance, V. R. Balkan, a former worker turned inspector, together with a union official, investigated an accident at his Moscow factory in 1937. Finding the cause to be improper testing of materials, the two fined the head of the production shop one hundred rubles, probably several days' pay, and placed a reprimand in the foreman's record.[158] The book that recounted this story was published in a guide for other union personnel and therefore encouraged similar action by workers.

These and many other examples show that for industrial hands the division between state and society was porous or vague, also the finding of a recent study of peasants and official positions on the collective farms.[159] Workers became instructors and inspectors and served on people's courts, rates and conflicts commissions, and similar bodies. In these roles they possessed authority over their peers and sometimes over their superiors as well. They could impose sanctions of their own or initiate proceedings in the regular courts. Such actions were an exercise of powers normally associated with the state. Workers who carried out authoritative functions could feel that the state was theirs in some fashion because it was; they were part of it. Workers who did not take part directly in institutions with state responsibilities could still appeal to such bodies, obtain a hearing, and typically receive a reasonable response.

While sane, calm, and sober, Soviet workers would not have dared to say that socialism was a poor system or that Stalin was an idiot. But bounds on speech allowed much open discussion of topics deeply significant to workers, including some aspects of production norms, pay rates and classifications, safety on the job, housing, and treatment by managers. This permitted discourse, and its results, often satisfying to industrial hands, occurred at a time when American workers in particular were struggling for basic union recognition,[160] which, even when they won it, did not necessarily provide much formal influence at the work place. Several men who had been employed in both Soviet and American factories told interviewers in the United States that plant conditions and atmosphere had been superior in the USSR.[161] Soviet workers were hardly better off or freer than their

American counterparts in the 1930s, but they had some important rights and opportunities, especially regarding criticism and decision making, which meant a lot to them.

Of course, Soviet industrial workers still struggled with profound poverty, abysmal working conditions in many cases, and tyrannical bosses in others. A director of a timber operation allegedly took workers to the job site at the point of a gun—but for this and other illegal acts he was condemned as a wrecker and sentenced to death in early 1939.[162] Young recruits for the obligatory labor-reserves program, which began in 1940, appeared almost like convicts in one photograph. Heads shaven and wearing uniforms, they were given ten minutes to march from their school to "practical exercises," which consisted of chopping wood in this example. As they marched, what looked like an officer walked beside them.[163] But this development had to do with the pressing needs of industry as the war approached.

Workers were sometimes forced to work on shifts they did not want or were pressured into overtime, though in some cases they protested vigorously.[164] Some were arrested arbitrarily and then returned to their jobs at reduced pay, under NKVD supervision, as a relatively mild form of forced labor.[165] It is impossible to say how many found themselves in this situation or how bad it really was. Occasionally they went without justification into the gulag or to their deaths.

The most important elements in determining the lot of workers, however, were their initiative, level of skill and experience, and personal relations with superiors, all of which varied tremendously, depending on human circumstances and workplace conditions. The industrial labor force continued to enjoy its most basic freedom, the ability to move and change jobs, on a broad scale until the war. Curtailment of this right resulted primarily from military needs, not from some fundamental imperative of the regime.

Far from basing its rule on the negative means of coercion, the Soviet state in the late 1930s fostered a limited but positive political role for the populace. In a system whose officials at virtually all levels felt tremendous pressures to juggle figures and lie to their superiors, frank information was of great value. If it came from workers, nominally the country's rulers, so much the better. Complaints and suggestions constantly flowed upward, giving the authorities at higher levels at least the illusion that they were in touch with the people. Central officials could appear to be the defenders of the common folk. As evidence cited here has already suggested, workers sometimes believed that that was true. An emigrant mason said that a worker "can write to the ministry and submit his complaint and the ministry will send an investigating commission and arrest the offender."[166] A former norm setter said in emigration that he had valued "the simplicity of relation" in the factories. "There they will never tell you: 'You are a worker and I am a director; you have to stand up when you talk to me.'" Anyone with a complaint could go to the plant director, to the chief of the factory's political department, or even to a member of the party Central Committee.[167]

There is, in fact, an example of a worker speaking directly to a CC member, K. Ryndin. When Ryndin toured the Cheliabinsk tractor factory in early 1938, a worker told him that he might learn a lot from the ordinary hands. "But you don't invite us to see you, and when you come to the factory, then around you there are so many bosses of all kinds, it's a dog's wedding, that no one can come up to you." The phrase about nuptials drew "laughter, noise" and approval from the CC plenum that heard the tale.[168]

In September 1936 the worker M. A. Panov wrote an angry letter to I. P. Rumiantsev, then first secretary of Smolensk oblast'. Panov had been "without a party card" for two years and lately had been out of work, too. After complaining to the Secretariat of the Council of Ministers, he had learned that his case had been referred to Rumiantsev. Ten days had gone by, but "you are still fooling around," Panov wrote to this local chieftain; "it's time to end this red tape and get down to work." Declaring, "You speak beautifully, but in fact it must be said that that's hot air," the worker announced that he would give Rumiantsev three days to act or he would complain to the party Central Committee. He made sure to add that he was not an "opportunist, Trotskyite, or Zinovievite, but one of our own."[169] Panov, like many other workers, thought that he had a right to criticize a high party official, then a member of the Central Committee, and to demand attention from him. Stalin had said, "Listen to the voice of the people," and his regime favored such positive elements in the system, for they encouraged greater productivity, satisfaction, and commitment to the state.

Workers on the Eve of the War

In the years just before the war, both the Terror and the Stakhanovite movement faded, while managerial authority revived. The press spoke frequently of the need to support managers and engineers, and the police ceased to arrest them so cavalierly.[170] These changes helped bring a long period of industrial turbulence to a close; with its passing, workers' opportunities to protest and participate in decision making declined.

Yet this loss of influence in the workplace was only relative to the levels of the preceding few years. Workers continued to protest firings to the rates and conflicts commissions, the union inspectors, and the courts.[171] Grievances still came to other officials, too, for instance, the 231 "toilers' complaints" to the Altai krai soviet for the period February 15–March 19, 1940.[172] In the 24 months following September 1937, the central committee of the communication workers' union received 2,007 complaints from workers about "incorrect" actions of managers. Of these, 432 were resolved in favor of the workers, 837 were rejected, and the rest were still "in process" at the time of the report.[173]

During Leningrad factory meetings in 1937–39, workers were outspoken about problems ranging from low pay through poor supply of materials to a firing after a conflict with a foreman. The worker Krumgol'ts castigated the management of the Leningrad mechanical factory in May 1939 for its "poor use of cadres" and "disorderly attitude toward people and work." He attacked the director for failure to "check decisions" in his shop. At the same session the worker Barzin related his firing as a "disorganizer" after a conflict with a foreman in which he had cursed the boss "Russian style." This description drew laughter from the audience.[174] In a city that had supposedly suffered at least as much as any other in the Terror, workers still criticized a director to his face and regained a job after berating a supervisor.

One émigré recalled that before the war his stepmother, a factory worker, "often scolded the boss" and also complained about living conditions but was never arrested.[175] John Scott attended a meeting at a Moscow factory in 1940 where workers were able to "criticize the plant director, [and] make suggestions as to how to increase production, improve quality, and lower costs."[176]

An incident from 1939 demonstrates even greater boldness on the part of a worker. During one of the periodic drives to get workers to buy government bonds, the party committee of a factory called in all the personnel to sign up. A witness remembered that "there was even a man we knew worked for [the] NKVD at the table. A girl came in—a Komsomolka. They gave her the standard speech—she had to work for nothing for a while. She just turned around, bent down, put her skirt over her head, and she said, 'Comrade Stalin and you all can kiss me whenever it is most convenient for you,' and she left. I am telling you, I saw that and I was numb with fear. All those men behind the table, they just sat silently. Finally, one of them said, 'Did you notice, she didn't have pants on?' and everybody started to laugh." The witness was numb with fear, though needlessly; the girl got away with her act.[177] The atmosphere of 1939 did not cow workers, and even an insult to Stalin did not result in arrest.

Aktiv meetings at Leningrad factories in 1940 were relatively calm. No charges of wrecking appeared, but worker participants continued to voice criticisms. A gathering at the Red Vyborzhets factory in June 1940, for instance, quietly but frankly covered problems in production. The worker Sheinin remarked that in the eight or nine years he had been there, this was the first meeting he had attended that was "devoted exclusively to economic problems."[178] In this sphere his right to be heard was intact.

Grigorii Tokaev was in charge of a laboratory dealing with aircraft technology in 1940–41. He was accused of sabotage, namely, wasting exactly thirteen minutes of his laboratory's time. At a meeting of the party cell attended by workers and scientists, the former jumped to his defense. A worker challenged an accusing scientist—hadn't Comrade Tokaev blocked the man's attempt at corruption? Another called the same scientist a liar.[179] In the city of Nikolaev in 1938 the director of a sanitation truck depot severely criticized a driver at an employees' meeting, with the goal of intimidating him and keeping him on the job. But the worker, who reported the story in emigration, asked the chief mechanic to defend him. After the mechanic praised the driver's conscientious work, "the director's mouth was immediately shut. He said he was misinformed." The driver left on the next day to take a better job.[180] In these and many other cases, workers behaved proudly and aggressively toward superiors; they stood firmly on their rights.

Of course dissatisfaction did exist. In March 1937 party members at the Bolshevik factory in Leningrad reported hearing one worker say to another, "You know, we are insignificant people, but those [administrators] are parasites, those sons of bitches."[181] Was this more than a typical resentment of social superiors that can be found around the world? A recent study of such statements concludes that workers felt deeply alienated from higher strata and from the regime. But like this book, the same investigation also shows that workers constantly took the trouble to protest to various organizations and periodicals, from which they demanded a thoughtful response.[182] Alienated people do not bother to express their grievances in this way any more than they bother to vote. During the 1930s American workers frequently voiced deep resentment about their "slavery" and the way their social superiors lived and behaved.[183] Yet by and large such critics did not become disenchanted with the political structure. Instead, they virtually worshipped Franklin Roosevelt and appealed to him or other government figures for help.

The psychologist Robert Coles, in conversations with lower-class American families over the course of many years, often encountered strong resentment toward the rich, liberals, intellectuals, and politicians—but intense expressions of patriotism frequently accompanied this feeling.[184] The same combination may well have occurred in the USSR under Stalin. Class or group antagonism does not necessarily lead to rejection of a system, particularly when those on the bottom receive some satisfaction from their complaints, have the ability to move, and occasionally exercise significant power over their superiors.

There was much to complain about and to resent in the USSR. Nonetheless, émigrés with experience in Soviet industry regularly pointed to positive aspects of the grievance structure and its responses to problems. Other material suggests that workers' attitudes toward their overall situation were often relatively positive by the eve of the war. One émigré recalled that life was getting better in 1940 and linked this change to people's willingness to fight for the regime.[185] Only thirteen years old at the time, and admittedly young to know how adults felt, he probably absorbed this mood from his father, who was a worker. Further evidence comes from a female chemist born in 1918. She also thought that 1940 was a good time: "There was no unpleasantness, there were no arrests, nobody was sent into exile, there were no denunciations in the newspapers, everybody was working."[186] These remarks accord well with the atmosphere at Leningrad and Moscow factory meetings in the same year. One observer noted that in 1939 the young workers of Leningrad were overwhelmingly loyal.[187] An émigré who had been a worker, then an engineer, believed that "immediately before the war and during the war even the non-Party element was cooperating willingly," though he tempered this statement with the opinion that older workers felt some antipathy to the regime.[188] The great optimism that John Scott found in Magnitogorsk at the same time has already been mentioned.

Workers' dreams of soaring high sometimes came true. "I will be a pilot," wrote a female weaver in her mill's newspaper in early 1937. And she was on her way, studying aviation part-time.[189] Coupled with the opportunities still available to seek other jobs, obtain education, and advance in a career, workers' chances to speak out and help shape the factory world must have meant a great deal to them.[190] Otherwise it is difficult to explain their willingness to volunteer for the army in 1941 (see Chapter 7); the level of Soviet war production, achieved under extraordinarily difficult circumstances; or the victory itself.

It may be correct to say that as a *class* Soviet workers were weak under Stalin.[191] But workers demonstrated solidarity, got their way against unpopular managers, and evinced an understanding that they were different from other social groups. Workers knew how to use the language of the regime in their own interests; if common "discourse," including the use of words, symbols, and symbolic actions, is a marker of class, then Soviet workers often displayed their "classness."

Workers probably cared considerably less about class than about material comforts, job security, polite treatment, the chance to move, and opportunities to speak out. Most of all, workers probably wanted high status in the workplace or, better yet, a way to rise to a higher social position. They definitely seized the many opportunities available under the Soviet regime to move up and out of their social milieu.[192]

Compromises, contradictions, and rapid changes were facts of Soviet factory life in the late 1930s. A few miles or blocks away from the Kremlin, managers had to figure out how to fulfill the plan and keep workers on the job at the same time. Ultimately, much of industrial life was not controlled by government or party decrees, which expressed pious wishes more often than they described successful results. In this context workers contributed their thoughts and exercised influence in their environment. Neither martyrs nor helpless puppets, they played a significant role in both the achievements of the period and its state-sponsored violence.

7

The Acid Test of Stalinism: Popular Response to World War II

At about 3:00 A.M. on Sunday, June 22, 1941, just as the first light began to spread across the northern European skies, German troops and satellite forces smashed across the Soviet borders. Some 4.6 million invaders were met by 2.9 million defenders.[1] Right from the start, the German campaign was a stunning success. The attackers quickly overran Soviet border posts, caught and destroyed the bulk of the defenders' air force on the ground, and pushed deep into the USSR. In many places Red Army units simply collapsed; communications and supplies were hopelessly disorganized. After a little more than four days, German armored units had penetrated more than 230 miles inside Soviet territory. On July 16 Smolensk fell, 500 miles into the USSR and only 250 from Moscow. The Germans surrounded Leningrad by September 8 and took Kiev on September 20. By November 27 they had entered the suburbs of Moscow and come within fifteen miles of the Kremlin.[2]

Then the desperate Soviet resistance stiffened, and enemy troops were thrown back with considerable losses. The battles before Moscow of late 1941 were probably decisive; the Wehrmacht never again wielded the force of the previous summer. Although German forces surged forward again in 1942, they did not achieve their strategic objectives. The tide turned against them forever with the defeat at Stalingrad in early 1943.

This chapter provides some background on the Red Army up to the summer of 1941 and then examines morale in the first five months of combat, when more than three million Soviet soldiers were captured.[3] In examining the army's conduct in the early fighting, the major issue is how much the surrenders stemmed from hatred of the regime and how much from more strictly military or wartime difficulties. Both German and Soviet sources, some newly opened but many available for decades, allow a systematic look at this question.

During World War II millions of people in the USSR had the choice of supporting their system or turning against it. Industrialization, purchased at such an immense cost since collectivization, would now have to prove its worth. In the struggle with Germany, Stalinism won, but was that because of its achievements or in spite of itself?

The Red Army in Peace and War, 1937-1941

Earlier chapters outlined the arrest of military officers in the late 1930s. However many fell in the Terror, the impact on the ability of the armed services to fight was huge. The problem extended beyond the loss of leadership: some of the army's best strategic and tactical thinkers disappeared, and fewer capable officers remained to train others.

The last point became crucial during the tremendous expansion of the Red Army. In 1936 its standing strength was about 940,000 men; in 1941 it numbered nearly 5 million. To command the added troops, probably at least 255,000 new officers were needed, not counting losses in the fighting of 1938–40 in the Far East, Poland, and Finland.[4] Even if as many as 23,000 officers were slain or permanently dismissed in the Terror, an additional 220,000 had to be found and trained before the Germans came.

Along with this expansion, the Soviet military simultaneously reorganized and switched to new weapons. After 1937 the old territorial units of the army were disbanded in favor of ones kept on active duty, and new generations of tanks, planes, and rockets were adopted. The training men had received for one kind of weapon might have been irrelevant to those they actually had to use when war broke out.[5]

Other European armies went through similar changes in the same period. But the Germans had some advantages in this race to prepare for combat. First, the old Weimar Republic's army had been limited to one hundred thousand men under the Versailles Treaty. But General Hans von Seeckt, like many another German, believed that that constraint was only temporary. He therefore made sure that the men entering the army were potential officers who could be used to command a much larger force when the treaty was quashed. This is exactly what happened after Hitler came to power. Second, the German Wehrmacht gained valuable experience fighting in Poland in 1939 and in Western Europe in the spring of 1940, in addition to developing superb confidence in those campaigns. Third, although there was some purging of German officers under Hitler, the vast majority of the corps came through the 1930s intact.

To further separate military matters from issues of morale in the invasion of 1941, the performance of Soviet armed forces from 1938 to 1940 must be mentioned. Having had a taste of Soviet territory in the Russian Civil War and having occupied Manchuria in 1931, toward the end of the decade the Japanese decided to test Red Army capabilities. Opinions differ on the quality and size of the Japanese forces involved in the major confrontation with the Red Army, which took place in July and August 1939 at a remote site called Nomonhan or Khalkin-Gol, on the Manchurian-Mongolian border.[6] But two Western studies agree that Soviet performance was excellent. The losers "admitted, grudgingly, that the Soviets were a first-class opponent."[7]

If the Red Army fought well against the Japanese, why did it do so poorly in the Finnish War of 1939–40? Leningrad, the second largest Soviet city and a center of industry and military production, was only twenty miles away from Finland and therefore within easy shelling range. Because of this inherent threat, the Soviet leadership wished to push back the Finnish border. The Finns presented no problem by themselves, but they had become quite friendly with the Germans during and after the Russian Civil War. Now, after the fall of Poland in September 1939 and the march of the Wehrmacht right to the western Soviet border, the Finnish issue became acute for Moscow (map 2). In addition, the Kremlin coveted nickel mines in the north of Finland. Stalin offered to trade a large piece of Soviet territory for land close to Leningrad, but the Finns refused.

A country with a population of about 183 million, counting former Polish citizens just incorporated into the USSR, then attacked a nation of less than 4 million. About one million Red Army troops opposed two hundred thousand Finnish soldiers.[8] And yet the fighting dragged on from November until March; Soviet losses were huge, and the world looked on in astonishment and even grim enjoyment as the courageous Finns not only held off the invaders but effectively counterattacked and took thousands of prisoners.

The key to the dismal Red Army performance in Finland lies in the peculiar conditions of that struggle. The short hours of daylight in the northern winter greatly hampered air support. And, unbelievably, Soviet troops were not trained to fight in Finnish conditions—a pathetic shortcoming for a country with so much snow and forest of its own. At first the attackers had no winter camouflage, so that they stood out dramatically against the snow. They had few competent ski troops and were probably overly mechanized, so that once heavy snow fell they were confined to the roads. Again, incredibly enough for a country so far north, Red troops and machines had inadequate protection from the cold. Many soldiers lacked even winter clothing. The whole story of preparations and initial combat is one of gross negligence and incompetence.[9]

The Soviet effort suffered as well from overconfidence. "Stalin did not deem it necessary to assign first-rate units to the campaign. . . . Many ill-trained reservists were used, some of whom—by their own admission—knew little more than

N

| 0 | 100 | 200 | 300 | KM. |
| 0 | 50 | 100 | 150 | 200 | MI. |

Norwegian Sea

NORWAY   SWEDEN   *Gulf of Bothnia*   FINLAND

White Sea

Belomorsk

L. Onega

L. Ladoga

Gulf of Finland

Leningrad

Tallinn

ESTONIA

Novgorod

North Sea

DEN.

Riga

LATVIA

USSR

Baltic Sea

LITHUANIA

Smolensk

1939   Vilnius

1945   1939   1939   Minsk

BEL.

Hamburg   Szczecin

Bialystok

Dnepr.

1945

Berlin   1939   Vistula   Warsaw   Brest   Pripyat   R.

1945   R.

GERMANY

Kiev

Frankfurt   1945

POLAND   1939

FRA.

Prague   1945   Krakow   L'vov   1939

CZECHOSLOVAKIA

UKRAINE

Munich   Vienna

SWITZ.   AUSTRIA   HUNGARY   ROMANIA   MOLDAVIA   Odessa

ITALY   YUGOSLAVIA

2. The Baltic Region in 1938

how to fire a rifle." Nor did the Red Army fight intelligently at first; it did not coordinate its different operations, so that, for example, tanks advanced without infantry support. The Finns then easily destroyed them with Molotov cocktails.[10] Soviet infantry mounted mass attacks against entrenched machine-gun positions, and artillery fire was "aimless."[11] The endless lakes and deep snow favored the Finnish small-group formations.

Some prisoners taken by the Finns indicated that they were basically hostile to the Soviet regime. Karelians, a branch of the Finns living in the USSR, perhaps naturally wanted to get back to the front to fight against the Red Army. They told their captors they hated the collective farms. Ukrainians also "spoke against the communists." The report of this dissent, however, does not specify the nature or frequency of such complaints nor does it mention problems among any other ethnic group.[12]

Nonetheless, the Red Army generally displayed high morale against the Finns. Soviet troops seldom surrendered, even in hopeless situations; on December 29, the Finns surrounded and annihilated the 163rd Division, taking five hundred prisoners but leaving five thousand dead.[13] When Soviet units were cut apart on January 5, 1940, "this should have led to the rapid destruction of the two enemy divisions, but instead *motti* [hedgehog positions] set in." The 18th Division was chopped into "numerous isolated pockets, each of which dug in and held fast." The other division also held. The Finns had expected to meet "shaken and demoralized Russians" but instead encountered "a toughness which, in its own way, was equal to their own and baulked them of the fruits of victory which should have followed a successful encirclement."[14]

Regarding the fierce fighting toward the end of December, one Finn said that "the houses were shot full of holes like sieves, hand grenades were thrown in, but when we tried to enter there was always some Russian alive who fired."[15] Yet the carnage took its toll on Red Army spirits: one Soviet veteran of the war told an interviewer that the troops entered the fighting in high spirits but that as "winter and time went on their mood and morale changed considerably."[16]

In short, for several months the Winter War was a gruesome display of ineptitude, overconfidence, and disaster—but also determination and bravery—on the Soviet side. In early 1940 the invaders finally reorganized, adopted more intelligent tactics, brought up more effective equipment, and massed artillery along the front. From then on, victory was only a matter of time.

Possibly Soviet troops believed that their huge country would eventually win and that surrender to the Finns would mean suffering at the hands of the Stalinist state sooner or later. But such an interpretation would fall far short of explaining the remarkable will to fight displayed by Soviet soldiers. The war did not reveal a people crushed or severely discontented with Stalinist rule. Even in a desperate situation, on foreign territory in a campaign they had been led to believe would be quick and easy, the Red Army continued to fight bravely. Something in their society had led them to that stance.

Following the Winter War, severe problems continued to plague Soviet military preparations. Apparently every expectation was of an easy victory against an invader. Under Stalin's direct influence, the army paid little attention to strategic defense. The enemy was to be stopped at the political frontier, where new fortifications were under construction in 1941, not at more logical positions farther back. Only 15 antitank guns were to be deployed per mile, an almost useless number against the 150 tanks that could be massed against them.[17]

Meanwhile, Soviet forces were slowly switching to modern weapons. The new KV and T-34 tanks, the best of any country's in the war, began to emerge from the factories in 1940; but just 243 KVs and 115 T-34s were built that year.[18] The story was similar for airplanes. To make matters worse, in early June 1941 only 9.8 percent of the fighter aircraft in use had aviation cannon, the most effective weapon against other planes.[19]

A report prepared by a special commission of the party Central Committee, detailed to watch over the transition from Kliment Voroshilov to Semyon K. Timoshenko as Commissar of Defense after the Finnish debacle, was deeply critical on a number of points. It cited the lack of a clear policy on the use of tanks, aviation, and parachute troops. Development of tank and mechanized forces was poor, too. At a command conference held in late December and early January 1940–41, top Soviet officers were not afraid to speak out and appraise the situation critically. They noted few improvements in recent months. Nevertheless, they expressed confidence that an attacker would quickly be destroyed. The exercises that followed, however, revealed serious problems in the quality of officers, quantity of equipment and ammunition, use of artillery, and deployment of troops.[20] Still, Stalin did not accelerate preparations for defense.

Out in the field, most units, lacking wireless communications, had to string wire, a dangerous and time-consuming practice. Where wireless was available, many officers did not know how to handle it. The Russians had more tanks than the Germans, but a minuscule number of those in the frontier area by June were the new models, only 508 KVs and 967 T-34s in all, according to the official Soviet history of the war. Of the old tanks, the BT-5s, BT-7s, T-26s, and so forth, only 27 percent were in working order by June 22.[21] And those that were functional might not be so for long; even in peacetime, many of the old models had only a *four-hour* engine life before needing major repairs.[22]

Training was also defective or too short in many cases. Tank crews for the new vehicles had often spent only one and a half or two hours actually driving their machines before the war began. Pilots in the Baltic military district had spent as few as fifteen hours in the air with the new aircraft, and in the Kiev district only four hours. In contrast, American pilots spent 150 hours aloft in their assigned planes before being allowed into combat.[23] New officers and recruits had been shoved into the ranks wholesale, and as much as 25 percent of the Red Army's strength of close to five million had eight months' training or less.[24] A further problem was that many officers had been with their units only a short time before June.[25] The Red Army was far from ready for the Germans.

On the other side, Hitler's forces had been preparing their onslaught for months. Their military activity in occupied Poland and in Finland began to increase by March 1941, and by May the chief of Soviet military intelligence estimated that one hundred German divisions were near the border.[26] Stalin began to receive new warnings from several quarters but ignored them all.

Soldiers' Response to the German Invasion, 1941

When the attack came on June 22, the Gensec at first would not believe it was the real thing. He ordered frontier troops not to fire back (map 3). For all that Stalin should have known of the invasion, it caught the men who had to fight by surprise; on the day before the onslaught, General Heinz Guderian, the arrogant and brilliant panzer commander, saw through binoculars that Red Army soldiers on the east bank of the Bug River were relaxing as bands played.[27]

Germany and its allies Romania, Hungary, and Slovakia—Spain and Italy eventually sent troops as well—had amassed 1.8 to 2.2 times the number of defenders along the Soviet borders.[28] Operating in conjunction with massive artillery and air assaults, German tanks smashed through Soviet defenses and drove deep behind the foremost units in great encircling pincers. The combination of tanks accompanied by motorized infantry and followed by ordinary foot soldiers destroyed Red Army communications and organization along with masses of soldiers. By noon of the first day, the Germans had annihilated twelve hundred enemy aircraft, most of them on the ground.[29] This gave a tremendous advantage to the attackers, allowing them not only to bomb and strafe at will but

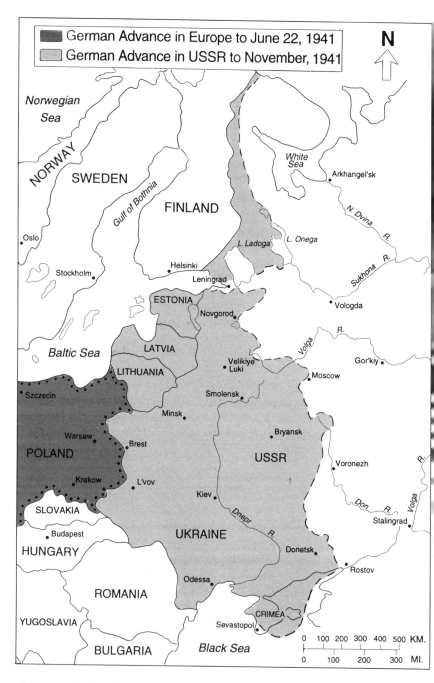

German Advance in Europe to June 22, 1941
German Advance in USSR to November, 1941

Norwegian Sea

NORWAY

SWEDEN

FINLAND

White Sea

Arkhangel'sk

N. Dvina R.

Oslo

Gulf of Bothnia

L. Ladoga

L. Onega

Sukhona R.

Stockholm

Helsinki

Leningrad

Vologda

ESTONIA

Novgorod

Baltic Sea

LATVIA

Velikiye Luki

Volga R.

Gor'kiy

LITHUANIA

Moscow

Szczecin

Smolensk

Minsk

Warsaw

Brest

Bryansk

POLAND

USSR

Voronezh

Krakow

L'vov

Kiev

R.

SLOVAKIA

Dnepr R.

Don R.

Volga

Stalingrad

Budapest

UKRAINE

Donetsk

HUNGARY

Rostov

ROMANIA

Odessa

CRIMEA

YUGOSLAVIA

Sevastopol

Black Sea

0 100 200 300 400 500 KM.

0   100   200   300 MI.

BULGARIA

3. The First Months of the German Invasion, 1941

also to carry out air reconnaissance without hindrance. They knew where Soviet forces were and what routes reinforcements were taking to the front.[30] The defenders blundered about, often in ignorance of where the Germans were, trying to restore communications and order; it was like a blind man trying to fight one who could see for miles. Between the first moments of the invasion and the stabilization of the front in mid-November, countless Soviet units could not reestablish effective communications, supply lines, and a chain of command. As we shall see, this situation had a profound effect on morale.

Not only was the June attack a surprise; a series of shocks continued into the fall. Trams filled with passengers were captured on the outskirts of Leningrad on September 16.[31] At Orel, south and slightly west of Moscow, the trams were still running when the Germans broke into the city on October 2.[32] Soviet armies kept reeling back, unable to create firm defensive lines. Red troops improvised everything, while the Germans kept their lines, communications, and control of the air intact.

Nor did Soviet field commanders fight particularly intelligently at first. Instead of massing the few good tanks together and thereby allowing them to protect one another and concentrate their firepower, officers used them "in dribs and drabs," which enabled the Germans to pick them off one at a time. If the T34 was a fine tank, it still fired its gun only once for every three German shells. In this phase of the war Soviet tank commanders were also the gunners, which obviously cut down on their ability to maneuver and fire at the same time. To make matters worse, there was only one radio transmitter per armored unit, located in the company commander's tank. Other vehicles had to watch the lead tank to know what to do. These difficulties made Soviet armor much less mobile than German.[33]

Contrasting the Winter War with the fighting in the summer of 1941 brings out a number of other factors in the Germans' favor. The Finnish terrain was all wrong for mechanized warfare, whereas much of the Soviet front was flat, open, treeless land, already baked hard by the sun. Defenders had nowhere to hide. Rivers are broad but sluggish. Camouflage was not an issue; German field gray blended reasonably well with the dry crops. The attack began on virtually the longest day of the year, long indeed at the latitude of Moscow, which in North America corresponds to the bottom of the Hudson Bay. Thus, in contrast to the disadvantages under which Soviet planes labored in the Finnish war, German aircraft could carry out reconnaissance and bombing during most of a twenty-four-hour period. In a country as small as Finland, local people who knew the territory could always be found. But in the vast expanse of the USSR, even the defenders usually fought over unfamiliar ground.

To be sure, German equipment and techniques were not without problems. The panzers were ultimately too light and their treads too narrow to function optimally in Russian conditions, especially in the mud of spring and fall. German bombers were also too light to deliver knockout blows and therefore played no strategic part in the war. Attack planning emphasized the leading role of tanks, so much so that there was always a danger of wide gaps opening between the panzers and the following infantry. Artillery fire was not as concentrated as it could have been, which reduced its effectiveness.[34] Finally, the German troops were a long distance from their main centers of supply and production, and they kept getting farther away as the summer and fall of 1941 went on. But all this mattered little in the early stages of the war; Soviet problems, compounded a thousand times by the rout that developed from the first hours of fighting, were the main factors in the situation.

In this maelstrom, eyewitnesses reported, Red Army soldiers' performance and reaction to the invasion varied tremendously, from resistance down to the last man to units marching in order to surrender to the Germans.[35] This confused picture alone should preclude any gross generalizations about Soviet morale and its relation to Stalinism.

Resistance varied according to several factors. Where the terrain was less favorable for German tanks and aircraft, as in the Baltic region, with its forests, streams, and swamps, Soviet troops acquitted themselves relatively well. The steppes of the Ukraine were a different story; this country was perfectly suited to large-scale tank operations. Here poor leadership on the command level also played a role. In the southern Ukraine, however, the competent hand of General M. P. Kirponos and the fact that he had some time to prepare for the enemy led to better performance of the Red Army.[36] The Belorussian front, straddling the route to Moscow, bore the heaviest German attacks and fared poorest. Yet there, if Soviet units could retreat into heavy woods or marshes, they sometimes fought on for months or even years.[37]

When the Red Army had a chance to dig in and resist from well-prepared positions, it often fought stubbornly. One example is the defense of the Brest fortress, which held out for several days after the Germans had swept around it. On the walls, Russians wrote messages about their determination to die rather than surrender. One read, "We are three men from Moscow—Ivanov, Stepanchikov, and Shuntiaev. We are defending this church, and we have sworn not to surrender. July 1941." Below that was written, "I am alone now. Stepanchikov and Shuntiaev have been killed. The Germans are inside the church. I have one hand-grenade left. They shall not get me alive." Another message read, "Things are difficult, but we are not losing courage. We die confidently. July 1941."[38] Most of these men kept their word; few prisoners were taken in the fortress.

But what about the three million who were captured in 1941? They can be divided into two major groups, those who were surrounded and those who were not. The first case typically involved the so-called cauldrons (*Kesseln*), rings that the Germans closed around great groups of Soviet units that summer and fall. The thirteen major cauldrons netted an estimated 2,465,000 prisoners, or almost 74 percent of all Soviet soldiers captured before the end of 1941.[39] Many lesser encirclements also took place, so that all but a small minority of the prisoners of war (POWs) for that year were caught in this fashion.

What happened in the cauldrons was almost like shooting fish in a barrel. First, German armor closed a ring; then tanks, infantry, and the Luftwaffe sliced the trapped forces to pieces. Red soldiers were cut off from the rest of the army, without food or ammunition. Soviet air drops were for the most part highly ineffective in view of enemy air superiority. Given these circumstances, troops surrendered not out of disloyalty but because they had been struggling for days against great odds, often with little or nothing to eat and no way to shoot back.

Considering the conditions under which soldiers fought inside the cauldrons, they often put up remarkable resistance. A good example was the great Kiev encirclement, which closed on September 16. German Army Group South, involved in this action, reported on September 20 that it had pierced the trapped units and divided them into three sections. In each there were "most strong attempts to break out to the east." The next day the Germans witnessed further strong efforts to break through; on the 22d the word "strong" was omitted, and by the 23d the report read, "The enemy has been broken into small groups, whose destruction is under way."[40] Alan Clark wrote of the Kiev cauldron that Soviet soldiers fought to the last round and then some, even with their teeth. "After five days of slaughter the first surrenders began," he noted.[41] A "high percentage" of the surrounded troops threw away their weapons, a German report stated, to try to pass as civilians and cross through enemy lines to the *east,* back to Soviet-held territory.[42]

Other German units also reported desperate Red Army attempts to break out of rings. Panzer Group I, for example, noted that on August 8 a "squadron" attacked an SS division and was "fully destroyed."[43] The 26th Infantry Division encountered similar resistance near the town of Filipovskoe at about the same time.[44]

It may be that German atrocities and murderous neglect of POWs stiffened Soviet resistance from the beginning of the invasion;[45] but information about their likely fate in German hands should have encouraged Red Army units to avoid combat at all costs and to reduce the risk of being captured. Yet in the examples just given, and indeed from general evidence on the early development of the war, Soviet troops were likely to counterattack. When they did, the slaughters that often resulted must have reduced fighting spirit, just as happened in the Finnish campaign.

Even in the absence of counterattacks or cauldrons, German air superiority gravely injured Soviet morale. A Red Army veteran recalled that at first the Germans had complete control of the air and that dive bombing produced widespread terror among his comrades. "You felt that every plane was coming down at you," he said. "It made a very terrible impression to see the German planes coming over every day flying quite freely and unafraid, taking photographs without interference and scouting and looking around."[46]

Stalin's son Iakov Djugashvili, a senior artillery lieutenant captured in mid-July, underscored this problem during his interrogation. The speed, exactness, and organization of the German forces had made a profound impression on Soviet soldiers, he said. They especially feared the Luftwaffe's attacks on troops moving to the front, so that Djugashvili felt it was more dangerous to be marching than to be in ground combat.[47] German and Soviet commanders alike recognized that air attacks behind Red Army lines greatly facilitated the invaders' progress.[48]

German tanks had something of the same effect on the defenders. Masters of the massed tank formation, the Wehrmacht used armor to such devastating effect that Soviet commanders soon coined a term for the response, "tank fright."[49] One Russian reported watching NKVD troops charge forward as other men retreated, to show that there were "still loyal Soviet citizens who were moving toward the front." But when the NKVD units saw German tanks, they too ran.[50]

The caliber of replacement troops also contributed to the Soviet collapse. A Russian captured on July 15 told his interrogators that he had had no prior military service, only a grand total of five days of training before being sent to the front. During his unit's march to the fighting, commissars were changed constantly, presumably owing to losses. These officials became fewer and lower in rank, until finally some of the new recruits, despite their rudimentary training, were asked to take positions as junior commanders.[51] Given the chaos and losses of the time, this tale may not be so unusual.

The most battle-worthy formations of the standing army had been deployed at or near the front, and these suffered immense casualties in the first attacks.[52] During the first three weeks of the invasion, 28 Soviet divisions were destroyed; 72 others suffered losses of over 50 percent of their strength.[53] There were other well-trained troops available, but until October 750,000 of these were held in the Far East for fear of a Japanese attack. As a result, after the first few weeks or even days of fighting, many of the soldiers sent against the Germans were poorly prepared. Among replacements for the 275th Artillery Division brought up between September 3 and 5, for example, were "many older untrained people." Having been issued weapons and uniforms, they marched directly into battle.[54]

A commissar's diary found by the Germans in early August asserted that "many reservists are traitors and there are many more deserters among them than among men called earlier."[55] It is more probable that these deserters were simply unprepared for combat and that they had not been welded into solid units. Because of the rapid infusion of new officers, the rank and file had not been able to develop trust in their leaders, something essential if soldiers are to risk their lives by obeying commands.

On occasion incompetent officers and the high casualty rate for good and bad ones alike turned the men into leaderless mobs. One captured Russian reported that "we were surrounded, thanks to our stupid commanders, and then the Germans started to pound us. Night and day they flew over us and bombed us. We were completely disorganized. Our leaders were dead or fled and without them we were absolutely useless."[56]

A former Soviet colonel mentioned another problem regarding officers. "In the first months of the German attack," he claimed, "many officers were under suspicion by their very [own] troops, by the very soldiers they had to command. Some of the officers were killed by their own troops who thought that they were spies."[57] He did not explain this remark. A report by Army Commander N. Voronov of April 1, 1940, to the Commissariat of Defense relates to this point: "In the army a situation has been created (after the year 1937) in which a commander does not feel confident in his actions: any subordinate at any moment can raise a fuss about anything which is unpleasant to him. [He can complain] along party or Komsomol lines, along the lines of the special organs, [he can] go complain to the political instructor or the military commissar, and the commander sometimes cannot even be guaranteed that a case against him will not start quickly."[58] Instead of suffering for his opinion, Voronov was later promoted to be the chief marshal of Soviet artillery.

Thus it appears that the Terror's effects did reach forward significantly into the war, but not in the way that orthodox writers have argued. Rather, troops had probably genuinely believed in the existence of enemies of the people before the war and had absorbed too readily the lesson that they had a right to complain; both attitudes led to serious disruption of the armed forces at a time when discipline was desperately needed.[59] Soviet troops may also have decided in the summer and fall of 1941 that their officers were traitors because of the horrendous slaughter and confusion.

Severe supply problems compounded every difficulty that the Red Army faced in the early months. One poignant desertion involved five Jewish soldiers, former Romanian citizens from Bukovina, an area annexed by the USSR in 1940. "Rations are bad," they told the Germans; "you get no bread from the unit. Everyone crossed the Dnepr unwillingly, because they were terribly afraid of being hungry there."[60] Of course, these men paid for their decision to avoid starvation by surrendering; the Germans executed all captured Jews and political commissars.

A regular army officer taken prisoner on August 8 told his interrogators that after encirclement he came to feel it was impossible to hold off German attacks. Besides, he had had nothing to eat for two days before capture.[61] Two Ukrainians who deserted in early August reported bad morale in their unit. "More than anything else, the rations in the last few days, except a few crackers, completely failed to appear."[62]

Captured in August in Estonia, a sailor who remained in the West after the war remarked that "on the Russian front there had been no bread, no meat, etc. Is there any wonder why so many Russian soldiers were taken prisoner?"[63] Surrendering to the Germans must have seemed better to many men than starving to death.

Besides these problems, the heavy Red Army losses took a toll on soldiers' spirits. Willingness to fight was high at first, a Major Konov told his interrogators, but as time went on the combination of casualties and retreat deflated morale.[64] One prisoner reported 70 percent losses in the 190th Artillery Division.[65] Dispatches of the German First Mountain Division mentioned laconically that from June 22 to June 26 "the small number of prisoners is explained by the fact that in the hard battle most of the enemy were shot."[66] The same division reported that around Vinnitsa from August 18 to 20 it took about 200 prisoners but killed about

850 in battle.[67] It is easy to imagine the spirits of the 200 survivors just before they were captured.

The fighting, however, was not as one-sided as such accounts might suggest. The Germans suffered 750,000 casualties in the first six months of the invasion, and many units were shattered. In spite of all their problems, the Soviet armed forces exacted a high price from the Wehrmacht for its victories.[68]

But this fact did not help Red Army prisoners. Orders regarding them and treatment of troops who had somehow escaped back to Soviet lines backfired and played a role in inducing surrender among some other soldiers. In August 1941 an order read to the troops stated that commanders who surrendered would be deemed traitors and shot if retaken; such actions had already occurred in many cases. Their families were also to be arrested. Rank-and-file soldiers who surrendered would be bombed by Soviet planes, and their families would lose all state assistance.[69] Sometimes troops who had been encircled but had broken out were shot by their own side. Certainly all this was a powerful incentive not to escape from German hands, and it sometimes appeared safer to surrender than to reach the Soviet lines again. Stalin's belief in enemies had once more hurt his cause.

Yet another factor, perhaps the most important one of all, severely damaged Soviet morale. A deceptively simple question is involved here: What do people fight for in any armed force? Studies of the Russo-German war seem to assume either that Soviet soldiers fought for Stalin, the regime, their homeland, or some combination of those or that troops chose to reject Stalinism and to surrender. Studies of motivation in military ranks, however, suggest that such broad considerations usually have little to do with why people actually risk their lives in combat and why they perform well or poorly.

General Edward Meyer, American Army Chief of Staff in the early 1980s, believes that "soldiers fight because they love one another within that squad." On the basis of platoon leaders' experiences in the Vietnam War, Colonel Dandridge Malone of the United States Army has argued that "there's some commitment to the larger unit and a little to the nation, but nowhere near as much as to the buddy and the squad."[70]

An investigation of German soldiers' motivation and morale during World War II maintains that their willingness to fight depended not on abstractions but on the cohesion of the smaller units, the squad, platoon, or company. A German sergeant captured toward the end of the war laughed at his American interrogators when they asked him about the role of his men's political opinions. "When you ask such a question," he replied, "I realize well that you have no idea of what makes a soldier fight. . . . If we think at all, it's about the end of the war and then home."[71]

The same study concluded that a man was likely to fight to the best of his ability as long as his "primary group" had leadership he could identify with and the unit supplied him with affection and social identity. When soldiers achieved "a high degree of intimacy" with their groups, they fought as long as possible. But when units were hastily organized and thrown into combat, as happened toward the end of the war, they fought much less effectively and surrendered more often. Soldiers in such outfits "carried with them the resentment and bitterness which the 'total mobilization' produced and which prevented the flow of affection necessary for group formation." Especially when men of different ages and backgrounds are concerned, some time has to elapse before loyalties to other groups "are at least put into the background" and military loyalty comes to the fore.[72] That is, soldiers recently called up require time and experience within the armed forces to focus on their units. Freshly inducted troops are not so willing to risk their lives, for politics or country, but they will eventually tend to do so for the troops next to them.

Such considerations apply to every army, and most certainly to the Soviet experience in the summer and fall of 1941. German attacks repeatedly broke Red Army units of all sizes into pieces, so that commanders had to organize new formations and call up reserves to fill the gaps.[73] Troops could hardly have had confidence in poorly trained officers or men near them whom they barely knew. Excluding formations that had been in service for some time, all the ingredients for degradation of morale existed among Soviet troops. These factors pushed to the surface as the fighting went badly, supply and command structures broke down, and the Germans poured steadily forward.

Serious objections to this analysis deserve mention here. Omer Bartov has argued that the concept of the primary group is irrelevant to the German experience on the Eastern Front; such groups disintegrated there in the fire storm that the Soviets, even as they fell back and died in greater numbers, directed against the Germans. Bartov maintains that the invaders had internalized Nazi propaganda about subhuman Slavs, ferocious Bolsheviks, and evil Jews. Fear of what such types would do to Germany if they ever reached it, projection of guilt for the troops' atrocities onto the victims, and extremely harsh discipline held the Wehrmacht together. Soldiers accepted Hitler's claim that the war was one of survival of ideologies.[74]

There is much merit to this view; yet the primary-group theory should still play an important role in analyzing Soviet performance. German units until the end of the war were rarely sliced apart the way the Red Army was in 1941, when retreat required constant ad hoc attempts to weld new fighting groups out of dazed individuals. Even Bartov occasionally suggests obliquely that loyalty to a primary group is desirable in war.[75] And the worst of the Soviet surrenders took place before the troops could have fully realized from their side that it was truly a war of ideological—and national—survival, a sense Bartov dates from the winter of 1941–42 for the German forces. Thus his work supplements rather than weakens the case for primary-group disintegration as a further cause of Soviet morale problems in the previous summer.

In any event, the truly remarkable feature of the early months of the war is that the Red Army did not collapse. Every time the Germans closed a cauldron and destroyed or captured the men in it, the next day would simply bring renewed fighting farther east. In spite of the numerous problems that weakened Soviet troops, the Germans spoke regularly of their "hard," "tough," or even "wild" resistance. One might object that there was something of a ritualistic flourish in such words, but the field reports are almost entirely free of rhetoric, a natural approach for exhausted men writing close to the front. Nor were these documents for public consumption; they were meant for other soldiers and professional purposes. This same recognition of Soviet determination to resist appears as well in the diary of General Franz Halder, Chief of the German Army General Staff, who wrote only for himself. Indeed, Halder was one of several Germans who viewed Soviet resistance as much tougher than anything his side had faced in Western Europe.[76]

A fair number of participants who later emigrated spoke of low morale and linked it to disloyalty.[77] As already noted, émigrés might be expected to show some antipathy toward the Stalinist regime. But others who remained abroad, including several captured during the war, reported that they had fought hard and surrendered only because of circumstances.[78]

Finally, the arrest of a relative or even of oneself did not invariably produce disloyalty or a desire to surrender; far from it. Although in such cases zeal to fight may not have come from love for things Soviet, it nonetheless further damages the old but uninvestigated assertion that state terror produced mass surrender.[79] V. I. Orlov was a "political worker in the guards," which were elite army units. He remembered in emigration that in spite of his doubts about his father's arrest and the Soviet standard of living, at the outbreak of the war he volunteered for the "active army."[80] This story is not uncommon.[81] In fact, numerous people who later emigrated noted enthusiasm for the Soviet cause in June 1941.[82]

Detailed evidence on the early months of the war more often than not describes strong Soviet resistance and loyalty in the initial stages of combat. If and when morale collapsed, leading to surrender, that occurred largely because of abysmal military and supply conditions, the way reserve units were placed in battle, or reorganizations of old units.

Civilian Response to the German Invasion

Because the Red Army was drawn from Soviet society, its behavior in 1941 already suggests much about the way civilians reacted to the Germans. But there is a persistent idea in the West, the twin of the notion that troops surrendered out of disloyalty, that civilians greeted the invaders as liberators on a grand scale.[83] In some areas they did bring flowers or bread and salt, the traditional Slavic tokens of welcome. Collaboration quickly began in some places, and peasants disbanded the collective farms. But a good deal of specific evidence either counters the idea of a widespread reception for the Germans or shows that it did not necessarily stem from hatred of Stalinism.

The more sophisticated Western treatments acknowledge that the Reich's forces were welcomed mainly in the newly acquired territories: the eastern section of prewar Poland, part of Romania, and the Baltic states. It is therefore necessary to examine those areas before the war. Latvia, Lithuania, and Estonia present no particular problems of interpretation. German influence in this region had been strong from the Middle Ages on; the cities and the land-owning class remained largely German down to the Revolution of 1917. Brought into the Russian Empire during the eighteenth century, the Baltic countries gained independence during the Civil War. Just as in Finland, the new governments in the region enacted land reform, giving farmsteads to the peasants. This, together with awakened nationalism and the fact that the Baltic peoples are Catholic or Lutheran, with only a sprinkling of Orthodox believers, made them value their independence keenly. When the Soviet Union annexed these three states for strategic reasons in the summer of 1940, strong hostility was inevitable. Several additional factors bolstered the Baltic peoples' welcome of the Wehrmacht the next summer: the Germans were the enemies of the USSR; their previous domination had become only the next-to-last oppression of the area, so that memories of it paled next to recent abuses by Soviet authorities; Germans still had religious and cultural ties to the local inhabitants; and the invaders' anti-Semitism evoked a degree of sympathy and supporting action against local Jews.[84]

A more important and complex story unfolded in the areas taken into the Soviet Union from Poland in September 1939. Ethnic Poles in the region were not the issue; their hatred for anything Soviet went back decades, their visceral distaste for anything Russian for centuries before that. It is the newly annexed Ukrainian population that deserves further comment.

This group had encountered severe problems in independent Poland. Of the country's 27 million inhabitants in 1921, 14.3 percent were Ukrainians.[85] Facing severe economic problems in the 1920s and 1930s, ethnic Poles struggled to rebuild their identity and their country after more than 120 years without statehood. The strain of this effort, together with deep, long-standing social divisions and ethnic tensions, led the country into a political swamp. By the middle of its second decade, the Polish government offered little in the way of a political program. The ruling group styled itself the "Non-Party Bloc for Cooperation with the Government," suggesting that it stood for "Poland" in some basic way and for its own right to run the country. "Even its more impartial defenders" often could not deny the bloc's "ideological poverty."[86]

But many Poles responded to dislocation and wounded pride the way other Europeans did: with virulent nationalism. This movement contributed powerfully to anti-Semitism,[87] though for our purposes anti-Ukrainianism is more important. During the Depression, ethnically Polish politicians and intellectuals sought scapegoats; they denounced Jews and Ukrainians for blocking "the Polish nation" from decent employment.[88]

In an effort to dampen what Polish authorities saw as the potentially disruptive effects of Ukrainian nationalism, they only made it worse. The number of elementary schools offering instruction in Ukrainian in East Galicia, the poorest part of a poor country and the most densely Ukrainian area, declined by 80 percent from 1921 to 1935.[89] The Polish government then began either to destroy Orthodox churches or to transfer them to other faiths. These policies further inflamed the feelings of Ukrainians, who correctly perceived an attack on their nationality.

Considering these pressures, the historian Antony Polonsky writes that "the majority of [Polish] Ukrainians began to look to Hitler for realization of their national objectives."[90] Ironically in light of his later savage assaults on the Slavs, by 1938 Hitler had gained a positive reputation among some Eastern European nationalists for his sponsorship of Slovak independence. This position was merely a ploy to split the Czechs and Slovaks and facilitate the German takeover of their entire country. No matter: when Hitler visited Vienna in March 1938, a group of nationalist Ukrainian exiles from Poland presented him with a wreath inscribed "To the Liberator of Small Peoples."[91] Given this background, much of the greeting for the Germans in the former eastern part of Poland during the summer of 1941 was rooted in Ukrainian nationalism per se and in the old frictions between Poles and Ukrainians.

Soviet behavior in the area just before the war also contributed strongly to a hopeful attitude toward the Germans. As Polish rule collapsed in September 1939 under the Wehrmacht's blows, the Red Army marched in from the east. Its zone, as agreed upon with the Reich, was the area most heavily populated by Ukrainians and Belorussians. At first, many of them welcomed the Soviets, though it is hard to say whether from enthusiasm or a desire to ingratiate themselves with a powerful new regime. Still others may have regarded the Red Army troops as protectors against the Germans; not all Ukrainians then felt that the Reich would be benevolent.[92]

Soviet authorities quickly moved to arrest anyone considered potentially disloyal in this highly strategic area, now the first line of defense against Germany. Perhaps 1.25 million people, about 9 percent of the region's population, were deported to places deep inside the USSR, often to gulag camps.[93] The impact of these actions on the local population is not entirely clear. A detailed study of what happened finds that the violence of the new regime was probably not particularly noticeable in the countryside, where more than 80 percent of the people lived. This was because "each hamlet or village was to a large degree an isolated universe" in which inhabitants settled old scores and grievances among themselves. Moreover, Soviet repression in the annexed territory was "selective rather than random. [It was] directed mostly against Polish officers, policemen, and landowners. These killings were simply not very visible; they occurred mostly on the roads or on rural estates, rather than in towns or villages where there would be many witnesses who would themselves feel threatened."[94] As the passage suggests, most victims of such murders, as well as of the deportations, were ethnic Poles. The majority of Ukrainians, Jews, and Belorussians may not have felt threatened by these acts.

But other factors may have turned many of them against the new rulers. First, even though collectivization was not imposed, it was obvious that the peasants would be heavily controlled by the state. Certainly the local inhabitants had heard of collectivization and feared that it was coming. In the meantime, the tightly knit peasant communities felt insulted by the Soviet authorities' habit of favoring "social inferiors," especially "youths and ruffians."[95] Finally, the poor appearance of Red Army troops and the way that the newcomers greedily snatched up all available consumer goods made a bad impression. Thus, developments in the area both during Polish rule and under the Soviets from 1939 to 1941 provided reasons for some initial welcome for the Germans.

As the Wehrmacht swept into the region, the invaders commented on the friendliness of inhabitants in former Poland. People around the town of Bilsk-Podlaski, especially peasants, were well disposed toward the conquerors.[96] But even in the areas newly incorporated into the USSR, the greeting was "partly" friendly.[97]

However, once German troops crossed the pre-1939 border into the "old" Soviet Ukraine, the reception became considerably cooler. Reinhard Heydrich, chief of the German security police, received regular summaries of civilian activity and response in occupied areas of the Soviet Union. A report of July 9 noted

> a fundamental difference between the former Polish and Russian territories. In the former Polish region, the Soviet regime was seen as enemy rule, so that in the two years of its activity it could still not fully create its [own] order in life. Hence the German troops were greeted by Polish ethnic groups as well as by the White Ruthenian population [apparently meaning Ukrainians and Belorussians] for the most part at least as liberators or with friendly neutrality. . . . The situation in the currently occupied White Ruthenian areas of the [old] USSR has a completely different basis. The statization of enterprises and trade as well as the collectivization of the peasantry was fully carried out. A White Ruthenian consciousness hardly exists or is weak because of Russification, communization, and among the rural population because of forced relocation of traditionally alien [to the communist regime] elements into the collective farms.[98]

This is a weak explanation of the different response as the Germans crossed the pre-1939 border. The traditional elements in the collective farms were alive and well and, by the invaders' own logic, should have led in providing a warm welcome.

Another report to Heydrich, dated July 12, was more perceptive. It argued that at first the population of the former Polish region had hoped that "Bolshevik rule" would introduce improvements, at least in cultural and traditional life. But "these hopes were bitterly disappointed." As a result, the Germans were greeted in a friendly way "on the part of the Ukrainian population."[99]

By the time information began to come back to Heydrich from the Minsk area, well into the old USSR, comments about response to the invaders sounded quite different. "The mood of the population is very low," though it was also described as wait-and-see. Running the gamut of possible reactions, the report concluded that the attitude of the "White Ruthenians" was friendlier (than that of the Russians, presumably) and that the population hoped for a "regulated life" as quickly as possible. But the actions of the field commander in the region, which speak loudest of all, indicate serious hostility toward the Germans; he had to order all men between the ages of eighteen and forty-five rounded up in order to prevent sabotage.[100] The 7th Panzer Division added to this picture on August 8 when it noted that "all revolts against the [Soviet] system have taken place outside central Russia."[101]

This evidence contradicts orthodox interpretations of Stalinism. Because the old USSR had been under it considerably longer and had, in the old views, suffered "total terror" and been "crushed," response to the Germans should have been much more favorable than in former eastern Poland, under Moscow's control less than two years. But the opposite occurred.

Soviet émigrés sometimes commented on the difference between their fellow citizens from the two sections of Ukraine. A Ukrainian truck driver from the old Soviet Union spoke "with great hatred against the Western Ukrainians," that is, the ones from the region taken from Poland in 1939.[102] A young Ukrainian tractor driver who left the USSR in 1950 "was roundly disgusted" when he met his first Ukrainian separatists in a displaced persons (DP) camp.[103]

A young woman whose nationality was unclear commented that "in the Ukraine, the Galicians have been engaging in strong separatist propaganda, but the Soviet Ukrainians just laugh at them."[104] A male émigré, probably a Russian, remarked that "the extreme Ukrainians here [in the DP camps] are those from Poland. The Poles treated them worse."[105] Such remarks make the influence of the pre-1939 period clear.

In any event, collective farmers reportedly often greeted the Germans warmly, even in the old USSR, because of their hatred for the Stalin regime. An old peasant near Leningrad supposedly commented, one week before the war began, "Now I expect salvation only from Hitler."[106] The peasants around Zuev were said to be happy in the summer of 1941 because the Germans had freed them from Stalin's regime.[107] According to a man from a state farm in the North Caucasus, everyone there awaited the Germans as liberators.[108] Such statements occur often in the sources.

It may well be that some reports of this type should be dismissed. Some émigrés may have made a psychological adjustment to departure by denigrating the country they left behind and establishing safety in numbers: "everyone" felt as they had and would have acted the same way.

The demographic structure of collective farmers may also have played a role in any genuine anti-Soviet feeling and its corollary, welcome for the Germans. A young man who left a farm to enter medical school remarked, "When I came back on summer vacations to the kolkhoz, I saw only old people. All of those who were young and strong left the kolkhoz and went to the town."[109] Another young man, who was about seventeen in 1941, lived on a collective farm before the war; he too remembered that the kolkhoz had only old people or those still in school.[110] The tremendous avenues of geographical and social mobility opened after the Revolution often benefited those who traveled along them, but taking the young and strong out of the collectives obviously put great burdens on those who remained behind. Many may have been embittered by this extra load.

Mobility out of the villages involved men more than women, and the flow of males into industry that characterized Russian life as early as the 1860s was reinforced in the 1930s. Men also went away to enter the army, of course. The result was that by the end of the decade there were 132 women on the kolkhozy for every 100 men.[111] This imbalance and its attendant problems may also have fostered dissatisfaction with the Soviet regime and the hope that the Germans would somehow be better. But obviously many kolkhozniki had fundamental reasons to hate the regime that had destroyed their old way of life as well as considerable numbers of their countrymen.

On the other hand, some developments from the mid-1930s to the eve of the war may have improved the peasants' attitude toward the state. Although evidence on this point is scanty, some material suggests that living standards were rising slowly but steadily in the Soviet zone after 1933, not only relative to the depths of the famine but in terms of some tangible progress toward general well-being. The émigré Fedor Belov, who lived on a Ukrainian collective farm, had no love for the Soviet regime as a whole. But he found that "in general, from the mid-1930s until 1941, the majority of kolkhoz members in the Ukraine lived relatively well. They were never in need of bread and other foodstuffs. If the market provided insufficient clothes and shoes, the shortage was made good by items made locally." Conditions on his own kolkhoz were especially favorable, although the higher demands for food deliveries from the farm in 1939–41 stirred up some dissatisfaction.[112]

The same story appears to have taken place in Belorussia. A collective farmer from that republic remembered that in 1934 his kolkhoz received purebred pigs that the government had purchased abroad. The farmers increased their herds of cattle and sheep through their own efforts and were able to build new cow and pig barns.[113] During the same period, a steady flow of tractors entered the country-side, which should have been a welcome change from the more difficult labor by hand and horse in the old days.

A recent American study of the collective farms from 1933 to 1937 argues that the kolkhoz order was improving by the middle of the decade. The state, having realized that it could not control the peasants' daily lives, began to regularize its demands on the farmers. In turn, the farmers "learned to maneuver within the system to escape its harshest effects." A series of concessions to the kolkhozniki, though not especially far-reaching, improved their material situation at least somewhat. The collective farm system "might have continued to stabilize"—by which the author means to have become less arbitrary, more favorable to peasants, and generally better—had not the preparations for war intervened.[114]

By the latter half of the 1930s, collective farmers had gained more say over who their chairpersons would be. They had also learned to denounce chairs and other officials they wished to get rid of.[115] The opportunities for villagers to criticize local conditions were intact in the late 1930s. In 1937 collective farmers wrote to Stalin and other officials with various complaints, for example, about poor food supply or about people who had suffered unjust fines.[116] An émigré who had been a Komsomol activist before the war and had visited many villages remembered that "the kolkhozniks always came to us with complaints. Told us how various things which should have been done have not been done." The Komsomol group would then take these complaints to the regional party secretary; "after that somebody would go to the village and straighten out things."[117] A former kolkhoznik recalled that "generally, you didn't feel much bureaucracy, and if you did, at least on the lower level you could criticize it easily."[118]

Although improvements on the collective farms hardly produced a comfortable life or overrode memories of collectivization,[119] they may have made many kolkhozniki in the old USSR feel that still better times were on the way. A survey of nonreturnees conducted after the war showed that 60 percent of the peasants among them expressed "some hostility to the Soviet system." But the authors who reported this figure noted that it was skewed in several ways: the atmosphere of the early Cold War inclined respondents to be more hostile to the USSR than the population at home would be; the nonreturnees as a group were more generally negative; and the sample did not include the youngest age groups. The study emphasized that from oldest to youngest, each successive age cohort accepted the Soviet system more than the one before had.[120] Therefore on the whole the young collective farmers on the eve of the war were more positively disposed toward Stalin's regime than were the nonreturnees surveyed in 1950–51. The increased dissatisfaction Belov noted in 1939–41 had to do with military needs and may have been perceived as no more than a temporary setback.

Although instances of a warm reception for the invaders seem to be recorded largely from villages, some urban dwellers also reacted sympathetically. A man from Dnepropetrovsk affirmed that people there were "all smiles" when the Germans came.[121] Just as for the peasants, some of this feeling clearly grew from suffering and dashed hopes under the Soviet regime.

But part of the welcome for the Germans stemmed from the perception that they had utterly defeated the Red Army, which retreated so quickly in many areas that the newcomers appeared likely to remain for a long time. Many of the defeated may have reasoned that it was better to make one's peace with the victors, just as some residents of eastern Poland had done in September 1939. One nonreturnee mentioned that during the summer of 1941, "defeatism set in among the population" in the last days before the Red Army moved further east.[122] Before the invaders reached Orel in early October "and everything that the Soviets had built fell overnight, they [local people] began to think that perhaps the Soviet power was a bad Power, and that perhaps it was better elsewhere."[123]

A Russian dairy-products expert believed that "90 percent of the population during the first days of the German campaign believed that Soviet power was at an end."[124] A man who said he had been a low-level NKVDist before the war recalled that by late 1941 "I thought positively . . . that they [Soviet authorities] would not return."[125] In Orel as early as June "there were no Soviet planes to oppose the Germans and they [local people] had the impression that everything was over when they saw how freely and uninterruptedly the German planes went about their business."[126] Other comments by émigrés echo these feelings.[127]

The experience of the summer of 1941 must have been terribly bitter and disillusioning for many people, since a major part of the rationale for the sacrifices of industrialization had been to make the USSR militarily powerful and to prevent invasion. This drive, much more than building some vague concept called socialism, was Stalinism's raison d'être. The system must have seemed all but bankrupt to many citizens during the initial German attack. Now, despite the hard work and miserable standards of living, the regime proved unable to keep the Germans from conquering a huge area. Just as for the issue of Red Army morale, the problem in analyzing civilian response to the Germans is to determine how much of any welcome arose from the discouraging military situation rather than from a basic antipathy to the Stalinist regime. In the evidence just given, the defeats of 1941 were the key factor in reducing faith in the Soviet system. As that happened, it was an easy step to greeting the Germans warmly.

There is yet another reason that Soviet people might have welcomed the Germans: anti-Semitism, a point of mutual outlook between some Slavs and the conquerors. As Jan Gross has noted, thousands of Poles helped the Germans round up Jews in occupied Poland during the war. The German victory was "received with joy in certain areas" of the country, and the Wehrmacht evoked "a friendly greeting from the population in many ethnically Polish hamlets and villages."[128] Perhaps some of this response had to do with prewar poverty and the hope that the Germans would improve the situation—if so, there was never a greater misunderstanding of intentions—but it probably stemmed more from the anti-Semitism that vanquished and victors had in common. As the commander of the largest Polish resistance movement, the Home Army, remarked in September 1941, "The overwhelming majority of the country is anti-Semitic."[129]

At that same moment, Ukrainians were collaborating with Germans in the mass slaughter of Jews at Babi Yar, a ravine outside Kiev. Russian anti-Semitism was in much the same category as Ukrainian. In the summer of 1941 Baltic peoples, particularly Lithuanians, as noted, quickly produced "partisan" units that either helped the Germans or acted on their own to round up Jews.[130] If the invaders appeared to be in the USSR to stay, some Gentiles may have reasoned, why not try to work with them in a way they understood? Perhaps there would be rewards and the hated Jews would be removed. These thoughts could also have led to some cooperation with the Germans on the eastern side of the pre-1939 border, as they appear to have done in Poland.

But the attitudes that the Soviet regime was finished in 1941 or that the Germans should be met favorably were only two of the varied civilian responses to the invasion. Another émigré recalled that after the Wehrmacht had taken the town of Feodosiia, in the Crimea, a Red Army expeditionary force briefly recaptured it. "But our joy was brief," she continued, because the Soviet troops were quickly driven out. "Our soldiers put up a frantic resistance," she added.[131] A former Red Army officer, whose love for the regime later fell so low that he defected in 1948, noted that the civilians in Baku, the capital of Azerbaijan, were "all patriotic" at the start of the war.[132]

Others reported mixed reactions in their areas. The young Ukrainian tractor driver mentioned earlier tried to evacuate east but could not cross the Dnepr River, so he went back to his village. There the elder, a traditional peasant leader, met the Germans with bread and salt.[133] A man from Leningrad maintained that "a certain part" of the intelligentsia, young workers, and students greeted the war with enthusiasm and patriotism. Some families, he wrote, were split between the fathers, who were more patriotic and nationalistic, and the children, who had seen "boredom and irrationality" everywhere. He also spoke of an antigovernment mood.[134]

A Jewish woman who worked as a pediatrician before June 1941 remembered that "the day that war was declared we met at the Komsomol meeting hall and everybody was asking to be sent to the front. It was all very sincere." But she also commented, "We heard people say, 'It won't be so terrible if the Germans come. If worse comes to worst we'll show them who the Jews are and they'll let us alone.'"[135]

Although some people welcomed the Wehrmacht, it is essential to bear in mind that the roads leading *east* were jammed with people fleeing ahead of the invasion.[136] Like the young man who tried to cross the Dnepr, other émigrés reported attempts to move in the same direction.[137] Finally, civilian response to the war included mass volunteering for the army by workers and others in the large cities. On June 22, before anyone from above had pressured them to do so, about one hundred thousand Leningraders volunteered for the militia. The same phenomenon occurred in Moscow and Kiev, though on a lesser scale.[138]

Soviet people had to make a crucial choice in 1941: Would they be loyal or disloyal to their government? Some chose one way, some another, for a great variety of reasons. Hatred for the Soviet system did exist, but it does not fully explain the welcome that some inhabitants showed the Germans. Antipathy to Stalinism certainly does not illuminate the coolness or resistance to the invaders that also occurred from the start.

There was no massive disloyalty among Soviet soldiers during the war. What did happen in 1941 was a colossal disaster that demoralized many troops and induced some to surrender after they had been surrounded and their units shattered. Often giving up was the only alternative to starvation. The most important story of the war for the Red Army was its astonishing determination to fight; this is why it won.

On the Soviet civilian side, attitudes toward the Germans and the war at the outset varied greatly. Some citizens greeted the invaders warmly, but even where this occurred, no one can say what percentage of the local inhabitants participated nor determine their reasons for doing so. Much of the welcome took place in the areas recently annexed by the USSR, the eastern part of old Poland or the formerly independent Baltic states.

At first people from the pre-1939 Soviet Union also sometimes favored the Germans. Here bitterness over collectivization, arrests during the Terror, and the lack of Western-style freedom played a role in making some civilians happy over the retreat of Soviet power. The terrible defeats of the summer of 1941, however, caused citizens to feel one or both of the following: that the Soviet regime had been totally defeated, and thus an accommodation with the victors was necessary; that all the sacrifices designed to keep invaders out had been in vain. Either outlook tended to damage faith in Stalin's rule for the time being and to prepare the ground for welcoming the Germans.

And yet, despite all the problems of 1941 and the profound flaws and violence committed in the name of Soviet socialism, people generally rallied to the regime when they needed to. Just as there was no absolute collapse of the Red Army, which continued to fight on in the face of defeat after defeat, the country's civilians experienced only occasional panic and psychic collapse. Overwhelmingly they continued to produce, often under extraordinarily difficult conditions, the guns, tanks, and weapons necessary for victory.[139] From the first days of combat, even before appeals to old-style patriotism began to issue from Moscow, this was the most important pattern of popular response to the war.

Conclusion

By the early 1990s, information about crimes under Stalin was old news in the former Soviet Union. Like Westerners, the educated Russian public felt it knew what his rule had been about and considered fear and coercion to be its essence. Assertions were common in and outside the old USSR that socialism—meaning, above all, Stalinism—had destroyed popular initiative, precluding meaningful change for a long time.[1]

From that position it was a short step to extremely condescending conclusions about the nature of the Russian people. Victims are helpless, and the helpless defective. Orlando Figes, a scholar of the Russian Civil War, wrote that since the eighteenth century the state, "instead of remoulding the Russians into industrious and conscientious 'Europeans,' . . . merely increased their 'Oblomovism' [referring to a lazy character in a nineteenth-century novel], their 'Asiatic' indolence and apathy."[2] The *New York Times* referred with apparent approval to educated Russians' use of the word *sovok,* meaning "dustpan," to describe citizens of a lower order: "a degraded species bred by serfdom, totalitarianism and especially its Soviet variant."[3] In light of such disdainful and far-reaching comments, a sense of people as actors and victims during the 1930s would help to reclaim their humanity.

Stalin has long served in the West, and now in liberal Russia as well, as an icon of evil. The documentary film *Stalin,* released in 1990, begins each segment with an animated sequence in which the Gensec is sitting at his desk. The camera pans in to a close-up of an hourglass in front of him. But instead of grains of sand, tiny skulls trickle down.[4] Such images of unlimited horror, repeated in this and other materials presented to the public, serve to vindicate history and politics in the West, itself a construct of virtue in contrast to Soviet malice.[5]

This book argues that Stalin was not guilty of mass first-degree murder from 1934 to 1941 and did not plan or carry out a systematic campaign to crush the nation. This view is not one of absolution, however: his policies did help to engender real plots, lies, and threats to his position. Then this fear-ridden man reacted, and overreacted, to events. All the while, he could not control the flow of people within the country, job turnover, or illegal acts by managers and many others. He was sitting at the peak of a pyramid of lies and incomplete information, and he must have known it. His power was constrained in fundamental ways, which contributed to his anxiety and tendency to govern by hit-and-run methods. His attitudes and deeds must be situated in a context of vast, popular suspicion generated in part by World War I and the Russian Civil War. Several conclusions follow: Stalin becomes more human than other have portrayed him. And his regime becomes less malevolent but possessed of greater popular support than is usually argued.

Yet this vision of Stalinism is ultimately more disturbing than the orthodox view, which depicts the loathsome state as a kind of machine operated by a handful of men and as the only real actor. Here not only a leader and a few fanatical followers are charged with crimes; instead, the interaction of society and a sometimes hysterical leadership produced repulsive acts in the late 1930s—though the public often considered these steps necessary to eliminate a grave threat.

This involvement in crimes does not mean that citizens should have resisted the regime but lacked the courage to do so. People thwarted central policy, often effectively, in a multitude of small and large ways. But popular attitudes toward enemies had been shaped by the past and the moment to the point that citizens broadly accepted the Terror as just; they did not want to resist it because, to a great extent, it was theirs. The nature of the Terror echoed their own experience and assessments of their situation. Sometimes individuals or groups prevented the appearance of the mentality that facilitated mass arrests, but once the contagion started, it took hold, until the mood exhausted itself and the leadership regained some of its senses.[6] Society was all too ready to panic, as happened in the witch crazes and during McCarthyism.

Under another leader, the Soviet regime might have steered people in a different direction; Lenin or Bukharin, for all their bloodthirstiness during the Civil War, would probably not have struck wildly at enemies fifteen years later. Stalin's mental difficulties seem present in his vacillation and lack of leadership in 1937–38 and at other times. His personality contributed greatly to the Terror, but if the situation of ordinary people had not primed them to follow his lead, the violence would have been much more limited. In many cases, incriminating material came to the NKVD from the public, and the police did not have to initiate matters.

Soviet people were not inherently cruel, any more than Western Europeans were during the witch crazes. But this investigation points to a distressing human inclination to panic and to believe in plots, which must then be crushed even at the cost of violating individuals' rights. The cases of Nazi Germany and Stalin's Russia indicate, too, that if substantial numbers of people decide a regime is worth supporting, they will ignore or excuse its most vicious deeds.

This attitude was easier to hold in the USSR than in Germany. During the Terror, Soviet officials at many levels, including policemen, believed that they were pursuing and handling actual criminals. Basic societal characteristics before the war, especially the low level of education, probably inclined the populace, even those who moved to cities, to believe in conspiracies.

People had the opportunity to speak out about local problems and conditions, especially in urban settings, though they did not usually express themselves frankly, if at all, on larger questions of national and foreign policy. Poor education and lack of adequate information played a role in restraining speech on such issues, along with fear of saying the wrong thing. But on local matters people were fairly quick to learn the unwritten though commonly known boundaries of public expression. These limits were largely self-imposed, probably because of a broad fear of enemies and of renewed internal disintegration. Privately Soviet citizens spoke much more openly, often claiming that they knew whom they could trust.[7]

The experience of criticizing anything during the 1930s presented to Soviet citizens the principle that they had a right to speak out, as well as to participate in some kinds of decisions. From there it was a matter of time; several key social developments; and increasing stability in housing and at work, with an attendant stronger commitment to improving present conditions, before the desire to have a meaningful voice in affairs became widespread and extended to policy matters, too. With increasing urbanization, rising levels of education, and a vast array of participatory agencies, Stalinism created the preconditions for perestroika. Marx was wrong about the contradictions of capitalism preparing its own demise; this thought applies more to socialism as practiced in the USSR and Eastern Europe after the war, in which society became too well educated and urbanized to stay within the constraints of the old authoritarian system. Educated city dwellers came to want and need a free flow of information much more than their rural forebears did. In this regard pressure for change began to build long before Mikhail Gorbachev emerged as leader.[8] He reflected this trend more than he caused it.

The reforms Gorbachev helped initiate in 1985 are usually seen as the antithesis of Stalinism; the Soviet Union was awakening from a long sleep, or nightmare, under totalitarianism.[9] Yet how could the same minds supposedly dulled by decades of terror produce the reform impulse and the energetic civil society that had emerged by the late 1980s? If we see no earlier roots for reform, we are reduced to the view that reform sprang suddenly from nowhere, or perhaps only from Gorbachev's brain. Given the scope of change after 1985, that argument would be absurd. It is more sensible to abandon the image of people held in thrall by their system and to look for the origins of the new era within society.

In the 1930s people criticized many things that were vitally important to them. Managers and administrators had to think for themselves to get anything accomplished and to stay out of the hands of the police. Every day they had to break the laws to survive and be productive, which often amounted to the same thing. Workers and managers, and just about everyone else, had to find ways around the demands of the government. They had to fiddle with norms and wages; devise ways to hire and fire people in violation of the spirit of the law, if not the letter; scrounge for materials and transportation; and find means of getting along with one another that were contrary to what was specified "from above." If we further recognize that the state never crushed society—indeed that the two cannot be easily separated and that they have always drawn from and influenced each other—then both the picture after 1985 and the period fifty years earlier become much more understandable.

The Soviet regime was hardly democratic. Nonetheless, it appears to have been reasonably well grounded, at least in the cities and among young people, as it entered the extreme test of World War II. Most of the surrenders of 1941 occurred after encirclements had produced desperate conditions; even peasant recruits generally fought hard for their country. The victory over Germany then conferred high legitimacy on Stalinism and seemed to justify the sacrifices of collectivization and industrialization.

At the same time, the idea of rule by terror under Stalin obscures the reasons why so many Russians came to oppose reform, with its major economic dislocation, by the early 1990s. Resistance to change has arisen not only among disgruntled bureaucrats and old-time communists, who fear the loss of their power and privileges, but also among people for whom the past held much that was positive.

Stalin's legacy is alive and important in the former USSR, for example, in the collective farms, where, ironically, there is now serious antipathy to change. Polls of Soviet, and now Russian, citizens have repeatedly asked their views of Stalin as a leader; the frequency of this question indicates anxiety among the elite about the possibility he is still popular. Here are some results in recent years:

—April 1989: 52 percent saw Stalin negatively (leaving 48 percent who did not).
—September 1991: asked if "Stalin was a great leader," 20 percent completely agreed; 8 percent more or less agreed.
—June–July 1992: 27 percent agreed completely with the same statement; 22 percent did more or less.[10] (President Boris Yeltsin's popularity, meanwhile, was slipping.)

It is impossible to say, and not particularly important, whether a majority saw Stalin positively at any point after his death. What is significant is that after two rounds of heavy criticism and the exposure of grotesque crimes under him, the first during Khrushchev's tenure between 1956 and 1964, a large portion of the citizenry still regarded him favorably. Certainly the increase in this respect from September 1991 to July 1992 had much to do with the rapidly deteriorating economic situation; people tended to look back at the good old days and mentally clean them up in contrast to the messy present. But equally clearly, they would not assess Stalin positively on a broad scale if something in their political culture, some positive memories of that period passed down despite repeated condemnations of it in the media, did not incline them to do so.

The recent polls probably do not accurately reflect the support that existed for Stalin in his lifetime, as shown in the widespread sorrow at the time of his death. Current surveys largely reach those who were children during the war or were born after it; most people who were adults during the conflict have died. The younger groups care less than older ones do about earlier legitimacy for the system, conferred by industrialization and the victory over the Germans. People born after the war have sought a less heroic legitimacy, one based on higher standards of freedom and well-being.

Older people often have a different view. Several years ago a relatively elderly man remarked, "Like all people of my generation, I respect Stalin."[11] In January 1992 a female custodian told a foreign reporter that "things are difficult. People want a strong government. The shelves are empty. . . . We were better off right after the war [after the immense devastation of 1941–45!]. People remember Stalin for that." The correspondent asked if people remembered that Stalin was responsible for the imprisonment and execution of millions. "'That was not Stalin,' she said, expressing an attitude often heard in Russia. 'It was the people around him. And it was in time of war.'"[12] Her remarks suggest that, like many people quoted earlier, she perceived state violence under Stalin as limited, not directed against the whole population. At a Moscow birthday party in November

1993, I heard an older woman speak of the "huge support" the vozhd′ enjoyed before the German invasion.

Such views are baffling to Stalin's victims and to many liberal Russians. In an interview in 1990, Galina Lewinson, herself arrested in the Terror, could not explain continuing support for him: "That's the trouble, and that's the question that we [the intelligentsia, in fact] can't answer ourselves."[13]

This book has addressed such perplexity. Lewinson implies the common view that massive injustice and tragedy were the major part or even the whole story of Stalinism. But statistics from Russian archives suggest that the scale of arrests and unnatural deaths under Stalin was not sufficient to induce general fear of the regime, even considering as indirect victims the friends and families of those taken away by the NKVD. The weight of impressionistic evidence found in many memoirs, interviews, and other accounts shows the same thing. More often than fearing the government in the late 1930s, people supported its campaign to root out enemies.

Galina Lewinson's question can therefore be answered this way: terror affected many citizens and caused great tragedy. But when it struck people down, it did not necessarily shake their relatives' and acquaintances' faith in the regime. In any case, terror touched a minority of the citizens, albeit a substantial one, and the violence was concentrated among the country's elite. Many citizens, however, did not experience or even notice the Terror except in newspapers or speeches.

The preceding paragraph may serve as a partial definition of Stalinism. More explicitly, it was in large measure a brutal and authoritarian system that caused suffering and death for millions. But for the bulk of the urban citizenry, who formed the economic and political center of gravity, those features were of secondary importance. For such people Stalinism provided important means of upward social mobility, participation, and criticism. Under the Gensec's rule, the country moved from backwardness to superpowerdom. All these developments must be seen in the context of a highly tense international atmosphere and of the legacy of fighting from 1914 to 1921, which included extreme brutalization and deep suspicions of others' intentions. These feelings also produced support for state violence. Without this background, Stalinism and the Great Terror are unthinkable.

A system of terror as described by theorists and other scholars has probably never existed. The model does not fit Nazi Germany. The most developed argument for such a system is E. V. Walter's *Terror and Resistance,* in which he discusses the reign of Shaka Zulu in the 1820s. But his treatment is based largely on accounts of British witnesses, who may not have been in a position to understand what they saw.[14] It is doubtful that any state could administer its people by imposing terror on them; assuming that a regime might try, severe contradictions and widespread avoidance behavior would quickly arise. Only an invading army might rule by terror, and then perhaps only for a limited time. Countries that become enemies of the West may be labeled systems of terror, but this judgment is of little help in understanding their internal workings or longevity.[15]

Stalinism in the second half of the 1930s was characterized not by reliance on any one practice but by a series of rapid, profound shifts. This pattern reflects the great ability of the country's leader to set policies in motion, if not to control their outcome. The Stalin of these pages was an evil man, but a man nonetheless. He did not emerge from childhood as vindictive, opportunistic, and power hungry— in short, as the master plotter.[16] Instead, he could and did change his behavior and political stance. The evidence is now strong that he did not plan the Terror. By 1935–36, the country had relaxed substantially in political terms. Coercion was steadily declining. Then came a huge new internal crisis and bloodletting. It too passed, although it left a gruesome trail. By late 1938, the regime admitted that many horrible mistakes had occurred. Once more the leadership reduced tension and curtailed the political use of law. Without the sharpening international situation of the years immediately preceding the war, more liberalization would have taken place.

There was never a long period of Stalinism without a serious foreign threat, major internal dislocation, or both, which makes identifying its true nature impossible. Was Stalinism therefore little more than crises and brutal responses to them? In answer, the trends of the calmer years between 1933 and the German invasion acquire great significance. Twice in that period amelioration in political life and use of the law, with the promise of even better to come, dominated the scene. But twice this direction was broken by unplanned events. Of course Stalin contributed much to the maliciousness of the period, but he did not need to rule by terror.

In the latter half of the 1930s, state and society in the USSR were intertwined. Led by an unbalanced man whom, unfortunately, many worshipped, Soviet people determined their own fate more than it was determined for them. Under tremendous pressure domestically and internationally, as well as from their bloody history, they were actors, victims, or sometimes both in quick succession. Their humanity produced a full range of deeds and emotions: lofty achievements and self-sacrifice, tragedy and indifference to it, hysteria and heinous crimes.

Abbreviations

BA	Bakhmetieff Archive of Russian and East European History and Culture, Columbia University
CDSP	*Current Digest of the Soviet Press*
GARF (formerly TsGAOR)	Gosudarstvennyi Arkhiv Rossiiskoi Federatsii
HI	Hoover Institution Archives
HP	Project on the Soviet Social System, Widener Library, Harvard University. "A" schedule interviews were life stories; "B" schedule interviews were on specialized topics, numbered sometimes in more than one volume. There are also folders of material at the Russian Research Center. If available, biographical data have been provided, using the project's designations. The interviews were translated into occasionally awkward English.
ITSK	*Izvestiia Tsentral'nogo Komiteta KPSS*
Komm., K	*Kommunist* (Kuibyshev)
Kom. Pravda	*Komsomol'skaia Pravda*
LGAOR	Leningradskii Gosudarstvennyi Arkhiv Oktiabri'skoi Revoliutsii i Sotsialisticheskogo Stroitel'stva
LPA-PAgstP	Partiinyi Arkhiv Goroda St. Peterburga, formerly Leningradskii Partiinyi Arkhiv
MN	*Moskovskie Novosti*
"NKVD SSSR"	N.K.V.D. SSSR (Po materialim byvshikh sotrudnikov NKVD SSSR), Nicolaevsky Collection, Hoover Institution Archives
NYT	*New York Times*
P	*Pravda*
RGAE-TSGANKh	Rossiiskii Gosudarstvennyi Arkhiv Ekonomiki, formerly Tsentral'nyi Gosudarstvennyi Arkhiv Narodnogo Khoziaistva
SA	Vsesoiuznaia Kommunisticheskaia Partiia (Bol'shevikov). Smolenskii Oblastnoi Komitet. The Smolensk Archives. The archival series is T87 unless otherwise indictated.
SIu	*Sovetskaia Iustitsiia*
SR	*Slavic Review*
Sob. zakonov	*Sobranie Zakonov i Rasporiazhenii Raboche-Krest'ianskogo Pravitel'stva Soiuza Sovetskikh Respublik*
TSGAMO	Tsentral'nyi Gosudarstvennyi Arkhiv Moskovskoi Oblasti
TSGARR (TSGA RSFSR)	Tsentral'nyi Gosudarstvennyi Arkhiv Rossiiskoi Respubliki
TSPA (RTSKhIDNI)	Rossiiskii Tsentr Khraneniia i Izucheniia Dokumentov Noveishei Istorii, formerly Tsentral'nyi Partiinyi Arkhiv
VP	*Voprosy Profdvizhenii*

All translations from sources cited in foreign languages are the author's.

Introduction

1. L. Gozman and A. Etkind, "Kul't Vlasti: Struktura Totalitarnogo Soznaniia," in *Osmyslit' kul't stalina* (Moscow: Progress, 1989), 337. They are referring to an article by Mikhail Gefter, "Stalin umer vchera," *Rabochii Klass i Sovremennyi Mir* 1 (1988).

2. Roy A. Medvedev, *Let History Judge: The Origins and Consequences of Stalinism*, rev. and expanded ed., ed. and trans. George Shriver (New York: Columbia University Press, 1989), 617. Unless otherwise specified, references are to this edition.

3. See Robert H. McNeal, *Stalin: Man and Ruler* (New York: New York University Press, 1988), 309.

4. E.g., Walter Laqueur, *Stalin: The Glasnost Revelations* (New York: Scribner's, 1990), 14, 227, 241. Laqueur emphasizes the role of terror in Stalinism but also mentions the leader's popularity.

5. Robert Conquest, *The Great Terror: Stalin's Purge of the Thirties* (New York: Macmillan, 1968); and Robert Conquest, *The Great Terror: A Reassessment* (New York: Oxford University Press, 1990). See also the following works by Roy A. Medvedev: *Let History Judge: The Origins and Consequences of Stalinism*, trans. Colleen Taylor, ed. David Joravsky and Georges Haupt (New York: Knopf, 1972); *K sudu istorii: Genezis i posledstviia stalinizma* (New York: Knopf, 1974); and *Let History Judge*, rev. ed.

6. In addition to the works cited in the previous note, see Laqueur, *Stalin;* Joel Carmichael, *Stalin's Masterpiece: The Show Trials and Purges of the Thirties, The Consolidation of the Bolshevik Dictatorship* (New York: St. Martin's, 1976); Adam B. Ulam, *Stalin: The Man and His Era* (New York: Viking, 1973). Ulam is exceptional in that he believes Stalin was not behind the Kirov murder. For treatments of the Terror that take the view outlined in the text and set the USSR into the theoretical context of totalitarianism, see Carl J. Friedrich and Zbigniew K. Brzezinski, *Totalitarian Dictatorship and Autocracy,* 2d ed. (Cambridge: Harvard University Press, 1965), 169; and Alexander Dallin and George W. Breslauer, *Political Terror in Communist Systems* (Stanford: Stanford University Press, 1970), 5.

7. Merle Fainsod, *Smolensk under Soviet Rule* (Cambridge: Harvard University Press, 1958).

8. Ibid., 379, 12.

9. Merle Fainsod, *How Russia Is Ruled,* rev. ed. (Cambridge: Harvard University Press, 1967), 437.

10. Joseph Berliner, *Factory and Manager in the USSR* (Cambridge: Harvard University Press, 1957).

11. Raymond Bauer and Alex Inkeles, *The Soviet Citizen: Daily Life in a Totalitarian Society* (Cambridge: Harvard University Press, 1959).

12. Examples of such reliance are Conquest, *The Great Terror: A Reassessment,* and Robert C. Tucker, *Stalin in Power: The Revolution from Above, 1928–1941* (New York: Norton, 1990). The case of the absent observer is Alexander Orlov, *The Secret History of Stalin's Crimes* (New York: Random House, 1953).

13. E.g., Medvedev, *Let History Judge,* 450–51.

14. MN, no. 7, February 12, 1989. Anna Akhmatova expressed much the same idea in her poem "Requiem," in *The Complete Poems of Anna Akhmatova,* expanded ed., trans. Judith Hemschemeyer, ed. Roberta Reeder (Boston: Zephyr Press, 1992), 386.

15. Recent studies of the tortuous history of totalitarianism as a term and its many definitions are Giuseppe Boffa, *The Stalin Phenomenon,* trans. Nicholas Fersen (Ithaca: Cornell University Press, 1992), 60–75; and Abbott Gleason, *Totalitarianism: The Inner History of the Cold War* (New York: Oxford University Press, 1995), esp. 121–42.

16. See, among other examples, Detlev J. K. Peukert, *Inside Nazi Germany: Conformity, Opposition, and Racism in Everyday Life,* trans. Richard Deveson (New Haven: Yale University Press, 1987); Leon Poliakov, *Harvest of Hate: The Nazi Program for the Destruction of the Jews of Europe* (Syracuse: Syracuse University Press, 1954), 18; Martin Broszat, *The Hitler State: The Foundation and Development of the Internal Structure of the Third Reich,* trans. John W. Hiden (London: Longman, 1981), 349–51, 357; Edward N. Peterson, *The Limits of Hitler's Power* (Princeton: Princeton University Press, 1969), esp. 443; and Milton Mayer, *They Thought They Were Free: The Germans, 1933–1945* (Chicago: University of Chicago Press, 1955).

17. See, e.g., Friedrich and Brzezinski, *Totalitarian Dictatorship,* esp. 15; Hannah Arendt, *The Origins of Totalitarianism,* new ed. (New York: Harcourt, Brace, 1966), 344; and Zbigniew K. Brzezinski, *The Permanent Purge: Politics in Soviet Totalitarianism* (Cambridge: Harvard University Press, 1956), 17, 27.

18. Dmitrii A. Volkogonov, *Triumf i tragediia: Politicheskii portret I. V. Stalina,* 2 vols. (Moscow: Novosti, 1989), vol. 1, pt. 2, p. 215.

19. See my "A Library Exhibit Offers Faulty 'Revelations' about Soviet History," *Chronicle of Higher Education* 39, no. 14 (November 25, 1992), B1.

20. Kennan Institute for Advanced Russian Studies, *Meeting Report* 8, no. 6 (n.d., but 1991), n.p.

21. Aleksandr Gel'man, "Vremia sobiraniia sil," *Sovetskaia Kul'tura,* April 9, 1988.

22. Among the new treatments of workers that develop these points are Francesco Benvenuti, "Stakhanovism and Stalinism, 1934–1938," CREES Discussion Papers, SIPS, no. 30, University of Birmingham, 1989; Hiroaki Kuromiya, *Stalin's Industrial Revolution: Politics and Workers, 1928–1932* (New York: Cambridge University Press, 1988); Lewis H. Siegelbaum, *Stakhanovism and the Politics of Productivity in the USSR, 1935–1941* (New York: Cambridge University Press, 1988); Donald Filtzer, *Soviet Workers and Stalinist Industrialization: The Formation of Modern Soviet Production Relations, 1928–1941* (Armonk, N.Y.: M. E. Sharpe, 1986); and Vladimir Andrle, *Workers in Stalin's Russia: Industrialization and Social Change in a Planned Economy* (New York: St. Martin's, 1988). A useful look at criticism and participation by workers in the 1920s is William J. Chase, *Workers, Society, and the Soviet State: Labor and Life in Moscow, 1918–1929* (Urbana: University of Illinois Press, 1987). On peasants in the 1930s, see Nellie Hauke Ohr, "Collective Farms and Russian Peasant Society, 1933–37," Ph.D. diss., Stanford University, 1990; Roberta Manning, "Peasants and the Party: Rural Administration in

the Soviet Countryside on the Eve of World War II," in *Essays on Revolutionary Culture and Stalinism: Selected Papers from the Third World Congress for Soviet and East European Studies,* ed. John W. Strong (Columbus, Ohio: Slavica, 1990); and Sheila Fitzpatrick, *Stalin's Peasants: Resistance and Survival in the Russian Village after Collectivization* (New York: Oxford University Press, 1994).

23. See J. Arch Getty, *Origins of the Great Purges: The Soviet Communist Party Reconsidered, 1933–1938* (New York: Cambridge University Press, 1985); on the postwar period, see Werner G. Hahn, *Postwar Soviet Politics: The Fall of Zhdanov and the Defeat of Moderation, 1946–53* (Ithaca: Cornell University Press, 1982); and William O. McCagg, Jr., *Stalin Embattled, 1943–1948,* (Detroit: Wayne State University Press, 1978).

24. The phrase is in Conquest, *Great Terror: A Reassessment,* 434.

Chapter One: The Police and Courts Begin to Relax, 1933–1936

1. On the 1920s, see, e.g., Chase, *Workers, Society;* Chris Ward, *Russia's Cotton Workers and the New Economic Policy: Shop-Floor Culture and State Policy, 1921–1929* (Cambridge: Cambridge University Press, 1990); and Lewis H. Siegelbaum, *Soviet State and Society between Revolutions, 1918–1929* (New York: Cambridge University Press, 1992).

2. Lars T. Lih, *Bread and Authority in Russia, 1914–1921* (Berkeley: University of California Press, 1990); and Orlando Figes, *Peasant Russia, Civil War: The Volga Countryside in Revolution (1917–1921)* (New York: Oxford University Press, 1989), esp. 29.

3. On the Whites' violence, see Richard Stites, *The Women's Liberation Movement in Russia: Feminism, Nihilism, and Bolshevism, 1860–1930* (Princeton: Princeton University Press, 1978), 318; Peter Kenez, "The Prosecution of Soviet History: A Critique of Richard Pipes' *The Russian Revolution,*" *Russian Review* 50, no. 3 (1991), 345–51; and Vladimir N. Brovkin, *Behind the Front Lines: Political Parties and Social Movements in Russia, 1918–1922* (Princeton: Princeton University Press, 1994).

4. Oliver H. Radkey, *The Unknown Civil War in Soviet Russia: A Study of the Green Movement in the Tambov Region, 1920–1921* (Stanford: Hoover Institution Press, 1976), chap. 11.

5. Boris Pasternak, *Doctor Zhivago,* trans. Max Hayward and Manya Harari (New York: Pantheon, 1958), 314–15.

6. Alfred Meyer, "The Impact of World War I on Russian Women's Lives," in *Russia's Women: Accommodation, Resistance, and Transformation,* ed. Barbara Evans Clements, Barbara Alpern Engel, and Christine D. Worobec (Berkeley: University of California Press, 1991), 211.

7. Evan Mawdsley, *The Russian Civil War* (Boston: Allen and Unwin, 1987), xi.

8. The phrase dates from at least the 1860s: Franco Venturi, *Roots of Revolution* (London: Weidenfeld and Nicolson, 1960), 289.

9. Peter Loewenberg, *Decoding the Past: The Psychohistorical Approach* (Berkeley: University of California Press, 1984), 248.

10. Tucker, *Stalin in Power,* 248.

11. Vsesoiuznaia kommunisticheskaia partiia, XVII s″ezd Vsesoiuznoi kommunisticheskoi partii (b.), 26 ianvaria–10 fevralia 1934 g., *Stenograficheskii otchet* (Moscow: Partizdat, 1934), 28.

12. From 1918 to 1922 the political police controlled some prison camps, then relinquished most to

the Commissariat of Justice. A new camp agency, GULAG, to be explained below, was created under the police in 1930; Michael Jakobson, *Origins of the Gulag: The Soviet Prison Camp System, 1917–1934* (Lexington: University Press of Kentucky, 1993), 111–19.

13. *Sob. zakonov,* no. 56, November 11, 1934, 801–02.

14. V. A. Tsikulin, *Istoriia gosudarstvennykh uchrezhdenii SSSR 1936–1965 gg.* (Moscow.: UPP MID, 1966), 222–23; "NKVD SSSR," b. (box) 294, f. (folder) 1, throughout.

15. *Ugolovnyi kodeks RSFSR redaktsii 1926 goda*: *S izmeneniiami do 1 iiulia 1931 goda* (Moscow: Sovetskoe zakonodatel'stvo, 1931), 22–24.

16. A. Repin, Manuscripts, BA, 243–44. Repin was a colonel in the NKVD border troops; he and A. Almazov were the same. His statement is confirmed in "NKVD SSSR," b. 294, f. 2, 293–94.

17. Peter H. Solomon, Jr., "Soviet Criminal Justice and the Great Terror," *SR* 46, no. 3/4 (1987): 392.

18. *Ugolovnyi kodeks RSFSR,* 65.

19. GARF, f. (fond) 8131, o. (opis') 27, d. (delo) 28. l. (list; or ll., listy) 16, n.d. This document refers to an order by the party Central Committee and the Council of Ministers (Sovnarkom) of August 8, 1933, on supervising the political police. The order itself has not been available to me.

20. Documents on display at the Library of Congress exhibit "Revelations from the Russian Archives," 1992 [hereafter cited as LC Documents], no. A21.16, "O poriadke proizvodstva arestov." Postanovlenie Soveta Narodnykh Komissarov Soiuza SSR i Tsentral'nogo Komiteta VKP (b) 17 June 1935.

21. Arkady Vaksberg, *Stalin's Prosecutor: The Life of Andrei Vyshinsky,* trans. Jan Butler, foreword by Robert Conquest (New York: Grove Weidenfeld, 1991), 15. Unfortunately, this popular work cites almost no sources.

22. Ibid., 13–31.

23. Eugene Huskey, "Vyshinskii, Krylenko, and the Shaping of the Soviet Legal Order," *SR* 46, nos. 3/4 (1987), 414.

24. Ibid.

25. *Sob. zakonov,* no. 36, July 19, 1934, 505–06, a resolution of the Central Executive Committee of the Supreme Soviet, the parliament. See also M. V. Kozhevnikov, *Istoriia sovetskogo suda 1917–1956 gody,* 2d ed. (Moscow: Gosiurizdat, 1957), 297–98.

26. GARF, f. 8131sch, o. 27, d. 70. ll. 103, 105, 106.

27. Huskey, "Vyshinskii," 428.

28. Andrei Vyshinskii, "Rech' t. Stalina," *SIu,* no. 18 (June 1935), 5. For other examples of the courts' rejection of political convictions in this period, see *SIu,* no. 33 (November 1936), 6, 7; and no. 31 (November 1936), 21.

29. GARF, f. 8131sch, o. 27, d. 73, ll. 228–35.

30. GARF, f. 8131sch, o. 27, d. 71, ll. 127–33.

31. In a letter to Molotov of May 26, 1936, Vyshinskii again asked that the NKVD be reined in regarding counterrevolutionary agitation; GARF, f. 8131sch, o. 27, d. 71, l. 242.

32. J. Arch Getty, Gabor T. Rittersporn, and Viktor N. Zemskov, "Victims of the Soviet Penal System in the Pre-war Years: A First Approach on the Basis of Archival Evidence," *American Historical Review* 98, no. 4 (October 1993), 1022.

33. Getty, *Origins,* 94.

34. "Sudebnaia praktika," *SIu,* no. 1 (January 1935), 24.

35. Shalaginov, "Dosudebnaia podgotovka dela—zalog kachestva," *SIu,* no. 5 (February 1935), 10. In 1934 in three rural districts forty-one presidents of kolkhozy, forty-three brigadiers, and four presidents of village soviets were convicted in only a few days, an example of "mistakes and excesses." Zaitsev, "O chem govorit praktika prokuratury i suda Cheliabinskoi obl. v uborochnoi i zernopostavkakh," *SIu,* no. 1 (January 1935), 7.

36. N. Lagovier, "Perestroika provoditsia slishkom medlenno i nereshitel'no. O sudebno-nadzornoi praktike prokuratury." *SIu,* no. 9 (March 1935), 5.

37. "Sniatie sudimosti s kolkhoznikov," *SIu,* no. 24 (August 1935), 2.

38. Shalaginov, "Dosudebnaia," 10.

39. Huskey, "Vyshinskii," 427.

40. "Signaly mest," *SIu,* no. 19 (July 1935), 17.

41. GARF, f. 3316, o. 2, d. 1837, ll. 2, 3.

42. GARF, f. 8131sch, o. 27, d. 71, l. 177. L. 190, a communication to Mikhail Kalinin, president of the USSR, of May 5, 1936, gives a total of 846,302 sentences reversed by then.

43. "Na doklade t. Krylenko," *SIu,* no. 11 (April 1935), 21.

44. Il'ia Il'f and Evgenii Petrov, *Sobranie sochinenii. Tom tretii. Rasskazy, fel'etony, stat'i, rechi 1932–1937. Vodevili i kinostsenarii* (Moscow: Gos. izd. khudozhestvennoi literatury, 1961), 364–68; originally in *P,* May 16, 1935.

45. *P,* August 14, 1935.

46. For theories of aggression, see Ted Gurr, with Charles Ruttenberg, *The Conditions of Civil Violence: First Tests of a Causal Model* (Princeton: Center of International Studies, 1967); and Eugene Burnstein and Philip Worchel, "Arbitrariness of Frustration and Its Consequences for Aggression in a Social Situation," in *Roots of Aggression: A Re-examination of the Frustration-Aggression Hypothesis,* ed. Leonard Berkowitz (New York: Atherton, 1969).

Chapter Two: Politics and Tension in the Stalinist Leadership, 1934–1937

1. Tucker, *Stalin in Power,* 212.

2. "O dele tak nazyvaemogo 'Soiuza marksistov-lenintsev,' " *ITsK,* no. 6 (1989), 103.

3. *Reabilitatsiia: Politicheskie protsessy 30–50-x godov* (Moscow: Izd. politicheskoi literatury, 1991), 334–443.

4. *ITsK,* no. 8 (1990), 203; no. 12 (1990), 185–98.

5. Ibid.

6. Tucker, *Stalin in Power,* 211–21.

7. Volkogonov, *Triumf i tragediia,* vol. 1, pt. 2, p. 86; "Letter of an Old Bolshevik," in Boris I. Nicolaevsky, *Power and the Soviet Elite: "The Letter of an Old Bolshevik" and Other Essays,* ed. Janet D. Zagoria (New York: Praeger, 1965), 30. Supposedly the record of conversations between Nikolai Bukharin and Boris Nicolaevsky in Paris in the spring of 1936, the "Letter" has served in the West as a key source for the purges but has been heavily criticized by Getty (*Origins,* 214–15). In the "Letter" the "Old Bolshevik" comments on the Moscow show trial of August 1936, but Bukharin returned home months before it began. Nicolaevsky said that the "Letter" was "originally written . . . as an account of my conversations with Bukharin." Then he added

"information from other sources, above all Charles Rappoport, a well-known French-Russian Communist" ("Letter," 9). It is therefore unclear how much of the "Letter" came from Bukharin, who was not then at the center of power, how much came from Rappoport, and how much was fancy.

8. Tucker, *Stalin in Power,* 212.

9. "O tak nazyvaemoi 'Antipartiinoi kontrrevoliutsionnoi gruppirovke Eismonta, Tolmacheva i drugikh,'" *ITsK,* no. 11 (1990), 63–73.

10. This is essentially the view of Robert C. Tucker in *Stalin as Revolutionary, 1879–1929: A Study in History and Personality* (New York: Norton, 1973), 69–91. For a different assessment of cultural influences on Stalin and the way he changed over time, see Ronald G. Suny, "Beyond Psychohistory: The Young Stalin in Georgia," *SR* 50, no. 1 (1991), 48–58.

11. Svetlana Alliluyeva, *Twenty Letters to a Friend,* trans. Priscilla McMillan (New York: Harper and Row, 1967), esp. 113.

12. *Stalin,* film by Thames Television, London, 1990.

13. Iris Bolton, "Families Coping with Suicide," in *Death and Grief in the Family,* ed. Thomas T. Frantz (Rockville, Md.: Aspen Systems Corp., 1984), 37. And see Marc Cleiren, *Adaptation after Bereavement: A Comparative Study of the Aftermath of Death from Suicide, Traffic Accident and Illness for Next of Kin* (Leiden, Netherlands: DSWO Press, 1991) 52–53, 184, 193. The degree of warning survivors had about a close relative's suicide has much to do with feelings afterward.

14. "Letter of an Old Bolshevik," 32–35.

15. On Kirov's purported liberalism, see, e.g., Tucker, *Stalin in Power,* 239. See Getty's criticism of this depiction of Kirov in *Origins,* 93.

16. G. A. Tokaev, *Betrayal of an Ideal* (Bloomington: Indiana University Press, 1955), 109, 241.

17. Anton Ciliga, *The Russian Enigma* (London: George Routledge and Sons, 1940), 120–21. Ciliga was a Croatian who spent the years 1926–36 in the USSR.

18. Tucker, *Stalin in Power,* 251.

19. "Skol'ko delegatov XVII s"ezda partii golosovalo protiv Stalina?" *ITsK,* no. 7 (1989), 114–21.

20. Well-known works that present this version are Tucker, *Stalin in Power,* 288–96; Conquest, *Great Terror: A Reassessment,* 37–52; and Medvedev, *Let History Judge,* 334–45.

21. *P,* November 4, 1991.

22. J. Arch Getty, "The Politics of Repression Revisited," in *Stalinist Terror: New Perspectives,* ed. J. Arch Getty and Roberta T. Manning (Cambridge: Cambridge University Press, 1993), 49.

23. Orlov, *Secret History,* 8–9, 10–19.

24. Getty, *Origins,* 207.

25. This is the opinion of Adam Ulam in *Stalin,* 385.

26. "O dele tak nazyvaemogo 'Moskovskogo tsentra,'" *ITsK,* no. 7 (1989), 69. Ezhov said this in March 1937 to the Central Committee; Stalin was there but did not contradict him.

27. LC Documents, marked I.9.I. at the bottom of the page, but part of the A12.9 series.

28. See, e.g., Tucker, *Stalin in Power,* 290.

29. *CDSP* 43, no. 8 (1991), 15.

30. Tucker, *Stalin in Power,* 289–90.

31. Tokaev, *Betrayal;* Ciliga, *Russian Enigma;* and Getty, *Origins.*

32. *Sob. zakonov,* no. 64, December 28, 1934, 913.

33. O. Fel'tgeim, "Konets ssylki," *Sovremennye zapiski* 68 (1939), 419.

34. "O dele tak nazyvaemogo 'Moskovskogo tsentra,'" 70.

35. "O tak nazyvaemom 'Antisovetskom ob″edinennom Trotskistsko-Zinov'evskom tsentre,'" *ITsK,* no. 8 (1989), 81.

36. Ciliga, *Russian Enigma,* 71, 282.

37. "O dele tak nazyvaemogo 'Moskovskogo tsentra,'" 85; and see Gabor Tamas Rittersporn, *Stalinist Simplifications and Soviet Complications: Social Tensions and Political Conflicts in the USSR, 1933–1953* (Philadelphia: Harwood, 1991), 73. In December 1934, 6,501 people were repressed: O. V. Khlevniuk, *1937-i: Stalin, NKVD i sovetskoe obshchesto* (Moscow: Respublika, 1992), 50. However, the average number arrested per month for counterrevolutionary crimes in 1934 was 7,535; in 1935 it was 9,078. See tables in the text.

38. *Leningradskaia Pravda,* March 20, 1935; cited in Getty, *Origins,* 265.

39. Letter from the secretary of the Western oblast' party committee, Shil'man, to district party committees (*raikomy*), marked "strictly secret," October 21, 1935, SA, b. (box) 44, r. (reel) 43, WKP (file number) 385, l. (list) 158.

40. See my "The Soviet Family during the 'Great Terror,' 1935–1941," *Soviet Studies* 43, no. 3 (1991), 553–74.

41. Tucker, *Stalin in Power,* 372.

42. Pierre Broué, *Trotsky* (Paris: Faillard, 1988), 703.

43. Ibid., 706.

44. Ibid., 709.

45. Getty, *Origins,* 119–20.

46. Broué, *Trotsky,* 711.

47. "O tak nazyvaemom 'Antisovetskom ob″edinennom trotskistsko-zinov'evskom tsentre,'" 82–83.

48. The suffix *shchina* added to a name in Russian signifies something deeply memorable, though almost always in a pejorative sense.

49. Getty, *Origins,* 116.

50. See Heather Hogan, *Forging Revolution: Metalworkers, Managers, and the State in St. Petersburg, 1890–1914* (Bloomington: Indiana University Press, 1993).

51. Boris A. Starkov, "Narkom Ezhov," in *Stalinist Terror,* 21–22.

52. Getty, *Origins,* 117–18.

53. Nadezhda Mandelstam, *Hope Against Hope: A Memoir,* trans. Max Hayward, introd. by Clarence Brown (New York: Atheneum, 1979), 322.

54. "Iz zapisnoi knizhki Borisa Ivanovicha Nikolaevskogo (Rasskazy A. F. Almazova)." Nicolaevsky Collection, HI, b. 233, f. 9, p. 2. Anna Larina, *This I Cannot Forget: The Memoirs of Nikolai Bukharin's Widow,* introd. by Stephen Cohen, trans. Garry Kern (New York: Norton, 1993), 268, reports that her husband was happy when Ezhov was appointed head of the NKVD: he "won't stoop to falsification," Bukharin said. Larina heard approval of the appointment "from many who knew" Ezhov.

55. "Letter of an Old Bolshevik," 48.

56. Orlov, *Secret History,* 161.

57. Volkogonov, *Triumf i tragediia,* vol. 1, pt. 2, p. 175.

58. *Rabochaia Moskva,* February 2, 1935.

59. "O partiinosti lits, prokhodivshikh po delu tak nazyvaemogo 'antisovetskogo pravotrot-skistskogo bloka,'" *ITsK,* no. 5 (1989), 73; "O tak nazyvaemom 'Antisovetskom ob"edinennom trotskistsko-zinov'evskom tsentre,'" 82; "O tak nazyvaemom 'Parallel'nom antisovetskom trotskistskom tsentre,'" *ITsK,* no. 9 (1989), 35; and "O dele tak nazyvaemogo 'Moskovskogo tsentra,'" 69, 85.

60. This is Getty's view in *Origins,* 38–57. Traditional views are Fainsod, *Smolensk,* 222–37, and Rigby, *Communist Party,* 200–10.

61. *Krasnoe znamia* (Tomsk), December 10, 1935, photo on p. 1.

62. TsPA (RTsKhIDNI), f. 17, o. 2, d. 561, l. 127, December 25, 1935.

63. Ibid.

64. Ibid., ll. 129–130.

65. Ibid., l. 129.

66. Ibid., e.g., ll. 143, 146, 162.

67. Ibid., ll. 133–34.

68. Ibid., ll. 10, 16, 18.

69. Ibid., l. 129.

70. *Trud,* March 21, 1936.

71. Ibid., July 18, 1936.

72. TsPA (RTsKhIDNI), f. 17, o. 2, d. 572, l. 70, June 3, 1936.

73. Ibid., l. 67; this would mean 9.4 percent of all members and candidates of the party as of December 1935.

74. Ibid., ll. 67, 68.

75. "Iz zapisnoi," 1–2 (separate pagination).

76. *P,* October 31, 1961; and Feliks I. Chuev, *140 besed s Molotovym: Iz dnevnika F. Chueva* (Moscow: Terra, 1991), 394. Chuev claims that his book is a record of conversations he had with Viacheslav Molotov. This particular recollection dates from January 9, 1981. Chuev's account of Molotov's remarks rings true when compared to other evidence and in light of his career as a staunch Stalinist.

77. "O tak nazyvaemom 'antisovetskom ob"edinennom trotskistsko-zinov'evskom tsentre,'" 85.

78. A. F. Almazov, "Itogovyi obzor NKVD," Nicolaevsky Collection, HI, b. 233, f. 8; A. Svetlanin (A. V. Likhachev), *Dal'nevostochnyi zagovor* (Frankfurt: Possev, 1953).

79. LPA-PAgStP, f. 1012, o. 1, d. 1004, l. 1, a meeting of the Kirov party *aktiv,* or core of activists, November 17, 1936.

80. SA, b. 38, r. 37, WKP 322, l. 140, meeting of August 19, 1936.

81. Nikita S. Khrushchev, *The Crimes of the Stalin Era: Special Report to the 20th Congress of the Communist Party of the Soviet Union,* annotated by Boris I. Nicolaevsky (New York: New Leader, 1962), S23.

82. E.g., Conquest, *Great Terror: A Reassessment,* 138.

83. TsPA (RTsKhIDNI), f. 17, o. 2, d. 575, l. 7 (printed 12).

84. Iosif Stalin, *Sochineniia,* 16 vols., ed. Robert H. McNeal (Stanford: Hoover Institution, 1967), 14:179.

ВАЗ

85. Hugh D. Hudson, Jr., *Blueprints and Blood: The Stalinization of Soviet Architecture, 1917–1937* (Princeton: Princeton University Press, 1994), 151–65.
86. LPA-PAgStP, f. 1012, o. 1, d. 1042, passim. This was a general meeting of the factory party organization.
87. SA, b. 38, r. 37, WKP 106, ll. 47, 66; my italics.
88. Getty, *Origins,* 152–53.
89. TsPA (RTsKhIDNI), f. 17, o. 2, d. 575, ll. 11–64 (printed 21–133). Subsequent quotations from the speech are also from this source.
90. Ibid., ll. 69–87 (148–67). Subsequent quotations in this section are also from this source.
91. Ibid., ll. 93a, 94 (193), 115 (231).
92. *Istochnik,* no. 0 (1993), suppl. to the journal *Rodina,* 23–25.
93. E.g., Conquest, *Great Terror: A Reassessment,* 167–69.
94. Judging by the account of Ordzhonikidze's last days in O. V. Khlevniuk, *Stalin i Ordzhonikidze: Konflikty v Politbiuro v 30-e gody* (Moscow: Rossiia Molodaia, 1993), 111–17, Stalin was more interested in pressuring Ordzhonikidze to adopt a militant stance toward enemies than in arresting him.
95. Getty, "Politics," 52–53.
96. TsPA (RTsKhIDNI), f. 17, o. 2, d. 612, vyp. (vypusk) 1, ll. 4–13.
97. Ibid., vyp. 2, ll. 1–8. Subsequent quotations from the speech are ibid., ll. 1–13.
98. Ibid., vyp. 3, l. 43.
99. Ibid., ll. 43, 20, 24.
100. Ibid., vyp. 1, ll. 67–68.
101. Ibid., vyp. 3, l. 23.
102. TsPA (RTsKhIDNI), f. 17, o. 2, d. 573, ll. 12–15.
103. TsPA (RTsKhIDNI), f. 17, o. 2, d. 612, vyp. 2, ll. 56–57.
104. Ibid., l. 59.
105. Ibid., l. 57.
106. Khlevniuk, *Stalin i Ordzhonikidze*, 72–73.
107. Larina, *This I Cannot Forget,* 312.
108. TsPA (RTsKhIDNI), f. 17, o. 2, d. 612, vyp. 2, ll. 86–87.
109. Stalin, *Sochineniia,* 14:189; the other quotations from this speech are cited on 191, 194, 197, 205, 211, 213, 214, 218, 221–22.
110. See, e.g., Ulam, *Stalin,* 431.
111. TsPA (RTsKhIDNI), f. 17, o. 2, d. 613, l. 3, a Central Committee resolution of March 3, 1937.
112. Stalin, *Sochineniia,* 14:226; the other quotations from this speech are quoted on 228, 232, 238, 243, 246.
113. TsPA (RTsKhIDNI), f. 17, o. 2, d. 612, vyp. 2, l. 96.
114. Ibid., vyp. 3, l. 101.
115. Ibid., vyp. 1, ll. 4–8.
116. SA, b. 38, r. 37, WKP 106, l. 52.
117. Tucker (*Stalin in Power,* 374, 381) mentions another officer arrested in July 1936, Dmitri Shmidt; he does not figure in recent Soviet accounts.
118. "Delo o tak nazyvaemoi 'antisovetskoi trotskistskoi voennoi organizatsii v Krasnoi Armii,'" *ITsK,* no. 4 (1989), 42–80.

119. Ibid., 45–46.

120. Ibid., 46–49.

121. F. Sergeev, "'Delo' Tukhachevskogo," *Nedelia,* no. 7 (1989), 10.

122. "Delo o tak nazyvaemoi 'antisovetskoi trotskistskoi voennoi organizatsii,'" 47.

123. Boris Viktorov, "'Zagovor' v Krasnoi Armii," in *Istoriia bez "belykh piaten": Daidzhest pressy, 1987–1988* (Leningrad: Chelovek, 1990), 254.

124. "Iz zapisnoi," 1–2 (separate pagination).

125. Almazov, "Itogovyi obzor NKVD."

126. Svetlanin, *Dal'nevostochnyi,* 25, 34, 35, and throughout.

127. HP no. 628, A, vol. 29, 11–12. This Russian male army officer was born about 1910; his father was a tsarist officer.

128. Tucker, *Stalin in Power,* 382; a slightly different version is in Conquest, *Great Terror: A Reassessment,* 198.

129. Tucker, *Stalin in Power,* 382.

130. *Le Temps,* December 13, 1938.

131. *London Times,* December 15, 1938.

132. Sergeev, "'Delo' Tukhachevskogo," 10.

133. Volkogonov, *Triumf i tragediia,* vol. 1, pt. 2, pp. 254–68.

134. Svetlanin, *Dal'nevostochnyi,* 91.

135. Tucker, *Stalin in Power,* 383–84; conversation with Roy Medvedev, March 13, 1988.

136. Anatolii Naumovich Rybakov, *Children of the Arbat,* trans. Harold Shukman (Boston: Little, Brown, 1988).

137. See Lynn Viola, "The Campaign to Eliminate the Kulak as a Class, Winter, 1929–1930: A Reevaluation of the Legislation," *SR* 45, no. 3 (Fall 1986), 503–24; and R. W. Davies, *The Socialist Offensive: The Collectivization of Soviet Agriculture, 1929–1930* (Cambridge: Harvard University Press, 1980).

138. The inhuman and virtually unchanging Stalin depicted by Tucker, Conquest, Ulam, and many others has lately been a popular image in anti-Stalinist Russian literature. See Margaret Ziolkowski, "A Modern Demonology: Some Literary Stalins," *SR* 50, no. 1 (1991), 59–69.

Chapter Three: The Political Police at Work in the Terror, 1937–1938

1. Aleksandr I. Solzhenitsyn, *The Gulag Archipelago, 1918–1956: An Experiment in Literary Investigation,* 2 vols., trans. Thomas P. Whitney (New York: Harper and Row, 1973), 1:68. Alexander Weissberg, *The Accused* (New York: Simon and Schuster, 1952), 89, dates this wave from the fall of 1937.

2. *Trud,* June 4, 1992.

3. Ibid.

4. *MN,* June 21, 1992.

5. GARF, f. 8131, o. 27, d. 145, ll. 49–57.

6. Getty, Rittersporn, and Zemskov, "Victims," 1023.

7. HP no. 3495, B5, vol. 10, reported no torture when he was arrested in 1929; no biographical data are available. HP no. 40, A, vol. 4, p. 44, said that when he was jailed in 1938 other prisoners told

him there was little or no beating before Ezhov took control of the police in September 1936. This respondent was a male Russian or Ukrainian born about 1900; he headed a research institute before his arrest. No. 106, B5, p. 18, recounted similar information; no biographical data available. No. 302, A, vol. 15, p. 13, who was arrested in 1931, did mention that he was beaten sometimes. On arrests in connection with the campaign to obtain gold, see Ciliga, *Russian Enigma,* 156. V. Pozdniakov, "Kak Ezhov prinimal NKVD," *Narodnaia Pravda,* no. 5 (1949), 22–23, writes that in November 1936 the new NKVD leadership put great pressure on officers in Moscow oblast' to "get confessions." However, he does not say that torture began at that time. Pozdniakov claimed that he had been an NKVD agent in the 1930s and that he heard the new policy announced at a meeting.

8. Petro G. Grigorenko, *Memoirs,* trans. Thomas P. Whitney (New York: Norton, 1982), 96. The account of this particular practice was reported by Grigorenko's brother, who was imprisoned where this torture occurred, though he was not a victim of it.

9. Nicholas Prychodko, *One of the Fifteen Million* (Boston: Little, Brown, 1952), 22. Prychodko worked in education; his father had been a well-to-do peasant.

10. Solzhenitsyn, 1:93–117.

11. Herbert Kelman and V. Lee Hamilton, *Crimes of Obedience: Toward a Social Psychology of Authority and Responsibility* (New Haven: Yale University Press, 1989), 19.

12. Michel Foucault, *Discipline and Punish: The Birth of the Prison,* trans. Alan Sheridan (New York: Vintage, 1979), 42.

13. Kelman and Hamilton, *Crimes of Obedience,* 16.

14. Peter H. Solomon, *Soviet Criminal Justice under Stalin* (Cambridge: Cambridge University Press, forthcoming), chaps. 4 and 5.

15. Carmichael, *Stalin's Masterpiece,* 186. Medvedev (*Let History Judge,* 396) says that 110 members were arrested and "destroyed."

16. Medvedev, *Let History Judge,* 396–413.

17. Conquest, *Great Terror: A Reassessment,* 297.

18. Teddy J. Uldricks, *Diplomacy and Ideology: The Origins of Soviet Foreign Relations, 1917–1930* (Beverly Hills: Sage, 1979), 173.

19. TsPA (RTsKhIDNI), f. 88., o. 1, d. 668, l. 34; a speech to the plenum of the Irkutsk city party committee, June 24, 1937. Addressing a congress of Georgian communists in May, Lavrenti Beria urged restraint and caution regarding former Trotskyists; Amy Knight, *Beria: Stalin's First Lieutenant* (Princeton: Princeton University Press, 1993), 76–77. *Pravda* quickly rebuked Beria, but his speech shows that even highly placed figures could interpret the February-March plenum as stressing moderation.

20. *P,* July 2, 1937.

21. HP no. 373, A, vol. 19, p. 14; this testimony was by the man's wife.

22. HP no. 402, B10, p. 2; no biographical data available. No. 91, A, vol. 7, pp. 36–37, reported that a man she knew, the chief bookkeeper in an airplane-parts factory, was exonerated. And see no. 122, B2, p. 1, who said that he had headed a Komsomol regional committee in the Urals. A man arrested in 1937 on political charges was acquitted in court; see no. 355, A, vol. 18, p. 12. No. 421, A, vol. 21, pp. 39–41, mentioned a Jewish jurist who was arrested in the same year but released.

23. V. N. Zemskov, "Arkhipelag GULAG glazami pisatel'ia i statistika," *Argumenty i Fakty,* no. 45 (1989), 2.

24. *P,* July 18, 1937.

25. Stalin, *Sochineniia,* 14:253–54.

26. Ibid., 262–63.

27. Khrushchev, *Secret Speech,* S32.

28. Alec Nove, "How Many Victims in the 1930s?—II," *Soviet Studies* 42, no. 4 (1990), 813.

29. Repin, Manuscripts, 254.

30. Roberta T. Manning, "Government in the Soviet Countryside in the Stalinist Thirties: The Case of Belyi Raion in 1937," *The Carl Beck Papers in Russian and East European Studies,* no. 301 (1984), 9.

31. Ibid., 2.

32. R. V. Ivanov-Razumnik, *The Memoirs of Ivanov-Razumnik,* ed. P. S. Squire (London: Oxford University Press, 1965), 149, wrote that an NKVDist told him that in Moscow alone three thousand investigators were at work in 1937–38. Robert Conquest, *Inside Stalin's Secret Police: NKVD Politics, 1936–1939* (Stanford: Hoover Institution Press, 1985), 6, extrapolates from Ivanov-Razumnik's claim to estimate 20,000–25,000 investigators for the whole USSR. Such figures now appear to be vastly exaggerated.

33. Vadim A. Denisov, "Zamechaniia k rukopisi po NKVD," Boris I. Nicolaevsky Collection, HI, b. 293, f. 11, p. 3.

34. Ibid., 14; HP no. 71, B5, pp. 3–4, said that in the Kalmyk Autonomous Republic about twenty NKVDisty worked per raion, but this included secretaries, typists, and jailers. No biographical data are available, but this respondent was interviewed in the Harvard Project as a specialist on the police.

35. SA, b. 29, r. 28, WKP 237, l. 74. A report of April 19, 1935, from the Belyi raion NKVD to the secretary of the raion party organization.

36. SA, T88, b. 4, r. 74, WKP 538, l. 6, a meeting of the oblast' party committee on July 4, 1936; see l. 8 for the meeting of February 25, 1936.

37. "NKVD SSSR," b. 296, f. 17, 19.

38. Ibid., b. 294, f. 2, 273.

39. HP no. 147, A, vol. 12, p. 12, a Russian male born about 1915. He was an army officer and then an NKVD officer from 1938 until his own arrest (for having given an uncle a false passport) in 1941. His family was from the prerevolutionary middle class.

40. The population figure is from the *Great Soviet Encyclopedia* (New York: Macmillan, 1973), 7: 31.

41. HP no. 105, B2, vol. 1, pp. 23–32, a Russian male born about 1918 or a little earlier. His father was a nobleman but a middle-class civil servant.

42. HP no. 105, B3, pp. 5–7.

43. *NYT,* January 3, 1992.

44. NKVD files are now open, but only to examine specific files of individuals, not internal directives and the like.

45. "Morning Edition," National Public Radio, January 10, 1992, transcript, p. 15.

46. *NYT,* January 3, 1992.

47. Stephen Kinzer, "East Germans Face their Accusers," *NYT Magazine,* April 12, 1992, 26.

48. "Morning Edition," 16.

49. Getty, *Origins,* 31.

50. *Soiuz rabotnikov sviazi SSSR. Tsentral'nyi komitet.* Resoliutsii III plenuma TSK soiuza rabotnikov sviazi (15–20 oktiabria 1938 g.). (Moscow: Izdanie TSK soiuza i Narodnogo komissariata sviazi, 1938), 12.

51. Manning, "Government," 31–32.

52. Konovalov, "Kazhdomu narodnomu sledovateliu—velosiped," *SIu,* no. 3 (January 1935), 11.

53. Kinzer, "East Germans," 27, 42.

54. "Molodezh' i NKVD," marked B-1377, no author, Nicolaevsky Collection, HI, b. 296, f. 13, p. 1.

55. HP no. 131, B10, p. 38, a Russian male sports teacher and program director born about 1911 to poor-to-average peasants.

56. HP no. 18, A, vol. 2, p. 31; no. 67, A, vol. 6, pp. 20–22; no. 29, A, vol. 3, pp. 12–14; no. 58, A, vol. 5, p. 11.

57. HP no. 1, A, vol. 1, p. 36, a Russian male army officer born between 1898 and 1906. His father was a government employee.

58. HP no. 64, A, vol. 6, p. 17, a Ukrainian male math teacher born about 1910. His family was from the old middle class.

59. HP no. 139, A, vol. 11, p. 9, a Russian female psychiatrist born in 1886 into a middle-class family. No. 353, B11, p. 14, a medical student; no other biographical data.

60. HP no. 139, p. 9; no. 353, p. 14; and no. 131, B10, p. 38.

61. HP no. 424, B11, p. 18; no biographical data available. No. 423, A, vol. 21, p. 14, a Ukrainian female teacher born about 1893 into the old middle class. No. 131, B10, p. 38; no. 454, A, vol. 23, p. 20, a Ukrainian male professor born about 1879, also from the middle class. No. 1313, A, vol. 33, p. 12, an Armenian female bookkeeper born about 1901 into the upper middle class.

62. Mandelstam, *Hope against Hope,* 34, 345.

63. J. K. Zawodny file, Twenty-six Interviews with Former Soviet Factory Workers, HI, set I, nos. 1, 3. Hereafter cited as set I or II with the respondent's number; this source is not paginated.

64. HP no. 342, A, vol. 18, pp. 21–22, a Ukrainian male auto mechanic born about 1913 into a family of poor-to-average peasants.

65. HP no. 20, A, vol. 2, p. 23, a Russian male lathe operator born about 1919 into a peasant family. And see no. 144, A, vol. 11, pp. 8–9; this Russian male, who was born about 1926 and worked in a railroad-car repair shop in 1941–42, did not even know if a spetsotdel existed there.

66. HP nos. 394, 108, 119, 138, 432, 130, 138, 345, 59.

67. HP no. 1, p. 1.

68. HP no. 287, A, vol. 15, pp. 6–7, a Russian male born about 1898 into the old middle class. And, for this same point regarding job changes, see no. 611, A, vol. 29, p. 24, a Ukrainian male construction engineer born about 1905 into the middle class; and no. 66, A, vol. 6, p. 26, a Russian male bookkeeper born about 1906 to a white-collar family.

69. Getty, *Origins,* 33.

70. A. A. Zhdanov, *Uroki politicheskikh oshibok Saratovskogo kraikoma* (Khabarovsk: Dal'giz, 1935), 38, 8.

71. Frank Lorimer, *The Population of the Soviet Union: History and Prospects* (Geneva: League of Nations, 1946), 149.
72. HP no. 97, A, vol. 7, pp. 13–14. This Ukrainian woman, born about 1914 into a family of well-off peasants, worked as a maid until 1937, then as a clerk in a food store.
73. HP no. 307, A, vol. 16, p. 11. This Russian male textile engineer and teacher was born about 1897 into the middle class.
74. One case was reported by HP no. 644, A, vol. 30, p. 31; a student before the war, she was a Ukrainian born around 1920 into the family of a government employee and tsarist officer. Two other such incidents, dating from 1930 and 1935, were reported by HP no. 1106, A, vol. 31, p. 9. This female Cossack, born about 1894 into a gentry family, worked in Khar'kov as a librarian.
75. HP no. 96, A, vol. 7, p. 4, a Russian male economic planner born around 1909. His father was a priest. Similar cases are in nos. 88, A, vol. 6, p. 7, and no. 93, A, vol. 7, p. 21.
76. HP no. 114, A, vol. 9, p. 10, a Russian male bookkeeper born about 1893 to a middle-class family.
77. HP no. 118, A, vol. 9, p. 5, a Ukrainian male born about 1910 into a poor-to-average peasant family and employed in a sanatorium.
78. HP no. 143, A, vol. 11, p. 23, a Russian male agronomist born about 1923. His father was a well-off peasant.
79. HP no. 1368, A, vol. 33, p. 10. This female Russian was born about 1905 into a family of poor-average peasants.
80. *Za Industrializatsiiu,* February 3, 1937, quoted in Andrle, *Workers,* 76.
81. HP no. 147, p. 62.
82. HP no. 105, B3, p. 24.
83. Tsikulin, *Istoriia,* 222.
84. See Conquest, *Inside Stalin's Secret Police,* 2, 28, 30, 86–87.
85. HP no. 147, 75–76.
86. "A. Dneprovets," untitled ms in the Aleksandr Vozniuk-Burmin file, BA, 16. "Dneprovets" appears to have been Vozniuk-Burmin.
87. HP no. 127, A, vol. 10, p. 7, a Russian male student born about 1924. The incident concerned his father.
88. David Remnick, "Letter from Moscow," *The New Yorker,* March 23, 1992, 68.
89. HP no. 147, A, vol. 12, p. 4; and no. 136, A, vol. 11, pp. 10–11, a Russian male born about 1903. His father was a noble and an army officer.
90. HP no. 149, A, vol. 12, pp. 38–39. This Russian male lawyer, from the prerevolutionary gentry, was born about 1899.
91. Repin, Manuscripts, 243–44. And see also his "Na sluzhbe v sovetskoi razvedke," Nicolaevsky Collection, HI, b. 233, f. 7, where he uses the name A. Almazov.
92. Kendall E. Bailes, *Technology and Society under Lenin and Stalin: Origins of the Soviet Technical Intelligentsia, 1917–1941* (Princeton: Princeton University Press, 1978), 422.
93. This is noted, e.g., by Weissberg, *Accused,* 81.
94. Vladimir D. Samarin, "The Soviet School, 1936–1942." In *Soviet Education,* ed. George Kline. (London: Routledge and Kegan Paul, 1957), 49. Solzhenitsyn, *Gulag,* 1:11, gives a similar story of a man who fled and lived elsewhere under his own name.

95. Eugenia Ginzburg, *Journey into the Whirlwind,* trans. Paul Stevenson and Max Hayward (New York: Harcourt, Brace, Jovanovich, 1967), 23, 166.

96. HP no. 371, B5, p. 34; no biographical data available.

97. HP no. 287, p. 9.

98. "Dneprovets," untitled ms, 7.

99. HP no. 67, A, vol. 6, p. 5. This Ukrainian newspaperman and screenwriter was born about 1910 into a noble family.

100. RGAE-TsGANKh, f. 7566, o. 1, d. 3537 b, l. 121. In another kombinat of the same date, of seven executives, none had been working more than three months (ibid., l. 211). Mikhail Boikov, *Liudi sovetskoi tiur'my,* 2 vols. (Buenos Aires: Seiatel', 1957), 1:334, claims that of 104 communists working for the Oil Institute in Groznyi, only 2, a guard and a cleaning woman, escaped arrest. Boikov was a young journalist when he was arrested in 1937.

101. HP no. 1495, A, vol. 35, p. 7, a Russian female school teacher born about 1918 into the old middle class.

102. K. Ivanenko, Manuscripts, "Shlema," BA, 1.

103. HP no. 432, A, vol. 21, p. 18, a Russian male employee at a machine-tractor station in the countryside, born about 1921 into a family of poor-to-average peasants.

104. HP no. 110, A, vol. 8, pp. 3, 15, a Russian male army officer from a worker's family, born around 1917. See also no. 56, A, vol. 5, pp. 8–9, an officer and the son of an officer, born about 1914, who reported that many of his arrested peers returned to duty in 1938–39.

105. HP no. 139, A, vol. 11, p. 5; see also no. 167, A, vol. 12, p. 4, a Russian male watchmaker born about 1904 into a middle-class family. See also HP no. 449, B11 p. 8, a Russian woman born about 1922 into a family of well-to-do peasants. She was a rank-and-file worker. Also HP no. 138, A, vol. 11, pp. 20–21; and no. 144, A. vol. 11, pp. 8–9.

106. N. Otradin, "Poputnye zametki," *Novoe Russkoe Slovo,* October 11, 1975.

107. Author's interview with Nikolai Alekseevich Avdeev, Nikita Ivanovich Chepel', Evgenii Leont'evich Gorushitel', and Konstantin Vasil'evich Pushkin, all former workers of the Likhachev (formerly Stalin) Auto Factory, Moscow, April 12, 1988.

108. Solzhenitsyn, *Gulag,* 1:71. Weissberg, *Accused,* 321, relates a story from 1938: all the males of a Romany (gypsy) band were arrested for stealing from a kolkhoz, even though they had been grazing their animals there with permission. Petr I. Iakir, in *Detstvo v tiur'me* (New York: Macmillan, 1972), 38–40, mentions another case of fifty Romany having been arrested at one time.

109. Ivan N. Minishki, "Illiuzii i deistvitel'nost'," BA, 272; Iakir, *Detstvo,* 28.

110. Rittersporn, *Stalinist Simplifications,* 205; and see "Les souvenirs d'un agent soviétique," *La Tribune de Genève,* December 14, 1949, in the Nicolaevsky Collection, HI, b. 295, f. 2. The article mentions "socialist competition" between the NKVD and military counterintelligence.

111. "O tom kak raionnye upravleniia NKVD poluchali 'tverdye zadaniia' po sozdaniiu kontr-revoliutsionnykh del po st. 58. ugolovnogo kodeksa"; marked no. V-825, Nicolaevsky Collection, HI, b. 296, f. 13, p. 12.

112. Vadim A. Denisov, "Organizatsiia, metody i tekhnika sledstviia v organakh gosbezopasnosti SSSR," Nicolaevsky Collection, HI, b. 293, f. 7, p. 5.

113. "Morning Edition," National Public Radio, February 26, 1992.

114. D. A. Volkogonov, "Fenomena Stalina," *Literaturnaia Gazeta,* no. 50, December 9, 1987, 13.

115. Denisov, "Organizatsiia," 5.

116. Volkogonov, *Triumf i tragediia,* vol. 1, pt. 1, p. 274.

117. Denisov, "Organizatsiia," 5.

118. A. T., "Tipy: Professor Makarov," BA, 3.

119. F. Beck and W. Godin [Konstantin Shteppa], *Russian Purge and the Extraction of Confession,* trans. Eric Mosbacher and David Porter (New York: Viking, 1951), 228–29, 168–69. These two writers, one Soviet and one German by origin, were both highly educated; Shteppa was a historian. Other examples are in A. T., "Manuscript," BA, 3–4; Abdurakhman Avtorkhanov, *Memuary* (Frankfurt: Posev, 1983), 519; Boikov, *Liudi,* 1:34; and Fedor Ivanovich Gorb, "Chernyi uragan," BA, 46.

120. Victor Kravchenko, *I Chose Justice* (New York: Scribner's, 1950), 232–33.

121. Tokaev, *Betrayal,* 178.

122. [Mikhail Gorokhov], "From the NKVD to the Polish Army," in David Dalin file (Dalin retained the original Russian spelling of his name for this file), BA, 18. Aleksandr Solzhenitsyn almost joined the NKVD as a young man; he had nothing against the organization at the time but wanted to pursue other interests. See his *Gulag,* 1:160.

123. [Gorokhov], "From the NKVD," 23.

124. And see the statements by an NKVD man in *An End to Silence: Uncensored Opinion in the Soviet Union: From Roy Medvedev's Underground Magazine Political Diary,* ed. and with an introduction by Stephen F. Cohen, trans. George Saunders (New York: Norton, 1982), 137–39.

125. Starkov, "Narkom Ezhov," 33, quoting TsPA (RTsKhIDNI), "Lichnoe delo Ezhova N. I."

126. "Les souvenirs," 5; G. Murat, "Chetvertyi kabinet," Nicolaevsky Collection, HI, b. 412, f. 37, p. 10. A letter from B. S. Konoplianko, who joined the NKVD in 1939, speaks of torture by "enemies of the people" within the police but not of the idea that no "enemies" existed in society (*Ogonek,* no. 5 [January 1988], 5). Finally, see Ioffe, *Odna noch',* 124–25.

127. I. G. R., "Pochemu ia bezhal iz Sovetskogo Soiuza," in B. M. Kuznetsov, *V ugodu stalinu: Gody 1945–1946,* 2 vols. (New York: Voennyi Vestnik, 1956), 1:54.

128. Israel K., the deputy director of a lumber enterprise, was arrested in August 1938. He was held for nine months and tortured but refused to sign a confession. At his "trial" a judge-general of a Military Collegium had the following response to his complaint about torture: "Well, what else could we do with you when you refused to sign?" In Sylvia Rothchild, *A Special Legacy: An Oral History of Soviet Jewish Emigrés in the United States* (New York: Simon and Schuster, 1985), 75–76.

129. "NKVD SSSR," b. 294, f. 1, 7.

130. HP no. 1720, A, vol. 37, p. 14, a Ukrainian female secretary born about 1898; she was the daughter of a priest. See also a similar story in no. 611, A, vol. 29, pp. 37–39.

131. Solzhenitsyn, *Gulag,* 1:160.

132. HP no. 65, B2, vol. 3, p. 10, a male born about 1900–03; no other biographical data.

133. HP no. 26, A, vol. 3, p. 13, a Russian male born about 1904 into a family of poor-to-average peasants. He became the chief engineer of a factory. See the same view expressed in a group discussion with four former Soviet executives, HP, B162 (folder materials in the Harvard Russian Research Center), B2, p. 10; and in no. 65, A, vol. 6, p. 7.

134. HP no. 105, B3, pp. 34–35.

135. HP no. 287, A, vol. 15, pp. 14–15.

136. Victor Kravchenko, *I Chose Freedom: The Personal and Political Life of a Soviet Official* (New York: Scribner's, 1946), 232–74; and HP no. 102, A, vol. 8, p. 18.

137. Valentina Bogdan, *Mimikriia v SSSR: Vospominaniia inzhenera 1935–1940 godov* (Frankfurt: Avtor, 1982), 143.

138. HP no. 105, B3, pp. 32–33.

139. Denisov, "Organizatsiia," 1–2.

140. SA, b. 44, r. 43, WKP 386, ll. 132–33.

141. HP no. 97, A, vol. 7, p. 14, told by a Ukrainian female worker born about 1914 into a family of well-off peasants. The sister was beaten while in custody. No. 85, A, vol. 6, p. 8, recounted the story of her father's arrest for two weeks in 1939 after his wife received letters from a White Guard cousin living abroad. The man arrested was an ordinary peasant.

142. HP no. 29, A, vol. 3, p. 33, a Belorussian male electrician born about 1909 into the family of a worker.

143. HP no. 190, A, vol. 14, p. 19, a Ukrainian male engineer born around 1915 into the family of a white-collar employee.

144. HP no. 23, B5, p. 4. This respondent, a superintendent of animal breeding for a network of six collective farms, was a Kalmyk male born about 1922 into a poor-to-average peasant family.

145. Victor Herman, *Coming Out of the Ice: An Unexpected Life* (New York: Harcourt, Brace, Jovanovich, 1979), 162.

146. Konstantin Shteppa, "Volna massovykh arrestov," Nicolaevsky Collection, HI, p. 33.

147. HP no. 431, A, vol. 21, p. 5; the respondent, who told this story about her uncle, was a Russian female born about 1923. Her father was a physician from the gentry.

148. Beck and Godin, *Russian Purge,* 42.

149. Nina Kosterina, *Dnevnik Niny Kosterinoi* (Moscow: Detskaia Literatura, 1964), 102.

150. HP no. 224, B5, p. 1; the respondent was a Mordvin man born in 1925. No other biographical data are available.

151. A. T., manuscript, "Fokin," 3–4, and "'Vzryvshchik Kremlia' Naidenov," 1–2.

152. Weissberg, *Accused,* 208.

153. HP no. 111, A, vol. 9, pp. 32–33, a Russian male school teacher born about 1920 into a middle-class family. A. T., "Tipy," 1, mentions the president of an oblast' party committee who, under arrest, denounced the whole apparatus of a raion agricultural department and half the oblast' collective farm presidents. Shteppa, "Volna," 29, mentions a somewhat similar story that led to the arrest of a factory director, a regional party secretary, and "very many" ordinary workers, peasants, and employees supposedly connected with a plot.

154. HP no. 99, A, vol. 7, p. 22, a Ukrainian male factory foreman born about 1909 into a family of well-off peasants.

155. HP no. 358, A, vol. 19, p. 6, a collective farmer born about 1925 into a family of poor-to-average peasants.

156. SA, b. 44, r. 43, WKP 386, ll. 132–33; and see HP no. 358, p. 6, who said that when collective farm peasants denounced their chair, the NKVD would always investigate.

157. Beck and Godin, *Russian Purge*, 195–97. A. V. Gorbatov, *Years Off My Life: The Memoirs of General of the Soviet Army A. V. Gorbatov* (London: Constable, 1964), 124, relates the story of the head of a railroad political department who incriminated three hundred people. He reasoned that "the worse it is, the better it is—like that it will all be cleared up more quickly."

158. Nikolai Borodin, *One Man in His Time* (New York: Macmillan, 1955), 219–21.

159. See Robert McCutcheon, "The 1936–1937 Purge of Soviet Astronomers," *SR* 50, no. 1 (Spring 1991), 100–17; and Hugh D. Hudson, Jr., "Terror in Soviet Architecture," *SR* 51 no. 3 (Fall 1992), 448–67.

160. Elizabeth Lermolo, *Face of a Victim*, trans. I. D. Talmadge (New York: Harper, 1955), 214–15; Boikov, *Liudi*, 2:86.

161. Weissberg, *Accused*, 348–49; S. Swianiewicz, *Forced Labour and Economic Development* (London: Oxford University Press, 1965), 17.

162. Nadezhda Ulanovskiia and Maia Ulanovskiia, *Istoriia odnoi sem'i* (New York: Chalidze, 1982), 135; Mikhail Shul'man, *Butyrskii dekameron*, 3 vols. (Tel Aviv: Effect, 1979–82), 1:10; L. Sheinin, "Iubilei," *Kom. Pravda*, November 15, 1964; HP no. 344, A, vol. 18, p. 12, a Cherkassian male worker, then student in a factory school, born about 1924; his father was a poor-to-average peasant. And see no. 391, B10, p. 5; no biographical data.

163. HP no. 359, A, vol. 19, p. 24. This Russian male, born about 1907, came from a family of poor-to-average peasants.

164. Ibid.

165. HP no. 45, A, vol. 4, p. 27, a Belorussian man born about 1911 into the middle class who became a school inspector and then commissar of education for the Belorussian Republic. And see HP no. 179, A, vol. 13, p. 23, a Russian theatrical director and writer born about 1901 into a noble family. Also no. 403, B10, p. 2, a man arrested in 1937 for three months who was not tortured; no biographical data available.

166. Boikov, *Liudi*, 1:241; see also 2:86.

167. G. A. Tokaev, *Comrade X* (London: Harvill, 1956), 2, 5, 7, 10, 20–21, 48.

168. Medvedev, *K sudu istorii*, 319.

169. HP no. 427, B5, p. 12; no biographical data available.

170. HP no. 24, A, vol. 3, p. 14. This man, born about 1913, claimed to have been from the Azerbaijani aristocracy.

171. HP no. 86, A, vol. 6, p. 17. This Azerbaijani male, born about 1911 into the middle class, worked as a butcher's helper.

172. See Eugene Victor Walter, *Terror and Resistance: A Study of Political Violence, with Case Studies of Some Primitive African Communities* (New York: Oxford University Press, 1969).

173. HP no. 147, A, vol. 12, p. 57; and Beck and Godin, *Russian Purge*, 163.

174. LC Document A.27.21, a letter from a group of jurists of October 1939 to A. A. Zhdanov, a member of the Politburo.

175. SA, Nicolaevsky Collection, HI, l. 89; "Otchet partiinogo komiteta Oshosdora UNKVD po Zap. Obl. za vremia s 22 maia 1936 g." This material from the Smolensk Archive is not contained in the National Archives collection.

176. SA, b. 44, r. 43, WKP 386, ll. 273–75, a letter to the secretary of the oblast' party committee from a former party member who joined it in 1918 and entered the OGPU in 1924.

177. SA, T88, b. 4, r. 74, WKP 538, l. 27, a meeting of the obkom, May 26, 1936. And see a similar reinstatement after a raion committee expelled a man who had been in the Red Army, the Cheka, and the OGPU; meeting of the obkom, January 4, 1936, ibid., l. 3.
178. SA, T88, b. 4, r. 74, WKP 538, l. 12; an obkom biuro meeting, June 25, 1936.
179. Ibid., July 23, 1936.
180. SA, b. 29, r. 28, WKP 238, l. 178, a letter from the obkom to raion secretaries and the head of the NKVD administration, October 4, 1937.
181. SA, b. 44, r. 43, WKP 386, l. 40, September 22, 1935. Sentence of the Voennyi Tribunal Pogranichnoi i Vnytrennei okhrany Zapadnoi oblasti i vyezdnoi sessii v g. Klintsy. See also ibid., l. 43, the obkom to the Central Committee of the Party, Special Sector, section 5, February 10, 1936.
182. A. Iakovleva, "Na raionnykh partiinykh sobraniiakh," *Komm., K,* no. 15, August 15, 1936.
183. SA, Nicolaevsky Collection, HI, protocol no. 7, closed session of the party committee, March 23, 1937, l. 131.
184. N. Klobukov, "Nekotorye vyvody," *Komm., K.,* no. 11, June 1937.
185. G. Rezepov, "Do kontsa ispravit' oshibki," *Komm., K.,* no. 11, June 1937.
186. P. Piiakin, "Bol'shevistskaia kritika," *Komm., K.,* no. 9, May 1938.
187. HP no. 163, B191, B5, p. 3; no biographical data.
188. HP no. 1296, A, vol. 33, pp. 6, 21. This Russian female singer and blueprint copyist was born about 1910 into the family of a tsarist colonel.
189. HP no. 1467, A, vol. 34, pp. 52–53. This Russian male civil engineer was born about 1910; his father was an engineer.
190. HP no. 1398, A, vol. 34, p. 16. This Ukrainian female railroad worker was born about 1905 to poor-to-average peasants.
191. Grigorenko, *Memoirs,* 79–84.
192. Ibid., 88–90. For a similar story about a military party group, see Roger R. Reese, "The Red Army and the Great Purges," in Getty and Manning, *Stalinist Terror,* 208.
193. HP no. 1720, A, vol. 37, pp. 4, 42–43.
194. Varlam Shalamov, *Kolymskie rasskazy* (London: Overseas Publications Interchange, 1978), 28.
195. Ibid., 159–60; similar accounts are in Solzhenitsyn, *Gulag,* vol. 2.
196. V. Petrov, "Kushan'e bez pripravy," Nicolaevsky Collection, HI, b. 279, f. 2, p. 1. Petrov spent five and a half years in Kolyma, beginning in mid-1936.
197. HP no. 1123, A, vol. 32, p. 12. This Russian male writer was born about 1916 into the family of a white-collar employee.
198. Boris Filippov, "Komissiia Koshketina. (Rasprava NKVD v Ukht-Pechorskom lagere v 1938 g.)," Nicolaevsky Collection, HI, b. 279, f. 5, p. 5.
199. Gustav Herling, *A World Apart,* trans. Joseph Marek (New York: New American Library, 1952), 63–64.
200. Margarete Buber (Neumann), *Under Two Dictators,* trans. Edward Fitzgerald (London: Victor Gollancz, 1949), 62–63.
201. Joseph Berger, *Nothing but the Truth* (New York: John Day, 1971), 124; and see Herman, *Coming Out,* 247.
202. Zemskov, "Arkhipelag GULAG," 2.

203. GARF, f. 9401s, o. 1a, d. 9, ll. 94–95, order 0072, February 17, 1936. For an example of Vyshinskii's complaints to Iagoda, see GARF, f. 8131sch, o. 27, d. 69, a letter of April 3, 1936. Such protests went back at least to 1934; see a letter to Stalin from I. Akulov, procurator of the USSR, June 4, 1934, on rapes, beatings, and shootings in the camps. Akulov asked that these problems be stopped (GARF, f. 8131sch, o. 27, d. 28, l. 29).

204. Lermolo, *Face,* 159.

205. Buber (Neumann), *Under Two Dictators,* 75. See also Ioffe, *Odna noch',* 68, for a similar observation.

206. Ioffe, *Odna noch',* 8.

207. Gorb, "Cherny," 46.

208. HP no. 385, A, vol. 19, p. 27. This Russian male journalist was born about 1911 into the family of a tailor.

209. Kravchenko, *I Chose Justice,* 249, 255, 258.

210. Ioffe, *Odna noch',* 71.

211. Boikov, *Liudi,* 1:333.

212. HP no. 354, B5, p. 4; no biographical data available.

213. A. Rakhalov, "Zhemchuzhina zapoliar'ia," BA, 49–50.

214. Ibid., 52, estimates 1,300; HP no. 385, B2, p. 2, gives a similar figure. See also Ioffe, *Odna noch',* 21 and 99, on such killings.

215. On these shootings, see, e.g., David J. Dallin and Boris I. Nicolaevsky, *Forced Labor in Soviet Russia* (New Haven: Yale University Press, 1947), 131; and Vladimir Petrov, *It Happens in Russia: Seven Years Forced Labour in the Siberian Goldfields* (London: Eyre and Spottiswoode, 1951), 172.

216. "Two Soviet Painters," Sergei Lvov's story, David Dalin file, BA, 130.

217. Buber (Neumann), *Under Two Dictators,* 110; in all likelihood the incident occurred in 1938.

218. "Two Soviet Painters," Sergei Lvov's story, 132. See also HP no. 21, B5, p. 12; no biographical data available.

219. Zemskov, "Arkhipelag GULAG," 2.

220. Repin, Manuscripts, 255.

221. HP no. 159, A, vol. 13, pp. 3, 9. This Avarets male tractor driver was born about 1910 to poor-to-average peasants. Buber (Neumann) also worked on a farm (*Under Two Dictators,* 80).

222. HP no. 417, A, vol. 21, pp. 3–4. This Russian male driver and woodworker was born about 1923; his father was a disadvantaged worker.

223. Herman, *Coming Out,* 208, 216–17.

224. Getty, Rittersporn, and Zemskov, "Victims," 1036–37.

225. Ibid.

226. HP no. 92, A, vol. 7, p. 11. This Russian male factory foreman was born about 1911 into a family of well-off peasants.

227. *Perekovka* (which means "reforging," in this case referring to the rehabilitation of criminals), the organ of the KVO Upravleniia Belbaltkombinata of the NKVD, January 15, 1936, in the Lavr Andreevich Lichin papers, BA.

228. *Perekovka,* January 15, 1935.

229. *Perekovka,* January 15, 1936.

230. Petrov, *It Happens,* 162–64, 171–72; and Mikhail Ivanovich Nil'skii, "Krov' v tundre," 44, in "Pobeg" (ms) and other papers, BA.

231. Swianiewicz, *Forced Labour,* 17.

232. HP no. 32, A, vol. 4, pp. 13, 18, 32. This Russian male was born no later than 1898 into a family of well-to-do peasants. He was a rank-and-file intellectual.

233. See Ginzburg, *Journey into the Whirlwind*; and Robert Conquest, *Kolyma: The Arctic Death Camps* (New York: Oxford University Press, 1979).

234. Petrov, *It Happens,* 186; Shul'man, *Butyrskii dekameron,* 1:47.

235. Gorbatov, *Years off My Life,* 129.

236. V. Pozdniakov, "Glavnoe upravlenie stroitel'stva Dal'nogo severa NKVD SSSR (Dal'stroi NKVD SSSR) (Po materialam inzhenera stroitel'stva g-na G.)," Nicolaevsky Collection, HI, b. 294, f. 8, pp. 294–98; p. 23 of the manuscript.

237. See Ginzburg, *Journey into the Whirlwind,* 367, 404–05.

238. Weissberg, *Accused,* 362–65.

239. Swianiewicz, *Forced Labour,* 206.

240. S. G. Wheatcroft, "On Assessing the Size of Forced Concentration Camp Labour in the Soviet Union, 1929–1956," *Soviet Studies* 33, no. 2 (April 1981), 270.

241. Getty, *Origins,* 163–71. Khlevniuk, *1937-i,* discusses cases of high-level emissaries from the center whipping up local party organizations to hunt for enemies more zealously.

242. One example was Pavel Postyshev in Ukraine and later in Kuibyshev oblast' (see chap. 4, this vol.).

Chapter Four: The Terror Ends

1. TsPA (RTsKhIDNI), f. 17, o. 2, d. 639, l. 3; a meeting of the Central Committee on January 14, 1938.

2. Ibid., ll. 3, 5.

3. Hiroaki Kuromiya, "Stalinist Terror in the Donbas: A Note," in Getty and Manning, *Stalinist Terror,* 217–18, details the devastation of the party in the Donbass. Rural party leaders also suffered greatly; see Daniel Thorniley, *The Rise and Fall of the Soviet Rural Communist Party, 1927–1939* (New York: St. Martin's, 1988), esp. 148.

4. TsPA (RTsKhIDNI), f. 17, o. 2, d. 639, l. 5.

5. Ibid., l. 6.

6. *P,* January 19, 1938; and see the editorial of January 22, which proclaimed the need to unmask "real," not "imaginary," enemies.

7. *P,* January 26, 1938.

8. GARF, f. 5446sch, o. 29, d. 178, December 15, 1937.

9. GARF, f. 8131sch, o. 27, d. 111, l. 13, letter from Vyshinskii to Molotov, n. d. (but early 1938), reply to a document of November 15, 1937.

10. GARF, f. 5446sch, o. 29, d. 179, ll. 191, 180, 195, 179, January–June 1938.

11. GARF, f. 8131sch, o. 27, d. 69, ll. 5–6, 7; January 19 and 24, 1938.

12. Ibid., d. 106, l. 19, January 24, 1938.

13. Ibid., d. 111, ll. 5–6, Vyshinskii to Stalin and Molotov, February 19, 1938.

14. GARF, f. 5446sch, o. 29, d. 179, l. 187, order no. 187–75, February 25, 1938.

15. GARF, f. 8131sch, o. 27, d. 111, l. 20, letter from Vyshinskii to Molotov, February 28, 1938. Vyshinskii wanted to add fifteen employees to deal with complaints.

16. Ibid., l. 46, Vyshinskii to Stalin and Molotov, March 13, 1938.

17. Ibid., d. 69, l. 14, Vyshinskii to Frinovskii (Ezhov's deputy), February 4, 1938; Vyshinskii's emphasis.

18. See, e.g., N. Sudarikov, "Klevetniki pered sovetskim sudom," *SIu*, no. 14, July 30, 1938, 16; A. Svidler, "Dela o klevete," *SIu*, nos. 20–21, November 5, 1938, 61.

19. GARF, f. 8131sch, o. 27, d. 106, ll. 44–45, protocol no. 14, March 22, 1938.

20. Ibid., d. 111, l. 118, Vyshinskii to Ezhov, March 17, 1938.

21. Ibid., l. 101, Vyshinskii to Malenkov at the Central Committee, March 29, 1938.

22. Ibid., d. 106, ll. 54, 66, 68, 84, 118, 170; protocol no. 57, October 7, 1938, l. 217, reports that in Sverdlovsk oblast' 36 percent of the cases checked were groundless. The document does not say whether these were counterrevolutionary cases.

23. GARF, f. 5446sch, o. 29, d. 179, l. 151, order 705/345, June 22, 1938.

24. GARF, 8131sch, o. 27, d. 106, l. 126, protocol no. 35, July 25, 1938.

25. Ibid., d. 145, ll. 107–09, part of the interrogation record of a former member of a troika. "Was it known to you that cases of arrestees after 1 August 1938 could not be brought [to the troiki]? Answer: "Yes, it was known to me."

26. *P,* August 2, 1938.

27. *P,* October 22, 1938.

28. Solomon, "Soviet Criminal Justice," 407.

29. A. Chuianov, *Na stremine veka: Zapiski sekretaria obkoma.* (Moscow: Politizdat, 1976), 42–48.

30. Ibid., 45.

31. For examples of reinstatements at this time, see A. N. Afinogenov, *Stat'i, dnevniki, pis'ma, vospominaniia* (Moscow: Iskusstvo, 1957), 167–80, 335, 337; *P,* January 2, 1938; *Komm., K.,* no. 10, May 1938; and Beck and Godin, *Russian Purge,* 200, for people released and reinstated in their jobs.

32. SA, b. 38, r. 37, WKKP 322, l. 14. Protocol no. 2, the Tumanovo RO of the NKVD, January 22, 1938.

33. Ibid., e.g., ll. 1–5, a meeting of April 11, 1938. This was an open, general gathering.

34. *The Great Purge Trial,* ed. and with notes by Robert C. Tucker and Stephen F. Cohen (New York: Grosset and Dunlap, 1965), 341, 660. On Bukharin at this moment, see Stephen F. Cohen, *Bukharin and the Bolshevik Revolution: A Political Biography, 1888–1938* (New York: Oxford University Press, 1973), 365–81.

35. *Krasnaia Kareliia* (Petrozavodsk), April 10, 1938.

36. As told by HP no. 144, p. 36.

37. Knight, *Beria,* 87–89; she adds that Ezhov was preparing a plot against Beria at this point, but her evidence is thin. Conquest, *Inside Stalin's Secret Police,* 70–79, tells a similar story about Ezhov's difficulties but without mentioning dismissed assistants.

38. GARF, f. 8131sch, o. 27, d. 116, l. 44, letter from Vyshinskii to Ezhov, October 11, 1938.

39. TsPA (RTsKhIDNI), f. 17, o. 3, d. 1003, ll. 85–86, "Ob arestakh, prokurorskom nadzore i vedenii sledstviia," a resolution of Sovnarkom and the CC, dated November 17, 1938, and signed by Molotov and Stalin.

40. GARF, f. 9401, o. 2, d. 1, ll. 2–4, order 00762, November 26, 1938.

41. TsPA (RTsKhIDNI), f. 17, o. 3, d. 1003, ll. 82–84, Ezhov to Stalin, November 23, 1938.

42. Ibid., ll. 34–35.

43. From an account by E. G. Feldman, cited in Medvedev, *Let History Judge*, 459–61. Medvedev would not allow me to examine his copy.

44. *ITsK*, no. 12 (1989), 89.

45. Alliluyeva, *Twenty Letters*, 7-8; Khrushchev, "Secret Speech," S34, S46, S50; and Medvedev, *On Stalin*, 100.

46. On Beria's reputation as a sex maniac, see Vaksberg, *Stalin's Prosecutor*, 291; and Evgenii Evtushenko, *Avtobiografiia* (London: Flegon Press, 1964), 103.

47. Alliluyeva, *Twenty Letters*, 137–38.

48. Other rumors concerning Beria and his relationship with Stalin are recounted in Nikolai Zhusenin, "Beriia," *Nedelia*, no. 8 (February 22–28, 1988); and S. Mikoian (son of A. I. Mikoian, a longtime Politburo member), "Sluga," *Kom. Pravda*, February 21, 1988. Beria was questioned by the party Presidium (Politburo) in 1953 and called an "enemy of the people"; "Plenum TsK," *ITsK*, no. 1 (January 1991), 146.

49. Knight, *Beria*, 35–50.

50. Medvedev, *Let History Judge*, 464.

51. Conquest, *Great Terror: A Reassessment*, 434–35; Zhusenin, "Beriia"; and Mikoian, "Sluga."

52. Khrushchev, "Secret Speech," S34–35.

53. Men'shagin, *Vospominaniia*, 38.

54. Weissberg, *Accused*, 324.

55. Evgenii Gnedin, "Sebia ne poteriat," *Novyi Mir*, no. 7 (1988), 180. Other high-ranking officials were also tortured after Ezhov's fall, for instance, Marshal Bliukher and Aleksandr Kosarev, head of the Komsomol; see Knight, *Beria*, 99.

56. Ivanov-Razumnik, *Memoirs*, 323; Ioffe, *Odna noch'*, 127; Avtorkhanov, *Memuary*, 56; Prychodko, *Fifteen Million*, 92; Beck and Godin, *Russian Purge*, 48.

57. Ivanov-Razumnik, *Memoirs*, 335–37.

58. Volkogonov, *Triumf i tragediia*, vol. 1, pt. 2, p. 301.

59. Solomon, "Soviet Criminal Justice," 408.

60. Men'shagin, *Vospominaniia*, 38–56.

61. Petro Grigorenko's brother was arrested but released in the course of one year, 1937. Petro took his stories about torture to an assistant of Vyshinskii's in early 1938. The procurator-general then moved to correct the situation. Grigorenko, *Memoirs*, 95–101.

62. "O rabote za 1939 god. Iz otcheta nachal'nika Upravleniia po nachal'stvuiushchemu sostavu RKKA Narkomata Oborony SSSR E. A. Shchadenko, 5 May 1940," *ITsK*, no. 1 (1990), 188–89.

63. Komal, "Voennye," 24, 25. There are slight discrepancies in the way his figures add up, but this is a matter of several hundreds.

64. Roger R. Reese, "The Red Army and the Great Purges," in Getty and Manning, *Stalinist Terror*, 199.

65. Komal, "Voennye," 24.

66. Interview with Major General of Justice V. Frolov, Deputy Chief Military Prosecutor of the USSR, CDSP 42, no. 42 (1990), 31.

67. Komal, "Voennye," 25.

68. *P,* June 22, 1989.

69. As calculated in the text. Reese, "Red Army," 199, gives a figure of 22,705 men discharged between 1937 and May 1940 whose fates are unknown. I cannot determine how Reese arrived at this total, but it is compatible with Komal's.

70. "O rabote za 1939 god," 189.

71. For earlier guesses of the number of officers purged, see Conquest, *The Great Terror: Stalin's Purge of the Thirties,* 228, 485; and John Erickson, *The Soviet High Comand* (New York: St. Martin's, 1962), 449, 451–52.

72. Ismail Akhmedov, *In and Out of Stalin's GRU: A Tatar's Escape from Red Army Intelligence* (Frederick, Md.: University Publications of America, 1984), 100.

73. HP no. 27, A, vol. 3, p. 20. This Russian male collective farmer was born about 1924 to peasants that were poor to well-to-do. Kravchenko, *I Chose Justice,* 172–77, relates the case of Andrei Lebid, arrested in December 1937; his case was reviewed twice, and he was released in 1941.

74. *SIu,* no. 2 (January 1939), 19.

75. E.g., see "Sudebnaia praktika," *SIu,* nos. 17–18 (May 1939), 59–60; no. 5 (March 1939), 71–72; no. 2 (January 1940), 40–41; and no. 18 (September 30, 1938), 48.

76. Solomon, "Soviet Criminal Justice," 409, 410n.

77. Ibid., 410.

78. Lev Kopelev, *To Be Preserved Forever* (Philadelphia: Lippincott, 1977), 182.

79. I. T. Goliakov, "XVIII s"ezd VKP(b) i zadachi sudebnykh organov," *SIu,* no. 8 (April 1939), 3–5.

80. GARF, f. 8131sch, o. 27, d. 118, ll. 25–37.

81. Ibid., ll. 65–67, from the head of the Leningrad oblast' NKVD Goglidze to Beria, December 25, 1938. See also d. 145, l. 138, a letter from the NKVD chief in the KASSR Burdakov to Merkulov, assistant head of the NKVD, July 16, 1939.

82. LC Document A.27.21, October 28, 1939.

83. GARF, f. 8131sch, o. 27, d. 145, ll. 129–32, Beria to Pankrat'ev, October 1, 1939, and Pankrat'ev's reply of the 27th. Note the delay of twenty-six days in responding.

84. E.g, ibid., o. 28, d. 60, ll. 183–84, 187–88, 189 ff.

85. Ibid., d. 46, l. 60, order 62–40s, March 23, 1940.

86. Ibid., d. 239, ll. 63–64, letter to Stalin, March 23, 1940.

87. Ernst Tallgren [S. Swianiewicz], "The Corrective Labor Camps," in Dallin and Nicolaevsky, *Forced Labor,* 9.

88. Swianiewicz, *Forced Labour,* 202.

89. Pozdniakov, "Glavnoe," 294–98 (p. 25 of the manuscript).

90. Petrov, *It Happens,* 121, 131.

91. Herling, *World Apart,* 100–01.

92. Buber (Neumann), *Under Two Dictators,* 80.

93. Kravchenko, *I Chose Justice,* 260–61.

94. Gorbatov, *Years,* 147; see also HP, no. 354, B5, p. 6.

95. Tallgren, "Corrective Labor," 9.

96. Such trials are mentioned in Avtorkhanov, *Memuary,* 615; Beck and Godin, *Russian Purge,* 169;

and Weissberg, *Accused*, 12. Trials of procurators or political or regular policemen are in *P*, October 22, 1938; *Krasnoe Znamia* (Tomsk), February 24, 1939; *Krasnaia Kareliia*, February 9, 1939; *Sotsialisticheskaia Iakutiia* (Iakutsk), February 12, 1939; and Murat, "Chetvertyi kabinet," 12.

97. *Krasnoe Znamia*, February 24, 1939.

98. *Krasnaia Kareliia*, February 9, 1939.

99. Conquest, *Inside Stalin's Secret Police*, 87.

100. HP, no. 40, pp. 44–45.

101. "Dneprovets," untitled manuscript, 32; his emphasis.

102. Mavrin, "Svetlaninskii dal'nevostochnyi zagovor," Nicolaevsky Collection, HI, b. 412, f. 6, p. 5.

103. H. G. Friese, "Student Life in a Soviet University," in *Soviet Education*, ed. George Kline (London: Routledge and Kegan Paul, 1957), 65–66.

104. *P*, December 3, 1938; *Kom. Pravda*, January 10, 1939.

105. HP no. 70, B2, p. 6. This man, born in the 1890s, was the shop head of a textile mill. His account of an investigative commission is confirmed by a former naval intelligence officer, HP no. 105, B3, p. 36.

106. HP no. 70, B2, p. 6.

107. Swianiewicz, *Forced Labour*, 144.

108. Ashot M. Arzumanian, *Taina bulata* (Erevan: Aiastan, 1967), 109–10; and Kravchenko, *I Chose Freedom*, 289–91. See also Ivanov-Razumnik, *Memoirs*, 354–55, for an investigator's careful concern for evidence in 1939.

109. HP no. 26, p. 39.

110. "Dneprovets," untitled manuscript, 31.

111. Gorbatov, *Years*, 152.

112. Conquest, *Inside Stalin's Secret Police*, 86–87.

113. HP no. 383, B5, p. 28; no biographical data available.

114. Tsikulin, *Istoriia*, 222–23.

115. Solomon, "Soviet Criminal Justice," 413.

116. *XVIII s''ezd vsesoiuznoi kommunisticheskoi partii bol'shevikov 10–21 marta 1939 g. Stenograficheskii otchet*, (Moscow: Gospolitizdat, 1939), 143–45, 399, 4.

117. Ibid., 519, 668.

118. Ibid., 519, 523.

119. Stalin, *Sochineniia*, 14:395; and Beria writing in *Kom. Pravda*, March 24, 1939.

120. *Kom. Pravda*, April 26, 1939.

121. Medvedev, *Let History Judge*, 458; Medvedev notes correctly, however, that Ezhov is not listed in the record of delegates.

122. Starkov, "Narkom Ezhov," 37–38.

123. On differences regarding foreign policy, see Tucker, *Stalin in Power*, 338–53. On Zhdanov and Molotov during the Terror, see Getty, *Origins*, 110–11, 129–30.

124. On these differences, see Hahn, *Postwar Soviet Politics*; and McCagg, *Stalin Embattled*.

125. See Viola, "The Campaign to Eliminate the Kulak."

126. Stalin mentioned enemies publicly only twice in 1938, in a February article; *Sochineniia*, 14:270, 272.

127. Ibid., 274–75.
128. Repin, Manuscripts, 245.
129. Boikov, *Liudi,* 2:235.
130. See, e.g., Sheila Fitzpatrick, "Stalin and the Making of a New Elite," *SR* 38, no. 3 (1979), 396–400; and Jerry F. Hough and Merle Fainsod, *How the Soviet Union Is Governed* (Cambridge: Harvard University Press, 1979), 170–77.
131. SA, b. 38, r. 37, WKP 323, ll. 7–188.
132. Rittersporn, *Stalinist Simplifications,* 11–12.
133. J. Arch Getty and William Chase, "Patterns of Repression among the Soviet Elite in the Late 1930s: A Biographical Approach," and Sheila Fitzpatrick, "The Impact of the Great Purges on Soviet Elites: A Case Study from Moscow and Leningrad Telephone Directories of the 1930s," both in Getty and Manning, *Stalinist Terror.*
134. Brzezinski, *Permanent Purge,* esp. 168.
135. Chuev, *140 besed s Molotovym,* 399, April 27, 1973.
136. See *Stalin's Letters to Molotov, 1925–1936,* ed. Lars T. Lih, Oleg V. Naumov, and Oleg V. Khlevniuk, foreword by Robert C. Tucker, trans. by Catherine A. Fitzpatrick (New Haven: Yale University Press, 1995), 200, letter no. 57, dated no earlier than August 6, 1930; 199–200, letter no. 56, August 2, 1930. The same sort of belief in enemies is evident (though the Russian editors disagree) in Stalin's letter to V. R. Menzhinskii, head of the OGPU, 195, n.d.
137. Lars T. Lih, introduction to *Stalin's Letters,* 10.
138. Nikita S. Khrushchev, *Khrushchev Remembers,* with an introduction, commentary and notes by Edward Crankshaw, trans. and ed. Strobe Talbott (Boston: Little, Brown, 1970), 20, 113–14.
139. Medvedev, *Let History Judge,* 862, citing an unpublished manuscript.
140. Quoted in Peter Gay, *Freud for Historians* (New York: Oxford University Press, 1985), 119.
141. Technically, a definition should refer to "paranoid state": "The paranoid lives in a state of chronic anxiety and fears the environment, which is seen as hostile and threatening"; Alfred M. Freedman, Harold Kaplan, and Benjamin Sadock, *Modern Synopsis of Comprehensive Textbook of Psychiatry/II.* 2d ed. (Baltimore: Williams and Wilkins, 1976), 489.
142. Chuev, *140 besed,* 390; interview of December 18, 1970.

Chapter Five: Fear and Belief in the Terror

1. Klara Agranovich-Shul'man, *Neobyknovennaia zhizn' odnoi zhenshchiny: Memuary* (New York: Avtor, 1981), 93. Agranovich-Shul'man was an actress and theater producer.
2. V. V. Tsaplin, "Statistika zhertv Stalinizma v 30-e gody," *Voprosy Istorii,* no. 4 (April 1989), 180.
3. See Getty, Rittersporn, and Zemskov, "Victims," 1017, 1022, for earlier high estimates.
4. V. N. Zemskov, "Ob uchete spetskontingenta NKVD vo Vsesoiuznykh perepisiakh naseleniia 1937 i 1939 gg.," *Sotsiologicheskie Issledovaniia,* no. 2 (1991), 75. Figures have been rounded.
5. Alec Nove, "How Many," 2:813, from archival materials recently collected in the USSR by S. Maksudov.
6. *NYT,* February 11, 1992.
7. GARF, f. 9401, o. 1, d. 4157, ll. 201–03.
8. Getty, Rittersporn, and Zemskov, "Victims," 1032.

9. Ibid., 1025.

10. See Stephan Merl, *Sozialer Aufstieg im sowjetischen Kolchossystem der 30er Jahre?* (Berlin: Duncker and Humblot, 1990), 100–07.

11. Solomon, "Soviet Criminal Justice," 400; for another case of this, see Ivanov-Razumnik, *Memoirs,* 344.

12. Laqueur, *Stalin,* 98. See also Jim Nichol, "Stalin's Crimes against the Non-Russian Nations: The 1987–1990 Revelations and Debate," *Carl Beck Papers,* no. 906 (1991). For Nichol, the issue of numbers "is unlikely to be solved through exhumations" (48).

13. Getty, Rittersporn, and Zemskov, "Victims," 1024, 1020.

14. E.g., Lorimer, *Population,* 133; and Barbara A. Anderson and Brian D. Silver, "Demographic Analysis and Population Catastrophes in the USSR," *SR* 44, no. 3 (Fall 1985), 517–36.

15. Steven Rosefielde, "Excess Mortality in the Soviet Union: A Reconsideration of the Demographic Consequences of Forced Industrialization, 1929–1949," *Soviet Studies* 35, no. 3 (July 1983), 387–405.

16. See Wheatcroft, "More Light."

17. Nove, "How Many," 2:813–14.

18. Brian P. Levack, *The Witch-Hunt in Early Modern Europe* (New York: Longman, 1987), 19; Christina Larner, *Witchcraft and Religion: The Politics of Popular Belief* (London: Blackwell, 1984), 26–28, 39. On the African slave trade, see David Henige, "Measuring the Immeasurable: The Atlantic Slave Trade, West African Population and the Pyrrhonian Critic," *Journal of African History* 27, no. 2 (1986), 312; and Philip D. Curtin, *The Atlantic Slave Trade: A Census* (Madison: University of Wisconsin Press, 1969), xiv.

19. Ruslan G. Skrynnikov, *Ivan the Terrible* (Gulf Breeze, Fla.: Academic International Press, 1981), 127–28, 147.

20. See the letters from Robert Conquest in *American Historical Review* 99, no. 3 (1994), 1038–40; and no. 5 (1994), 1821, followed in both cases by responses from J. Arch Getty, Gabor T. Rittersporn, and Viktor Zemskov.

21. Antonov-Ovseyenko, *Time of Stalin,* 216.

22. E.g., Mandelstam, *Hope against Hope,* 57.

23. Ilya Ehrenburg, *Memoirs: 1921–1941,* trans. Tatiana Shebunina in collaboration with Yvonne Kapp (Cleveland: World, 1964), 426.

24. Ibid., 423.

25. I am indebted for this phrase and this thought to Robert C. Tucker.

26. Fainsod, *Smolensk under Soviet Rule,* 303, 422. Some peasants wept for Kirov but hated Stalin and wished that he had been killed; others expressed "malicious satisfaction" at Kirov's death (Fitzpatrick, *Stalin's Peasants,* 17–18, 291).

27. See Medvedev, *Let History Judge,* 336.

28. Beck and Godin, *Russian Purge,* 21.

29. Tokaev, *Betrayal,* 278–79.

30. Shul'man, *Butyrskii dekameron,* 1:248–51.

31. Andrew Smith, *I Was a Soviet Worker* (London: Hale, 1937), 254–55. Smith was a radical American worker who fled the United States to escape a political trial.

32. William Campbell, *Villi the Clown* (Boston: Faber and Faber, 1981), 29.

33. Lev Kopelev, *The Education of a True Believer,* trans. Gary Kern (New York: Harper and Row, 1980), 300.

34. Berger, *Nothing but the Truth,* 55.

35. Avtorkhanov, *Memuary,* 443. Avtorkhanov was from a small Caucasian mountain village.

36. Kravchenko, *I Chose Freedom,* 206; see Medvedev's similar opinion in *K sudu,* 336; Vladimir and Evdokia Petrov accepted the show trials' charges: *Empire of Fear* (New York: Praeger, 1956), 47, 131. Kravchenko's family was poor before the Revolution; his father was a revolutionary railroad worker. Medvedev was born in 1925; his father was a Marxist philosopher. The Petrovs were managerial employees and translators for the NKVD in the 1930s. Vladimir was from a poor Siberian peasant family.

37. Weissberg, *Accused,* 7; "a period of emotional recuperation was interrupted in August 1936" by the announcement of the trial (1). Weissberg was an Austrian engineer.

38. Mandel'stam, *Hope against Hope,* 336. This man was furious at what he considered deceit but not at terror.

39. Fitzpatrick, *Stalin's Peasants,* 296–312.

40. Shul'man, *Butyrskii,* 1:xiii–xiv.

41. Raisa Berg, *Sukhovei: Vospominaniia genetika* (New York: Chalidze, 1983), 49; she speaks of "four blessed years" (32), from 1935 to 1939. Berg's father was a professor and academician; she was a geneticist. Minishki, "Illiuzii," 131, 136–37. In April 1937 Minishki, who had been technical director of a factory, was happy about a substantial promotion (137).

42. Antonov-Ovseyenko, *Time of Stalin,* 228, 231.

43. Margarete Buber did note that her husband, the prominent German communist Heinz Neumann, feared arrest even before arriving in the Soviet Union in early 1935. She found that in that year the "atmosphere in Moscow was already stifling. Former political friends no longer dared visit each other" (Buber (Neumann), *Under Two Dictators,* 15). The later carnage among German communists may have colored this comment, and she notes many party members arrested in 1937–38 who had not felt fear or sensed impending arrest before they were incarcerated. Avtorkhanov expected arrest for two years before it finally occurred in October 1937, yet he also said that he was not even sure then that he would be picked up (Avtorkhanov, *Memuary,* 505).

44. As noted, this and other evidence counters the view that within the party from December 1934 to early 1937 tension constantly increased; Fainsod, *Smolensk under Soviet Rule,* 222–37; and Rigby, *Communist Party Membership,* 200–01, 210.

45. Lidiia Shatunovskaia, *Zhizn' v Kremle* (New York: Chalidze, 1982), 92, 95.

46. Solzhenitsyn, *Gulag Archipelago,* 1:68. Eugenia Ginzburg wrote, "So it began—that accursed year [1937]," in her *Journey into the Whirlwind,* 35. Ginzburg was a member of the party elite and a university teacher in Kazan'.

47. Weissberg, *Accused,* 89.

48. A version of this joke is in Medvedev, *On Stalin,* 102.

49. Beck and Godin, *Russian Purge,* 146.

50. Shatunovskaia, *Zhizn',* 102.

51. Ibid., 101. Bailes, *Technology and Society under Lenin and Stalin,* 422, notes that the old technical "specialists," usually nonparty and educated before the Revolution, fared much better in the Terror than other prerevolutionary elites. Valentina Bogdan and her husband, both nonparty specialists, were not arrested; see her *Mimikriia v SSSR.*

52. Grigorenko, *Memoirs*, 44.

53. A. T., "Tipy," 3. Ginzburg wrote, "As we all knew, the closer you had been to prominent Communists, the longer your sentence" (Ginzburg, *Journey into the Whirlwind*, 318).

54. B. Ivanov, "Pochemu my ne khotim vozvrashchat′sia v SSSR," David Dalin (sic) file, BA, 13.

55. Beck and Godin, *Russian Purge*, 98–147. Weissberg, *Accused*, 5, gives a broader set of categories than Beck and Godin's.

56. Kravchenko, *I Chose Justice*, 196–97.

57. HP no. 24, B5, B162, p. 24.

58. HP no. 415, A, vol. 20, p. 67. This Russian male foreman in a milk plant was born about 1903 to poor-to-average peasants.

59. Akhmedov, *In and Out of Stalin's GRU*, 104. Akhmedov was from a poor Tatar family.

60. John Scott, *Behind the Urals: An American Worker in Russia's City of Steel* (1942; reprint, Bloomington: Indiana University Press, 1973), 195. Scott had been a student in Wisconsin before traveling to Magnitogorsk to work as a welder.

61. Grigorenko, *Memoirs*, 75. And see Mark Von Hagen, "Soviet Soldiers and Officers on the Eve of the German Invasion: Towards a Description of Social Psychology and Political Attitudes," *Soviet Union/Union Sovietique* 18, nos. 1–3 (1991), 92–93.

62. See, e.g., Fitzpatrick, "Stalin and the Making of a New Elite," 396–400; and Hough and Fainsod, *How the Soviet Union Is Governed*, 170–77.

63. SA, b. 49, rf. 48, WKP 440, l. 145; meeting of the Shamilovo party cell for November 14, 1937.

64. Ibid., ll. 143, 170. I have not been able to locate later Shamilovo protocols.

65. Bogdan, *Mimikriia*, 238.

66. Dneprovets, untitled manuscript, BA, 16. "Dneprovets" worked in the local *militsiia*. Resistance to promotion or fear of it are in Aleksandr Dmitrievich Belozerov, "Memoirs," BA, 111. Another worker believed that it was dangerous to become prominent; Eugenia Hanfmann and Helen Beier, *Six Russian Men: Lives in Turmoil* (North Quincy, Mass.: Christopher, 1976), 64.

67. HP no. 351, A, vol. 18, p. 19, a Ukrainian male lathe operator, born about 1906 to poor-to-average peasants.

68. HP no. 165, A, vol. 2, p. 13; no biographical data.

69. Professor Hiroaki Kuromiya, conversation with author, April 1993, Bloomington, Ind.

70. On the difficulties of Donbass production, see Roberta T. Manning, "The Soviet Economic Crisis of 1936–1940 and the Great Purges," in *Stalinist Terror*, 125–26.

71. *Vechernii Leningrad*, January 10–March 29, 1990.

72. Getty, Rittersporn, and Zemskov, "Victims," 1030.

73. A. T., "Tipy," 1.

74. HP no. 71, B5, p. 34.

75. HP no. 421, A, vol. 21, p. 22. See also David L. Hoffman, "The Great Terror on the Local Level: Purges in Moscow Factories, 1936–1938," in *Stalinist Terror*, esp. 165. Kuromiya's "Stalinist Terror" does not assign a prominent role to arrests of workers. See also Aleksandr Vozniuk-Burmin, untitled manuscript, BA, 7, 16, among other examples.

76. Inkeles and Bauer, *Soviet Citizen*, 48–49, 108.

77. HP no. 470, A, vol. 23, p. 25. This was a Russian male engineer and construction supervisor, later head of construction for the Donbass mine trust, born about 1913. His own arrest followed that of the man he mentioned.

78. HP no. 403, B10, p. 18.

79. Mandelstam, *Hope against Hope*, 13; after serving his sentence, Kuzin was appointed "to a very good academic post."

80. Herman, *Coming out of the Ice*, 66.

81. Conquest, *Great Terror: A Reassessment*, 270.

82. Mikhail Ivanovich Nil'skii, "Manuscripts," ["Pobeg" and other stories], BA, 76.

83. Kravchenko, *I Chose Justice*, 158.

84. Evgeniia Ginzburg believed that innocent people were being arrested in 1937, but she applied that idea only to communists; *Journey into the Whirlwind*, 36–37. Kravchenko, *I Chose Freedom*, 212, refers to alarm among workers in 1937 in regard to arrests, but only to party men sleeping in their clothes in expectation of arrest (215). Bogdan, *Mimikriia*, 130, said that she and her husband feared arrest; however, they were left at liberty.

85. Akhmedov, *In and Out*, 104; Bogdan, *Mimikriia*, 130, says she and her husband knew innocents were being arrested.

86. Weissberg, *Accused*, 309; yet he still believed that justice would be done. He knew other prisoners who remained convinced that their cases were mistakes and that they would be released (205, 269, 284, 295). For similar reactions, see also Buber (Neumann), *Under Two Dictators*, 28, 35, 40, and esp. 84; Gorbatov, *Years*, 117–18, 134; A. T., "Tipy," 1; Kravchenko, *Justice*, 178–80; Vasily Grossman, *Forever Flowing*, trans. by Thomas P. Whitney (New York: Harper and Row, 1972), 104–05; Shul'man, *Butyrskii*, 1:18; and Ginzburg, *Into the Whirlwind*, 96, 102–03, 107, 111, 120, 122–24, 144, 154–55.

87. Ivanov-Razumnik, *Memoirs*, 311, 316.

88. Antonov-Ovseyenko, *Time of Stalin*, 231.

89. Beck and Godin, *Russian Purge*, 24; Bogdan, *Mimikriia*, 110.

90. Solzhenitsyn, *Gulag*, 1:160–61.

91. Pavel Kuznetsov, "Why I did not return to the USSR," David Dalin file, BA, 3.

92. People exchanged many jokes that were critical of the economy and politics and discussed issues frankly with family and friends; see my "Soviet Family" and "Social Dimensions of Stalinist Rule: Humor and Terror in the USSR, 1935–1941," *The Journal of Social History* 24, no. 3 (1991).

93. Nikita Malysh, "Why I did not return to my country: The story of a Red Army Officer," David Dalin file, BA, 3.

94. Andrei Manchur, "Pochemu ia ne vozvrashchaius' v SSSR," David Dalin file, BA, 2–3.

95. Lena Moroz, "The Road of the Young," David Dalin file, BA, 7.

96. Raisa Orlova, *Memoirs*, trans. Samuel Cioran (New York: Random House, 1983), 61.

97. HP no. 378, A, vol. 19, p. 24 This respondent was a rank-and-file worker born about 1926 into the middle class. See also no. 12, A, vol. 2, p. 6; this was a Russian male meteorologist, born about 1997, based near Sevastopol. His father was a priest.

98. "Effect of Treason Trials on Army Morale," memorandum by Philip R. Faymonville, U.S. military attaché in Moscow, February 24, 1937, U.S. Military Intelligence Reports: The Soviet Union, 1919–1941, microfilm, reel 3, pp. 339–40 (Fredrick, Md.: University Publications of America, 1984).

99. Gorbatov, *Years*, 103.

100. Lidiia Chukovskaia, *Opustel'yi Dom: Povest'* (Paris: Librairie des Cinq Continents, 1965), 52, 59; see also 50. The novel is also called *Sofiia Petrovna*. Chukovskaia's father was the translator and writer Kornei Chukovskii.
101. Prychodko, *Fifteen Million,* 21. Prychodko worked in education; his father had been a well-off peasant.
102. Grigorenko, *Memoirs,* 36.
103. HP no. 9, A, vol. 1, p. 45. This Belorussian woman, born about 1920 into the family of a mechanic, was a student before the war. A friend who had served in grain collections told her stories of people dying.
104. Kuznetsov, "Why," 3.
105. HP nos. 149, 147, 11, 1684, 1664, 395 AS (NY) 1760, 135 B5, and others.
106. John Hazard, interview with author, Oxford, Ohio, May 11, 1991. Jack Miller, a British economist who lived in Moscow in 1936–37, reported that students in a planning institute, who were mostly in their thirties, were not at all worried about the arrests, either in terms of their own safety or out of pity for those taken. There were no arrests among these students before Miller left the institute in September 1937. See his "Soviet Planners in 1936–37," in *Soviet Planning: Essays in Honour of Maum Jasny,* ed. Jane Degras and Alec Nove (Oxford: Blackwell, 1964), 118–19. I thank Lars Lih for this citation.
107. HP no. 105, A, vol. 8, pp. 3, 4, 11.
108. Bogdan, *Mimikriia,* 108–11.
109. Markoosha Fischer, *My Lives in Russia* (New York: Harper and Bros., 1944), 151, 163–65.
110. A. Lunin, "Kak sozdaiutsia 'Sputniki'," BA, 14.
111. K. Petrus, *Uzniki kommunizma* (New York: Chekhov, 1953), 169. See also belief in enemies in Rothchild, *Special Legacy,* 78, 79, 75.
112. HP no. 345, A, vol. 4, p. 14 of government section. This Belorussian male, a pupil before the war, was born about 1828 into the family of poor-to-average peasants. HP no. 93, A, vol. 7, pp. 22, 26, believed the official communications he heard.
113. Friese, "Student Life," 71.
114. HP no. 6, A, vol. 1, p. 46. This Russian male medical student and lab technician was born no earlier than 1920. He came from a collective farm and his parents were middle peasants.
115. Aleksandr Solzhenitsyn, "The Way," an unpublished manuscript quoted in Michael *Scammell, Solzhenitsyn: A Biography* (New York: Norton, 1984), 105.
116. Scammell, *Solzhenitsyn,* 105, 111; see also HP no. 1053, A, vol. 31, p. 11, for similar complacency. This Russian male actor was born about 1897 into a family of gentry.
117. [Gorokhov], "From the NKVD to the Polish Army," Dalin File, BA, 23.
118. Orlova, *Memoirs,* ix, 63.
119. Dmitri Panin, *The Notebooks of Sologdin,* trans. John Moore (New York: Harcourt Brace Jovanovich, 1976), 15. Panin maintained that he had been deeply anti-Soviet from childhood.
120. Kopelev, *Education of a True Believer,* 122. Kopelev was from a well-educated and relatively well-off Kievan family.
121. Kravchenko, *I Chose Justice,* 251.
122. Chukovskaia, *Opustel'yi Dom,* 70.
123. Lidiia Chukovskaia, *Protsess iskliucheniia (Ocherk literaturnykh nravov)* (Paris: YMCA Press,

1979), 10; the second quotation is from *Politicheskii dnevnik,* 2 vols. Vol. 1, 1964–70 (Amsterdam: Fond Im. Gertsena, 1972), 57.

124. Shatunovskaia, *Zhizn',* 268.

125. Mandelstam, *Hope against Hope,* 51, 33, 68, 132, 162, 220, 254, 309, 316, 297, 23, 28, 44, 96, 113, 287, 332–33.

126. E.g., Kravchenko, *I Chose Justice,* 165–66.

127. Ibid., 204.

128. Inkeles and Bauer, *Soviet Citizen,* 245.

129. Robert D. Grey, Lauri A. Jennisch, and Alanna S. Tyler, "Soviet Public Opinion and the Gorbachev Reforms," *SR* 49, no. 2 (1990), 265. Their sources were Soviet people who emigrated to the United States between 1979 and 1982. Almost all urban, 95 percent were Jews. This group probably favored freedom of speech more than citizens in the USSR, especially after exposure to American life. Nevertheless, 23.6 percent agreed and 21.7 percent strongly agreed that "it is necessary to keep dangerous ideas from the public."

130. Philip Lawrence Harriman, *Handbook of Psychological Terms* (Totowa, N.J.: Littlefield, Adams, 1965), 169, 194.

131. M. H. Erdelyi and B. Goldberg, "Let's Not Sweep Repression under the Rug: Towards a Cognitive Psychology of Repression," in J. F. Kihlstrom and F. J. Evans, eds. *Functional Disorders of Memory* (Hillsdale, N.J.: Erlbaum, 1979), 364, 360. Sigmund Freud, *Introductory Lectures on Psycho-Analysis,* trans. and ed. James Strachey (New York: Norton, 1966), 366.

132. Erdelyi and Goldberg, "Let's Not Sweep Repression," 360.

133. I base this conclusion on conversations with Dr. Michael Miller, a psychiatrist, of Fairfield, Ohio.

134. G. Mandler, *Mind and Emotion,* reprint with corrections (Malabar, Fla.: Krieger, 1982), 82.

135. Erdelyi and Goldberg, "Let's Not Sweep Repression," 375.

136. See Poliakov, *Harvest of Hate,* 18; Broszat, *Hitler State,* 349–51, 357; Peterson, *Limits of Hitler's Power,* esp. 443; Peukert, *Inside Nazi Germany*; and Mayer, *They Thought They Were Free.*

137. See, e.g., Boikov, *Liudi,* 1:88; Beck and Godin, 93, 221–22; Minishki, "Illiuzii," 141; and Petrov, *It Happens in Russia,* 65–66.

138. The phrase and the idea are used in Hélène Carrère d'Encausse, *A History of the Soviet Union, 1917–1953.* Vol. 2, *Stalin: Order through Terror,* trans. Valence Ionescu (New York: Longman, 1981).

139. Khrushchev, *Khrushchev Remembers,* 114.

140. Medvedev, *Let History Judge,* 624.

141. *Vozhatyi,* April 4, 1938, 5.

142. HP no. 111, A, vol. 9, p. 35.

143. HP no. 64, B2, vol. 1, pp. 13–14. A. Finn, *Experiences of a Soviet Journalist* (New York: Research Program on the USSR, 1954), 7, reports that censors once discovered in *Izvestiia* a swastika visible if a light was held behind the page. This must have been in 1937 or early 1938.

144. HP no. 284, A, vol. 15, p. 19. This Ukrainian male movie projectionist was born about 1915 into a family of well-off peasants. See also a similar story told by HP no. 1720, A, vol. 37, p. 14, a Ukrainian woman born about 1898 into a priest's family; she worked as a secretary.

145. Chukovskaia, *Opustel'yi dom*, English version, *The Deserted House*, trans. Aline B. Werth (Belmont, Mass.: Nordland, 1967), 92.

146. Beck and Godin, *Russian Purge*, 114.

147. SA, Nicolaevsky Collection, HI, protocol no. 7, closed session of March 23, 1937, l. 129.

148. Ibid., l. 128.

149. HP no. 1124, A, vol. 32, p. 17, a Russian female stenographer born about 1892 into the gentry. She reported this story about an acquaintance.

150. As asserted by Conquest, *Great Terror: A Reassessment*, 434.

151. Scott, *Behind the Urals*, 264.

152. See, e.g., SA, b. 14, WKP 106, ll. 55, 60; b. 14, WKP 110, l. 185; b. 62, r. R67, WKP 107, l. 94, all from 1937.

153. *P*, December 4, 1938. The enemies meant here were probably the false denouncers stressed for many months.

154. *P*, December 2, 1938. For other articles that implied endorsement of criticism from below, see *P*, July 4, October 2 and 3, 1939.

155. David Joravsky, *The Lysenko Affair* (Cambridge: Harvard University Press, 1970), 124, 108.

156. Berg, *Sukhovei*, 51.

157. Solzhenitsyn, *Gulag*, 1:160–61.

158. Kravchenko, *I Chose Freedom*, 345; for a similar case, see Berger, *Nothing but the Truth*, 180–81.

159. See my "Social Dimensions."

160. Various textbooks on Soviet history put the case this way; e.g., Basil Dmytryshyn, *USSR: A Concise History*, 4th ed. (New York: Scribner's, 1984), 157–202; M. K. Dziewanowski, *A History of Soviet Russia*, 2d ed. (Englewood Cliffs, N.J.: Prentice-Hall, 1985), 200–14; Geoffrey Hosking, *The First Socialist Society: A History of the Soviet Union from Within* (Cambridge: Harvard University Press, 1985), 149–226; and Woodford McClellan, *Russia: A History of the Soviet Period*, 2d ed. (Englewood Cliffs, N.J.: 1990), 129–56. Expressions like "total terror" and "total fear" can be found in Arendt, *Origins of Totalitarianism*, 466, and Friedrich and Brzezinski, *Totalitarian Dictatorship*, 169.

161. Kosterina, *Dnevnik*, 9–31. Kosterina had a good time on the holiday of November 7, 1936, for example, and enjoyed herself a great deal as late as May 1, 1938 (ibid., 17–18, 43). She was aware that "something is happening" as arrests take place in the summer of 1937 but indicates no fear about them (29).

162. Agranovich-Shul'man, *Neobyknovennaia zhizn'*, 87.

163. Scammell, *Solzhenitsyn*, 96.

164. Bogdan, *Mimikriia*, 123–24. The American Timbres family had many good times with one another and with Soviet citizens from October 1936 until the father became ill in May 1937; Harry and Rebecca Timbres, *We Didn't Ask Utopia: A Quaker Family in Soviet Russia* (New York: Prentice-Hall, 1939), to 267.

165. G. Arkitin, "Politicheskie nastroeniia naseleniia g. Leningrada v leto 1941 g.," BA, 4–7. Anna Ivanovna M., "Why I did not Return to the USSR," BA, omits arrests in her account of why she remained in Western Europe after the war; she speaks instead of poverty, hard work, and excessive time spent listening to propaganda. As already noted, Andrei Manchur also emphasized economic factors, not terror, in his disillusionment.

166. Kopelev, *Education,* 123.
167. Tokaev, *Betrayal,* 131.
168. Scott, *Behind the Urals,* 205.
169. Solzhenitsyn, *Gulag,* 1:160.

Chapter Six: Life in the Factories

1. This view of the Soviet period draws on an old tradition of analysis regarding the tsarist state and society. See, e.g., the classic prerevolutionary work of V. O. Kliuchevsky, *A Course in Russian History: The Seventeenth Century,* trans. Natalie Duddington (Chicago: Quadrangle, 1968), 8; and Richard Pipes, *Russia under the Old Regime* (New York: Scribner's, 1974), 21. For older treatments of workers in this period, see Manya Gordon, *Workers before and after Lenin* (New York: Dutton, 1941); Arvid Brodersen, *The Soviet Worker: Labor and Government in Soviet Society* (New York: Random House, 1966); Solomon M. Schwarz, *Labor in the Soviet Union* (New York: Praeger, 1951); and Robert Conquest, *Industrial Workers in the USSR* (New York: Praeger, 1967). Some more recent studies echo this approach in fundamental ways; see, e.g., Walter D. Connor, *The Accidental Proletariat: Workers, Politics and Crisis in Gorbachev's Russia* (Princeton: Princeton University Press, 1991).
2. Newer treatments of the subject include Connor, *Accidental Proletariat;* Benvenuti, "Stakhanovism and Stalinism"; Kuromiya, *Stalin's Industrial Revolution;* Filtzer (who sometimes affirms older views), *Soviet Workers;* and Andrle, *Workers in Stalin's Russia.*
3. Workers' criticism has figured in studies like Siegelbaum's *Stakhanovism* but has generally been a peripheral concern.
4. Lorimer, *Population,* 147, 149.
5. *Naselenie SSSR za 70 let* (Moscow: Nauka, 1988), 161.
6. Siegelbaum, *Stakhanovism,* 18; and Moshe Lewin, *The Making of the Soviet System: Essays in the Social History of Interwar Russia* (New York: Pantheon, 1985), 225.
7. Kuromiya, *Stalin's Industrial Revolution,* 213–14.
8. Gordon, *Workers,* 268.
9. Siegelbaum, *Stakhanovism,* 215.
10. Schwarz, *Labor,* 177.
11. Janet Chapman, *Real Wages in Soviet Russia since 1928* (Cambridge: Harvard University Press, 1963), 176.
12. Gordon, *Workers,* 141.
13. Siegelbaum, *Stakhanovism,* 215; Schwarz, *Labor,* 143, gives slightly different figures.
14. See Mark Von Hagen, *Soldiers in the Proletarian Dictatorship: The Red Army and the Soviet Socialist State, 1917–1930* (Ithaca: Cornell University Press, 1990), 275, 287, on peasant recruits' strong curiosity and desire to see the city and escape patriarchal control.
15. Quoted in Connor, *Accidental Proletariat,* 39–40.
16. The story of HP no. 147, who was not a peasant by birth but from the middle class, is still indicative of this tendency. His father was executed in 1931 and his mother disappeared after her arrest in the 1930s. The son, however, became a battalion commander, forgot about his parents, and thought that "Soviet power was the best in the world" before the war.

17. Stephen Kotkin, *Magnetic Mountain: Stalinism as a Civilization* (Berkeley: University of California Press, 1995), 250–51, 254, 265, 273.

18. Schwarz, *Labor,* 163.

19. Andrle, *Workers in Stalin's Russia,* 41.

20. John Barber, "The Impact of Rural Migrants on the Soviet Working Class, 1928–1941," paper presented to the Social Science Research Council Conference on Industrialization and Change in Soviet Society, University of Michigan, 1988, 8.

21. Scott, *Behind the Urals,* 233.

22. TsGAMO, f. 6852, o. 1, d. 367, l. 15, for an example of livestock and gardens kept at a factory outside Moscow in 1935.

23. Gordon, *Workers,* 203.

24. See, e.g., Chase, *Workers, Society.*

25. Jay B. Sorenson, *The Life and Death of Soviet Trade Unionism, 1917–1928* (New York: Atherton, 1969), 253.

26. Chase, *Workers, Society,* 275–85.

27. *Voprosy Truda,* no. 9 (1930), 21, quoted in Kuromiya, *Stalin's Industrial Revolution,* 207.

28. Filtzer, *Soviet Workers,* 111–12.

29. Schwarz, *Labor,* 98–100.

30. Filtzer, *Soviet Workers,* 234–35.

31. Conquest, *Industrial Workers,* 9, 14; Schwarz, *Labor,* 98–100.

32. SA, b. 12, r. 11, WKP 84, l. 71, a factory directors' conference of May 23, 1935; GARF, f. 7952, o. 5, d. 65, l. 87, an engineer at Kuznetsk; Zawodny, I/5, an electrician and then a shop chief; and I/8, an accountant in a Ukrainian factory.

33. I. V. Paramonov, *Uchit'sia upravliat': Mysli i opyt starogo khoziaistvennika,* 3d ed. (Moscow: Ekonomika, 1977), 118. Paramonov was a manager in the coal, construction, and other industries in the 1930s and 1940s.

34. HP no. 470, p. 4.

35. Filtzer, *Soviet Workers,* 54, 112.

36. Ibid., 112–13.

37. Andrle, *Workers in Stalin's Russia,* 133.

38. Filtzer, *Soviet Workers,* 112–13.

39. Ibid., 137, 54.

40. Kuromiya, *Stalin's Industrial Revolution,* 200–10.

41. Filtzer, *Soviet Workers,* 135.

42. Ibid., 239.

43. Zawodny, II/17.

44. LGAOR, f. 2140, o. 21, d. 330, ll. 10–11.

45. Filtzer, *Soviet Workers,* 144, 141.

46. "O kontrole nad provedeniem v zhizn' ukaza presidiuma verkhovnogo soveta SSSR ot 26 iiunia 1940," *ITsK,* no. 1, 1990, 186.

47. Conquest, *Industrial Workers,* 15.

48. HP no. 74, p. 63; no. 26, p. 62.

49. On the beginnings of the Stakhanovite movement, see Siegelbaum, *Stakhanovism,* 66–86; and

Semen Gershberg, *Stakhanov i stakhanovtsy,* 2d ed. (Moscow: Izdatel'stvo politicheskoi literatury, 1985), 9–31.

50. The waitress is pictured in *Krasnoe Znamia* (Tomsk), February 5, 1939; the mail carrier's photograph is in ibid., November 29, 1938. GARF, f. 5451, o. 19, d. 227, l. 28, mentions a Stakhanovite women's hairdresser.

51. The conventional interpretation of the movement is, e.g., in Nicholas V. Riasanovsky, *A History of Russia,* 4th ed. (New York: Oxford University Press, 1984), 502.

52. Siegelbaum, *Stakhanovism,* 280.

53. RGAE-TsGANKh, f. 7995, o. 1, d. 577, l. 11; d. 333, l. 149; f. 7622, o. 1, d. 251, l. 29; O. A. Ermanskii, *Stakhanovskoe dvizhenie i stakhanovskie metody* (Moscow: Gosudarstvennoe Sotsial'no-Ekonomicheskoe Izdatel'stvo, 1940), 230.

54. N. Tkachuk, "Iz praktiki massovogo kontrolia na gorkovskom avtozavode im. Molotova," *VP,* no. 4 (1935), 74–77.

55. Filtzer, *Soviet Workers,* 184. On the meaning of norms in this period, see my "Reassessing the History of Soviet Workers: Opportunities to Criticize and Participate in Decision-Making," in *New Directions in Soviet History,* ed. Stephen White (Cambridge: Cambridge University Press, 1992), 167–68.

56. *Tikhookeanskaia Zvezda,* July 16, 1936.

57. Siegelbaum, *Stakhanovism,* 262. There was constant pressure from above on managers and unions to bring workers to the level of fulfilling norms; see, among many examples, V. Chekryzhov and L. Kaminer, "Itogi peresmotra norm vyrabotki v mashinostroenii," *Profsoiuzy SSSR,* no. 7 (July 1939), 51, which refers to a resolution of the eighth plenum of the National Trade Union Council.

58. RGAE-TsGANKh, f. 4086, o. 2, d. 4731, l. 14. This is an undated letter to Lazar Kaganovich, Commissar of Heavy Industry, from the head of the auto-tractor division of the commissariat, Merkulov; data are given through October 1938.

59. *Industrializatsiia severo-zapadnogo raiona v gody vtoroi i tret'ei piatiletok, 1933–1941 gg., dokumenty i materialy* (Leningrad: Leningradskii Gosudarstvennyi Universitet, 1969), 87.

60. TsGAMO, f. 5687, o. 1, d. 42, l. 38.

61. For examples of workers' involvement in determining the new norms, see RGAE-TsGANKh, f. 7604, o. 8, ed. khr. (edinitsa khraneniia) 33, l. 30, for the branch conference of the linen industry in April 1936; and D. Mochalin, "Uchastie proforganizatsii v peresmotre norm v transportnom mashinostroenii," *VP,* no. 3 (March 1936), 82–83.

62. *Tikhookeanskaia Zvezda,* June 15, 1936.

63. RGAE-TsGANKh, f. 7622, o. 1, d. 54, l. 208. This is from the branch conference of the auto-tractor industry, February 1936.

64. *Trud,* March 6, 1928, quoted in Lewis Siegelbaum, "Masters of the Shop Floor: Foremen and Soviet Industrialisation," in *Stalinism: Its Nature and Aftermath* (London: Macmillan, 1992), 140.

65. Ermanskii, *Stakhanovskoe dvizhenie,* 246; see also RGAE-TsGANKh, f. 4086, o. 2, ed. khr. 3365, l. 280, to the division of labor of the metal industry from the Kaganovich factory, Moscow.

66. Ermanskii, *Stakhanovskoe dvizhenie,* 246; RGAE-TsGANKh, f. 7604, o. 8, ed. khr. 33, l. 154, the otdel pen'kozavodov GUPDI, dating from early 1936; ibid., f. 4086, o. 2, ed. khr. 3286, l. 8, from

the conference of the transportation department of the Commissariat of Heavy Industry, March 1936.

67. RGAE-TsGANKh, f. 4086, o. 2, ed. khr. 3286, l. 10: one factory recommended a 61 percent increase in a norm, but the conference raised it 33 percent. In another case a factory recommended a 46 percent rise, but the conference chose 23 percent.
68. See Michael Burawoy, *The Politics of Production: Factory Regimes under Capitalism and Socialism* (London: Verso, 1985). 10, 183, 287, on norms in other countries.
69. Ibid., 10–18 passim and 131.
70. *Tikhookeanskaia Zvezda*, May 26, 1936.
71. HP no. 99, A, vol. 7, p. 16; a male Ukrainian worker, foreman, then foremen's supervisor, born about 1909 to well-off peasants. And see HP no. 456, A, vol. 23, pp. 9–10, a male Ukrainian miner born about 1919 into a tsarist officer's family.
72. Siegelbaum, "Masters," 127, 141.
73. E.g., Zawodny, II/20; Hanfmann and Beier, *Six Russian Men*, 77.
74. LGAOR, f. 2140, o. 21, d. 265, ll. 10–11, February 19, 1940.
75. RGAE-TsGANKh, f. 7604, o. 8, ed. khr. 117.
76. Ermanskii, *Stakhanovskoe dvizhenie*, 330. At one Donbass mine in 1938, thirty-five norms were lowered even though the old ones were being filled by 150–160 percent; A. Minevich, "Uporiadochit' zarabotnuiu platu v kamennougol'noi promyshlennosti," *Profsoiuzy SSSR*, nos. 8–9 (August–September 1939), 73–74.
77. N. M. Shvernik, "O rabote profsouizov po zarabotnoi plate," *Profsoiuzy SSSR*, no. 12 (August 1938), 17.
78. *Pervoe vsesoiuznoe soveshchanie rabochikh i rabotnits-stakhanovtsev, 14–17 noiabria 1935 g. Stenograficheskii otchet* (Moscow: Partizdat, 1935), 165.
79. Ibid., 151.
80. TsGAMO, f. 6852, o. 1, d. 290, l. 40, the Moscow oblast' administration of glass and chemical plants, December 17, 1935.
81. TsGARR (TsGA RSFSR), f. 52, o. 1, ed. khr. 14, l. 60, stenographic record, December 8, 1935.
82. Ibid., l. 18.
83. Ibid., d. 19, ll. 47–48, Stenogramma I otraslevoi konferentsii rabotnikov farforno-faiansevoi promyshlennosti, April 9, 1936.
84. "O bor'be organov," *SIu*, no. 13 (May 1935), 14; a resolution of March 9, 1935.
85. See Siegelbaum, *Stakhanovism*, 91–92.
86. TsGARR (TsGA RSFSR), f. 52, o. 1, d. 19, l. 54.
87. F. Voropaev, "Profrabotu na transporte—na uroven' stakhanovskogo dvizheniia," *VP*, no. 2 (February 1936), 17.
88. M. Voskresenskaia and L. Novoselov, *Proizvodstvennye soveshchaniia—shkola upravleniia (1921–1965 gg.)* (Moscow: VTsSPS Profizdat, 1965), 92.
89. Ibid., 91.
90. Ibid., 94.
91. *Profrabota po-novomu: Rasskazy predfabzavkomov, tsekhorgov i gruporgov* (Moscow: Profizdat, 1936), 81.
92. R. Sabirov, "Kak profgruppa stala sploshnoi Stakhanovskoi," *VP*, no. 1 (January 1936), 66–67.

See A. Egipov, "Stakhanovskie sutki, piatidnevki i dekady na Podol'skom zavode," *VP*, no. 2 (February 1936); and L. Rovskii, "Kak ne nado pomogat' stakhanovskomu dvizheniiu," *VP*, no. 2 (February 1936), on revived production conferences in Podol'sk and Khar'kov.

93. On the tensions Stakhanovism created in the factories, see my "The Stakhanovite Movement: The Background to the Great Terror in the Factories, 1935–1938," in *Stalinist Terror*.

94. Interview with former workers of the Likhachev Auto Factory, Moscow, April 12, 1988.

95. Borodin, *One Man*, 253–54.

96. This same popularity with workers may well have helped save Victor Kravchenko. See also HP no. 16, B2, vol. 3, p. 31. This Russian man, who worked as a supervisor of foremen, was born about 1914 into a middle-class family.

97. See my "Stakhanovite Movement," 147–48; and Robert Maier, *Die Stachanov-Bewegung 1935–1938: Der Stachanovismus as Tragendes und Verschaerfendes Moment des Stalinisierung der Sowjetischen Gesellschaft* (Stuttgart: Franz Steiner, 1990), 93, 230–32.

98. See my "Reassessing," 176.

99. Degot', "Dela, sviazannye s soprotivleniem stakhanovskogo dvizheniiu," *Slu*, no. 14 (May 1936), 3.

100. *P*, March 26, 1936.

101. G. K. Ordzhonikidze, *Stati i rechi*, 2 vols. (Moscow: Gospolitizdat, 1956–57), 2:709. These remarks were in his speech to the conference of leading Stakhanovites.

102. Ibid., 771; a speech to the directing soviet of Narkomtiazhprom, June 26, 1936.

103. *Slu*, no. 11 (April 1936), 8–9.

104. Stalin, *Sochineniia*, 14:98.

105. TsGAOR, f. 5451, o. 19, d. 227, ll. 113, 116. This file is VTsSPS, reports from central committees of unions, 1935.

106. HP no. 1497, A, vol. 35, p. 18, a Russian male mining engineer born about 1909; his father was a tsarist army officer.

107. TsGARR (TsGA RSFSR), f. 52, o. 1, ed. khr. 16, ll. 140–41, a report of December 10, 1935. See a similar case involving an engineer in 1935 in GARF, f. 7952, o. 5, d. 66, l. 4.

108. HP no. 65, B2, vol. 3, pp. 29–30. The respondent was a construction engineer probably born sometime between 1900 and 1903; no other biographical data were available.

109. Ibid., 30.

110. HP no. 639, A, vol. 30, p. 13; no. 13, A, vol. 2, p. 10; no. 92, A, vol. 7, p. 5; no. 190, A, vol. 14, pp. 14–15; no. 65, B2 vol. 3, p. 30, reported that except for the time the "whore" got Lenin's works, "you could not observe any isolation of Stakhanovites from the rest of the workers."

111. P. Moskatov, "Pomoch' stakhanovtsam dal'she razvernut' stakhanovskoe dvizhenie," *VP*, no. 17 (September 1937), 18.

112. RGAE-TsGANKh, f. 7995, o. 1, d. 578, l. 113. Stenogramma soveshchaniia v Glavstankoinstrumente, September 29, 1937.

113. *Svobodnyi Proletarii*, June 16, 1937.

114. See, e.g., GARF, f. 5457, o. 26, d. 8, l. 6, December 15, 1934, the linen industry; ibid., d. 11, l. 1, January 23, 1935; LPA-PAgStP, f. 1012, o. 1, d. 975, l. 91, the Kirov metal factory, February 10, 1935; ibid., d. 1010, l. 11, July 8, 1936; ibid., f. 77, o. 1, d. 261, l. 39, Bolshevik factory, October

15, 1936; the newspaper *Daesh' Traktor* of the Gorkii auto factory, June 28, 1937; and LPA-PAgStP, f. 77, o. 1, d. 318, l. 98, party committee of the Bolshevik factory, June 18, 1941.

115. GARF, f. 5457, o. 26, d. 585, l. 1, stenographic record of the all-union conference of Stakhanovites in the linen industry, February 5, 1939.

116. RGAE-TsGANKh, f. 4086, o. 2, d. 4265, ll. 2–5.

117. David L. Hoffmann, *Peasant Metropolis: Social Identities in Moscow, 1929–1941* (Ithaca: Cornell University Press, 1994), 107, 115.

118. E.g., Zawodny, I/2, I/11.

119. Ibid., I/8.

120. Ibid., II/15.

121. *Tikhookeanskaia Zvezda,* July 21, 1935.

122. *Svobodnyi Proletarii,* March 8, January 17, and February 25, 1937.

123. *Kirovets,* January 17, 18 and February 14, 1937.

124. Stalin, *Sochineniia,* 14:238; see also 86–87, 100–01, 131, 232.

125. Quoted in Ermanskii, *Stakhanovskoe dvizhenie,* viii, emphasis in the original. No date was given for the *Pravda* statement, but the foreword to the book was written in December 1938.

126. I have heard such remarks numerous times; e.g., from Francesco Benvenuti, during his commentary on a paper I gave at the Fourth World Congress for Soviet and East European Studies, Harrogate, England, July 25, 1990.

127. HP no. 470, pp. 16–17. See also similar comments by no. 56, p. 18, and no. 517, p. 16.

128. HP no. 611, pp. 18–19.

129. SA b. 44, r. 43, WKP 386, 389. There is even a case of a member of the NKVD having been removed from his job and arrested following a complaint about his abuse of power: ibid., WKP 386, l. 43, February 10, 1936.

130. Ibid., ll. 314–20, 288.

131. Stalin, *Sochineniia,* 14:62, a speech to graduates of the Red Army Academy, May 4, 1935.

132. SA, b. 12, r. 11, WKP 84, l. 122, stenogramma soveshchaniia gorodskikh organizatsii pri gorkome, June 3, 1935.

133. M. Taub, "Kak zabotiatsia o liudakh na elektrostantsiiakh Uzbekistana," *VP,* no. 9 (September 1935), 73–76.

134. Zawodny, II/19.

135. *Tikhookeanskaia Zvezda,* July 2, 1937.

136. For another example of local officials' attitudes, see *Rabochaia Moskva,* September 27, 1935, in which a worker charged that she was fired because she criticized the director of her factory. The local union organization would not help her.

137. *Kodeks zakonov o trude,* 2d ed., with changes to October 1, 1938 (Moscow: Profizdat, 1938), 44, 155–56.

138. Soiuz rabochikh bumazhnoi promyshlennosti SSSR. Tsentral'nyi komitet, *Otchet tsentral'nogo komiteta professional'nogo soiuza rabochikh bumazhnoi promyshlennosti. 1973–1939 gg.* (Moscow: Profizdat, 1939), 44.

139. Zawodny, II/13.

140. RGAE-TsGANKh, f. 7622, o. 1, d. 202, ll. 1–7.

141. Zawodny, II/16.

142. Ibid., II/17.

143. GARF, f. 5457, o. 26, d. 306, l. 24, an election meeting of the factory party committee and workers of the spinning shop of the Kazan' linen factory named after Lenin, June 26–28, 1937. See a similar case in ibid., l. 6, at the same factory, July 2–3, 1937. These were secret ballots.

144. Ibid., d. 11, l. 59; a decision of a plenum of the factory committee at Svobodnyi Proletarii, June 11, 1935.

145. Ibid., d. 789, l. 79; the oblast' committee of the Smolensk linen workers, May 27, 1941. For a similar case, see ibid., l. 110, from Kalinin oblast' same industry.

146. Ibid., d. 281, ll. 12–13; the Sverdlovsk oblast' committee of the linen industry, December 17, 1937.

147. RGAE-TsGANKh, f. 7995, o. 1, d. 580, ll. 12–15; a resolution of the presidium of the Central Committee of the union of workers of the lathe and tool industry, February 16, 1938.

148. As told to me by the émigré economist Aaron Katsenelenboigen at a conference on the Great Terror held at Michigan State University, May 1986.

149. LGAOR, f. 6276, o. 21, d. 4, ll. 9, 13, April 16, 1937.

150. "Praktika mest," *Slu,* no. 23 (August 1935), 12.

151. *Tikhookeanskaia Zvezda,* July 22, 1936. The Justice representatives promised to investigate workers' complaints about holidays, poor ventilation, mistakes in calculating pay, and lack of help with technical study.

152. *Aleksandr Kosarev: Sbornik vospominanii* (Moscow: Molodaia Gvardiia, 1963), 105.

153. *Desiatyi s''ezd vsesoiuznogo leninskogo kommunisticheskogo soiuza molodezhi, 11–21 aprelia 1936 g.: Stenograficheskii otchet,* 2 vols. (Moscow: Partizdat TSK VKP (b), 1936), 1:73–74.

154. TsPA (RTsKhIDNI), f. 88, o. 1, d. 616, l. 1, September 25, 1936.

155. LPA-PAgStP, f. 77, o. 1, d. 318. Workers also complained to a party committee in SA, Nicolaevsky, l. 158, April 20–22, 1937.

156. *Svobodnyi Proletarii,* April 22, 1937. One hundred eighty-four people took part in an election meeting, twenty-seven of whom were nominated for the factory committee; discussion cut that number to fifteen, and nine were elected.

157. By June 1937 more than 150,000 "public inspectors," not all workers, were active in the USSR. T. Tirzbanrut, "Likvidirovat' posledstviia vreditel'stva v okhrane truda," *VP,* no. 11 (June 1937), 23.

158. *Profaktivisty rasskazyvaiut o svoei rabote* (Moscow: Moskovskii oblastnoi komitet professional'nogo soiuza rabochikh metalloizdelii, 1937), 30.

159. Ohr, "Collective," 272.

160. Sidney Fine, *Sit-Down: The General Motors Strike of 1936–1937* (Ann Arbor: University of Michigan Press, 1969), 29–54.

161. E.g., Zawodny, II/17, II/23.

162. *Krasnaia Chuvashiia* (Cheboksary), March 5, 1939.

163. *Altaiskaia Pravda* (Barnaul), June 10, 1941.

164. GARF, f. 5457, o. 26, d. 427, l. 32; meeting of young Stakhanovites of the linen industry in Ivanovskaia oblast', August 29, 1938.

165. *Biulleten' VTsSPS,* no. 15, August 1936, 7.

166. HP no. 119, p. 9.

167. HP no. 189, p. 58.

168. TsPA (RTsKhIDNI), f. 17, o. 2, d. 612, vyp. 3, l. 55; the Central Committee meeting of March 4, 1938.

169. SA, b. 44, r. 43, WKP 386, l. 326; no date on the letter, but it was marked received on September 17, 1936.

170. See, e.g., G. M. Il'in, "Novyi pod"em sotsialisticheskogo sorevnovaniia," *Stakhanovets,* no. 11 (1938), 34. Il'in was director of Moscow's Hammer and Sickle factory.

171. "Sudebnye dela o lodyriakh i rvachakh," *Slu,* no. 4, February 1939, 31–32; *Slu,* no. 14, July 1939, 6.

172. *Altaiskaia Pravda* (Barnaul), March 27, 1940.

173. Tsentral'nyi komitet professional'nogo soiuza rabotnikov sviazi, *Otchet tsentral'nogo komiteta professional'nogo soiuza rabotnikov sviazi. Sentiabr' 1937-sentiabr' 1939 gg.* (Moscow: Profizdat, 1939), 69–70.

174. LGAOR, f. 1633, o. 15, d. 394, l. 37, a meeting at the Krasnyi Vyborzhets plant, September 5, 1937; ibid., f. 1253, o. 3, d. 81, ll. 50–51, a meeting of June 3, 1938, at the Leningrad metal plant; and d. 99, ll. 30-31, a meeting at the Leningrad mechanical factory on May 6, 1939. Workers also criticized managers by name in Magnitogorsk in June 1938; RGAE-TsGANKh, f. 4086, o. 2, d. 4344, ll. 4, 8, 9.

175. HP no. 153, A, vol. 12, pp. 31–32.

176. Scott, *Behind the Urals,* 264.

177. Zawodny, II/19.

178. LGAOR, f. 1633, o. 15, d. 485, l. 29. Actually, as early as June 3, 1938, there was a calm discussion of the factory's situation involving workers and the new director at the Leningrad metal factory: ibid., f. 1253, o. 3, d. 81, ll. 50–51.

179. Tokaev, *Comrade X,* 148.

180. HP no. 1215, A, vol. 32, p. 12; a Ukrainian male rank-and file-worker and driver born about 1900; his father was a well-to-do peasant (58).

181. LPA-PAgStP, f. 77. o. 1, d. 264, l. 60; a closed party cell meeting at the Bolshevik factory, Leningrad, 30 March 30, 1937.

182. Sarah Davies, "Constructing Social Identities: Popular Representations of the Self and Other in Leningrad, 1934–41," presented at the conference "Everyday Life in Russia, 1921–1941: The Formation of Soviet Subjectivity," St. Petersburg, August 1994.

183. *"Slaves of the Depression" : Workers' Letters about Life on the Job,* ed. Gerald Markowitz and David Rosner (Ithaca: Cornell University Press, 1987), esp. 7.

184. Robert Coles, *The Political Life of Children* (Boston: Atlantic Monthly Press, 1986), 252–59.

185. HP no. 153, p. 54.

186. HP no. 59, p. 29.

187. Arkitin, "Politicheskie," 4–7.

188. Zawodny, II/16; this comment was essentially repeated in II/13, who added, "The workers understand the fact that we have to build and build and build." Perhaps older workers were more disgruntled partly because, unlike so many of their fellows, they had not been promoted out of their situation. Kotkin, *Magnetic Mountain,* details enthusiasm and social support for the regime, despite some coercion, throughout the 1930s (93, 200–01, 223, 230).

189. *Svobodnyi Proletarii*, January 6, 1937.

190. On education and upward social mobility, see Sheila Fitzpatrick, *Education and Social Mobility in the Soviet Union, 1921–1934* (Cambridge: Cambridge University Press, 1979).

191. Filtzer, *Soviet Workers*, 254; Connor, *Accidental Proletariat*, 43–44, makes the same point.

192. Sheila Fitzpatrick, *The Russian Revolution, 1917–1932* (New York: Oxford University Press, 1982), argues that to lower-class people the revolution meant opportunity to move up in society. Her *Education and Social Mobility* shows how often they took the opportunity.

Chapter Seven: The Acid Test of Stalinism

1. Mikhail Heller and Aleksandr M. Nekrich, *Utopia in Power: The History of the Soviet Union from 1917 to the Present*, trans. Phyllis B. Carlos (New York: Summit, 1986), 371–72, state that German troop strength alone was 3.3 million. Albert Seaton, *The Russo-German War, 1941–1945* (New York: Praeger, 1971), 61–62, writes that 3.2 million Germans and about 400,000 allied troops were involved in the invasion. G. Kumanev, in *P*, June 22, 1989, claims that 5.5 million enemy troops faced one-half that number on the Soviet side. In the first echelon of German troops were 103 divisions, of which 10 were tank; opposing them in the first rank of Soviet units were 56 infantry and cavalry divisions.

2. Many works outline the campaigns of 1941; see, e.g., John Erickson, *The Road to Stalingrad: Stalin's War with Germany*, vol. 1 (London: Weidenfeld and Nicolson, 1975); Paul Carell (a pseudonym), *Hitler Moves East: 1941–1945* (Boston: Little, Brown, 1964); Alan Clark, *Barbarossa: The Russian-German Conflict, 1941–1945* (New York: William Morrow, 1965); and Alexander Werth, *Russia at War, 1941–1945* (New York: Avon, 1964).

3. Christian Streit, *Keine Kameraden: Die Wehrmacht und die sowjetischen Kriegsgefangenen, 1941–1945,* new ed. (Bonn: J. H. W. Dietz, 1991), 83, lists 3.35 million prisoners by mid-December. Apparently Streit has attempted to correct for the possibility of double counting by the Germans. Seaton, *Russo-German War*, 208n, simply says the number "exceeded three million." *Grif sekretnosti sniat: Poteri vooruzhennykh sil SSSR v voinakh, boevykh deistviiakh i voennykh konfliktakh: Statisticheskoe issledovanie* (Moscow: Voennoe izdatel'stvo, 1993), 336–37, claims that German figures include party and Soviet officials captured, plus civilian men of military age. The Germans in the fall of 1941 reported capturing 665,000 east of Kiev, but the whole southwestern front comprised only 627,000 troops, of whom 150,000 escaped encirclement. The total of missing and captured soldiers in the entire Russo-German war was 4,559,000. The Germans may have exaggerated the number of military prisoners they took, but Alexander Dallin used their materials to calculate a total of about 5.7 million for the entire war (Dallin, *German Rule in Russia, 1941-1945: A Study of Occupation Policies* [New York: St. Martin's, 1957], 427).

4. Roger Reese, "A Note on a Consequence of the Expansion of the Red Army on the Eve of World War II," *Soviet Studies* 41, no. 1 (January 1989), 137.

5. Ibid.

6. Larry W. Moses, "Soviet-Japanese Confrontation in Outer Mongolia: The Battle of Nomonhan-Khalkin Gol," *Journal of Asian History* 1, no. 1 (1967), 70, notes the high caliber of the Japanese forces. But Alvin D. Coox, *Nomonhan: Japan against Russia, 1939* (Stanford: Stanford University Press, 1985), esp. 175, considers the Japanese troops to have been poorly equipped.

7. Coox, *Nomonhan,* 1089–91; Moses, "Soviet-Japanese Confrontation," also describes good Soviet performance.

8. Erickson, *Road to Stalingrad,* 13.

9. Anthony F. Upton, *Finland, 1939–1940* (Newark, Del.: University of Delaware Press, 1979), 57; Allen F. Chew, *The White Death: The Epic of the Soviet Finnish Winter War* (East Lansing: Michigan State University Press, 1971), 22.

10. Chew, *White Death,* 21–22, 62–63.

11. Erickson, *Road to Stalingrad,* 14.

12. V. Zenzinov, *Vstrecha s Rossiei* (New York: International University Press, 1945), 14–16.

13. Chew, *White Death,* 109; see also 64.

14. Upton, *Finland,* 69, 84.

15. Chew, *White Death,* 55.

16. HP no. 395, pp. 57–58.

17. Erickson, *Road to Stalingrad,* 29.

18. Ibid., 33.

19. Kumanev in *P,* June 22, 1989.

20. Erickson, *Road to Stalingrad,* 40–46.

21. Werth, *Russia at War,* 148–49.

22. Erickson, *Road to Stalingrad,* 46.

23. Werth, *Russia at War,* 149.

24. Seaton, *Russo-German War,* 17–18.

25. Reese, "Note," 138.

26. Seaton, *Russo-German War,* 15.

27. Heinz Guderian, *Panzer Leader,* trans. Constantine Fitzgibbon (New York: Dutton, 1952), 153.

28. Nekrich and Heller, *Utopia,* 372; Werth, *Russia,* 150, claims a German superiority of four to one or five to one in the main areas of attack.

29. Erickson, *Road to Stalingrad,* 119.

30. General Franz Halder, Chief of the German General Staff, wrote in his diary on June 24, "The enemy air force is completely out of the picture after the very high initial losses (reports speak of 2,000)" (Halder, *The Private War Journal of Generaloberst Franz Halder* [Nuremberg: Office of Chief of Counsel for War Crimes, 1946], 167). However, this was not quite true; Halder noted on July 17 that Army Group North reported enemy air superiority (249). Nonetheless, the Germans dominated the skies in the first months of the war.

31. Erickson, *Road to Stalingrad,* 193.

32. E.g., see I. Gebirgs-Division. I C. Einsatz Russland. Band 1. Anlagen zum Tätigkeitsbericht vom 22.6–10.7.41. National Archives, microfilm (hereafter cited as NA), T 315, r. (roll) 44, fr. (frames) 548–49, July 24, 1941, on the surprise of the German attack at Niemirow; see also Werth, *Russia,* 228n, on the surprise at Orel on October 2.

33. Carell, *Hitler,* 79–80.

34. Seaton, *Russo-German War,* 71–75.

35. Dallin, *German Rule,* 63; and James Lucas, *War on the Eastern Front, 1941–1945: The German Soldier in Russia* (New York: Stein and Day, 1979), 52.

36. On the fighting in the Baltic, see Harrison Salisbury, *The Nine Hundred Days: The Siege of*

Leningrad (New York: Avon, 1969), 189–223; day-to-day fighting on all fronts is covered in the works by Seaton, Erickson, Carell, and Clark, among others.

37. Erickson, *Road to Stalingrad,* 242–43; and Gerhard Weinberg, "The Yelnya-Dorogobuzh Area of Smolensk Oblast," in *Soviet Partisans in World War II,* ed. John A. Armstrong (Madison: University of Wisconsin Press, 1964), 400.

38. Carell, *Hitler,* 44. And Pz AOK I, Morgen- u. Abendmeldungen der Abteilung Ic als Anlage zum Tätigkeitsbericht Ic. Panzer AOK I, Ia/Ic. Beilage 5. 22.6–31.10.41. NA T 313, r. 9, fr. 7235656, reported that "as long as he [the enemy] occupied a prepared position, he fought stubbornly."

39. Streit, *Keine Kameraden,* 83; but Fischer, *Soviet Opposition,* 3, cites a German figure of 2,053,000 prisoners taken before November 1, which would include all the large cauldrons. This smaller total of all prisoners taken would mean that an even higher proportion of prisoners was captured in the rings.

40. Heeresgruppe Süd. Kriegstagebuch II. Teil. Band 4. 16.Sept.41–5.Okt.41. NA, T 311, r. 258, fr. 624–660, 20.9–23.9.41. But on the next day the group met stiff resistance at Perekop.

41. Clark, *Barbarossa,* 142–43.

42. Heeresgruppe Süd fr. 623, September 19, 1941; see also Pz AOK I Panzergruppe I, T 313, r. 9, fr. 7235665, June 26, 1941, for another report of the same phenomenon.

43. Reported in ibid., fr. 7235758, August 5, 1941.

44. 6. Infanterie Division Ic. NA, T 315, r. 308, fr. 165, August 11, 1941.

45. Streit, *Keine Kameraden,* 83, 86–87.

46. HP no. 118, A, vol. 9, pp. 39–40, a Ukrainian male born about 1910, a poor-to-average peasant from a family of the same. A similar story from the Novgorod area is in "Liudi vne zakona," no author; file in HI, 5, written in 1942 in the Bergen-Belsen prisoner-of-war camp by a man captured in 1941.

47. 4. Panzer Division. Ia, Ic, Tätigkeitsbericht, Anlage I, Band I. Fortsetzung. NA, T 315, r. 206, fr. 248, July 19, 1941.

48. 6. Infanterie Division, NA, T 315, r. 308, fr. 40. A circular from Generalkommando des VIII Fliegerkorps, Commanding General Richthofen. A captured captain said on July 13, 1941, "Supply situation bad, effectively destroyed by the German air force" (4. Panzer Division, NA, T 315, r. 206, fr. 226).

49. Erickson, *Road to Stalingrad,* 162.

50. HP no. 470, B10, p. 45, a Russian male born about 1913 who was a construction engineer before the war.

51. 4. Panzer Division, NA, T 315, r. 206, fr. 241, July 15, 1941.

52. I. Gebirgs Division, NA, T 315, r. 44, fr. 1055, August 5, 1941; interview with Colonel Prokol'ev, artillery. He described "newly brought-up reservists, some of whom had not served for ten years, with a one-month refresher course. Very little fighting ability." See also I. Korps. Gen. Kdo. I. AK. [General Staff of the Corps], Anlage zum Kriegstagebuch I.A.K. Tätigkeitsbericht vom 1.II.41–31 March 1942. NA, T 314, r. 47, fr. 279, indicates that Soviet active divisions were stationed along the frontier.

53. Kumanev in *P,* June 22, 1989.

54. Panzer AOK I, T 313, r. 9, fr. 7235851, September 9, 1941; Carell, *Hitler,* 152, writes that south of Naro-Fominsk many captured soldiers were members of workers' battalions raised in Moscow.

HP no. 445, A, vol. 22, p. 13, an army officer born about 1919 into an officer's family, remembered that in August in his unit around Velikie Luki most men were reservists fresh from civilian life. He also claimed that most of them did not know Russian. See also 7. Panzer Division. Tätigkeitsbericht der 7. Panzer-Division. Abt. IC. Russland I. Anlagen zu I. Abschnitt: 1 June 1941–7 August 1941, NA, T 315, r. 436, fr. 952, July 30, 1941.

55. 4. Panzer Division, T 315, r. 206, fr. 343, August 5, 1941. Nevertheless, the same diary noted that after encirclement two battalions were "real heroes" and attacked tanks. After at least five days of encirclement, the commissar reported bad morale.

56. HP no. 1486, A, vol. 34, pp. 7–8. This Russian male, born about 1901, was a chief engineer in a canning factory.

57. HP no. 341, A, vol. 18, p. 14, a Soviet colonel born about 1898 into a poor-to-average peasant family.

58. Quoted in Kumanev, *P*, June 22, 1989.

59. Mark Von Hagen provides evidence of soldiers', including junior officers', belief that higher officers were often enemies of the people in the Great Terror. During the Red Army's campaigns of 1939–40 in Finland, Romania, and eastern Poland, he notes "political officers' reports of a rise in the frequency of attempts by soldiers to kill commanding officers" (Von Hagen, "Soviet Soldiers," 93–94, 98).

60. I. Gebirgs Division, T 315, r. 44, fr. 799, 31.VIII.41. A captured Turkmen remarked, "Everyone is afraid of hunger."

61. 4. Panzer Division, T 315, r. 206, fr. 334, August 9, 1941.

62. 7. Panzer Division, T 315, r. 436, August 8, 1941.

63. HP no. 481, A, vol. 24, pp. 30–31, a Russian male government employee born about 1909 to well-to-do peasants.

64. 4. Panzer Division, T 315, r. 206, fr. 393, August 24, 1941.

65. I. Panzerarmee, T 313, r. 10, fr. 7236204, August 1, 1941.

66. I. Gebirgs Division, T 315, r. 44, fr. 184, June 27, 1941.

67. Ibid., fr. 535, August 18–20, 1941.

68. Omer Bartov, *Hitler's Army: Soldiers, Nazis, and War in the Third Reich* (New York: Oxford University Press, 1991), 35–37.

69. Catherine Andreyev, *Vlasov and the Russian Liberation Movement: Soviet Reality and Emigré Theories* (London: Cambridge University Press, 1987), 34.

70. Quoted in James Fallows, *National Defense* (New York: Random House, 1981), 109–11.

71. E. A. Shils and M. Janowitz, "Cohesion and Disintegration in the Wehrmacht in World War II," *Public Opinion Quarterly* 12 (1948), 284.

72. Ibid., 284–88.

73. On reorganized units, see, e.g., 4. Panzer Division, T 315, r. 206, fr. 314–15, 4.8.41; a Lt. Mitrofanov related two separate reorganizations he experienced in the fighting; after some very bloody losses, he and seven others decided to desert to the Germans. HP no. 126, A, vol. 10, pp. 9–10, a Russian male born about 1920, an officer whose family was "superior intellectual." This respondent reported that units were broken up "to strengthen the morale of the soldiers." The tactic did not work. Similar problems are recounted in I. Gebirgs Division, T 315, r. 44, fr. 1055, August 5, 1941; and HP no. 118, A, vol. 9, pp. 32–34.

74. Bartov, *Hitler's Army,* 4–6 and throughout; and his *The Eastern Front, 1941–1945: German Troops and the Barbarisation of Warfare* (New York: St. Martin's, 1986), 31 and throughout.

75. Bartov, *Hitler's Army,* 28, 30.

76. Halder, *Private War,* 183, June 29; August Haussleitner, *An der mittleren Ostfront* (Nuremberg: Schrag, 1942), 48. A captain of the 18th Panzer Division wrote about the first days of the campaign that "there was no feeling, as there had been in France, of entry into a defeated nation. Instead there was resistance, always resistance, however hopeless" (quoted in Clark, *Barbarossa,* 56). A German report of early August 1941 remarked that in contrast to the West, where surrounded troops usually surrendered readily, encircled Soviet units resisted "until the complete exhaustion of their ability to fight" (RH 2/2582, Militär Archiv, Freiburg [now Potsdam], Germany, Beantwortung des am 4.8.41 übergebenen Fragebogens OKH Fremde Heere Ost, 20).

77. E.g., HP no. 379, A, vol. 19, p. 27, a Russian female born about 1927, a disadvantaged worker from a family of the same; no. 416, A, vol. 21, p. 18, a Don Cossack born about 1908, an electrical lineman from a family of well-off peasants; no. 420, A, vol. 21, p. 29, a female of German descent born about 1923, a rank-and-file intellectual whose father was a landowner and officer before the Revolution; and no. 373, A, vol. 19, p. 58, a Russian female born around 1891, a biologist in charge of a laboratory whose family was prerevolutionary gentry. Such statements may have been affected by émigrés' psychological interest in denigrating their homeland and the fact they were speaking at the height of the Cold War, often with an eye to emigrating to the United States. The family backgrounds of the respondents just listed may have inclined them against the Soviet regime from its inception.

78. Bauer and Inkeles, *Soviet Citizen,* 30–33. Even members of General Andrei Vlasov's Russian Army of Liberation made this claim. See Andrei Georgevich Aldan, *Armiia obrechennykh* (New York: Trudy arkhiva Russkoi Osvoboditel'noi Armii, 1969), 12; and "Pis'mo voennoplennykh," in Kuznetsov, *V ugodu Stalinu,* 1:91. The last source noted that many prisoners had been wounded at the time of capture. See also HP no. 66, A, vol. 6, pp. 25–26, a Russian male born in 1906, a bookkeeper from a white-collar family; no. 136, A, vol. 11, p. 78, a Russian male born in 1903, a graduate of an NKVD school who became an army officer and whose father was a nobleman and officer; and no. 345, A, vol. 4, p. 28, a Belorussian male born in 1928, a poor-to-average peasant from the same background. Vlasov himself repeatedly fought his way out of encirclements in 1941, only to be captured in yet another one in July 1942. But even then he was taken only after he had wandered in forests for two weeks (Andreyev, *Vlasov,* 22–37).

79. E.g., HP no. 341, A, vol. 18, pp. 15–16. This former colonel was arrested for fourteen months in 1937–38 and in 1941 fought "not for the Bolsheviks" but for the motherland. "I wanted to shoot myself, I didn't want to be captured," he said.

80. Vladimir I. Orlov, "Moia ispoved'," Nicolaevsky Collection, HI, b. 232, f. 9, p. 2.

81. There were many such cases. Besides the colonel just mentioned, see HP no. 385, A, vol. 19, p. 97, a Russian male born about 1911, a government official from a tailor's family; and no. 117, A, vol. 9, p. 47, a Ukrainian male army officer born about 1922 to well-off peasants; Kosterina, *Diary,* 190; Petrov, *It Happens in Russia,* 277. Beck and Godin, *Russian Purge,* 127–28, opined that many who had been arrested "gave their utmost for the Soviet Union during the war." See also Berger, *Nothing but the Truth,* 205; and Borodin, *One Man,* 280.

82. Among many examples, see Orlova, *Memoirs,* 43; Kopelev, *Education,* 219; Ruth Turkov

Kaminska, *I Don't Want to Be Brave Anymore* (Washington, D.C.: New Republic Books, 1978), 44; and Kurilov, "Why I did not return," 14.

83. See, e.g., the textbook by David MacKenzie and Michael W. Curran, *A History of Russia and the Soviet Union,* 3d ed. (Chicago: Dorsey, 1987), 740.

84. Roundups of Jews happened extensively in Lithuania; see Harry Gordon, *The Shadow of Death: The Holocaust in Lithuania* (Lexington: University Press of Kentucky, 1992); and Peter Lawrence, "Why Lithuania? A Study of Active and Passive Collaboration in Mass Murder in a Lithuanian Village, 1941," in *Why Germany? National Socialist Anti-Semitism and the European Context,* ed. John Milfull (Oxford, England: Berg, 1993).

85. M. K. Dziewanowski, *Poland in the Twentieth Century* (New York: Columbia University Press, 1977), 87.

86. Ibid., 92.

87. Ibid., 93; Celia S. Heller, *On the Edge of Destruction: The Jews of Poland between the Two World Wars* (New York: Columbia University Press), 90–94.

88. Edward Wynot, Jr., "'A Necessary Cruelty': The Emergence of Official Anti-Semitism in Poland, 1936–39," *American Historical Review* 76, no. 4 (1971), 1035–58.

89. Jan Tomasz Gross, *Polish Society under German Occupation: The Generalgouvernement, 1939–1944* (Princeton: Princeton University Press, 1979), 19.

90. Antony Polonsky, *Politics in Independent Poland, 1921–1939: The Crisis of Constitutional Government* (New York: Oxford University Press, 1972), 459–62. See also John A. Armstrong, *Ukrainian Nationalism* (New York: Columbia University Press, 1955), 26–27.

91. Polonsky, *Politics,* 477.

92. Jan Tomasz Gross, *Revolution from Abroad: The Soviet Conquest of Poland's Western Ukraine and Western Belorussia* (Princeton: Princeton University Press, 1988), 20–23. A Red Army man said people welcomed Soviet troops; HP no. 193, B2, vol. 2, pp. 6–7; no biographical data. See also HP no. 489, B 191 B4, 1; no biographical data.

93. Gross, *Revolution,* xiii.

94. Ibid., 42–43.

95. Ibid., 56.

96. Records of the Reich Leader of the SS and Chief of the German Police (Reichsfuehrer SS und Chef der Deutschen Polizei). Ereignismeldungen UdSSR. NA, T 175, r. 233, fr. 2721425, July 5, 1941.

97. Ibid., fr. 2721370–71.

98. Ibid., fr. 2721453–4, July 1, 1941.

99. Ibid., fr. 2721482–3, July 12, 1941.

100. Ibid., fr. 2721478, July 12, 1941.

101. 7 Panzer Division. Panzer Gruppe 3. Abt. Ia. Zentralrussland. NA, T 315, r. 436, fr. 1196, August 11, 1941.

102. HP no. 103, A, vol. 8, p. 65, a Ukrainian male tractor driver born into a well-off peasant family about 1900.

103. HP no. 133, A, vol. 10, p. 2, a Ukrainian male tractor driver born about 1923 into a family of poor-to-average peasants.

104. HP no. 130, A, vol. 10, p. 33, a Russian female worker in a chocolate factory born about 1920; her father was a worker.

105. HP no. 517, A, vol. 26, p. 57.
106. Arkitin, "Politicheskie," 5.
107. "Respublika Zueva," 3.
108. HP no. 1706, A, vol. 37, p. 47 a Russian male worker born about 1913, the son of a Cossack officer.
109. HP no. 6, A, vol. 1, p. 42, a Russian male laboratory technician born after 1920 into a family of "middle peasants."
110. HP no. 27, p. 43.
111. Merl, *Sozialer Aufstieg,* 260.
112. Fedor Belov, *The History of a Soviet Collective Farm* (New York: Praeger, 1955), 18–19; on his kolkhoz, see 15–19.
113. G. M. Kovalev, "Oni byli pervymi," in *V nachale bol'shogo puti: Memuarnyi sbornik* (Minsk: Uradzhai, 1975), 281.
114. Ohr, "Collective Farms," iv, 105, 4, 70, 72, 92.
115. Merl, *Sozialer Aufstieg,* 100, 106–08, writes that farmers could not select kolkhoz presidents but details removals of these officials after complaints from ordinary farmers. See also Ohr, "Collective Farms," 99–100, 105, 117.
116. "Pis'ma iz derevni: God 1937-i," *Kommunist,* no. 1 (1990).
117. HP no. 240, A, vol. 14, p. 34, a Russian male born about 1922 or 1923 into a family of well-off peasants. He was in a military academy on the eve of the war.
118. HP no. 30, A, vol. 4, p. 7, a Russian male kolkhoz president was born about 1906 into a family of well-off peasants.
119. See Fitzpatrick, *Stalin's Peasants.*
120. Inkeles and Bauer, *Soviet Citizen,* 265, 274.
121. HP no. 1354, A, vol. 33, p. 75, a Ukrainian female teacher born about 1917. Her father was a teacher and tsarist officer.
122. HP no. 33, B6, p. 2.
123. HP no. 41, B2, vol. 1, p. 5.
124. HP no. 287, p. 31.
125. HP no. 34, A, vol. 4, p. 11, a Russian male born about 1911 into a middle-class family. He finished technical school, then joined the NKVD.
126. HP no. 41, B2, vol. 1, p. 3.
127. HP no. 20, B 191 B6, p. 3; and no. 526, A, vol. 27, p. 36, a Ukrainian male engineer born about 1911 into the middle class.
128. Gross, *Polish Society,* 184, 126.
129. Gross, *Polish Society,* 184.
130. Records of the Reich Leader, r. 233, fr. 2721399, July 2, 1941; fr. 2721402, July 2, 1941, a report from Wilno (Vilna).
131. Anna Ivanovna M., "Why I did not return to the USSR," 6.
132. Borodin, *One Man,* 264–69.
133. HP no. 133, A, vol. 10, p. 70.
134. Arkitin, "Politicheskie," 17.
135. Rothchild, *Special Legacy,* 212, the story of Anna D.

136. Werth, *Russia at War,* 160–61.
137. HP no. 1757, B2, vol. 2, p. 6; no biographical data available. L. V. Dudin, "Vospominaniia o Kieve pri Nemtsakh," Nicolaevsky Collection, HI, b. 232, f. 10, p. 54, remembered that in Kiev "everyone who could started to run" when the Germans were reported to be about fifty miles west of the city.
138. Richard Bidlack, "Workers at War: Factory Workers and Labor Policy in the Siege of Leningrad," *Carl Beck Papers,* no. 902 (1991).
139. Lend-lease aid to the USSR was substantial but did not involve weaponry for the most part. Domestic production provided most guns, tanks, shells, and so on; see Werth, *Russia at War,* 574–77.

Conclusion

1. Viacheslav Chornovil, then leader of the opposition in Ukraine, said that the "Russian people have been so ruined by socialism that you cannot do anything with them" (*The Economist,* December 5, 1992, 4).
2. Orlando Figes, "Stalin's Oblomovs," *Times Literary Supplement,* January 13, 1995.
3. *NYT,* March 28, 1993. *Sovok* can also mean "soviet," but that was not its usage here. See also Alexander Kabakov, "A Whole Society of Dissidents," *Moscow Times* 2, no. 38, international weekly edition, February 5, 1995, 37.
4. *Stalin,* Thames Television.
5. E.g., *Revelations from the Russian Archives,* catalog of an exhibition held at the Library of Congress, June–July 1992 (Washington, D.C.: Library of Congress, 1992); and *Stalin,* directed by Ivan Passer (Home Box Office Film, 1992).
6. For other resistance to the general mood of 1937–38, see *Oni ne molchali,* compiled by A. V. Afanas'ev (Moscow: Politizdat, 1991).
7. See my "Soviet Family" and "Social Dimensions."
8. Moshe Lewin, *The Gorbachev Phenomenon: A Historical Interpretation* (Berkeley: University of California Press, 1988).
9. E.g., as portrayed in the title and text of Geoffrey Hosking, *The Awakening of the Soviet Union* (Cambridge: Harvard University Press, 1990).
10. Stephen White, *Gorbachev and After,* 3d ed. (Cambridge: Cambridge University Press, 1992), 231, gives the first poll. The surveys of 1991 and 1992 were mentioned in a talk by Boris Grushin, director of the Vox Populi Public Opinion Research Service in Moscow, published by the Kennan Institute for Advanced Studies, *Meeting Report* 10, no. 2 (1992), 3.
11. *Stalin,* Thames Television; for citizens' positive comments on Stalin, see also *60 Minutes,* transcript, vol. 22, no. 21, for February 11, 1990.
12. *NYT,* January 3, 1992.
13. *60 Minutes,* February 11, 1990.
14. Walter, *Terror and Resistance.*
15. See, e.g., Samir al-Khalil, *Republic of Fear: The Inside Story of Saddam's Iraq* (New York: Pantheon, 1989). Of course, grotesque violence has occurred in Iraq, but much more than that keeps Saddam Hussein in power. In recent years Iraq's enemy status has dampened discussion in

the West of the other side of life there, including economic development, increased social services, upward social mobility, and land reform. See Phebe Marr, *The Modern History of Iraq* (Boulder, Colo.: Westview Press, 1985), 247–81.

16. Again, see Tucker, *Stalin as Revolutionary,* 69–91; cf. this treatment to Suny, "Beyond Psycho-history."

Glossary of Names and Key Terms

Article 58 major article of the criminal code of the Russian Republic that dealt with counterrevolutionary activity.

Beria, Lavrentii Pavlovich a Georgian. Became head of the political police in November 1938. Executed as a spy in 1953.

Bukharin, Nikolai a leading member of the Politburo in the 1920s and key figure in driving Leon Trotsky out of the Communist Party. Labeled a rightist by Stalin in 1928 for his defense of independent peasants. Executed in 1938.

Central Committee (CC) the second highest body of the Communist Party, composed of about 140 members in the late 1930s.

chistki literally, "cleansings"; used in reference to the purges of the Communist Party.

Dashnaks an Armenian nationalist movement active in the early twentieth century.

Ezhov, Nikolai Ivanovich head of the political police from September 1936 to November 1938. Executed in 1940.

Gensec abbreviation for general secretary (leader) of the Communist Party, the position Stalin held from 1922 until his death. This term came to refer to him.

gulag the acronym of Glavnoe Upravlenie Lageriami, the Main Administration of Corrective Labor Camps of the political police.

Iagoda, Genrykh from 1932 until September 1936, head of the OGPU and then the NKVD (q.v.). Executed in 1938.

Kamenev, Lev a leading Politburo member in the 1920s. His career moved in tandem with Zinoviev's (q.v.), including his execution in August 1936.

Kirov, Sergei a longtime communist official. Became party chief in Leningrad in 1926 and a full member of the Politburo in 1930. Assassinated on December 1, 1934.

kolkhoz a collective farm in which the state owns the land and employees are paid by shares of the annual profits, if any. Peasants maintain small private plots and some livestock.

kombinat a group of enterprises (for example, of coal mines) organized as one economic unit.

Komsomol Kommunisticheskii Soiuz Molodezhi (Communist Youth League), a communist organization for young people between fifteen and twenty-six years of age.

krai a small territorial unit; or, in Siberia, a vast one.

Krylenko, Nikolai Civil War hero and People's Commissar of Justice in the 1930s. Executed as an enemy of the people in 1938.

narkom abbreviation of Narodnyi Komissar (People's Commissar). Head of a commissariat (ministry).

Narodnyi Komissariat Vnutrennykh Del People's Commissariat of Internal Affairs, the NKVD, which from 1934 to 1941 included the political and civil police as well as other agencies.

obkom oblastnoi komitet, *oblast'* (q.v.): committee of the Communist Party. Responsible for key decisions on politics and all spheres of life.

Ob"edinennoe Gosudarstvennoe Politicheskoe Upravlenie (OGPU) Unified State Political Administration, the name of the political police from 1923 until 1934.

oblast' an administrative unit roughly equivalent to a province. Oblast' party secretaries, following Soviet usage of "secretary" in the political sphere, were the leaders in these units. As such they were usually members of the party Central Committee.

Old Bolsheviks members of the Communist Party who had joined before the seizure of power in October 1917.

Ordzhonikidze, Grigorii (Sergo) a Georgian. Politburo member and Commissar of Heavy Industry until his suicide in February 1937.

Piatakov, Grigorii a key figure in Soviet industrialization; assistant to Ordzhonikidze in the Commissariat of Heavy Industry in the 1930s. A leading Trotskyite in the 1920s. Executed in 1937.

Politburo the highest body of the party, consisting of some fifteen full and candidate (nonvoting) members in the 1930s.

Procuracy the Soviet equivalent of the American attorney general's office. Responsible for investigating and trying crimes.

raion small administrative unit within an oblast'.

raikom Communist Party committee of a raion.

Russian Social Democratic Party the Russian Marxists. Split in 1903 into the Bolshevik and Menshevik wings. Divided irrevocably and became bitter enemies during the course of 1917.

seksoty (from *sekretnye sotrudniki*) secret coworkers, that is, stool pigeons for the political police.

Sovnarkom Soviet (council) of People's Commissars; the cabinet of ministers.

Supreme Soviet the parliament.

troika a three-person judicial board that handled political cases; disbanded, at least nominally, in 1934. Revived in 1936 and finally abolished in November 1938.

Trotsky, Leon Lenin's chief lieutenant in 1917 and organizer of the Red Army. A leading Politburo member in the 1920s until his ouster in 1926; exiled abroad in 1929. An ardent critic of Stalin's rule in the 1930s. Murdered in Mexico by an agent of Stalin's in 1940.

Tukhachevskii, Marshal Mikhail N. a leading military commander and thinker, formerly a colonel in the tsarist army. Switched to the Reds in the Civil War. Executed in 1937.

vozhd' leader, a term reminiscent of Führer.

vrediteli literally, "wreckers"; used to refer to saboteurs.

Vyshinskii, Andrei an ethnic Pole and a Menshevik from 1905 to 1917. Procurator-general (attorney general) of the USSR from 1935 to 1939 and chief prosecutor of the Moscow show trials. Later deputy foreign minister, then minister.

Zinoviev, Grigorii a leading Politburo member in the 1920s; formed the United Opposition with Trotsky in 1926. Ousted from the Politburo in July of that year. Rehabilitated into good standing several times. Executed after the first Moscow show trial, August 1936.

Index